# THE LIFE OF
# ST. PATRICK
## AND HIS PLACE IN HISTORY

## JOHN B. BURY

DOVER PUBLICATIONS, INC.
Mineola, New York

Published in Canada by General Publishing Company, Ltd., 30
Lesmill Road, Don Mills, Toronto, Ontario.
Published in the United Kingdom by Constable and Company,
Ltd., 3 The Lanchesters, 162–164 Fulham Palace Road, London W6
9ER.

*Bibliographical Note*

This Dover edition, first published in 1998, is an unabridged
republication of the work first published by Macmillan and Co.,
Ltd. (London and New York) in 1905. The Introduction, by Liam
de Paor, is new.

*Library of Congress Cataloging-in-Publication Data*

Bury, J. B. (John Bagnell), 1861–1927.
    The life of St. Patrick and his place in history / John B. Bury.
        p.    cm.
    Originally published: London : Macmillan and Co., 1905.
With new introd.
    Includes bibliographical references and index.
    ISBN 0-486-40037-9 (pbk.)
        1. Patrick, Saint, 373?–463?   2. Christian saints—Ireland—
Biography.   I. Title.
BR1720.P26B87   1998
270.2'092—dc21
[B]                                                               97-44209
                                                                      CIP

Manufactured in the United States of America
Dover Publications, Inc., 31 East 2nd Street, Mineola, N.Y. 11501

# CONTENTS

## CHAPTER VI

## CHAPTER VII

## CHAPTER VIII

## CHAPTER IX

## CHAPTER X

# CONTENTS

## APPENDIX A—Sources

## APPENDIX B—NOTES

## APPENDIX C—EXCURSUS

# CONTENTS

## MAPS

# PREFACE

PERHAPS the scope of this book will be best understood if I explain that the subject attracted my attention, not as an important crisis in the history of Ireland, but, in the first place, as an appendix to the history of the Roman Empire, illustrating the emanations of its influence beyond its own frontiers; and, in the second place, as a notable episode in the series of conversions which spread over northern Europe the religion which prevails to-day. Studying the work of the Slavonic apostles, Cyril and Methodius, I was led to compare them with other European missionaries, Wulfilas, for instance, and Augustine, Boniface, and Otto of Bamberg. When I came to Patrick, I found it impossible to gain any clear conception of the man and his work. The subject was wrapt in obscurity, and this obscurity was encircled by an atmosphere of controversy and conjecture. Doubts of the very existence of St. Patrick had been entertained, and other views almost amounted to the thesis that if he did exist, he was not himself, but a namesake. It was at once evident that the material had never been critically sifted, and that it would be necessary to begin at the beginning, almost as if nothing had been done, in a field where much had been written.

This may seem unfair to the work of Todd, which in learning and critical acumen stands out pre-eminent from the mass of historical literature which has gathered round St. Patrick. And I should like unreservedly to acknowledge that I found it an excellent introduction to the subject. But it left me doubtful about every fact connected with Patrick's life. The radical vice of the book is that the indispensable substructure is lacking. The preliminary task of criticising the sources methodically had never been performed. Todd showed his scholarship and historical insight in dealing with this particular passage or that particular statement, but such sporadic criticism was no substitute for methodical *Quellenkritik*. Hence his results might be right or wrong, but they could not be convincing.

It is a minor defect in Todd's *St. Patrick* that he is not impartial. By this I mean that he wrote with an unmistakable ecclesiastical bias. It is not implied that he would have ever stooped to a misrepresentation of the evidence for the purpose of proving a particular thesis. No reader would accuse him of that. But it is clear that he was anxious to establish a particular thesis. He does not conceal that the conclusions to which the evidence, as he interpreted it, conducted him were conclusions which he wished to reach. In other words, he approached a historical problem, with a distinct preference for one solution rather than another; and this preference was due to an interest totally irrelevant to mere historical truth. The business of a historian is to ascertain facts. There is something essentially absurd in his wishing that any alleged fact should turn out to be true or should turn out to be false. So far as he entertains a wish of the kind, his attitude is not critical.

The justification of the present biography is that it rests upon a methodical examination of the sources, and that the conclusions, whether right or wrong, were reached without any prepossession. For one whose interest in the subject is purely intellectual, it was a matter of unmixed indifference what answer might be found to any one of the vexed questions. I will not anticipate my conclusions here, but I may say that they tend to show that the Roman Catholic conception of St. Patrick's work is, generally, nearer to historical fact than the views of some anti-Papal divines.

The fragmentary material, presenting endless difficulties and problems, might have been treated with much less trouble to myself if I had been content to weave, as Todd has done, technical discussions into the story. It was less easy to do what I have attempted, to cast matter of this kind into the literary shape of a biography—a choice which necessitated long appendices supplying the justifications and groundwork. These appendices represent the work which belongs to the science of history; the text is an effort in the art of historiography.[1]

It should be needless to say that, in dealing with such fragmentary material, reconstructions and hypotheses are inevitable. In ancient and mediæval history, as in physical science, hypotheses, founded on a critical examination of the data, are necessary for the advancement of knowledge. The reconstructions may fall to-morrow, but, if they are legitimate, they will not have been useless.

[1] I may be permitted to remark that in vindicating the claims of history to be regarded as a science or *Wissenchaft*, I never meant to suggest a proposition so indefensible as that the presentation of the results of historical research is not an art, requiring the tact and skill in selection and arrangement which belong to the literary faculty. The friendly criticisms of Mr. John Morley in the *Nineteenth Century and After*, October 1904, and of Mr. S. H. Butcher in *Harvard Lectures on Greek Subjects* (1904), Lecture VI., show me that I did not sufficiently guard against this misapprehension.

The future historian of Ireland will have much to discover about the political and social state of the island, which is still but vaguely understood, and the religion of the Scots, about which it may be affirmed that we know little more than nothing. These subjects await systematic investigation, and I have only attempted a slight sketch (Chapter IV.), confining myself to what it seemed possible to say with tolerable safety on the chief points immediately relevant to the scope of this monograph. But, notwithstanding the dimness of the background, I venture to hope that some new light has been thrown on the foreground, and that this study will supply a firmer basis for the life and work of Patrick, even if some of the superstructures should fall.

The two maps are merely intended to help the reader to see the whereabouts of some places which he might not easily find without reference to the Ordnance Survey. I consulted Mr. Orpen's valuable map of Early Ireland (unfortunately on a small scale) in Poole's *Historical Atlas of Modern Europe*. But he has used material which applies to a later period, and I have not ventured to follow him, for instance, in marking the boundary between the northern frontiers of the kingdoms of Connaught and Meath.

It was fortunate for me that my friend Professor Gwynn was engaged at the same time on a "diplomatic" edition of the records contained in the *Codex Armachanus*, which constitute the principal body of evidence. With a generosity which has placed me under a deep obligation, he put the results of his labour on the difficult text at my disposal, and I have had the invaluable help and stimulus of constant communication with him on many critical problems arising out of the text of the documents.

Since the book was in type I have received some communications from my friend Professor Rhŷs which suggest a hope that the mysterious Bannauenta, St. Patrick's home, may perhaps be identified at last. I had conjectured that it should be sought near the Severn or the Bristol Channel. The existence of three places named Banwen (which may represent Bannauenta) in Glamorganshire opens a prospect that the solution may possibly lie there.

J. B. BURY.

# INTRODUCTION

ST. PATRICK is of special, indeed unique, interest for the historian of Late Antiquity. He is the only person, among all those who lived in the British Isles in the fifth century of our era, who left us extended items of writing, in the form of two letters. Unfortunately, neither letter is as informative as we would like about his life, times, or circumstances, but they are all we have. One letter, quite short, is a denunciation and excommunication of a petty British ruler, whose soldiers had captured and sold into slavery some Christians recently baptized by Patrick. The other, a longer document, is a defense (against charges not clearly stipulated) of Patrick's personal and financial integrity and of his work of preaching the Christian Gospel in Ireland.

This second letter is addressed to senior ecclesiastics in Britain, and reveals in passing that Patrick himself was British, the son of a fairly well-to-do landowner who was a deacon of the Church and was also an official of standing within the administrative system established by the Romans. As a boy, Patrick had been captured in a raid on his home and taken to Ireland as a slave, but he had escaped after some years. As he saw it himself, he was divinely inspired to return there with the Christian message.

In the course of time, Patrick became the center of a more and more elaborated legend and the conversion of Ireland was attributed to him. The church of Armagh, which he was said to have founded, claimed primacy among Irish churches and collected materials—lists of names, stories, hagiography, annalists' reconstructions—to support that claim and to enhance the fame of Patrick himself. In the seventh and eighth centuries historians and ecclesiastical propagandists did their best to construct plausible narratives with such materials. They left puzzles to intrigue modern historians and propagandists, and in the nineteenth century there was controversy (of keen interest in that time) as to whether St. Patrick had been truly ecclesiastically Roman or had been, on the contrary, a primitive Protestant.

At that point the subject attracted the attention of the classical historian J. B. Bury, "not," as he explains in his preface, "as an important crisis in the history of Ireland, but, in the first place, as an appendix to the history of the Roman Empire." John Bagnell Bury was born on October 16, 1861, the son of the Rev. Edward John Bury, rector of Clontibret, County

Monaghan, in Ireland. His father taught him Latin, beginning when he was four years old, and he excelled in Greek at Foyle College in Derry. He took a double first class degree in classics and philosophy at Trinity College, Dublin, and went on to a scholarly career, spent mainly in Cambridge and devoted largely to the study of problems in classical history and literature. In particular he devoted much attention to the history of the later Roman Empire. He also wrote, among other books, *A History of the Papacy in the Nineteenth Century*, *A History of Freedom of Thought* and *The Idea of Progress: An Inquiry Into Its Origin and Growth*. In 1905 he turned to what subsequently came to be referred to as "the problem of St. Patrick"—partly in an endeavor to take the matter out of the area of nineteenth-century religious and sectarian controversy.

Bury died in 1927. For many years it seemed that he had indeed solved the problem, more or less. His work *The Life of St. Patrick* established an orthodoxy which still, with modifications, commands allegiance among some scholars, though in the past half century there has been much revision of its conclusions, and indeed of the evidential material on which it is founded. Bury wholly succeeded in terms of bringing an impartial and extremely well informed mind to bear on the question and handling the evidence fairly and judiciously.

His method was to sift through the materials of various kinds that had been gathered together in the early Middle Ages under the name of Patrick. He exercised an experienced judgment in deconstructing myth and legend, drawing on his wide knowledge of fifth-century Europe, and synthesizing as best he could a fifth-century history of Ireland from the evidence of the annals and of pseudo-historic tales. The result is a model of this type of reconstruction of the past from unpromising materials. Bury's work is careful, readable, and, in its general thrust, a very plausible narrative of the life and times of the man who was to be honored for more than a thousand years as Ireland's patron saint. He had the advantage, as he acknowledged, that his friend and colleague John Gwynn was at the same time preparing a "diplomatic" edition of the ninth-century Book of Armagh, which great manuscript contains, among other material, a collection of Patrician texts and notes. Bury had ready access to current scholarship on the early Irish sources and he brought to his task his own wide and deep knowledge of that Romanized world from which St. Patrick came.

The student of St. Patrick must therefore turn to Bury both for information and for example, but Bury has by no means had the last word on this subject. His masterly synthesis held its own without serious challenge until a new scholarly—and at times fierce—controversy sprang up with the publication in 1942 of *The Two Patricks*, a lecture delivered by T. F. O'Rahilly to the Dublin Institute for Advanced Studies. The main course of the controversy can be traced in the long summary, and argumentative, paper published by D. Binchy in *Studia Hibernica*, volume 2, in 1962: "Patrick and his biographers: ancient and modern." Subsequent full-length studies of the question, which should be consulted by the serious inquirer into these matters, include R.P.C. Hanson's *St. Patrick—His Origins and Career* and E. A. Thompson's *Who Was St. Patrick?*

The new perspective provided by the research of the present century mainly is based on a more rigorous criticism of the Irish sources. We can no longer, for example, take Irish fifth-century annals as contemporary, or even near contemporary, with the events they record. They are reconstructions, embodying much guesswork, made by scholars and disputants of the seventh and eighth centuries, who sought to cast their interpretation of earlier times in annalistic form. Nor can we take at face value the work of seventh-century hagiographers such as Muirchú and Tírechán, both of whom produced accounts of Patrick in the service of the claims of Armagh. Bury, of course, by his training and background, well understood the importance of the criticism of sources. However, he did not have available to him the results of the work on early Irish texts that has been done by numerous scholars over the past ninety years, and he was led into undue reliance on secondary and tertiary sources for want of better ones. Our picture of fifth-century Ireland is very different now from what it was at the start of the twentieth century.

Bury's approach was sound: he worked inward from the outer world—the late Roman Empire—thus moving from the known to the unknown. His grasp of the significance of the fact that the first bishop of the Irish Christians was not Patrick, but Palladius, sent by Pope Celestine I in 431, is sure and steady, and he has a valuable discussion of the Palladian mission in the early part of his book. His exemplary method is revealed in the appendices, where he discusses in detail many difficulties in the evidence.

The Irish was not the first Christian Church established outside the bounds of the Roman Empire, but the circumstances of its foundation were quite different from those obtaining in Ethiopia or eastern Germany, and it is not too much to say that understanding what happened in Ireland in the course of the fifth century will contribute much to understanding the origins of what we have come to know as "Europe" (an entity quite different from the ancient polity and *imperium* that surrounded the

Mediterranean Sea). This is what Bury grasped. He stepped outside the confines of "national" history (which often obscured vision) and took as his themes the interaction of Roman and non-Roman cultures and that extraordinary process of transformation—whose consequences are still working themselves out in our world—by which an esoteric Judeo-Christian tradition of transcendence breathed life into barbarian Europe and created a vital and aggressively active civilization.

Bury's *Life of St. Patrick* is a monument of enlightened scholarship and is of permanent value.

Liam de Paor

Dublin, September 1997

# CHAPTER I

## ON THE DIFFUSION OF CHRISTIANITY BEYOND THE ROMAN EMPIRE

THE series of movements and wanderings, settlements and conquests, which may be most fitly described as the expansion of the German and Slavonic races, began in the second century A.D., and continued for well-nigh a thousand years, reshaping the political geography and changing the ethnical character of Europe. The latest stage in the process was the expansion of the northern Germans of Scandinavia and Denmark, which led to the settlements of the Vikings and Danes in the west and to the creation of the Russian State by Swedes in the east. The general movement of European history is not grasped if we fail to recognise that the invasions and conquests of the Norsemen which began towards the close of the eighth century are the continuation of the earlier German expansion which we are accustomed to designate as the Wandering of the Peoples. It was not till this last stage that Ireland came within range of this general transformation, when, in the ninth century, Teutonic settlements were made on her coasts and a Teutonic kingdom was formed within her borders. Till then she had escaped the stress of the political vicissitudes of Europe. But, four centuries before, a force of another kind had drawn her into union with the continent and made her a part of the Roman world, so far as the Roman world represented Christendom. Remaining still politically aloof, still impervious to the influence of higher social organisation, the island was swept into the spiritual federation, which, through the act of Constantine, had become closely identified with the Roman State. This was what the Roman Empire did for Ireland, not directly or designedly, but automatically, one might say, through the circumstances of its geographical position. The foundation of a church in Ireland was not accomplished till the very hour when the Empire was beginning to fall gradually asunder in the west ; and so it happens that when Europe, in the fifth century, is acquiring a new form and feature, the establishment of the Christian faith in the outlying island appears as a distinct, though modest, part of the general transformation. *Ab integro saeclorum nascitur ordo*, and Ireland, too, has its small place in the great change.

To understand the conversion of Ireland, which we are here considering as an episode in the history of Europe, we must glance at the general conditions of the early propagation of the Christian idea.

It would not be easy to determine how much Christianity owes to the Roman Empire, and we can hardly imagine what the rate and the mode of its progress through southern and western Europe would have been if these lands had not been united and organised by the might of Rome.  It is perhaps not an exaggeration to say that the existence of the Empire was a condition of the success of a universal religion in Europe; and it is assuredly true that the hindrances which the Roman Government, for two centuries and a half, opposed to its diffusion, by treating it as the one foreign religion which could not be tolerated by the State, were more than compensated by the facilities of steady and safe intercourse and communication, which not only helped the new idea to travel, but enabled its preachers and adherents to organise their work and keep in constant touch with one another.

The manner in which this faith spread in the west, and the steps in its progress, are entirely hidden from us; we can only mark, in a general way, some stages in the process.[1]  We know that there were organised communities in Gaul in the second century, and organised communities in Britain at the end of the third; but in neither of these countries, it would seem, did the religion begin to spread widely till after its official recognition by the Emperor Constantine.  At the end of the fourth

[1] For the expansion of Christianity in the first three centuries see Harnack's invaluable work *Die Mission und Ausbreitung des Christentums in den ersten drei Jahrhunderten* (1902).

century there were still large districts in Gaul, especially in the Belgic provinces, which were entirely heathen. In this respect Gaul and Britain present a notable contrast to the other great Atlantic country of the Empire. In the Spanish peninsula Christianity made such rapid strides, and the Spaniards adapted it so skilfully to their pagan habits, that before the time of Constantine Spain had become, throughout its length and breadth, a Christian land.

It could not be expected that, while there were still within the Roman frontiers many outlying districts where the new religion had not penetrated, the western churches could conceive the design of making any systematic attempt to convert the folks who lived beyond the borders of the Empire. The first duty of the bishops of Gaul and the bishops of Britain, if they undertook any missionary work, was to extend their faith in the still heathen parts of their own provinces. The single conspicuous case in which it reached a northern people, independent of the Empire, is significant, for it exhibits the kind of circumstances which helped this religion to travel. The conversion of the West Goths in Dacia was not inaugurated by any missionary zeal on the part of the Church, but came to pass through the means of Christian captives whom the people had carried off in their invasions of Asia Minor in the middle of the third century. The "apostle" Wulfilas, whose work led to the general conversion of the Goths, sprang from a Cappadocian family which had thus been led into captivity, and had lived for two generations in Gothic land. Gothic in spirit and sentiment, as he was Gothic in name, he devoted himself to spreading the gospel of the Christians among his people. His work was recognised and supported at Constantinople, but the fact remains that the conversion of the Goths was due to the hostilities which had brought Christian captives to their land, and not to missionary enterprise of the Church. The part which captives played in diffusing a knowledge of their religion is, in this instance, strikingly exemplified. The conversion of the kingdom of Iberia under Mount Caucasus is another case. The story that it became Christian in the reign of Constantine through the bond-slave Nino, who is still revered there as the "enlightener and apostle of Georgia," rests upon evidence only two generations later, and must have a foundation in fact.[1] And even if the tale is not accepted literally, its existence illustrates the important part which Christian captives played in the diffusion of their creed. This is expressly observed by the author of the treatise *On the Calling of the Gentiles.* "Sons of the Church led captive by enemies made their masters serve the gospel of Christ, and taught the faith to those to whom the fortune of war had enslaved them." [2]

---

[1] Rufinus, *Hist. ecc.* ii. 7. For the Georgian legend of Nino see *Life of St. Nino,* translated by Marjory and J. O. Wardrop, in Oxford *Studia Biblica et Ecclesiastica,* vol. v. (1900).

[2] *De Vocatione Gentium,* ii. 32.

The same nameless writer, who composed his work in the fifth century, notices another channel by which knowledge of his religion was conveyed to the barbarians. Foreign soldiers, who enlisted in the army of the Empire, sometimes came under Christian influences in their garrison stations, and when they returned to their own homes beyond the Imperial frontier they carried the faith with them.[1]

That the silent and constant intercourse of commerce was also a means of propagation beyond the limits of the Empire cannot be doubted, though commercial relations and conditions in ancient and mediaeval history are among the hardest to realise because ancient and mediaeval writers never thought of describing them. The foundation of the Abyssinian church, however, exhibits the part which merchants, as well as the part which captives, might take in propagating a religious faith; and fortunately we possess an account which was derived directly from one of the captives who was concerned in the matter.[2]

A party of Greek explorers who had been sailing in southern seas landed on the coast of Abyssinia and were slaughtered by the natives, with the exception of two youths who were spared to become slaves of the king. One served him as cup-bearer, the other, whose name was Frumentius, as secretary;

---

[1] On the other hand it may be questioned whether the army itself did anything to diffuse Christianity within the Empire. In the west certainly its chief significance in the history of religion was what it did to spread the solar, Mithraic worship. Cp. Harnack, *op. cit.* 268, 388.

[2] Rufinus, *Hist. ecc.* i. 9.

and after the king's death his son's education was
entrusted to these two men. Frumentius used his
influence to help the Roman merchants who traded
with Abyssinia to found a Christian church. He
was afterwards permitted to return to his own
country, but he resolved to dedicate his life
to the propagation of Christianity in Abyssinia,
and having been consecrated by Athanasius at
Alexandria as Bishop of Axum, the Abyssinian
capital town, he returned thither to foster the new
church.

This course of events illustrates both the way in
which captives helped to spread Christianity abroad,
and also how the intercourse of trade could lead to
the planting of Christian communities in lands outside the Empire. It illustrates the fact that up to
the sixth century the extension of that faith to the
barbarians was not due to direct efforts or deliberate
design on the part of the Church, but to chapters of
accidents which arose through the relations, hostile
and pacific, of the Empire with its neighbours.
The "mission" to the Gentiles was, in practice,
limited by the Church to the Roman world, though
the heads of the Church were always ready to recognise, welcome, and affiliate Christian communities
which might be planted on barbarian ground by the
accidents of private enterprise.

It was only after the Roman Empire had become
officially Christian through the memorable decision
of Constantine, that the conversion of neighbouring

states (with the striking exception of Armenia)[1] really began; just after that change the victorious religion began to spread generally in Gaul and Britain. The work of Frumentius and the work of Wulfilas were alike subsequent to the revolution of Constantine. It would be difficult to estimate how great was the impetus which this religion derived, for the acceleration of its progress, from its acceptance by the head of the Roman State. But while it is evident that the Church gained immeasurably within the Empire by her sudden exaltation, it is perhaps generally overlooked how her changed position aided Christianity to pass out beyond the Empire's borders. We touch here on a fact of supreme importance—not less important, but more likely to escape notice, because it cannot be stated in terms of definite occurrences:—the enormous prestige which the Roman Empire possessed in the minds of the barbarian peoples who dwelt beyond it. The observant student who follows with care the history of the expansion of Germany and the strange process by which the German kingdoms were established within the Empire in western Europe, is struck at every step by the profound respect which the barbarians evinced for the Empire and the Roman name throughout all their hostilities and injuries. While they were unconsciously dismembering it, they believed in its impregnable stability;

[1] Armenia was already Christian at the beginning of the fourth century in the days of Maximin.—Eusebius, *Hist. ecc.* ix. 8. 2.

Europe without the Empire was unimaginable; the dominion of Rome seemed to them part of the universal order, as eternal as the great globe itself. If we take into account this immeasurable reverence for Rome, which is one of the governing psychical facts in the history of the "wandering of the nations," we can discern what prestige a religion would acquire for neighbouring peoples when it became the religion of the Roman people and the Roman State. We can understand with what different eyes the barbarians must have regarded Christianity when it was a forbidden and persecuted doctrine and when it was raised to be a State religion. It at once acquired a claim on their attention; it was no longer merely one among many rival doctrines current in the Empire. Considerations of political advantage came in; and political motives could sway barbarians, no less than Constantine himself, in determining their attitude to a religious creed. And the fact that the Christian God was the God of that great Empire was in itself a persuasive argument in his favour. Could a people find any more powerful protector than the Deity who was worshipped and feared by the greatest "nation" on earth? So it seemed to the Burgundians, who embraced the Roman religion, we are told,[1] because they conceived that "the God of the Romans is a strong helper to those who fear Him." The simple barbarians did not reason too

[1] Socrates, *Hist. ecc.* vii. 30.

curiously. It did not occur to them that the Eternal City had achieved her greatness and built her empire under the auspices of Jupiter and Mars. There can be little doubt that, if the step taken by Constantine had been postponed for a hundred years, we should not find the Goths and the Vandals professing Christianity at the beginning of the fifth century.

Among the independent neighbours of the Roman Empire, Ireland occupies a singular place as the only part of the Celtic world which had not been gathered under the sceptre of Rome.[1] It may be suspected that an erroneous opinion is prevalent, just because it lay outside the Empire, that this outlying island was in early times more separate and aloof from Europe than its geographical position would lead us to suppose. The truth is that we have but lately begun to realise the frequency and prevalence of intercourse by sea before historical records begin. It has been but recently brought home to us that hundreds and hundreds of years before the Homeric poems were created, the lands of the Mediterranean were bound together by maritime communication. The same thing is true of the northern seas at a later period. It is absurd to suppose that the Celtic conquerors of Britain and of Iverne burned their ships when they had reached

---

[1] The island of Man is indeed another exception. The Scottic colonisation of north-western Britain (Argyle, etc.) was comparatively late, but before the middle of the fifth century (see below, chap. ix. p. 192).

the island shores and cut themselves off from intercourse with the mainland from which they had
crossed. And we may be sure that it was not they
who first established regular communications. We
may be sure that the pre-Celtic peoples of south
Britain and the Ivernians, who gave its name to
Ireland, knew the waterways to the coasts of the
continent. The intimate connexion of the Celts of
Britain with their kinsfolk across the Channel is
amply attested in Caesar's history of the conquest
of Gaul; and in the ordinary histories of Britain
the political connexion, which even took the shape
of a Gallo-British kingdom, has hardly been duly
emphasised. Ireland was further, but not far.
Constant relations between this island and Britain
were inevitable through mere proximity, but there
is no doubt that regular communication was also
maintained with Gaul[1] and with Spain. Whatever
weight may be allowed to the Irish semi-mythical
traditions which point to ancient bonds between
Ireland and Spain—and in judging them we must
remember that the Ivernians are of the same
Mediterranean race as the Iberians—it is, for the
Celtic period, highly significant to find Roman

[1] Professor Rhŷs thinks that it was to Ireland, more than to Britain, that
the Gallic Druids went to learn their art, and that Caesar (in *B.G.* vi. 13) was
badly informed; and he has recently stated this view in *Studies in Early
Irish History* (*Proceedings of British Academy*, vol. i.), p. 35. It is
remarkable that, apart from Caesar's assertion, the only evidence for Druidism
in southern Britain pertains to the island of Anglesey (Tacitus, *Ann.* xiv. 29),
and Professor Rhŷs holds that in the first century A.D. Anglesey (Mona) was
not yet Brythonic. Druidism in the Isle of Man is attested by a stone
inscribed *Dovaidona maqi Droata* "(the burial-place) of Dovaido, son of (the)
Druid." See Professor Rhŷs in the *Academy* for August 15, 1890.

geographers regarding Ireland as midway between Spain and Britain,[1] a conception which seems to point unmistakably to direct intercourse between Irish and Spanish ports. But the trade of Ireland with the Empire is noticed by Tacitus,[2] and is illustrated by the knowledge which Romans could acquire of its geography. Ptolemy, in the second century, gives an account of the island, which, disfigured though it is, and in many parts undecipherable through the corruption of the place-names, can be tested sufficiently to show that it is based upon genuine information.

It does not surprise us that in our Roman records we hear no syllable of any relations with Ireland, when we remember how meagre and sporadic are the literary records of Roman rule in Britain from the time of Domitian to the premature close. We know, indeed, that at the very outset the question had been considered whether Ireland should be occupied or not. A general of Domitian thought the conquest ought to be attempted, but the government decided against his opinion.[3] The question has been asked why the Romans never annexed it? The

---

[1] Tacitus, *Agricola*, c. 24, medio inter Britanniam atque Hispaniam sita. Cp. Caesar, *B.G.* v. 13. The notice in Orosius (*Hist.* i. 2, § 72) of the lighthouse at Brigantia in north-western Spain as built *ad speculam Britanniae* is noteworthy. Compare the remarks of Professor Rhŷs, *op. cit.* p. 47.

[2] Tacitus, *ib.* aditus portusque per commercia et negotiatores cogniti.

[3] Tacitus, *ib.* The policy recommended by Agricola, who considered one legion sufficient to hold the island, was based partly on the ground of political expedience. The conquest of Ireland, he thought, would have a similar wholesome effect on Britain to that which the conquest of Britain had on Gaul, by removing the spectacle of liberty (*si Romana ubique arma et uelut e conspectu libertas tolleretur*).

answer is simple. After the time of Augustus no additions were made to Roman dominion except under the stress of political necessity. Britain was annexed by the generals of Claudius for the same reason which prompted Julius to invade it,—political necessity, arising from the dangerously close bonds which united the Britons with the Gauls. The inference is that in the case of Ireland there was no such pressing political necessity. The Goidels of Ireland were a different branch of the Celtic race, and the Britons could find in Ireland no such support as the Gauls found in Britain. This explanation accords with the fact that till the middle of the fourth century the Irish or Scots are not named among the dangerous invaders of the British province; they are not named at all.

But it would be a false inference from this silence to suppose that the government in Britain had not to take political account of their western neighbours. Ireland was well on the horizon of the Roman governors, and Irish affairs must from time to time have claimed their attention. The exile, of whom Agricola made much, was not, we might surmise, the last Irish prince who sought in Britain a refuge from enemies at home. But one important measure of policy has escaped oblivion, though not through Roman records. In the third century, it would seem, an Irish tribe which dwelled in the kingdom of Meath was driven from its land. The name of this tribe, the Dessi, still lives in their

ancient home—the district of Deece.[1]     Some of
them migrated southward to the lands of the Suir
and the Blackwater, where their name likewise
survives in the districts of Decies.[2]     But others
sought new abodes beyond the sea, and they settled
largely in South Wales.     The migration of the
Dessi rests on the records of Irish tradition, but it
is confirmed by the clear evidence of inscribed
stones which attest the presence of a Goidelic
population in south-western Britain.     Here we have
to do with an act of policy on the part of the
Roman Government similar to the policy pursued
in other parts of the Empire.     A foreign people was
allowed to settle, perhaps under certain conditions
of military service,[3] on the south-western sea-board.
Nor need these Goidelic settlers have consisted only
of the Dessi, or the settlements have all been made
at one time, and there seem to have been other
settlements in Somerset, Devonshire, and Cornwall.[4]

General considerations, then, supported by
particular fragments of evidence which exist, would
prepare us to learn, as something not surprising, but
rather to be expected, that, by the end of the fourth
century, Christians, and some knowledge of the
Christian worship, should have found their way to
the Irish shores.     Beyond the regular intercourse
with Britain, Gaul, and Spain there was the special
circumstances of the Irish settlements in south-west

---

[1] The baronies of Upper and Lower Deece, in Co. Meath.
[2] Decies within Drum, and Decies without Drum, in Co. Waterford.
[3] See note, Appendix B.     [4] *Ib.*

Britain—a highroad for the new creed to travel;[1]
and the great invasion in the middle of the fourth
century, which will be mentioned in the next
chapter, must have conveyed Christian captives to
Ireland. In the conversion of this island, as elsewhere, captives played the part of missionaries. It
will not then amaze us to find, when we reach the
fifth century, that men go forth from Ireland to be
trained in the Christian theology. It will not
astonish us to learn that Christian communities
exist which are ripe for organisation, or to find this
religion penetrating into the house of the High
Kings. We shall see reasons for supposing that
the Latin alphabet had already made its way to
Ireland,[2] and the reception of an alphabet generally
means the reception of other influences from the
same source.[3] For the present it is enough to
have brought the relations of the Empire to Ireland
somewhat into line with its relations to other independent neighbours.

[1] It seems probable that Pelagius sprang from these Gaelic settlers in
Britain.   See below, p. 43.

[2] See below, cap. viii. *ad fin.*

[3] Un peuple n'emprunte pas l'alphabet des voisins s'il n'a pas à correspondre
avec eux. . . . Qui donc constate un emprunt de monnaie et d'alphabet, en
tous temps et en tous lieux, peut affirmer un échange de produits et d'idées
(V. Bérard, *Les Phéniciens et l'Odyssée*, i. p. 20).

# CHAPTER II

## THE CAPTIVITY AND ESCAPE OF PATRICK

### § 1. *Parentage and Capture*

THE conversion of Ireland to Christianity has, as we have seen, its modest place among those manifold changes by which a new Europe was being formed in the fifth century. The beginnings of the work had been noiseless and dateless, due to the play of accident and the obscure zeal of nameless pioneers; but it was organised and established, so that it could never be undone, mainly by the efforts of one man, a Roman citizen of Britain, who devoted his life to the task.

The child who was destined to play this part in the shaping of a new Europe was born before the close of the fourth century, perhaps in the year 389 A.D. His father, Calpurnius, was a Briton; like all free subjects of the Empire, he was a Roman citizen; and, like his father Potitus before him, he bore a Roman name. He belonged to the middle class of landed proprietors, and was a decurion or member of the municipal council of a Roman town. His

home was in a village named Bannaventa, but
we cannot with any certainty identify its locality.[1]
The only Bannaventa that we know lay near
Daventry, but this position does not agree with an
ancient indication that the village of Calpurnius was
close to the western sea.  As the two elements of
the name Bannaventa were probably not uncommon
in British geographical nomenclature, it is not a rash
assumption that there were other small places so
called besides the only Bannaventa which happens
to appear in Roman geographical sources, and we
may be inclined to look for the Bannaventa of
Calpurnius in south-western Britain, perhaps in the
regions of the lower Severn.   The village must
have been in the neighbourhood of a town possessing a municipal council of decurions, to which
Calpurnius belonged.   It would not be right to infer
that it was a town with the rank of a *colonia*, like
Gloucester, or of a *municipium*, like St. Albans;
for smaller Roman towns, such as were technically
known as *praefecturae, fora*, and *conciliabula*, might
be managed by municipal councils.[2]

To be a decurion, or member of the governing
council, of a Roman town in the days of Calpurnius
and his father was, throughout the greater part of
the Roman dominion, an unenvied dignity.  Every
landowner in a municipality who did not belong
to the senatorial class was obliged to be a decurion,
provided he possessed sixteen acres or upwards;

---

[1] See Appendix C, 1.          [2] See note, Appendix B.

and on these landowners the chief burden of imperial taxation fell. They were in this sense "the sinews of the republic." They were bound to deliver to the officials of the imperial treasury the amount of taxation levied upon their community ; it was their duty both to collect the tax and to assess the proportion payable by the individual proprietor. In the fourth century, while the class of great landed proprietors, who were mainly senators and entirely free from municipal obligations, was increasing, the class of small landowners diminished in numbers and declined in prosperity. This decline progressed rapidly, and the imperial laws which sought to arrest it suggest an appalling picture of economic decay and hopeless misery throughout the provinces. The evils of perverse legislation were aggravated by the corruption and tyranny of the treasury officials, which the Emperors, with the best purposes, seemed powerless to prevent. Men devised and sought all possible means of escaping from the sad fate of a decurion's dignity. Many a harassed taxpayer abandoned his land, surrendered his freedom, and became a labourer on the estate of a rich landlord to escape the miseries of a decayed decurion's life. We find the Emperor Maxentius punishing Christians by promoting them to the dignity of a decurion.

It is unknown to us whether the municipal classes in Britain suffered as cruelly as their

brethren in other parts of the Empire. The
history of this island throughout the last century
of Roman rule is almost a blank. It would be
hazardous to draw any inferences from the agri-
cultural prosperity of Britain, whose corn-fields,
notwithstanding the fact that large tracts of land
which is now under tillage were then woodland,
sometimes supplied the Roman legions on the
Rhine with their daily bread. But it is possible,
for all we know, that members of the British
municipalities may have enjoyed a less dreary lot
than the downtrodden decurions of other provinces.

There was one class of decurions which seems
to have caused the Emperors considerable per-
plexity. It was those who, whether from a
genuine religious motive or in order to shirk the
municipal burdens, took orders in the Christian
Church. A pagan Emperor like Julian had no
scruple in recalling them sternly to their civil
duties, but Christian Emperors found it difficult
to assert such a principle. They had to sustain
the curial system at all costs, and yet avoid
giving offence to the Church. Theodosius the
Great laid down that the estates of decurions
who had become presbyters or deacons before
a certain year should be exempt from municipal
obligations, but that those who had taken orders
after that year should forfeit their lands to the State.
He qualified this law, however, by a later enact-

ment, which provided that if the presbyter or deacon had a son who was not in orders, the son might keep the paternal property and perform the accompanying duties.

Now Calpurnius belonged to this class of decurions who had sought ordination. He was a Christian deacon, and his father before him had been a Christian presbyter. And it would seem as if they had found it feasible to combine their spiritual with their worldly duties. In any case, we may assume that the property remained in the family ; it was not forfeited to the State.

Whether the burdens laid upon them from Milan or Constantinople were heavy or light, Calpurnius and his fellows in the northern island were keenly conscious that the rule of their Roman lords had its compensations. For Britain was beset by three bold and ruthless foes.[1] The northern frontier of the province was ever threatened by the Picts of Caledonia. Her western shores dreaded the descents of the Gaels and Scots of Ireland, while the south and east were exposed to those Saxon freebooters who were ultimately to conquer the island. Against these enemies, ever watching for a favourable opportunity to spoil their rich neighbour, the Roman garrison was usually a strong and sure protection for the peaceful Britons. But favourable opportunities sometimes came. Potitus, at least, if not

[1] See Appendix C, 2, for the following account of the invasions of Britain.

Calpurnius, must have shared in the agonies which Britain felt in those two terrible years when she was attacked on all sides, by Pict, by Scot, and by Saxon, when Theodosius, the great Emperor's father, had to come in haste and put forth all his strength to deliver the province from the barbarians. In the valley of the Severn the foes whom men had to dread now were Irish freebooters, and we need not doubt that in those years their pirate crafts sailed up the river and brought death and ruin to many. Theodosius defeated Saxon, Pict, and Scot, and it would seem that he pursued the Scots across the sea, driving them back to their own shores. The Court poet of his grandson sings how icebound Hiverne wept for the heaps of her slain children. After this, the land had peace for a space. Serious and thoroughgoing measures were taken for its defence, and an adequate army was left under a capable commander. Men could breathe freely once more. But the breathing space lasted less than fifteen years. The usurpation of the tyrant Maximus brought new calamities to Britain. Maximus assumed the purple (A.D. 383) by the will of the soldiers, who were ill-satisfied with the government of Gratian ; and if the provincials approved of this rash act, they perhaps hoped that Maximus would be content with exercising authority in their own island. But even if Maximus did not desire a more spacious field for his ambition, such a course

was perhaps impracticable.   It would have been
difficult for any usurper to maintain himself, with
the adhesion of Britain alone, against the power
of the lord of the West.   Probably the best chance
of success, the best chance of life, for the tyrant
lay in winning Gaul.   And so Maximus crossed
the Channel, taking the army, or a part of it, with
him.   His own safety was at stake ; he recked
not of the safety of the province ; and whatever
forces he left on the shores and on the northern
frontier were unequal to the task of protecting the
island against the foes who were ever awaiting
a propitious hour to pounce upon their prey.
Bitterly were the Britons destined to rue the
day when Maximus was invested with the purple.
Denuded of defenders, they had again to bear the
inroads of Pict, Saxon, and Scot.   Rescue came
after the fall of Maximus (A.D. 388), and the son
of their former defender, the Emperor Theodosius,
empowered his most trusted general, Stilicho, to
make all needed provision for the defence of
the remote province.   The enemies seem to
have escaped, safe and sated, from the shores of
Britain before the return of the army ; no fighting
devolved on Stilicho ; he had only to see to works
of fortification and defence.   But it was high time
for legions to return ; Britain, says a contemporary
poet, was well-nigh done to death.

The woes and distresses of these years must
have been witnessed and felt by Calpurnius and his

household, and they must have experienced profoundly the joy of relief when their country was
once more defended by an adequate army. It was
probably just before or just after this new period
of security had begun that a son was born to
Calpurnius and his wife Concessa.[1] It may have
been the habit of the native provincials to give their
children two names, a Latin name, which stamped
them as Romans, as well as a British name, which
would naturally be used in home life. Calpurnius
called his son Patricius.[2] But if Patricius talked as
a child with his father and mother the Brythonic
tongue of his forefathers, he bore the name of Sucat.
He was thus double-named, like the Apostle Paul,
who bore a Roman as well as a Jewish name from
his youth up.[3] But another Roman name, Magonus,
is also ascribed to Patrick; and possibly his full
style—as it would appear in the town registry when
he should come of age to exercise the rights of a
citizen—was Patricius Magonus Sucatus. Such a
name would be strictly analogous to that of
a Roman historian of Gothic family who lived in a
later generation, Renatus Profuturus Frigeridus.[4]

As the son of a deacon, Patrick was educated in
the Christian faith, and was taught the Christian
scriptures. And we may be sure that he was
brought up to feel a deep reverence for the Empire

---

[1] *Circa* A.D. 389 ; see Appendix C, 3.
[2] See note, Appendix B.
[3] There is no evidence, and no probability, that the name Paul was
adopted on his conversion, or that it had anything to do with Sergius Paullus.
[4] Frigeridus is Gothic Frigairêths.

in which he was born a freeman and citizen, and to regard Rome as the mighty bulwark of the world—

qua nihil in terris complectitur altius aether.

This feeling comes out in his writings ; it may have been strengthened by the experiences of his life, but the idea must have been with him from his very cradle.   Peaceful folk in Britain in those days could have imagined no more terrible disaster than to be sundered from the Empire ; Rome was the symbol of peace and civilisation, and to Rome they passionately clung.   The worst thing they had to dread from year to year was that the Roman army should be summoned to meet some sudden need in another province.

But as Patrick grew up, the waves were already gathering, to close slowly over the island, and to sweep the whole of western Europe.   The great Theodosius died, and his two feeble successors slumbered at Milan and Constantinople, while along all the borders, or even pressing through the gates, were the barbarians, armed and ready, impressed by the majesty of Rome, but hungry for the spoils of the world.   Hardly was Theodosius at rest in his tomb when Greece was laid waste by the Goths, and Athens trembled at the presence of Alaric.   But men did not yet realise, even in their dreams, the strange things to come, whereof this was the menace and the presage.   When the rumour of Alaric and his Goths reached the homesteads of Britain, it must have struck men's ears as a thing far off, a trouble in which they could have no part. And the danger that stole upon the Empire was muffled and disguised. Alaric was a Goth, but at the same time he was an imperial general, a Master of Soldiers, a servant of the Roman State, profoundly loyal to the Empire, the integrity of which he was undermining.

A few years later Britain was startled by sudden tidings. Alaric and his Goths had entered Italy itself; the Emperor Honorius was trembling on his throne, and the armies of the west must hasten to defend him. The message came from Stilicho, the general on whose strength and craft the safety of western Europe in these years depended, and one Britannic legion obeyed the summons to Italy. The islanders must again have been sick at heart in daily expectation of the assaults of their old enemies.

Those enemies were not asleep, and they rose up presently to take advantage of the favourable time. At this point we encounter an Irish king, whose name is famous in the obscure history of his own land. King Niall was the High-king of Ireland in the days of the rebellion of Maximus, and may possibly have joined in the marauding expeditions which vexed Britain during those years. His deeds are enveloped in legend, but the exalted notion which his countrymen formed of his prowess is expressed in the vain tale that he invaded Gaul and conquered as far as the Alps. To the annals

of the Empire king Niall is as unknown as the
princelings of remotest Scythia, but in Britain his
name must have been a familiar word.   The tradition that he died out of his own country, but slain
by the hand of a fellow-countryman, can hardly fail
to be founded on fact; and when the Irish annals
tell us that he met his death " by the Sea of Wight,"
there is nothing in the circumstances of the time
which forbids us to believe the record.   If the date
assigned to his death, A.D. 405, is roughly correct,
this last hosting of Niall was made before the
Roman army had finally left the island, but during
the disorders which preceded its departure.

It may have been at this crisis[1] in the history of
Britain that the event happened which shaped the
whole life of the son of Calpurnius, who had now
reached the age of sixteen, in his home near the
western sea.   A fleet of Irish freebooters came to
the coasts or river-banks in the neighbourhood seeking plunder and loading their vessels with captives.
Patrick was at his father's farmstead, and was
one of the victims.   Men-servants and maid-servants
were taken, but his parents escaped ; perhaps they
were not there, or perhaps the pirates could not
carry more than a certain number of slaves, and
chose the young.

Thus was Patrick, in his seventeenth year, carried
into captivity in Ireland—"to the ultimate places of
the earth," as he says himself, as if Ireland were

[1] For date see Appendix C, 3.

severed by half the globe from Britain. The phrase shows how thoroughly, how touchingly Roman was Patrick's geographical view. The Roman Empire was the world, and all outside its fringe was in darkness, the ultimate places of the earth.

## § 2. *Captivity and Escape*

Of all that befell Patrick during his captivity in Ireland we know little, yet the little knowledge we possess is more immediate and authentic than our acquaintance with any other episode of his life, because it comes from his own pen. But at the outset we encounter a puzzling contradiction between Patrick's own words and the tradition which was afterwards current in Ireland as to the place of his bondage.[1]

When the boats of his captors reached their haven, Patrick was led—so we should conclude from his own story—across the island into the kingdom of Connaught, to serve a master in the very furthest parts of the "ultimate land." His master dwelled near the wood of Fochlad, "nigh to the western sea," in north-western Connaught, to this day a wild and desolate land, though the forest has long since been cleared away. A part of this bleak country belonged to Amolngaid, who afterwards became king of Connaught, and it is still called by his name, Tir-awley, "the land of Amoln-

---

[1] See Appendix C, 4.

gaid." But the wood of Fochlad was probably of larger extent than the district of Tirawley ; it may have stretched over Mayo to the western promontory of Murrisk. Here, we should perhaps suppose, close to Crochan Aigli, the mount which has been immemorially associated with Patrick's name,[1] the British slave served his master for six years.

But our other records transport us to a distant part of Ireland, far away from the forest of Fochlad, to Pictish soil near the eastern coast of Ulster. Here in the lands east of Lough Neagh, the old race, driven eastward from central Ulster, still held out. The name Ulaid, which originally designated the whole of northern Ireland—even as now in its Danish form of Ulster—had come to be specially applied to the eastern corner, whither the true Ulidians had been driven. It seemed now to be the true Ulaid. Within the borders of Ulidia, in this restricted sense, there was a marked division. In the extreme north were the Scots, and in the south were the Picts. The small land of the Scots was known as Dal-riada, and the larger land of the Picts as Dal-aradia.[2] It is supposed that both peoples, those known as Scots and those known as Picts, represented the older races, which possessed Ireland before the coming of the Goidelic invaders, whose language ultimately prevailed throughout the whole island.

[1] Croagh Patrick, close to Westport.

[2] Dalriada = north Antrim ; Dalaradia = south Antrim and Down. The Latin form, Ulidia, is used in this book for Ulaid in the narrower meaning.

Here, it was believed and recorded, Patrick
served a master whose name was Miliucc. His
lands and his homestead were in northern Dalaradia, and Patrick herded his droves of pigs on
Mount Miss. The name of this mountain still
abides unchanged, though by coalescing with *sliabh*,
the Gaelic word for "mountain," it is slightly disguised in the form Slemish. Not really lofty, and
not visible at a distance of many miles, yet, when
you come within its range, Mount Miss dominates
the whole scene and produces the impression of
a massive mountain. Its curious, striking shape,
like an inverted bowl, round and wide-brimmed,
exercises a sort of charm on the eye, and haunts
one who is walking in the valley of the Braid,
somewhat as the triangular form of Pentelicus,
clear-cut like the pediment of a temple, follows one
about in the plain of Athens.

It was in this valley of the Braid and on the
slopes of Miss that, according to the common
tradition and general belief, Patrick for six years
did the bidding of his lord.[1] But it is certain,
from his own words, that he served near the
forest of Fochlad. An attempt may be made
to reconcile the contradiction by assuming that
he changed masters, and that, having dwelled at
first in the west, he was sold to another master
in Dalaradia;[2] but his own description of his bond-

---

[1] It has been conjectured that Miliucc's dwelling was on the hill of
Skerry, on the northern side of the Braid ; see below, p. 86.
[2] Another possible theory is mentioned in Appendix C, 4.

age seems hardly compatible with such a conjecture. The simplest solution seems to be a frank rejection of the story which connected his captivity with Mount Miss in the land of the Picts.

While he ate the bitter bread of bondage in a foreign land, a profound spiritual change came over him. He had never given much thought to his religion, but now that he was a thrall amid strangers, "the Lord," he says, "opened the sense of my unbelief." The ardour of religious emotion, "the love and fear of God," so fully consumed his soul that in a single day or night he would offer a hundred prayers; and he describes himself, in woodland or on mountain-side, rising from his bed before dawn and going forth to pray in hail, or rain, or snow.

> His contemplation was above the earth,
> And fixed on spiritual object.

Thus the years of his bondage were also the years of his "conversion," and he looked back upon this stage in his spiritual development as the most important and critical in his life.

But he was homesick, and he was too young to abandon hope of deliverance and escape from the wild outland into which fate had cast him. He longed and hoped, and we may be sure that he prayed, to win his way back within the borders of the Roman Empire. His waking hopes came back to him at night as responsive voices in his dreams. He heard a voice that said to him in his

*skeptical*
*naturalist*

sleep, "Thou doest well to fast; thou shalt soon
return to thy native land." And another night it
said, "Behold, thy ship is ready." Patrick took
these dream-voices for divine intimations, and they
heartened him to make an attempt to escape.
Escape was not easy, and was beset with many
perils. For the port where he might hope to find
a foreign vessel was about a hundred and eighty
miles from his master's house. Patrick, in describing his escape, does not name the port, but
we may conjecture that it was Inver-dea, at the
mouth of the stream, which is now called the Vartry,
and reaches the sea near the town of Wicklow.
The resolution of attempting this long flight, with
the danger of falling into the hands of some other
master, if not of being overtaken by his own, is
ascribed by Patrick to the promptings of a higher
will than his. He escaped all dangers and
reached the port, where he knew no man. But at
all events he had chosen the season of his flight
well. The ship of his dreams was there, and was
soon to sail. It was a ship of traders; their cargo
was aboard, and part of the cargo consisted of
dogs, probably Irish wolf-hounds. Patrick spoke
to some of the crew, and made a proposal of service.
He was willing to work his passage to the port to
which the vessel was bound. The proposal seems
to have been at first entertained, but afterwards
the shipmaster objected, and said sharply, "Nay,
in no wise shalt thou come with us." The dis-

appointment, as safety seemed within grasp, must have been bitter, and Patrick turned away from the mariners to seek the lodging where he had found shelter. As he went he prayed, and before he finished his prayer he heard one of the crew shouting behind him, "Come quickly, for they are calling you." The shipmaster had been persuaded to forego his objections, and Patrick set sail from the shores of Ireland with this rough company.

To what country or race the crew belonged we are not told; we learn only that they were heathen. They wished to enter into some solemn compact of abiding friendship with Patrick, but he refused to be adopted by them. "I would not," he says, using a quaint phrase,[1] "suck their breasts because of the fear of God. Nevertheless I hoped of them that they might come to the faith of Christ, for they were heathen, and therefore I held on with them."

They sailed for three days before they made land. The name of the coast which they reached is hidden from us, and there is something very strange about the whole story. The voyage was clearly un-eventful. They were not driven by storm or stress of weather out of their course to some undesired shore. There is nothing in the tale, as Patrick tells it himself, to suggest that the ship did not reach the port to which it was bound. Yet when they landed, their way lay through a desert, and they journeyed through the desert for eight and

[1] See note, Appendix B.

twenty days in all.  Their food ran short, and at
last starvation threatened them ; many of their dogs
were exhausted and left to die on the wayside.
Then the shipmaster said to Patrick, "Now, O
Christian, thou sayest thy God is great and
almighty.  Why then dost thou not pray for us ?
For we are in danger of starvation, and there is
no likelihood of our seeing any man."  And Patrick,
in the spirit of the missionary, replied, "Nothing is
impossible to the Lord, my God.  Turn to him
truly, that he may send you food in your path this
day till ye are filled, for he has plenty in all places."
Presently a drove of pigs appeared on the road, and
the starving wayfarers killed many, and rested there
two nights, and were refreshed.  They were as
ready as Patrick himself to believe that the appearance of the swine was a miraculous answer to his
prayer, and he won high esteem in their eyes.

As Patrick slept here, his body satisfied, after
long privation, by a plenteous meal, he had a dream,
which he remembered vividly as long as he lived.
He dreamed that a great stone fell upon him, and
that he could not move his limbs.  Then he called
upon Elias,[1] and the beams of the rising sun awoke
him, and the feeling of heaviness fell away.  Patrick
regarded this nightmare as a temptation of Satan,
and imagined that Christ had come to his aid.
The incident has a ridiculous side, but it shows

---

[1] The association of Saint Elias with the sun was due to the resemblance
of the name to the Greek ἤλιος.

the intense religious excitement of Patrick at this period, ready to see in the most trivial occurrence a direct interposition from heaven; and we must remember how in those days dreams were universally invested with a certain mystery and dread.

For nine days more Patrick and his companions travelled through deserted places, but were not in want of food or shelter; on the tenth they came to the habitations of men. Patrick had no thoughts of remaining with them longer than he needed. He had heard in a dream a divine voice answering his thoughts and saying, "Thou shalt remain with them two months." This dream naturally guided him in choosing the time of his escape. At the end of two months he succeeded in releasing himself from his masters.

In his description of this strange adventure he leaves us to divine the geography as best we may, for he relates it as if it had happened in some nameless land beyond the borders of the known world. But the circumstances enable us to determine that the ship made for the coast of Gaul. It can be shown that its destination was not Britain, and Gaul is the only other land which could have been reached in three days or thereabouts. The aim of the traders with their Irish dogs must have been to reach southern Europe, and the place of disembarkation would naturally have been Nantes or Bordeaux. The story of the long faring through a wilderness might be taken to illustrate the condition of western

and south-western Gaul at this period.[1] For much
about the time at which Patrick's adventures
happened, Gallic poets were writing heartbreak-
ing descriptions of the desolation which had been
brought upon this country by the great invasion of
Vandals and Sueves and other barbarous peoples.
The Vandals and Sueves had indeed already left
it to pass into Spain, but they had left it waste.
Strong castles, walled cities, sings one poet, could
not escape; the hands of the barbarians reached
even lonely lodges in dismal wilds and the very
caves in the hills. "If the whole ocean," cries
another, "had poured its waters into the fields of
Gaul, its vasty waves would have spared more than
the invaders."

But even in the exceptional conditions of the
time, it is surprising that a party, starting from a
port on the west coast and travelling to the Mediterranean, should have walked for four weeks without seeing a human abode and in dire peril of
starvation. We must suppose that they avoided,
deliberately and carefully, beaten roads, and perhaps
made considerable halts, in order to avoid encounters
with roaming bands of the Teutonic barbarians.

Though Patrick did not mention the scene of his
journey in the narrative which he left behind him,
he used to tell his disciples how he had "the fear of
God as a guide in his journey through Gaul and
Italy." This confirms the conclusion, to which the

[1] See Appendix C, 6.

other evidence points, that Gaul was the destination
of the crew, and also intimates that he travelled with
his companions through Gaul to Italy.  It was in
Italy, then, we must suppose, that he succeeded in
escaping from them.

The book in which he described this episode
was written by Patrick, as we shall see hereafter,
when he was an old man.  He rigidly omitted all
details which did not bear upon his special purpose
in writing it.  The whole tale of his captivity and
escape, undefined or vaguely defined by landmarks
or seamarks, as if the places of the adventures had
no name or lay beyond the range of all human
charts, is designed to display exclusively the
spiritual significance of those experiences.  That
the land of his captivity was Ireland, this was indeed
significant ; but otherwise names of men and places
were of no concern and might be allowed to drop
away.  Patrick, in reviewing this critical period of
his life, reproduces the select incidents as they
impressed him at the moment, contributing, as he
believed, to his own spiritual development, or illustrating the wonderful ways in which Heaven had
dealt with him.

# CHAPTER III

## § 1. *At Lérins*

PATRICK has not told us where, or in what circumstances, he parted from his companions, nor has he related his subsequent adventures. When he found himself free his first thought would have been, we should suppose, to make his way back to his home in Britain. We saw that he probably succeeded in escaping from his fellow-travellers in Italy, and his easiest way home might in that case have been by the coast road through Liguria and Provence to Marseilles. From whatever quarter he started, he seems to have reached the coast of Provence. For here at length, amid perplexing, broken clues, we have a definite trace of his path ; here at length we can fix an episode in his life to a small plot of ground.

In the later part of the fourth century the influence of the Eastern on the Western mind had displayed itself not only in theological thought, but also in the spread of asceticism and the foundation of

monastic societies, especially through the influence
of men like Ambrose, Martin of Tours, and Jerome.
In choosing their lonely dwelling-places, the eyes of
anchorets did not overlook the little deserted islands
which lay here and there off the coast in the western
Mediterranean.   Island cloisters studded the coast
of Italy "like a necklace" before the end of the
fourth century, and soon they began to appear off
the coast of Provence.   It was perhaps while Patrick
was a slave in Ireland that a traveller, weary of the
world, came back from the east to his native Gaul,
and, seeking a spot where he might found a little
society of monks who desired to live far from the
turmoil of cities, he was directed to the uncouth
islet of Lerinus, which no man tilled or approached
because it was infested by snakes.   Honoratus took
possession of it and reclaimed it for cultivation.
Wells were dug, and sweet water flowed "in the
midst of the bitterness of the sea."   Vines were
planted and cells were built, and a little monastic
community gathered round Honoratus, destined
within a few years to be more illustrious than any
of the older island cloisters.   Lerinus is the outer-
most of the two islands which lie opposite to the
cape of Cannes, smaller and lower than its fellow
Lero, which screens it from view, bearing at the
present day the name of the man who made it significant in history.[1]   It is difficult to realise as one
walks round it to-day and sees a few stones, relics

---

[1] St. Honorat.—Lero is Ste. Marguerite.

of its ancient monks, that at one time it exercised a great if unobtrusive influence in southern Gaul. Its peaceful, sequestered cells, "withdrawn into the great sea," *in mare magnum recedentia*, had a wonderful attraction for men who had been ship-wrecked in the tumbling world, or who desired unbroken hours for contemplation—*vacare et videre.*

Patrick found a refuge in the island cloister of Honoratus, and in that island we are for the first time treading ground where we have reason to think that he lived for a considerable time. We should like to know the circumstances of his admission to this community, but his own picture of the state of his mind enables us to understand how easily he could have been moved by the ascetic attractions of the monastery to interrupt his homeward journey and lead a religious life in the *sacrae solitudines* of Lerinus for a few years.

Among the men of some note who sojourned in the monastery in its early days was Hilary, who afterwards became Bishop of Arelate; Maximus, who was the second abbot, and then Bishop of Reii; Lupus, who subsequently held the see of Trecasses; Vincentius, who taught and wrote in the cloister; and Eucherius, who composed, among other works, a treatise in praise of the hermit's life. Eucherius had built a hut for himself and his wife Galla, aloof from the rest of the brotherhood, in the larger island of Lero. It was remembered how one day Honoratus sent a messenger across in a boat with a letter on a wax tablet, and Eucherius, seeing the abbot's writing, said, " To the wax you have restored its honey."

As the monastic spirit grew and spread, many a stranger set his face to Lerinus, hoping, as men hoped greatly in those days, that "he might break through the wall of the passions and ascend by violence to the kingdom of heaven." Among those who joined the new society was Faustus, a compatriot of Patrick. But it is unknown whether he was at Lérins at this time ; perhaps he was still only a child, for we first hear of him in the abbot-ship of Maximus, who succeeded Honoratus,[1] and whom he himself was destined to succeed.[2] Faustus had enjoyed an education such as Patrick never acquired. He was a student of ancient philosophy, and a master of style, as style was then understood. He was afterwards the valued friend and corre-spondent of the greatest man of letters of that century, Sidonius Apollinaris. Crude and rustic must Patrick have seemed to his fellow-countryman, if they met at Lérins. Yet to-day the name of Faustus has passed out of men's memory, and Patrick's is familiar in the households of western Christendom, and in far-western Christendom beyond the ocean.

There can be no doubt that the years which he spent at Lérins exercised an abiding influence on Patrick. He was brought under the spell of the monastic ideal ; and though his life was not to

---

[1] A.D. 426.　　　　[2] A.D. 433.

be sequestered, but out in the active world of
men, monastic societies became a principal and
indispensable element in his idea of a Christian
Church.    It is improbable that during these years
of seclusion he was stirred, even faintly, by the idea
of devoting himself to the work of spreading
Christianity in the barbarous land associated with
his slavery and shame.    But he was profoundly
convinced that during the years of his bondage he
had been held as in the hollow of God's hand ; whatever hopes or ambitions he may have cherished in
his boyhood must have been driven from his heart
by the stress of his experience, and in such a frame
of mind the instinct of a man of that age was to turn
to a religious life.    At Lérins, perhaps, his desire,
so far as he understood it, was to remain a monk ;
*uenire ad eremum summa perfectio est.*    But there
were energies and feelings in him which such a life
would not have contented.    At the end of a few years
he left the monastery to visit his kinsfolk in Britain,
and there he became conscious of the true destiny of
his life.

## § 2. *At Home in Britain*

When Patrick returned to his old home, his
kinsfolk welcomed him "as a son," [1] and implored
him to stay and not part from them again.    But if
he had any thought of yielding to their persuasions,

---

[1] His own expression "as a son" shows that *parentes* here means kinsfolk,
not parents, and justifies the inference that his parents were dead.

it was dismissed when he became aware, all at once, that the aim of his life was determined. The idea of labouring among the heathen, which may have been gradually, though quite unconsciously, gathering force and secretly winning possession of his brain, suddenly stood full-grown, as it were, face to face with him in a sensible shape. In a vision of the night it seemed to him that he saw a man standing by his side. It was a certain Victoricus. We may suppose that Patrick had made this man's acquaintance in Gaul, and that he was interested in Ireland, but his only appearance in history is in Patrick's dream. To the dreamer he seemed to have come from Ireland, and in his hand he held a bundle of letters. "And he gave me one of these, and I read the beginning of the letter, which contained 'the voice of the Irish.' And as I read the beginning of it, I fancied that I heard the voice of the folk who were near the wood of Fochlad, nigh to the western sea. And this was the cry: 'We pray thee, holy youth, to come and again walk amongst us as before.' I was pierced to the heart and could read no more; and thereupon I awoke." This is the dreamer's description of his dream. But, as the story was told in later days, the cry that pierced his heart was uttered by the young children of Fochlad, even by the children still unborn. There is nothing of this in Patrick's words, yet the tradition betrays a true instinct of the significance of the dream. It brings out more intensely and pathetically how the forlorn condition of the helpless unbaptized, condemned to everlasting punishment by the doctrine of the Church, could appeal irresistibly to the pity of a Christian who held that rigorous doctrine.

This doctrine was closely connected with the question which, at this time, above all other questions, was agitating western Christendom ; and, strange to say, the controversy had been opened by a man of Irish descent. It is possible that, as some claim, Pelagius was born in Ireland, but the evidence rather points to the conclusion that he belonged to an Irish family settled in western Britain. His name represents, doubtless, some Irish sea-name such as Muirchu, "hound of the sea." While Patrick was serving in Ireland, Pelagius was in Rome, thinking out one of the great problems which has constantly perplexed the meditations of men, and promulgating a view which arrested the interest or compelled the attention of leaders of theological opinion from York to Carthage, from Carthage to Jerusalem. For some years the Roman Empire echoed with his fame.

Pelagianism is not one of those dull, lifeless heresies which have no more interest than the fact that they once possessed for a short space the minds of men a long while dead. At this period the onward movement of human thought was confined within the lines of theology, couched in theological language, and we must distinguish those questions which, like the Arian and Pelagian, involve speculations of perpetual human interest from controversies

which touch merely the formulae of a special
theology.   We need not enter upon the actual
course of the debate in which Pelagius and Augustine represented two opposed tendencies of religious
and philosophic thought, destined to reappear in the
time of the Reformation, but we are concerned
with the general significance of the questions involved.   The chief and central principle of Pelagius
was the recognition of freewill as an inalienable
property of human nature.   In every action a man
is free to choose between good and evil, and his
choice is not determined, and has not been pre-
determined, by the Deity who originally gave to
man that power of choosing.   Pelagius regarded
freewill as the palladium and surrogate of the dignity
of human nature.   This view logically excluded the
doctrine of original sin, inherited from Adam, as well
as the doctrine of predestination ; it implied that
infants are born sinless, and that baptism is not
necessary to save them from hell ; it implied that it
was perfectly possible, however difficult, for a man
who had not embraced the Christian faith, or been
bathed in the mystical waters of baptism, to lead a
sinless life.   It is clear that this thesis, as the
opponents of Pelagius saw and said, struck at the
very root of the theory of the "Atonement"—at
least as the "Atonement" was crudely conceived by
the Church in dependence on the old Jewish story
of the fall of Adam.   Pelagius does not seem to
have succeeded in really working his theory of

human nature into the Christian system, which he fully accepted, and this was the logical weakness of his position in the theological debate.

Pelagius was not a mere speculator. Himself a monk and rigorous liver, he had in view the practical aim of raising the morality of Christians, and his particular view of human nature and "sin" bore directly on this practical aim. For if the purpose of religion is to realise the ideal of holiness and draw men up, above the level of commonplace sensual life, to high and heavenly things, and if the doctrine of sin was framed by the Church with this view, it might well have seemed to an observer that there lay a practical danger in such a doctrine. There was a danger that, if men were taught that they were born evil and impotent to resist evil by efforts of their own nature, the moral consciousness would be stifled and paralysed by a belief so dishonouring to humanity. The assertion of the freedom of the will by Pelagius, and his denial of innate sin, represent a reaction of the moral consciousness against the dominance of the religious consciousness, and although he speaks within the Church, he is really asserting the man against the Christian, defending the honour of the "reasonable creature."[1]

To the surveyor of the history of humanity this is the interest which Pelagius possesses, an interest which is generally obscured in the dust of controversy. He was the champion of human nature as such,

---

[1] Pelagius, *Letter to Demetrias*, Migne, *P.L.*, xxxii. 1100.

which the Christian Church, in pursuance of its high objects, dishonoured and branded as essentially depraved. He was the champion of all the good men who lived " on the ridge of the world," as men of his own race would have said, before ever Jesus was born, of all those whose minds were fixed on invisible things, of all the noble and sinless pagans, were they many or few. This was the merit of Pelagius, to have attempted to rescue the dignity of human nature oppressed by the doctrine of sin ; and we who realise how much our race owes to the peoples of antiquity may feel particular sympathy with him who dared to say that, before Jesus, sinless men had lived upon earth.[1] Of few men have the Celts of Ireland or Britain better reason to be proud than of the bold thinker who went forth to speak holy words for humanity against the inhuman side of the Christian faith. He was ranged against the authorities of Augustine and Jerome, but he was not fond of fighting ; he wished to keep the whole question out of the region of dogma, and let it remain a matter of opinion ; he never sought to get his own views sanctioned by a council of the Church. But the strife and the defeat are of subordinate interest. What interests us is that Pelagius, himself originally stimulated by Rufinus, stimulated thinking men throughout the West, and induced many to

---

[1] Prosper has an epigram on the thesis that the whole life of non-Christians is sin :

> Perque omnes calles errat sapientia mundi
> Et tenebris addit quae sine luce gerit.

(Epig. 83, ed. Migne, 51, p. 524.)

modify their views about freewill and congenital
sin.

The repose of Lérins was not uninvaded by the
sounds of this debate, and some of its more notable
monks showed hereafter that they had been profoundly influenced by the arguments of Pelagius.
The subject therefore must have been familiar to
Patrick; and the terrible doctrine, impugned by the
Scottish heretic, that infants, being sinful at their
birth, incur the everlasting punishment of the wicked
until they are redeemed through the mysterious
rite of baptism, might well affect his imagination.
Nothing could have done more to quicken his
concern for the unbaptized people by the western
sea than a vivid realisation of this doctrine.

The self-revealing dream convinced Patrick that
he was destined to go as missioner and helper to
Ireland—*ad ultimum terrae*, to the limit of the
world. Yet he felt hesitation and uncertainty, dis-
trusting his own fitness for such an enterprise, conscious of the defective education of his youth; and
he felt a natural repugnance to return to the land
of captivity. His self-questionings and diffidence
were in the end overcome by the mastering instinct of his soul; and to his religious imagination
the instinct seemed to speak within him, like an
inner voice, confirming his purpose. Such experiences befall men of a certain cast and mould when
an impulse, which they can hardly justify when they
weigh it in the scales of the understanding, affects

them so strongly that it seems the objective compulsion or admonition of some external intelligence.


### § 3. *At Auxerre*

It is probable that when he was finally convinced of the destination of his life, and knew that he must seek the woods of Fochlad, Patrick did not tarry long in Britain, but returned to Gaul in order to prepare himself for carrying out his task. It was necessary not only to train himself, but to win support and countenance for his enterprise from influential authorities in the Church. Even if Patrick had been already in clerical orders, it would have been the mere adventure of a wild fanatic, and would have excited general disapprobation, to set sail in the first ship that left the mouth of the Severn for the Irish coast, and, trusting simply in his own zeal and the divine protection, set out to convert the heathen of Connaught. Such were not the conditions of the task which he aspired to perform. He knew that, if he was to succeed, he must come with support and resources and fellow-workers, accredited and in touch with the Christian communities which already existed in Ireland. He needed not only theological study and the counsels of men of leading and light, but material support and official recognition.

At this time the church of Autissiodorum seems to have already won a high position in northern

Gaul through the virtues of its bishop, Amator. It was soon to win a higher fame still through the greater talents of Amator's successor. The town of Autissiodorum, situated on the river Yonne, is no exception to the general rule that the towns of Gaul have preserved the old Gallic names, whether place-names or tribe-names, throughout Roman and German domination alike; and Auxerre, like most towns in Gaul, unlike most towns in Britain, has had a continuous life through all changes since the days when it was Patrick's home in the reign of Honorius and Valentinian. For it was Auxerre that Patrick chose as the place of his study; perhaps he was introduced to Amator by British ecclesiastics. It may be that there was some special link or intimacy between the church of Auxerre and one of the British sees. But it is not unlikely that there was a further motive in determining Patrick's choice. Perhaps some particular interest had been exhibited at Auxerre in the Christian communities of Ireland. There is, in fact, evidence which points to the conclusion that Auxerre was a resort of Irish Christians for theological study. Patrick was ordained deacon by Bishop Amator before long, and it would seem that two other young men, who were afterwards to help the spread of Christianity in Ireland, were ordained at the same time. One of them was a native of south Ireland; his Irish name was Fith, but he took the name of Iserninus. The nationality of his

companion, Auxilius, which the Irish made into
Ausaille, is unknown.

*14 yrs*    Fourteen years passed, at the smallest computation, from the ordination of Patrick till the day
came for setting forth to his chosen task. This
long delay can hardly be accounted for by the
necessities of an ecclesiastical training. There
must have been other impediments and difficulties.
He intimates himself that he was not encouraged.
Those to whom he looked up for counsel considered
his project rash and himself unqualified for such a
work. His *rusticitas*, or want of liberal education,
was urged against him; and perhaps a failure to
win support is a sufficient explanation of the delay.

At all events Patrick, one would suppose, had a
discreet, if not a sympathetic, guide in the head of
the church of Auxerre. Amator had been succeeded
by one who was to bear a more illustrious name in
the ecclesiastical annals of Gaul. Germanus is a
case, common in Gaul and elsewhere at this period,
of a distinguished layman who held office in the
State exchanging secular for ecclesiastical office.
In the year 429 it devolved upon him to visit
Britain, and this enterprise must have had a
particular interest for Patrick. The poison of the
serpent Pelagius, as his opponents named him, had
been spreading, in a diluted form, in the island;
some of the writings of its British advocates are
still extant. The orthodox pillars of the British
Church were alarmed, and they sent pressing mes-

sages across the sea to invite their Gallic brethren
to send able champions over to overcome the
heresy. It was probably to Auxerre and Troyes,
in the first instance, that they made their appeal,
and it is recorded that at a synod held at Troyes
it was decided that Germanus should proceed to
Britain along with Lupus, Bishop of Troyes, who
had been formerly a monk of Lérins. Whatever
may be the truth about this alleged Gallic synod,
Germanus went with higher authority and prestige ;
for he went under the direct sanction of Celestine,
the Bishop of Rome. We learn that this sanction
was gained by the influence of the deacon Palladius,
who may possibly have been a deacon of Germanus.
The authoritative mission from Gaul seems to have
crushed the heretics, and their doctrine was compelled to hide its head in Britain for a few years to
come.

Celestine was approached soon afterwards on a
subject which touched Patrick more closely than the
suppression of heresy in Britain. His attention
was drawn to the position of the Christian communities in Ireland. The man who interested himself in this matter was the same deacon, Palladius,
who had interested himself in the extirpation of
British Pelagianism. It is remarkable that this
first appearance of Irish Christianity in ecclesiastical
history should be associated, both chronologically
and in the person of Palladius, with the Pelagian
question. Now we may be sure that some overture

or message had come from the Christian bodies in
Ireland, whether to Britain, or Gaul, or to Rome
itself; for the Bishop of Rome would hardly have
sent them a bishop unless they had intimated that
they wanted one.[1]    It is, then, not impossible,
though it is not proven, that the motive of the Irish
Christians in taking such a step at this moment
may have been the same Pelagian difficulty
which had caused the appeal from Britain.[2]    The
question, which must have occurred sooner or later,
of organising the small Christian societies of Ireland
may possibly have been brought to a head by the
Pelagian debate.    And if the Pelagian heresy had
gained any ground in Ireland, nothing would have
been more natural than that the fact should have
come before the notice of Germanus while he was
dealing with the same question in Britain.

This conjecture, which is suggested unconstrain-
edly by the general situation, may supply us with
the key for reading between the lines of a passage
in Patrick's autobiographical sketch.    He complains
of the treachery of a most intimate friend, whom he
does not name, but who seems, from the circumstances, to have been an ecclesiastic, whether of
Britain or Gaul.    To this friend he had communicated his inmost thoughts,—*credidi etiam animam,*
—and had evidently received sympathy from him in
regard to his cherished plan of working in Ireland.

[1] Compare Celestine, *Ep.* iv. (Migne, *P.L.*, l. 434), nullus inuitis detur
episcopus.
[2] The conjecture is due to Professor Zimmer.

His friend had told him emphatically that he must be made a bishop. And afterwards, when the question of choosing a bishop for Ireland practically arose, his friend was active in urging his claims. Now it was in Britain that the matter was discussed when Patrick's friend, though Patrick himself was not there, showed such loyal zeal in his behalf. Here, then, we have an incident which exactly fits into the situation when Germanus was fighting against heresy in Britain in A.D. 429. If this heresy existed in Ireland, it was an element in the problem with which Germanus had to deal, even with regard to British interests solely; for, if the false doctrine were permitted to spread unchecked in the Irish communities, it might constitute a serious danger to the neighbouring church in Britain. If, as was most likely to occur, orthodox members of the Irish communities sent representatives to Germanus while he was in Britain and asked for some intervention, the question of sending a bishop to guide the Irish Christians in the right path and organise their society became at once practical and urgent. This then, it seems reasonable to suggest, may have been the occasion on which Patrick's friend designated him as the suitable man for the post.

The opportunity for which Patrick had been waiting long seemed to have come at last. Probably a certain interest in Irish Christianity had been already felt in Gaul, and especially at Auxerre; but

it was now brought under the notice of the head of
Christendom.   There seemed a prospect now for
Patrick to undertake the work on which he had set
his heart under high sanction and with sufficient
support.   But Celestine's choice fell on another.
The deacon Palladius, who had been active in
these affairs, was prepared to go to Ireland, and
Celestine consecrated him bishop for the purpose
(A.D. 431).   The choice, if it was Celestine's own,
was perfectly natural.   We must remember that the
first and chief consideration of Celestine was the
welfare and orthodoxy of Irish believers, not the
conversion of Irish unbelievers.   He was called
upon to meet the need of the Christian communities; the further spreading of the faith among
the heathen was an ulterior consideration.   The
qualification, therefore, which he sought in the new
bishop may not have been burning zeal for preaching to pagans, but rather experience and capacity
for dealing with the Pelagian heresy.   Palladius had
taken a prominent part in coping with this heresy
in Britain, and it is a probable conjecture that
he had accompanied Germanus thither.   Possibly
representatives of the Irish Christians may have
intimated that they wished for his appointment.

## § 4. *Palladius in Ireland* (A.D. 431-2)

The brief chronicle of the visit of Palladius to
Ireland is that he came and went within a year.   It

is generally assumed that he had not the strength
or tact to deal with the situation; that he departed
in despair; that his mission was a failure.   But our
evidence hardly warrants this conclusion.   We are
told that he proceeded from Ireland to the land of
the Picts in north Britain, and died there.   But we
cannot be sure that he did not intend to return.   It
is with north Leinster [1] and the hills of Wicklow that
tradition associates the brief episode of Palladius.
But we may be tempted to suspect that the expedition of Palladius to the country of the Picts was not
an abandonment of Ireland, but was, on the contrary,
part of his work in Ireland, and that it was not the
Picts of north Britain, but some Christian communities existing among the Picts of Dalaradia in
north Ireland, who were the object of his concern.
The most probable conclusion seems to be that the
episcopate of Palladius in Ireland was cut short, not
by a voluntary desertion of his post, but by death.

We should like to know where were the dwelling-
places of the Christians to whom Palladius was sent.
Between the port where Wicklow of the Vikings
now is, the port where Palladius landed, and the
lonely glen of the two lakes by whose shores a cluster
of churches was afterwards to spring up, stretched
the lands of the children of Garrchu, and tradition
said that the chief of this tribe regarded Palladius
with disfavour.   But his short sojourn is also

---

[1] The old kingdom of Leinster, or Laigin, was south of the Liffey, and in
this book "Leinster" is used in this sense (not equivalent to the modern
province, which includes the old kingdom of Meath).   See below, chap. iv.

associated with the foundation of three churches.
It is possible that we may seek the site of a little
house for praying, built by him or his disciples, on
a high wooded hill that rises sheer enough on the
left bank of the river Avoca, close to a long slant-
ing hollow, down which, over grass or bushes, the
eye catches the glimmer of the stream winding in
the vale below, and rises beyond to the higher hills
which bound the horizon.    Here may have been
the " House of the Romans," Tech na Róman, and
Tigroney, the shape in which this name is concealed,
may be a memorial of the first missioner of Rome.
But farther west, beyond the hills, we can determine
with less uncertainty another place which tradition
associated with the activity of Palladius, in the
neighbourhood of one of the royal seats of the lords
of Leinster.    From the high rath of Dunlavin those
kings had a wide survey of their realm.    Standing
there, one can see westward to Mount Bladma,
and northward, across the Plain of Liffey, into the
kingdom of Meath.    More than a league eastward
from this fortress Palladius is said to have founded
a church which was known as the " domnach " or
" Lord's house " of the High-field, *Domnach Airte*,
in a hilly region which is strewn with the remnants
of ancient generations.    The original church of this
place has long since vanished, and its precise site
cannot be guessed with certainty, but it gave a
permanent name to the place.    At Donard we feel
with some assurance that we are at one of the

earliest homes of the Christian faith in Ireland, not the earliest that existed, but the earliest to which we can give a name.

There was a third church, seemingly the most important of those which Palladius is said to have founded, Cell Fine, "the Church of the Tribes," in which his tablets and certain books and relics which he had brought from Rome were preserved. Here, and perhaps here only, in the place, unknown to us, where his relics lay, was preserved the memory of Palladius, a mere name. Whatever his qualities may have been, he was too short a time in Ireland to have produced a permanent impression. The historical significance of his appearance there does not lie in any slight ecclesiastical or theological successes he may have accomplished. It is significant because it was the first manifestation in Ireland of the authority of Rome. The secular arm of Rome, in days when Rome was mightier—the arm of Agricola, the arm of Theodosius—had never reached the Scottic coast; it was not till after the mother of the Empire had been besieged and despoiled by barbarian invaders that her new spiritual dominion began to reach out to those remote shores which her worldly power had never sought to gain. The coming of Palladius was the first link in the chain which bound Ireland — for some centuries loosely—to the spiritual centre of western Europe.

But when, seeking vainly for traces of this first

comer in the vales of the children of Garrchu or on the holy hill of Donard, we see the memorials in earth and stone of days before Palladius, we are reminded that, if his coming is significant, it is a fact more important still that no secular messengers of Rome had come before him.   The superstitious and primitive customs of the island were protected and secured, pure and uncontaminated, by the barrier of sundering seas.   If one of the early Roman Emperors had annexed Ireland to their British provinces, ideas of city life and civil government and administration would have been introduced which might have proved a more powerful solvent than Christianity of Celtic and Iberian barbarism. A Roman colonia, a number of Roman towns with municipal organisation, might, in a couple of hundred years, have produced a greater change in civilisation than all the little clerical communities which sprang up in the three or four centuries after the coming of Palladius.   It would have been the task of the Roman government to put an end to the incessant petty wars between the kingdoms and tribes, *pacisque imponere morem*.   But the absence of such civilising influence protected and preserved the native traditions, and the curiosity of those who study the development of the human mind may be glad that Ireland lay safe and undisturbed at the end of the world, and that Palladius, nearly a hundred years after the death of Constantine, was the first emissary from Rome.

## § 5. *Consecration of Patrick* (A.D. 432)

The appointment of Palladius as bishop for the
Scots had naturally affected the plans of Patrick.
There was no longer any motive for delay in setting
about the accomplishment of his project.    There
was no reason why, with the support of Auxerre
and Bishop Germanus, he should not set forth, along
with whatever coadjutors he could muster, and,
under the auspices of the new bishop, begin the
conversion of the heathen.    All was arranged for his
enterprise in the following year (A.D. 432), and the
tradition is that he had already set out from Auxerre,
accompanied by Segitius, an elderly presbyter, when
the news reached Gaul that Palladius was dead.
The announcement was brought by some of the
companions of Palladius, and Patrick's plans were
once more interrupted.    But only for a moment.
The circumstances seem to imply that there was
a distinct understanding that he was to be the
successor of Palladius, and Germanus consecrated
him bishop immediately.    And so it came about
that, in the end, he started for the field of his work
invested with the authority and office which would
render his labours most effective.[1]

Considerable preparations had, doubtless, been
necessary.    To carry out the ambitious scheme of
converting heathen lands, there was needed not
only a company of fellow-workers, but a cargo of

---

[1] See Appendix C, 9, on Patrick's consecration.

"spiritual treasures" and ecclesiastical gear for the equipment of the new communities which were to be founded.[1] Money and treasure were indispensable, and however simple Patrick's faith may have been in the intrinsic potency of the gospel which he was inspired to preach, he was a man of thoroughly practical mind, and he knew that silver and gold and worldly wealth would be needed in dealing with pagan princes, and in the effective establishment of clerical communities.

The foregoing account of Patrick's setting forth for the field of his labours is based on a critical examination of the oldest sources. In later times men wished to believe that he, too, like Palladius, was consecrated by Celestine.[2] Such a consecration seemed both to add a halo of dignity to the national saint and to link his church more closely to the apostolic seat. We have no means of knowing whether Patrick set out before or after the death of Celestine,[3] but in any case the pious story is inconsistent with the oldest testimonies. Nor, even if there were room for doubt, would the question

[1] No better illustration of this can be found than Pope Gregory's provision for the mission of Augustine to England, as recorded in Bede, *Hist. ecc.* i. 29 ; he sent, besides fellow-workers, "uniuersa quae ad cultum erant ac ministerium ecclesiae necessaria, uasa videlicet sacra, et vestimenta altarium, ornamenta quoque ecclesiarum, et sacerdotalia uel clericilia indumenta, sanctorum etiam apostolorum ac martyrum reliquias, necnon et codices plurimos."

[2] It has recently been held, more plausibly but erroneously, that Patrick was on his way to Rome when the news of the death of Palladius overtook him. See Appendix C, 8.

[3] Celestine probably died July 27, and Xystus succeeded July 31, 432. These dates have been determined by M. Duchesne, *Liber Pontificalis*, i. pp. ccli.-ii.

involve any point of theoretical or practical importance.   By virtue of what had already happened,
Ireland was, in principle, as closely linked to Rome
as any western church.   The circumstances of the consecration and mission of Palladius were significant ;
but whether his successor was ordained at Rome or
at Auxerre, whether he was personally known to
the Roman pontiff or not, was a matter of little
moment.   It will not be amiss, however, to dwell
more fully on the situation.

The position of the Roman see at this period in
the Western Church is often wrongly represented,
or vaguely understood.   At the end of the fourth
century the bishops of Rome, beyond their acknowledged primacy in Christendom, possessed at least
two important rights which secured them a large
influence in the ecclesiastical affairs of the western
provinces of the Empire.[1]   The Roman see was
recognised by imperial decrees of Valentinian I. and
Gratian as a court to which clergy might appeal
from the decisions of provincial councils in any part
of the western portion of the Empire.   Of not
less practical importance was another distinctive
prerogative, which, though not recognised by any
formal enactment, was admitted and acted upon by
the churches of the west.   The Roman Church was

---

[1] It is probable that excommunication by a Roman bishop was also recognised as universally binding.   The question whether the popes had the right
of annulling sentences pronounced by provincial councils on bishops, depends
on the question of the authenticity of the Council of Sardica.   See J. Friedrich,
*Sitzungsber.* of the Bavarian Academy, 1901, 417 *sqq.* ; E. Babut, *Le concile
de Turin*, 75.

*Role of state*

regarded as the model church, and when doubtful points of discipline arose, the bishops of the Gallic or other provinces used to consult the Bishop of Rome for guidance, not as to a particular case, but as to a general principle. The answers of the Roman bishops to such questions are what are called *decretals.* No decretals are preserved older than those of Damasus,[1] and perhaps it was in his pontificate that the practice of such applications for advice became general. The motive of the custom is evident. It was to preserve uniformity of discipline throughout the Church and prevent the upgrowth of divergent practices. But those who consulted the Roman pontiff were not in any way bound to accept his ruling. The decretal was an answer to a question ; it was not a command. Those who accepted it were merely imitating the Roman see ; they were not obeying it.

The appellate jurisdiction, and the decretals which were gradually to be converted from letters of advice into letters of command, were the chief foundations on which the spiritual empire of Rome grew up. But in the latter part of the fourth century its nascent authority was confronted by a serious danger in the shape of a rival. When Milan instead of Rome became the imperial residence in Italy, the see of Milan assumed immediately a new importance and prestige. Its bishop soon came to be regarded as an authority to which appeals might be addressed,

[1] A.D. 366-384.

as well as to the Bishop of Rome. This new dignity was justified by the personality of Ambrose, who then occupied the see, but it was due to the presence of the Augustus. If his presence had been lasting, it is possible that Mediolanum would have become in regard to Rome what Constantinople became, because it was the Imperial city, in regard to Alexandria and Antioch. But the danger passed away when the Emperor Honorius migrated to Ravenna, though the consequences of the transient rivalry of Milan with Rome can be traced for a few years longer.

For the further development of the spiritual authority of Rome two things were necessary—tact and imperial support. Bishop Zosimus possessed neither, and his brief pontificate did as much as could be done within two short years to injure the prestige of the apostolic seat. He was smitten on one cheek by the synods of Africa, he was smitten on the other by the Gallic bishops at the Council of Turin.[1] He intervened in the Pelagian controversy, and was obliged to eat his own words. But his inglorious pontificate remains a landmark,[2] because he was the first to make a strenuous attempt to exercise sovran rights which the western churches had never admitted or been asked to admit—rights which a more competent pontiff afterwards secured. The indiscretions of Zosimus were atoned for by more

---

[1] See Babut, *Le concile de Turin* (1904), a valuable work.

[2] This has been well brought out by M. Babut.

moderate successors, but the most consummate tact and adroitness would never have won the powers of intervention which he had claimed and the Gallic bishops had repudiated, if Pope Leo had not gained the ear of the Emperor. In A.D. 445, one of the greatest dates in the history of the growth of the papal power, the Emperor Valentinian III. conferred on the Bishop of Rome sovran authority in the western provinces which were still under imperial sway.[1]

But in the meantime, though southern Gaul might resist Zosimus and disregard Celestine when they attempted to assert a right of control, though Celestine might discern in the power of the see of Arles and in the tendencies of the monks of Lérins forces adverse to Roman influence, no Gallic bishop would have thought of questioning the appellate jurisdiction or the moral authority of the Roman see, as exercised before the days of Zosimus. Germanus of Auxerre might sympathise with Hilary of Arles in his struggle with Pope Leo, but in dealing with heresy in Britain he had acted cordially with Pope Celestine. No one could ascribe more importance than Vincentius of Lérins to the decisions of the "apostolic seat."[2] It would be a grave mistake to infer from the disputes which cluster round Arles that the bishops of Gaul had ceased in any way to acknowledge the older claims of Rome or to reverence it as the head of Christendom.

---

[1] *Novella*, xvi.   [2] *Commonitorium*, ii. 33, 34.

When a new ecclesiastical province was to be added to western Christendom, it was to Rome, naturally, that an appeal would be made. It was to the Bishop of Rome, as representing the unity of the Church, that the Christians of Ireland, desiring to be an organised portion of that unity, would naturally look to speed them on their way. His recognition of Ireland as a province of the spiritual federation of which he was the acknowledged head, would be the most direct and effective means of securing for it an established place among the western churches. If, then, they asked Celestine either to choose a bishop for them, or to confirm their own choice and consecrate a bishop of their choosing, they adopted exactly the course which we might expect. But once this step was taken, once the Roman bishop had given his countenance and sanction, it was a matter of indifference who consecrated his successor. There was significance in the consecration at Rome of the first bishop of the new province ; there would have been no particular significance in such a consecration in the case of the second any more than in the case of the third. It was an accident that Patrick was consecrated in Gaul. If Palladius had not been cut off, and if Patrick had proceeded, as he intended, to Ireland in the capacity of a simple deacon, he might afterwards have been called to succeed Palladius by the choice of the Irish Christians and received episcopal ordination wherever it was most convenient. The essential point is that by the sending of Palladius, Ireland had become one of the western churches, and therefore, like its fellows, looked to the see of Rome as the highest authority in Christendom.    Unless, at the very moment of incorporation, they were to repudiate the unity of the Church, the Christians of Ireland could not look with other eyes than the Christians of Gaul at the appellate jurisdiction of the Roman bishop, and the moral weight of his decretals.

*Note the shift.*

# CHAPTER IV

## POLITICAL AND SOCIAL CONDITION OF IRELAND

NOWHERE more conspicuously than in Ireland have secular institutions determined the manner in which the Christian religion spread and increased. The introduction of that religion effected no social revolution; it introduced new ideas and a new profession, but society steadily remained in the primitive stage of tribal organisation for more than a thousand years after the island had become part of Christendom.[1]

Ireland was divided into a large number of small districts, each of which was owned by a tribe,[2] the aggregate of a number of clans or families which believed that they were descended from a common ancestor. At the head of the tribe was a "king," who was elected from a certain family. Below the king were four social grades within the tribe. There were the nobles,[3] who were distinguished by the

---

[1] The chief source for the social and economic conditions of ancient Ireland is the collection of the *Ancient Laws of Ireland* (6 vols., 1865-1901). A clear account of the general framework of society, with interesting details and illustrations, will be found in Dr. Joyce's *Social History of Ireland*, vol. i.

[2] *Tuath* = people, tribe, tribal district.      [3] *Flaith* = noble.

possession of land.   These were the only members
of the tribe, besides the king, who had land of their
own.   After them came those who had wealth in
cattle and other movable property,[1] but were only
tenants of the land on which they lived.   Below
these were freemen, who had no property either in
soil or in cattle, but farmed lands for which they
paid rent.   The lowest grade consisted of herds and
labourers of various kinds, who were not freemen,
but were regarded as members of the tribe and
entitled to its protection.   There was also another
class of slaves who did not belong to the tribe,
consisting of strangers—such as fugitives, bought
slaves, and captives.   Patrick belonged to this
class, *fudirs* as they were called, in the days of his
bondage.

Originally all the land must have belonged to
the tribe.   But at the time with which we are
concerned, part of the arable land was the private
property of the king and the nobles.   There were,
however, certain restrictions on this proprietorship
which show that, theoretically, all the land was
still considered as in a certain sense tribal.   The
chief of these was that the proprietor could not
alienate his land without the consent of the tribe.

The limits of these small tribal kingdoms can be
still approximately traced, for they are represented,
for the most part, by the baronies of the modern
map, and the names of the baronies in many cases

---

[1] The *bó-aires*.

preserve the names of the tribes. The inspection of a map on which the baronies are marked will convey a general idea of the number and size of the small kingdoms which formed the political units of the island. These kingdoms varied greatly in size ; the tribes varied in numbers and importance. But each kingdom, whether large or small, managed its own affairs. The self-government of the tribes, and the complicated organisation of the clans and families within them, were the most important and fundamental social facts. But the tribal units were grouped together loosely in a political organisation of an elaborate kind, consisting in degrees of overlordship.

Thus the king of Cashel was king over all the kingdoms of Munster ; the under-kings owed him tribute and service in war, and he had certain obligations to them.[1] The king of Connaught and the king of Laigin held the same position in regard to the kings of those provinces, and the King of Tara exercised similar overlordship over the kings of Meath. But the king of Tara was also overlord of all the kings of Ireland, and his superior position was designated by the title "Árd-rí," High King.

The kings of Cashel, Connaught, and Laigin are

---

[1] The tributes and presents which are due from the under-kings to the over-kings, the donations which the over-kings owe to the under-kings, the privileges which the various kings possess, are the subject of the *Book of Rights* (edited and translated by O'Donovan, 1847), which still awaits a critical investigation. It is easy to see that it was compiled in Munster in the tenth century, but it was based on older material of high antiquity, and clearly reproduces the general character of the mutual relations which theoretically bound together the Irish kingdoms.

usually described as provincial kings. For the
island was regarded as consisting of five provinces
or "fifths." Connaught, Mumu, and "Ultonia"
corresponded, with some minor differences, to
Connaught, Munster, and Ulster of the modern
map ; while Leinster represents the two remaining
fifths, Laigin in the south and Meath in the north.
But it does not appear that in historical times there
was any king who held the same position in the
province of Ulster which the king of Cashel held in
Munster. The northern province consisted of three
large kingdoms, which seem to have been wholly
independent, Aileach, Oriel, and Ulaid.[1] The
kings of these territories were all alike overlords
of under-kings ; they were all alike subject to the
High King ; but they were as independent of one
another as they were of the king of Connaught.
The king of Ulaid was not under the king of
Aileach, as the king of Thomond or the king of
Ossory was under the king of Cashel.[2]

Ireland then was organised, theoretically, in an
ascending scale of kings and over-kings. There was
the High King at the head of all. Below him were
six over-kings, the king of Cashel, the king of

[1] The king of Aileach was so called because his palace was at Aileach,
near Londonderry. His territory was north Ulster to the Bann. Ulaid was
east Ulster ; Oriel, south Ulster.

[2] This is clearly to be inferred from the *Book of Rights*, where no relations
or mutual obligations are mentioned as existing between the three Ulster kings.
Nor was there, since the destruction of the old Ulidian kingdom in the third
century, any name to designate the whole province, for Ulaid was confined to
the kingdom in the east of Ulster. The use of Ultonia to describe the
province, as distinguished from Ulidia = Ulaid, is of course merely a literary
convention.

Connaught, the king of Laigin, the king of Aileach, the king of Ulaid, and the king of Oriel. Below these were the tribal kings, but in some cases there were intermediate grades, kings who were overlords of several small territories. For example, several of the small kingdoms in north Munster formed an intermediate group, the kingdom of Thomond. It is clear that this system must have grown up by degrees through conquest, and one remarkable practice illustrates its origin. It was the habit of the over-kings to take hostages from the under-kings, as a surety for the fulfilment of their obligations. This was such an important feature of the political system that a house for the custody of hostages was an almost indispensable addition to a royal palace. The "mound of the hostages" is still shown at Tara.[1]

But though the general theory of the system is clear, it would be difficult to say how far it was a reality at any particular period, or how far the elaborate scheme of obligations and counter-obliga- tions, binding on the kings of all ranks, was intended to be enforced. The ceaseless warfare which marks the annals of Ireland suggests that these bonds were a cause of trouble rather than a source of union.

Of the political relations existing in Ireland in the fifth century we know practically nothing. The most important fact seems to be that the descendants

[1] See Petrie, *Tara Hill*, 135.

of King Eochaid,[1] and particularly the family of his son Niall, both of whom had been High Kings, were winning a decided preponderance in the northern half of the island. When Patrick came to Ireland, a son of Niall was on the throne of Tara; his cousin was king of Connaught; one of his sons gave an abiding name to a large territory in north Ulster;[2] other sons were kings of lesser kingdoms in Meath. Family connexions of this kind were no permanent, or even immediate, guarantee of union; but it is probable that at this time, through the predominance of his near kindred, a prudent High King, such as Loigaire, son of Niall, seems to have been, may have been able to exert more effectual and far-reaching influence than many of his forerunners and successors. We shall have occasion to observe that his reign seems to have been a relatively peaceful period, if such an epithet can be applied to any epoch of Irish history. Whatever may have been the measure of the High King's authority, it was unquestionably desirable for the new bishop, in pursuing his designs, to secure his favour or neutrality. But the political situation and the mutual relations of the higher potentates had, we may fairly surmise, no decisive or serious effect on the prospects of the religion which was now about to become firmly established in the land. Those prospects depended

---

[1] His date, according to the Annals, was A.D. 358-366; Niall reigned A.D. 379-405; his nephew, Dathi, 405-428; and then his son, Loigaire, 428-463. For Amolngaid (Dathi's brother), king of Connaught, see Appendix C, 14.

[2] Tyr-connell.

mainly, if not entirely, upon gaining the tribal kings and the heads of families. The king of Ulidia, or the King of Ireland himself, might suffer or encourage the strange worship in his own immediate territory, might himself embrace the faith, but beyond that he could only recommend it; and though his example might indeed do much, he could not force any under-king and his tribe to tolerate the presence of a Christian community in their borders.

It was not political relations but the tribal system and economic conditions that claimed the study of a bishop who came not merely to make individual converts, but to build up a sacerdotal society. A church and a priesthood must have means of support, and in a country where wealth consisted in land and cattle it was plain that, if the church was to become a stable and powerful institution, its priests and ministers must have lands secured for their use. But land could be obtained only through the goodwill of those who possessed it, and therefore it was impossible to plant a church in any territory until some noble who owned a private estate had been persuaded to accept the Christian baptism and to make a grant of land for ecclesiastical use, with his tribe's consent. The conversion of the landless classes, slaves, or farmers, or even the lords of herds, could not lead to the foundation of churches and the maintenance of sacerdotal institutions. The success of Patrick's enterprise depended on the kings of the tribes and the chiefs of the clans.

There was another reason also why Christianity could not hope to make considerable progress until the heads of society had been converted. Strong tribal sentiment, expressed in the devotion of the tribesmen to the king of the tribe, of the clansmen to the chief of the clan, was the most powerful social bond; and while, if a chief accepted the new faith, his clan would generally follow his example, it was not likely that if he rejected it many of his followers would dissociate themselves from his action. Thus on every account the process of establishing the Christian worship and priesthood in Ireland must begin from above and not from below.

We know little of the religious beliefs and cults in Ireland which the Christian faith aspired to displace. It there was any one divinity who was revered and worshipped throughout the land it was probably the sun. There seem to have been no temples, but there were altars in the open air, and idols were worshipped, especially in the form of pillar-stones. Various gods and goddesses play a part in the tales of Irish mythology, but it is not known whether any of these beings was honoured by a cult. There was no priesthood, and it seems certain that there was no organised religion which could be described as national.

Heathenism of such a kind could oppose no formidable resistance to the weapons of such a force as the organised religion which had swept the Roman Empire. Heathenism is naturally

tolerant; and, when there is no powerful sacerdotal order jealous of its privileges and monopoly,
a new superstition is readily entertained. It must
be admitted as probable that the morality which the
Christian faith enjoins, and the hopes which it offers,
would hardly have appealed to heathen peoples or
taken possession of their minds if it had not engaged
their imaginations by mysteries and rites. It was,
above all, these mysterious rites—baptism, without
which the body and soul were condemned to everlasting torment, and the mystical ceremony which is
known as the Eucharist—that stamped the religion
as genuine in the eyes of barbarians. And it is to
be observed that Christianity, while it demanded
that its converts should abandon heathen observ-
ances and heathen cults, did not require them to
surrender their belief in the existence of the beings
whom they were forbidden to worship. They were
only required to regard those beings in a new light,
as maleficent demons. For the Christians them
selves, even the highest authorities in the Church,
were as superstitious as the heathen. The belief in
the *sidhe*, or fairies, which was universal in Ireland,
was not affected by Christianity, and survives at the
present day. Thus the spreading of the new religion
was facilitated by the circumstance that it made no
attempt to root out the heathen superstitions as intellectual absurdities, but only aimed at transcending
and transforming them, so that fear of deities should
be turned into hatred of demons.

*Reaction to 'gods' — devils.
'superstition'*

The chief pretenders to the possession of wizardry and powers of divination in Ireland were the Druids,[1] who correspond, but not in all respects, to the Druids of Gaul. They joined to their supernatural lore innocent secular learning, skill in poetry, and knowledge of the laws and history of their country. They gave the kings advice and educated their children. The high value which was attached to their counsels rested naturally on their prophetic powers. They practised divination in various forms, with inscribed rods of yew, for instance, or by means of magic wheels.[2] They could raise the winds, cover the plains with darkness, create envelopes of vapour,[3] which rendered those who moved therein invisible. Though learned in things divine, they did not form a sacerdotal class; and in their religious functions they might be compared rather to augurs than to priests. It was their habit to shave their heads in front from ear to ear and to wear white garments. It was inevitable that these men should be unfriendly to the introduction of new beliefs which threatened their own position, since it condemned the practice of divination and those kindred arts on which their eminent power was

---

[1] The derivation of the word *druid* (nom. *drui*, gen. *druad*) is uncertain. Perhaps, as Professor Rhŷs holds, Druidism was not of Celtic origin, and the word " was adopted by the Celts from some earlier population conquered by them " (see his " Studies in Early Irish History," in *Proceedings of the British Academy*, vol. i. p. 8). *Druidecht* is the Irish for magic. For the functions and powers of the Druids some excellent pages in Dr. Joyce's *Social History*, I. c. ix., may be recommended; illustrations and references will be found there.

[2] Mug Ruith, servant of the wheel, was the name of a mythical Druid.

[3] The *Feth Fiada*.

based.   But their opposition could not be effective, because they had no organisation.

The fact, then, that the Christian Church, by its recognition of demons as an actual power with which it had to cope, stood in this respect on the same intellectual plane as the heathen, was an advantage in the task of diffusing the religion. The belief in demons as a foe with which the Church had to deal was expressed officially in the institution of a clerical order called exorcists, whose duty it was, by means of formulae, to exorcise devils at baptism.[1]   Patrick had exorcists in his train, and it was not unimportant that the Christian, going forth to persuade the heathen, had such equipments of superstition.   He was able to meet the heathen sorcerer on common ground because he believed in the sorceries which he condemned.[2]   He was as fully convinced as the pagan that the powers of magicians were real, but he knew that those powers were strictly limited, whereas the power of his own God was limitless.   Patrick could never have said to an Irish wizard, as children of enlightenment would now say, "Your magic is imposture; your

[1] For these superstitious ceremonies at baptism cp. Duchesne, *Origines du culte chrétien*, pp. 296-7 (the exorcism of salt), 299, 317 ; cp. 349.

[2] In the remarkable ancient Irish Christian incantation, the Lorica, ascribed to St. Patrick (see Appendix A, 5), the Trinity, Angels, Prophets, and other Christian powers are invoked, but also " might of heaven, brightness of sun, brilliance of moon, splendour of fire, speed of light, swiftness of wind, depth of sea, stability of earth, firmness of rock," to intervene between him who repeats the spell when he arises in the morning and " every fierce merciless force that may come upon my body and soul ; against incantations of false prophets, against black laws of paganism, against false laws of heresy, against deceit of idolatry, *against spells of women and smiths and druids*, against all knowledge that is forbidden [so Atkinson] the human soul."

spells cannot really raise spirits or control the forces of nature; you cannot foretell what is to come." He would have said, "Yes, you can do such miracles by the aid of evil powers, but those powers are subject to a good power whose religion I preach, and are impotent except through his permission." This point of mental agreement between the Christian priest and the heathen whom he regarded as benighted, their common belief in the efficacy of sorcery, though they put different interpretations on its conditions,[1] was probably not an insignificant aid in the propagation of the Christian religion. It may be said, more generally, that if Christianity had offered to men only its new theological doctrine with the hope of immortal life and its new ethical ideals, if it had come simple and unadorned, without an armoury of mysteries, miracles, and rites, if it had risen to the height of rejecting magic not because it was wicked but because it was absurd, it could never have won half the world.

It was natural that the spread of new religious ideas should excite the misgivings of the Druids, but so long as the new doctrine was professed only here and there in isolated households, they could hardly

---

[1] M. Réville, dealing with the third century, puts this very well. "Chacun croit sans le moindre difficulté à toutes les merveilles et à toutes les folies. On dirait même que plus une pratique est merveilleuse, plus elle a de chance d'être admise sans contestation. Chose singulière ! les adeptes des religions opposées ne contestent pas la réalité des miracles allégués par leurs adversaires : Celse admet les miracles des chrétiens, et ceux-ci ne se refusent pas à admettre les miracles païens ; des deux parts on attribue aux mauvais esprits les merveilles invoquées par les adversaires" (*La Religion à Rome sous les Sévères*, p. 131).

gauge its force or estimate the danger.  It is not
unlikely that shortly before the coming of Palladius
they awoke to the fact that a faith, opposed to their
own interests, was gaining ground, for, at the same
time, the Christian communities were discovering
that they deserved and required a bishop and an
ecclesiastical organisation.   The apprehension of
the Druids may be reflected in a prophecy attributed
to the wizards of the High King.    They foretold
that a foreign doctrine would seduce the people,
overthrow kings, and subvert the old order of
things, and they designated the preacher of the
doctrine in these oracular words :[1] " Adze-head will
come with a crook-head staff; in his house, with
hole-head robe, he will chant impiety from his table;
from the front (eastern) part of his house all his
household will respond, So be it, so be it."    It
would not be legitimate to build any theory on an
alleged prophecy, when we cannot control its date.
But we may admit, without hesitation, that this
ancient verse, which was assuredly composed by a
pagan, contains nothing inconsistent with the tradition that it was current before the coming of Patrick.
There is nothing to stamp it as an oracle _post eventum._
The knowledge which it shows of Christian usages
was accessible to the Druids, inasmuch as Christianity
was already known, had already won converts, in
Ireland.   And if, as we have seen reason to believe,
the Christians of Ireland negotiated for the appoint-

[1] See note, Appendix B.

ment of a bishop a year or two before the sending of Palladius, there would be no difficulty in supposing that the Druids at this juncture, aware that a leader was expected, expressed their apprehensions in this form.   But whatever be the truth about the oracle, whether it circulated in the mouths of men before the appearance of Palladius and Patrick, or was first declared at a later period, it possesses historical significance as reflecting the agitation of heathenism, roused at length to alarm at the growth of the foreign worship.

*Synthesis — practical plans & supernatural power*

# CHAPTER V

## IN THE ISLAND-PLAIN, IN DALARADIA

THE spot where the river Vartry, once the Dee, reaches the coast, just north of the long ness which runs out into the sea at Wicklow, has a historical interest because this little river mouth, now of no account, was a chief port of the island in ancient times for mariners from south Britain and Gaul, a place where strangers and traders landed, and where the natives could perhaps most often have sight of outlandish ships and foreign faces. It was the port where Patrick would most naturally land coming from south Britain; but in any case he could hardly do otherwise than first seek the region where Palladius had briefly laboured. This would naturally be the starting-point, the place for studying the situation, forming plans, perhaps opening negotiations. But there is no record of this first indispensable stage in the new bishop's work, and our ignorance of his relations to these communities in southern Ireland is one of the most unhappy gaps in our meagre knowledge of his life. He has no sooner landed in the kingdom

81

of Leinster than tradition transports him to the
kingdom of Ulidia.

We must see where this tradition—this Ulidian
tradition—would lead, though we cannot allow it to
guide us blindly. There are two connected narratives
professing to describe important passages of Patrick's
work in Ireland. One of these[1] contains some
genuine, unvarnished records as to Christian communities which he founded. The other[2] is compact of
stories which it is difficult to utilise for historical
purposes, though it be admitted that they have
elements of historical value. The most striking
parts of it are pure legend, but they are framed in a
setting which might include some literal facts. And
the historical background is there, though we have
to allow for some distortion by anti-pagan motives.
But the difficulty which meets the critic here is due
to the circumstance that he has no sufficient records
of a genuine historical kind to guide him in dealing
with this mixed material. Most of those who have
undertaken to deal with it have adopted the crude
and vain method of retaining as historical what is
not miraculous. There is much which we can securely
reject at once, but there are other things which,
while we are not at liberty to accept them, we must
regard as possibly resting on some authentic basis.
We have not the data for a definite solution. It has
seemed best, then, to reproduce the story, to criticise
it, and point out what may be its implications.

[1] The *Memoir* by Tírechán.      [2] The *Life* by Muirchu.

If we stand on the steep headland which towers above the sea halfway between the Danish towns of Wicklow and Dublin, the eye reaches from the long low hill prominence under which the southern town is built, northward to the island of Lambay. A little beyond, hidden from the view and close to the coast, are some small islets which in ancient days were known as the isles of the Children of Cor. If we could see these minute points of land, we should be able to take in, with a sweep of the eye, the first stage of St. Patrick's traditional journey when he steered his boat northward from the mouth of the Dee to bear his message to the woods and glens of Ulidia. The story tells that he landed on one of these islets, which has ever since been known as Inis Patrick. The name attests an association with the apostle. It might be said that, if he travelled to Ulidia by sea, as he may well have done, it was a natural precaution, in days when travellers might be suspected as outlaws or robbers, to land for a night's halt on a desert island rather than on the coast, where churlish inhabitants might give a stranger no pleasant welcome. From the island which bears his name he continued his course along the coast of Meath, past the mouth of the Boyne, and along the shores of Conaille Muirthemni, which formed the southern part of the Ulidian kingdom. This was the country where in old days Setanta,[1] the lord of the march, is said to have kept watch and ward over

[1] Cuchullin of legend.

the gates of Ulster. But it was in more northern parts of the Pictish kingdom that Patrick's purpose lay, and he steered on past the inlet which was not yet the fiord of the Carlings, past the mountainous region of southern Dalaradia, till he came to a little land-locked bay, which in shape, though on a far smaller scale, and not flanked by mountains, resembles the Bay of Pagasae. But the sea-portal to Lake Strangford, as it is now called, is a much narrower strait [1] than the mouth of the Greek gulf. Patrick rowed into this water, and landed, he and those that were with him, on the southern shore of the bay at the mouth of the Slan stream, which till recent years was known by its old name.[2] They hid their boat, we are told, and went a short distance inward from the shore to find a place of rest. Had they rowed farther westward and followed, past salt marshes, the banks of the winding river Quoile, they would have soon come to a great fortress, Dún Lethglasse. But of the country and the country's folk the tale supposes that they knew nought. A swineherd espied the strangers from his hut, and, supposing them to be thieves and robbers, went forth and told his master. The region is embossed, as it were, with small hills, and one of the higher of these hills was the master's abode. Dichu was the name of this man of substance, and he was one of those "naturally good"

---

[1] Then called Brene Strait.
[2] The Slaney (see Appendix B, note). It flows from L. Money past Raholp.

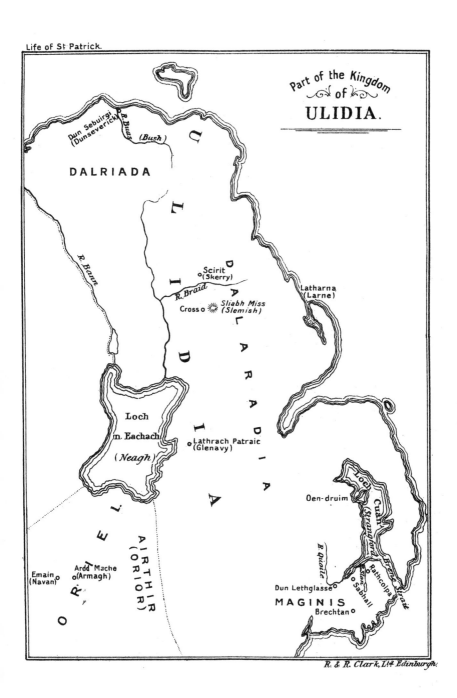

Part of the Kingdom
of
ULIDIA.

DALRIADA

U L I D I A

DAL ARADIA

*Dun Sebuirgi*
(Dunseverick)

*R. Buss*

(Bush)

*R. Bann*

Scirit
o (Skerry)

*R. Braid*

Crosso o ☀ *Sliabh Miss*
(Slemish)

Latharna
(Larne)

Loch

m. Eachach

(Neagh)

Lathrach Patraic
(Glenavy)

Oen-druim

*Loch Cuan*

*Strangford*

*Brene Strait*

*R. Quoile*

Ratticolpa o
o Saul
o Sabhall

Dun Lethglasse o

MAGINIS

Brechtan o

O R G E L I

A I R T H I R
(ORIOR)

Emain o
(Navan)

Ardd Mache
o (Armagh)

*R. & R. Clark, Ltd Edinburgh.*

men whom Patrick, though he was not a Pelagian, may have been prepared to find among pagan folk. At the tidings of his herd, Dichu was prepared to slay the strangers, but when he looked upon the face of Patrick he changed his mind and offered hospitality. Then Patrick preached to him and he believed, the first convert won by the apostle in the land of the Scots.

Before we ask the questions that naturally rise in the mind when we hear a tale like this, we must accompany the saint on a further stage in his progress. He tarried with Dichu only a few days, for he was impatient to carry out a purpose which he cherished of revisiting the scene of his thraldom and the home of his old master Miliucc in the extreme north of Dalaradia. He left his boat in the keeping of Dichu and journeyed by land through the country of the Picts till he saw once more the slopes of Mount Miss. Miliucc still lived, and Patrick wished to pay the master from whom he had fled the price of his freedom. It is not suggested that he deemed it necessary, even after so many years, thus to legalise his liberty and secure himself against the claim of a master to seize a fugitive slave. The suggestion seems rather to be that he hoped to convert Miliucc to the Christian doctrine, and that the best means of conciliation was to recognise his right. But the heathen chief, hearing that he was approaching with this intent, and seized with a strange alarm lest his former slave should by some irresistible spell constrain him to embrace a new religion against his will, resorted to an extreme device. Having gathered all his substance together into his wooden house, he set fire to the building, and perished with it. The flames of the unexpected pyre met Patrick's eyes as he stood on the south-western side of Mount Miss,[1] and his biographer pictures him standing for two or three hours dumb with surprise and grief. " I know not, God knows," he said, using a favourite phrase, " whether the posterity of this man shall not serve others for ever, and no king arise from his seed." Then he turned back and retraced his steps to the habitation of Dichu.

The funeral pyre of Mount Miss[2] sends our thoughts over sea and land to a more famous pyre at Sardis. The self-immolation of the obscure Dalaradian kingling belongs to the same cycle of lore as that of the great Lydian monarch whose name became a proverb for luxury and wealth. Croesus built a timber death-pile in the court of his palace to escape the shame of servitude to an earthly conqueror; Miliucc sought the flames to avoid the peril of thraldom under a ghostly master.

---

[1] It has been conjectured that the stronghold of Miliucc was on the hill of Skerry, north of Slemish, on the other side of the Braid valley. Muirchu says that Patrick saw the conflagration from the south side of Slemish. We may interpret south to mean south-west. A cross, mentioned by Muirchu, was erected on the spot where the legend supposed Patrick to have stood, and the memory of this is still preserved in the name of the townland of Cross, on a hill to the west of Slemish.

[2] Dr. W. Stokes, taking the story literally, suggests that Miliucc committed self-destruction as " a mode of vengeance " (*Book of Lismore*, p. 295).

But in both cases the idea of a king dying solemnly
by fire is taken from some old religious usage and
introduced by legendary fancy into an historical
situation. And in this case fancy has wrought
well and fitly. The desperate pyre of Miliucc is
a pathetic symbol of the protest of a doomed
religion.

The "island-plain"[1] of Dalaradia and the districts about Dún Lethglasse claimed to have been
the part of Ireland in which Patrick began his work
of preaching and baptizing heathen men. He abode
there and his religion grew ; and inhabitants of those
places in later days, when his memory had been
glorified, pleased themselves by the thought that he
"chose out and loved" this plain. He established
himself securely here with the help of his friend
Dichu, who, though apparently not the lord of
Dún Lethglasse, was clearly a chieftain of influence
and authority in that region. Dichu granted
Patrick a site for a Christian establishment on a hill
not far from the fortress, and a wooden barn was
said to have been turned into a place of Christian
worship. The rustic association has been preserved
in the name, which has remained ever since, *Sabhall*
or *Saul*, a word said to be borrowed[2] from the
Latin *stabulum*—cattle-stall or sheepfold.

We cannot suppose that the history of St.

---

[1] *Mag-inis*, later known as Lecale (*Leath Cathail*), now the baronies of
Lower and Upper Lecale. It is accurately described as a peninsular plain.

[2] But meaning *barn*.

Patrick's first plunge into his missionary work was so simple, or so fully left to the play of chance, as this naive tale represents. It belongs to a class of tales which are characteristic of history in its uncritical stage, tales which invert the perspective and magnify some subordinate incident to be the main motive and purpose of the actors, ignoring the true motive or depressing it to the level of an accident. Such tales, which abounded, for instance, in the records of Hellas, are often accepted as literally true if they hang together superficially, and if the particular incidents are natural or even possible. A deeper criticism displays their incredibility. The epic simplicity of Patrick's journey may be true to outward circumstances, but it is not possible to believe that he went out so purely at a venture, like one in a romance who fares forth, on a quest indeed and with a purpose, yet content to leave his course to be guided by fortune, without previous plan or calculation. The sole motive of Patrick's northern journey is represented here as the hope of persuading his old master to become a Christian, whereas its actual and important result, the missionary work in southern Ulidia, appears almost as an accidental consequence. The hard historic fact which underlies the story is the work of Patrick in Ulidia and the foundation of Saul; and the story is evidently the Ulidian legend of this beginning of a new epoch in Ulidian history. Recognising this, we are unable to trust the story even so far as to infer that Ulidia was the first scene of Patrick's missionary activity, as the Ulidians claimed. We can neither affirm this nor deny it; but we must observe that, according to another tradition, which has just as much authority, he began his work in the kingdom of Meath. We have already seen reason to reject the tradition that the place of Patrick's captivity was in north-eastern Ireland, and we may now see this record in a new light, as part of an attempt of the Ulidian Christians to appropriate, as it were, Patrick to themselves, to associate with their own land the bondage of his boyhood and to make it the stage of his earliest labours.

There is one point in the story which can be accepted. It can be shown that Dichu, the proprietor of Saul, was a real person. He was the son of Trechim, and his brother Rus was a man of influence who lived at Brechtan, which is still Bright, a few miles south of Saul. But was this region so completely unprepared for the reception of the new faith as the legend represents? Was the Christian idea a new revelation to the chieftains of Dalaradia, borne for the first time by Patrick to those shores? It seems more probable that there were some Christian communities there already and that the land was ripe for conversion. It has been pointed out above that it was perhaps in this land of the Picts that Palladius died. If this were so—but we are treading on ground where certainty is unattainable—we might accept without much hesitation the Ulidian claim that, when Patrick left Leinster, his first destination was Ulidia. For it would be the first duty of the new bishop of the Christians in Ireland to visit and confirm the Christian communities which existed. The force of the argument depends on the fact that two different lines converge to a fixed point. The action of Palladius, the first bishop of Ireland, in leaving Leinster and sailing "to the land of the Picts," and the Ulidian tradition that Patrick also travelled directly from Leinster to the land of the Picts, may find a common solution in the hypothesis that the Christian faith had already taken root in Dalaradia.

Other churches in the neighbourhood of Saul claimed to have been planted by Patrick, one at Brechtan, the place of Dichu's brother, another at Rathcolpa, which is still Raholp. Brechtan was the church of his disciple, Bishop Loarn; and Tassach, his artificer, who made altars and other things which were needed for his religious rites and the furnishing forth of his oratories, was installed at Rathcolpa. These three places, associated intimately with the first growth of Christianity in the Ulidian kingdom, Saul, Brechtan, and Rathcolpa, are ranged, within a short distance, on the eastern side of the Dún, which, a place of some note in Ireland's secular history, was destined to win importance as a

religious centre. But no church was founded
there by St. Patrick, though his name was afterwards to become permanently attached to it.
The most interesting remains of past ages at
Down-patrick are not ecclesiastical, but the "down"
or dún itself, a great mound encircled by three
broad ramparts on the banks of the Quoile,
one of the most impressive of ancient Irish earthworks.

The most irreproachable contemporary evidence
could hardly testify more clearly to the deep impression that St. Patrick made upon the dwellers
of the Island-plain than the fact that their
mythopoeic instinct was stirred, at a very early
stage, to explain one of the natural features of
their country by the miraculous powers of their
teacher. According to one story an uncivil and
grasping neighbour seized two oxen of St. Patrick,
which were at pasture. The saint cursed him:
"Mudebrod! thou hast done ill. Thy land shall
never profit thee." And on the same day the
sea rushed in and covered it, and the fruitful soil
was changed into a salt marsh. The motive of
such tales is to account for the origin of the salt
marshes which mark the northern border of the
island-plain on the shores of Lake Strangford,[1]

[1] There is a second story (also recorded by Muirchu), clearly inspired by
the same motive. Patrick was resting near Druimbo (in the north of Mag
Inis, and close to a salt marsh), and he heard the noise of pagans who were
busily engaged in making an earthwork. It was Sunday and he commanded

and they show that the figure of St. Patrick had inspired popular imagination in those regions at an early period.

them to cease from work.   When they refused he cursed them : " Mudebrod ! may your work not profit you ! " and the sea rushed in, as in the other story, and the work was destroyed.   The curse *mudebrod* (or *mudebroth*) has not been explained.

# CHAPTER VI

## IN MEATH

### § 1. *King Loigaire's Policy*

IT has been already pointed out that the Roman terminus did not mark the limit of Roman influence. That influence extended beyond the bounds of the Empire. The existence of the majestic Empire was a fact of which its free neighbours had to take cognisance, and which impressed itself on their minds as one of the great facts of the universe. They were forced into intercourse, whether hostile or peaceful, with the Roman republic. We have seen that it must have affected the folks of Ireland who were the neighbours of the British and Gallic provinces, though severed by narrow seas. The soil of that island had indeed never been trodden by Roman legions, but its ports were not sealed to the outer world, and from the first century the outer world practically meant the Roman world. The men of Ireland in the fourth century must have conceived their island as lying just outside the threshold of a complex of land and sea, over which the power of Rome stretched to bounds almost inaccessible to their imagination. When the grasp of Rome relaxed or her power grew weak in the neighbouring provinces of Britain, the Irish speedily became aware, and, like the Germans, failed not to seize opportunities for winning spoil and plunder; but, though they appear in Roman records as wasters and enemies, this does not imply that they had no respect and veneration for Rome and her civilisation. The compatibility of veneration with hostile behaviour on the part of barbarians is shown by the attitude of the Germans in all their dealings with the Empire which they dismembered. We may be sure that the Iberians and Celts of Ireland, who were certainly not inferior in intelligence to the Germans or less open to new ideas, were qualified to admire the majesty of the Roman name and to feel curiosity about the immense empire which dominated their horizon. Some of their own folk, as we saw, had found new habitations in Roman territory,[1] and thus formed a special channel for Roman influence to trickle into the free island.

The chief influence was the infiltration of the Christian religion. The adoption of this religion by the Imperial government in the fourth century must have had, as we have seen, a sensible effect

[1] See above, chap. i. p. 14.

in conferring prestige on Christianity beyond the
boundaries of the Empire.    It became inevitable
that the favoured creed should henceforth be
closely associated with the Empire in the idea of
barbarians and regarded as the Roman religion.
Hence that religion acquired, on political grounds,
a higher claim on their attention.

We must realise the force of these general considerations in order to understand the policy of the
High King who sat on the throne of Ireland
throughout the whole period of Patrick's work in
the island.    Loigaire had succeeded about five
years before Patrick's arrival (A.D. 428).    He was
son of King Niall, who had been slain in Britain,
perhaps in the very year in which Patrick had
been carried into captivity.    Niall's immediate
successor was his nephew, Dathi, who reigned for
twenty-three years, and likewise found death beyond
the sea.[1]    But Dathi, it would seem, went forth as
a friend, not as a foe, of Rome.    He led a host to
help the Roman general Aetius to drive back the
Franks from the frontiers of eastern Gaul, and he
was struck by lightning.    The expedition of Dathi
has an interest not only from the Irish, but also
from the Roman point of view.    It illustrates the
wide view of Aetius.    It shows us how he looked
to all quarters for mercenary help; if he relied on
the Huns, whom he was hereafter to smite so
hard, he also invited auxiliaries from Scottia.

[1] See Appendix C, 11.

From the Irish side, it illustrates the fact that Ireland was within the Roman horizon.

The reign of Loigaire lasted thirty-six years, and it marks a new epoch in Irish history. The part which Loigaire himself played in bringing about this change has been underrated. His statesmanship has been obscured by tradition, but is revealed by interrogation of the scanty evidence.

The first difficulty is one which meets us at all stages of early Irish history. It is impossible to determine the compass of the power and authority of the High Kings in the under-kingdoms. It seems probable that Loigaire was able to exercise as much influence, at least in northern Ireland, as was permitted to any king by the political and social organisation of the country. We have seen that the efforts of his grandfather, Eochaid, and his father, Niall, had extended the power of the family throughout a great part of north Ireland. His cousin, Amolngaid, was king of Connaught. His brothers and half-brothers were petty kings.[1]

Whatever the authority of Loigaire was, he seems to have used it in the interests of peace. So far as we can judge from the evidence of the Annals, his reign was a period of peace. He was indeed the perpetual enemy of the king of Leinster, and on three occasions at least there was war between them. On the first, Loigaire was victorious; on the second, he was taken prisoner;

---

[1] See above, cap. iv. p. 72.

on the third, he was slain. But apart from this fatal feud we do not hear of wars, and we do not hear that he ventured upon expeditions over sea or took advantage of the difficulties of Britain, engaged then in her struggle with the invaders who were to conquer her.

A pacific policy harmonises with the record— though a warlike policy would not contradict it— that in his reign and under his auspices a code of native laws was constructed. This code, entitled the *Senchus Mór*, still exists, changed and enlarged, and something will be said of it in another place. It seems probable that the idea of this national work was due to the example and influence of the Roman Empire. There is no direct evidence that this was so, but it is a remarkable coincidence that the reign of the king to whom the Irish code is ascribed concurs with the reign of the Emperor Theodosius, whose lawyers gathered the imperial edicts into the code called by his name. It cannot be thought improbable that this coincidence is significant, and that the influence of Rome is responsible for the earlier code of the Scot no less than for the later codes of Goth, Burgundian, and Frank. The synchronism struck the native annalists, and they expressed it in a clumsy way by placing the composition of the Irish law-book in the very year in which the Code of Theodosius was issued (A.D. 438). That may be taken as a naive unhistorical expression of a true discernment that the idea of the Code of Loigaire and his colleagues came directly or indirectly from the Empire.

The way in which the Roman world made its influence felt in Ireland should be compared with the ways in which it exerted influence over other adjacent countries. Let us take, for instance, Russia. Neither Russia nor Ireland ever passed for a moment under the rule of Caesar. Both states were neighbours of the Empire, and for the kings of Tara as for the princes of Kiev the Empire was the eminent fact in the political worlds with which they were acquainted. In both cases the intercourse of trade, varied by warfare, prepared the way for the ultimate reception of some of the ideas of the higher culture of Rome. But there was one essential difference, due to political geography. Ireland was of little consequence or account in the eyes of the Caesars of Old Rome, and it was only now and then, as in the days of Valentinian I., that they were called upon to give it a thought; whereas for the Caesars of the New Rome the existence of the Russian state, from its creation in the ninth century, was an important fact which entered permanently into the calculations of their foreign policy. The contrast between the presence of political relations in one case and their almost complete absence in the other is reflected in the contrast between the circumstances of the victory of Christianity in

Russia and in Ireland. In Russia the faith of the Empire made, as it were, a solemn entry through the public portals of the State ; in Ireland it entered privately through postern gates, and conquered from within. In Russia it was imposed upon his subjects by their prince Vladimir, who at the same time married a sister of the Roman Augusti ; in Ireland it was only tolerated, when its success had begun, by the chief king, whose very name most probably never fell upon the ears of the Augustus at Ravenna. But in both cases the introduction of the religion was only a part, though the most important and effective part, of a wider influence diffused from the Empire.

The great question with which Loigaire had to deal was the spread of Christianity in his dominion, a question which confronted barbarian kings just as it confronted Roman Emperors, and might be as embarrassing and critical for Loigaire in his small sphere as it had proved for the ecumenical states-men Diocletian and Constantine. It is clear that in the days of Theodosius II. the moment had come when the High King of Ireland was con-strained to adopt a definite attitude. If, as seems possible, it was in the south of Ireland, in the realms of Leinster and Munster, that this religion had hitherto made most progress, then, so long as it was tolerated by the sovereigns of those king-doms, the High King might ignore it. But once it began to spread sensibly in his own immediate kingdom of Meath, as king of Meath he could not ignore what in other parts of Ireland the lord of all Ireland might pass over; the time had come when he had to decide whether he would oppose or recognise Christian communities and Christian priests.

For most barbarian kings this question would be equivalent to another, Shall I myself adopt the foreign faith? It argues in Loigaire exceptional ability and objectivity of vision that he was capable of separating his own personal view from his kingly policy. He was not drawn himself to the creed of Christ; he held fast to the pagan faith and customs of his fathers; but this did not hinder him from recognising the great and growing strength of the religion which had overflowed from the Empire into his island. He saw that it had already taken root, and we may be certain that its close identification with the great Empire, the union of Christ with Caesar, was an imposing argument.[1] But if King Loigaire resolved on a policy of toleration, and was ultimately prepared to "regularise" the position of the Christian clerics, it is not unlikely that at first he may have been inclined to adopt a different attitude. It must have been difficult for him to withstand the influence of the Druids, who naturally put forth all their efforts to check the advance of the dangerous doctrine which had come from over seas to destroy their profession, their religion, and their

[1] Compare what has been said above in chap. i. p. 9.

gods. Tradition recorded their prophecies that the new faith, if it were admitted, would subvert kings and kingdoms. In legend, as we shall see, Loigaire appears as following the counsels of his Druids, resolving to slay Patrick, and yielding only when the sorcery of the Christian proved stronger than the sorcery of the heathen magicians. It is possible that this tale may reflect facts in so far as Loigaire may have been inclined to persecute before he adopted his policy of even-handed toleration. We must not leave out of our account the circumstance that, as in the case of Frankish Chlodwig and English Ethelbert, there were probably friends of the Christian religion in the king's own household.

Ethelbert indeed was not like Loigaire. He, too, began with the resolve to remain true to his own gods, while he granted licence to the priests of his wife's creed to do their will in his realm. Before two years had passed, however, the English king forsook the old way himself and was initiated in the Christian rites, while the Irish king never abandoned the faith of his fathers. But Ethelbert's wife, like Chlodwig's, was a Christian, while of Loigaire's we cannot say what gods she worshipped; we have only the record that she was a native of Britain, and, for all we know, she may have been dead when Patrick arrived on the scene. Yet the fact that he had a British wife may supply a point of contact between the Irish king and the Empire and help to explain his tolerant attitude to the Roman religion. But he had also a British daughter-in-law, and here, if the main facts of the following story are true, we may fairly seek a co-operating influence.

In mid Meath, on the banks of the river Boyne, where it winds in one of its loveliest curves through the plain to the west of the royal hill of Tara, a small Christian settlement arose, perhaps soon after Patrick's arrival in Ireland. The place was called the "ford of the alder," and the name of the tree, Trim, still clings to it. In this spot Fedilmid, son of King Loigaire, had his dwelling, and his wife was a lady of Britain, who, if not already a Christian, must have had some knowledge of the established religion of the Empire of which Britain was still in name a province. Trim, according to its own tradition, was the scene of one of Patrick's most important successes.

The naive story relates that Lomman, one of Patrick's British fellow-workers, sailed up the Boyne and landed at the Ford of the Alder. In the morning Fedilmid's young son, Fortchernn,[1] sallied forth and found Lomman reading the Gospel. Immediately the boy believed and was baptized, and remained with Lomman till his mother came out

---

[1] This name is the same as the British Vortigern (Welsh Gwrtheyrn), and the original Goidelic form was similar. It occurs in Ogam inscriptions, thus: ... Maqi Vorrtigern⟨i⟩, on a stone of Ballyhank (near Cork), now in the Dublin Museum (Rhŷs, *Proc. of R.S.A.I.*, pt. i. vol. xxxii. p. 9, 1902).

to seek him. She was delighted to meet a fellow-countryman, and she, too, believed and returned to her house and told Fedilmid all that had befallen their son. Then Fedilmid conversed with Lomman in the British tongue, and believed with all his household. He consigned Fortchernn to the care of Lomman, to be his pupil and spiritual foster-child, and made a donation of his estate at Trim to Patrick and Lomman and Fortchernn.

Though the details of this story cannot be taken literally, it may probably preserve correctly some of the main facts—that Fortchernn became a pupil of Lomman and embraced the spiritual life; that Fedilmid made the donation, and that the British princess played a part in the episode. But tales of this kind are prone to represent circumstances, which were really due to design, as the effect of chance. It is possible that the British princess was already a Christian, and that, just as Augustine travelled to Kent by the invitation of its Gallic queen, so Lomman rowed to Trim at the call of its British mistress. In any case we may be sure that Lomman's coming to the Ford of the Alder was not fortuitous, but was arranged by him and Patrick with forethought and purpose. The result was of high importance. It gave Patrick a strong position and prestige in Meath by establishing a Christian community with which the son and grandson of the High King were so closely associated.

## § 2. *Legend of Patrick's Contest with the Druids*

The bitter hostility of the Druids and the relations of Loigaire to Patrick were worked up by Irish imagination into a legend which ushers in the saint upon the scene of his work with great spectacular effect. The story represents him as resolving to celebrate the first Easter after his landing in Ireland on the hill of Slane, which rises high above the left bank of the Boyne at about twelve miles from its mouth. On the night of Easter eve he and his companions lit the Paschal fire, and on that self-same night it so chanced that the King of Ireland held a high and solemn festival in his palace at Tara where the kings and nobles of the land gathered together. It was the custom that on that night of the year no fire should be lit until a fire had been kindled with solemn ritual in the royal house. Suddenly the company assembled at Tara saw a light shining across the plain of Breg from the hill of Slane.[1] King Loigaire, in surprise and alarm, consulted his magicians, and they said, "O king, unless this fire which you see be quenched this same night, it will never be quenched; and the kindler of it will overcome us all and seduce all the folk of your realm." And the king replied, "It shall not be, but we will go to see the issue of the matter, and we will put to death those who do such sin against our kingdom." So he had nine chariots

---

[1] The distance of Tara from Slane is about ten miles.

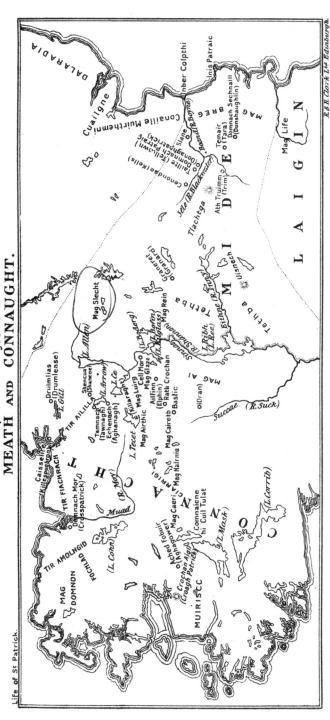

Map of the Kingdoms of
MEATH and CONNAUGHT.

Life of St Patrick.

R & R Clark Ltd Edinburgh.

yoked, and, with the queen and his two chief
sorcerers and others, he drove through the night
over the plain of Breg.    And in order to win magic
power over them who had kindled the fire, they
wheeled lefthandwise, or contrariwise to the sun's
course.    And the magicians arranged with the king
that he should not go up to the place where the fire
was kindled, lest he should afterwards worship the
kindler thereof, but that the offender should be
summoned to the king's presence at some distance
from the fire, and the magicians should converse
with him.    So the company dismounted out of
range of the fire, and Patrick was summoned.    And
the sorcerers said, " Let none arise at his coming,
for whoever rises will afterwards worship him."
When Patrick came and saw the chariots and
horses, he quoted the words of the Psalmist, " Some
in chariots and some on horses, but we in the name
of the Lord."    One of the company, and one only—
his name was Erc—rose up when Patrick appeared,
and he was converted and Patrick blessed him (and
he was afterwards buried at Slane).    Then the
sorcerers and Patrick began to converse and dispute ;
and Lochru, one of the enchanters, uttered strong
words against the Christian faith.    And Patrick,
looking grimly at him, prayed to God that the
blasphemer should be flung into the air and dashed
to the ground.    And so it befell.    Lochru was lifted
upwards and fell upon a stone, so that his head was
dashed in pieces.    Then the king was wroth and

said, "Lay hands upon the fellow." And Patrick, seeing the heathen about to attack him, cried in a loud voice, "Let God arise, and let his enemies be scattered." Then a great darkness fell and the earth quaked, and in the tumult the heathen fell upon each other, and the horses fled over the plain, and of all that company only the king and queen, and Lucetmael, the other sorcerer, and a few others survived. Then the queen went to Patrick and besought him, saying, "O mighty and just man, do not destroy the king! He will come and kneel and worship your god." And the king, constrained by fear, bent his knee to Patrick and pretended to worship God. But afterwards he bade Patrick to him, purposing to slay him; but Patrick knew his thoughts, and he went before the king with his eight companions, one of whom was a boy. But as the king counted them, lo! they were no longer there, but he saw in the distance eight deer and a fawn making for the wilds. And the king returned in the morning twilight to Tara, disheartened and ashamed.

The framers of this legend had an instinct for scenic effect. The bold and brilliant idea of the first Easter fire flashing defiance across the plain of Meath to the heathen powers of Tara, and the vision of the king with his queen and sorcerers setting forth from their palace in the depth of night with chariots and horses, and careering over the plain, as Ailill and Maeve of pagan story might have suddenly

driven in headlong course against the Hound of
Ulaid, is a picture not unworthy of the best of those
nameless story-makers who in all lands, working one
cannot tell where or how, transfigure the facts of
history.    The calendar is disregarded.    The idea is
that Easter is to replace Beltane, the Christian to
overcome the heathen fire ; and it is a matter of no
import that the day of Beltane was the first day of
summer, which could never fall on Easter Eve.[1]
But incongruous though the circumstances are, the
scene is well conceived to express the triumph of
the new faith, and certain general historical facts
are embodied, namely, the hostility of the Druids and
the personal distaste of the king for the foreign
creed.

And the imaginary coincidence of the pagan with
the Christian festival has a historical interest of its
own.    Down to modern times we find the ancient
heathen customs of Europe observed in different
countries on different days.    In some regions they
were transferred to Christian feasts like Easter and
Pentecost, elsewhere the old heathen days were
preserved.    When the old practice was adapted to
the frame of the new faith, the change was silent
and unrecorded, but this Irish legend, by its impossible junction of the two festivals, may be said to

---

[1] Yet more remote from the Paschal season was the feast of Samhain at
the close of autumn (November 1), when on the hill of Tlachtga, not far from
Trim, a fire was kindled, from which, tradition says, all hearths in Ireland
were lit.    It was at Samhain too, according to tradition, that the High Kings
used to hold such high festivals at Tara as are designated in the story.    See
note, Appendix B.

embody unconsciously a record of such a change.
We can detect here, in the very act as it were, the
process by which pagan superstitions which insisted
on surviving were sometimes adopted into the
Christian calendar.

The story has a sequel which tells how Patrick
strove with the other enchanter. On the morrow,
that is, Easter day, Loigaire, with kings and princes
and nobles, was feasting in his palace, when Patrick
with five companions suddenly appeared among
them, though the door was shut.[1] He came to
preach the Word, and the king invited him to sit at
meat. Lucetmael, the Druid, in order to prove him,
poured a noxious drop into the cup of Patrick, and
the saint blessed the cup, and the liquor was frozen
to ice, except the drop of poison, which remained
liquid, and fell out when the cup was turned upside
down. Then he blessed the cup again, and the
drink returned into its natural state.

Then the magician said, "Let us work miracles
on the plain; let us bring down snow upon the
land." Patrick said, "I will not bring down aught
against the will of God." And the magician by his
incantations brought snow waist-high upon the plain.
"Now remove it," said the saint. "I cannot," said
the Druid, "till this hour upon the morrow." "You
can do evil," answered the saint, "but not good,"

---

[1] This incident is obviously suggested by St. John xx. 19, 26. When St.
Columba went to the palace of King Brude the closed gates opened of their
own accord (Adamnan, *V. Col.* ii. 35).

and he blessed the plain, and the snow vanished without rain, or mist, or wind. And all applauded and marvelled. Then in the same way the Druid brought darkness down over the plain, but he could not dissipate it, and Patrick dissipated it.

Then said the king, " Dip your books in the water, and we will worship him whose books come out unspoiled." Patrick was willing to accept this test, but the sorcerer refused on the ground that Patrick worshipped water as a god, meaning its use in baptism. Then the king proposed the same test with fire instead of water ; but the Druid said, " No, this man worships fire and water alternately." But all these parleyings were only preliminary, leading up to the main issue, which is closely connected with the events of the previous night. Patrick proposed an ordeal, which was accepted. His pupil Benignus and the magician were placed in a hut built half of green and half of dry wood. Benignus, clothed in the magician's garment, was placed in the dry part, and Lucetmael, wearing the garment of Patrick, in the green part. And the hut was set on fire in the presence of all. Then Patrick prayed, and the fire consumed the magician, leaving Patrick's robe unburnt, but it did not hurt Benignus, though it burnt the magician's robe from about him. Then Loigaire was fain to kill Patrick, but he was afraid.

Having discerned that one of the motives of the whole legend is the adoption in the Christian Church, in connexion with the Easter festival, of those fire-customs and sun-charms which were associated throughout Celtic, as throughout Teutonic, Europe with certain days in spring or early summer, we can hardly avoid recognising in this ordeal a memory of the custom of burning a victim on those days. This victim was thought to represent the spirit of vegetation, and its ashes were carried forth and scattered in the fields to make them fruitful. Originally the victim was human, but as time went on, either a mock victim, such as a straw man, was substituted, or he who was chosen to die and decked out for sacrifice was rescued at the brink of the fire. In the Eiffel country, by the Rhine, for instance, the custom was long maintained of heaping brushwood round a tall beech-tree, and forming a framework known as the "burg" or the "hut," and a straw man was sometimes burned in it.[1] We can hardly doubt that the chief ceremonial of the Beltane celebration, the burning of the spirit of growth—whether represented by a man or by a mock man, whether in a dress of leaves or in a framework of green or dry wood— was the motive which suggested the story of this ordeal. In the story the motive has lost its particular significance, and but for its connexion with the opposition between Easter and Beltane might escape detection.

The envelopment of a motive of somewhat the same kind in a setting which purposes to be historical, and in which the motive entirely loses its meaning,

---

[1] See note, Appendix B.

has an instructive parallel in the famous story of the funeral pyre of king Croesus. The fundamental motive of that story is the burning of the god Sandan,[1] but the incident has been wrought into a historical context so as to disguise its origin, and the tale was largely accepted as literal fact. But Cyrus was as innocent of dooming his defeated foe to a cruel death as Patrick was of burning his Druid rival. In both cases the true victims of the legendary flames were spirits of popular imagination.

The story bears the stamp of an early origin. It is a common fallacy that legends attach themselves to a figure only after a long lapse of time, and that the antiquity of biographies may always be measured by the presence or absence of miracles. The truth is that those men who are destined to become the subjects of myth evoke the mythopoeic instinct in their fellows while they are still alive, or before they are cold in their graves. When once the tale is set rolling it may gather up as time goes on many conventional and insignificant accretions of fiction, and the presence or absence of these may indeed be a guide in determining the age of a document. But the myths which are significant and characteristic are nearly contemporary; they arise within the radius of the personality to which they relate. The tale of Patrick's first Easter in Ireland and his dealings with the king is eminently a creation of this kind.

[1] See note, Appendix B.

In this legend of Patrick's dealings with the High King there is one implication which harmonises with other records,[1] and which, we cannot doubt, reflects, while it distorts, a fact.    Patrick visited Loigaire in his palace at Tara, but he went as a guest in peace, not as a hostile magician and a destroyer of life. The position which the Christian creed had won rendered a conference no less desirable for the High King than for the bishop who represented the Church of the Empire.    Loigaire agreed to protect Patrick in his own kingdom, though he resisted any attempts that were made to convert him.    No cross should be raised over his sepulchre; he should be buried, like his forefathers, standing and accoutred in his arms.

But the place of the Christian communities in the society of Ireland, their rights and obligations, and the modifications of existing customs and laws which the principles and doctrines of their religion demanded, raised questions which could not well be settled except in a general conclave of the kings and chief men of the island.    Now it was a custom of the High Kings to hold occasionally a great celebration, called the Feast of Tara, to which the under-kings were invited.    It was an opportunity for discussing the common affairs of the realm.    Such an occasion is evidently contemplated in the legend, and the Annals record that a Feast of Tara was held

---

[1] Tírechán, p. 308, perrexitque ad civitatem Temro ad Loigairium filium Neill iterum quia apud illum foedus pepigit ut non occideretur in regno illius.

towards the close of Loigaire's reign. It is therefore possible that at such an assembly the religious
question was marked as a subject of deliberation,
and the bishop was invited to be present. If so, the
general issue of the debate must have been that
Christian communities were recognised as social
units on the same footing as families, but that
Christian principles could not alter the general
principles of Irish law. This brings us to the chief
monument of Loigaire's reign, the legal code, the
construction of which may well have been discussed
and resolved on at one of the general assemblages
at Tara.

## § 3. *Loigaire's Code*

Loigaire did for Ireland what Euric did for
the Visigoths, Gundobad for the Burgundians,
Chlodwig for the Salian Franks; and we have
already observed that to him probably, as to them,
the idea of compiling a written legal code came from
the Roman Empire. The *Senchus Mór*, as the
code was called, has not come down in its primitive
form; it has been remodelled, worked over, and
overlaid with additions by subsequent lawyers; but
a critical examination of the evidence leaves little
room for doubt that in its original shape it was,
as tradition held, composed under the auspices of
Loigaire. As it was to be valid for Ireland, and
not merely for Meath, it was necessary for the High
King to act in consort with the provincial kings, and

tradition mentions as his coadjutors Corc, king of Munster, and Daire of Orior.[1]

If the view is right that the initiation of such a code was due to the influence of Roman ideas, it would be not unnatural or surprising that the Christian bishop and Roman citizen, who represented more than any other man in Ireland the ideas of Roman civilisation, should have been consulted, though the construction of the law-book was a matter for native experts. But there was another reason why Patrick would naturally have been taken into the counsels of the kings and lawyers. The spread of Christianity and the foundation of Christian communities throughout the land rendered it imperative for the secular authorities to define the status of the clergy and fix the law which should be binding on all. A new society had been established, recognising laws of its own, which differed from the laws of the country ; and this threatened to create a double system, which would have been fatal to order. Either the spirit of the Mosaic law must be allowed to transform the ancient customs of the land, or the Christians must resign themselves to living under principles opposed to ecclesiastical teaching.

It is possible that Patrick made an attempt to revolutionise the Irish system of dealing with cases of manslaughter, to abolish the customs of composition by fine and private retaliation, and make it an offence punishable by death. But if he made

[1] See Appendix C, 12.

such an attempt it was unsuccessful, and it would probably have received little support from his native converts. The principle of primitive societies that bloodshedding was a private offence which could be atoned for by payment of a composition—a principle which Greek societies were discarding in the seventh century B.C.—prevailed in Ireland so long as Ireland was independent, and the Irish Church was perfectly content.

Among the experts who are said to have taken part in compiling the code was the poet Dubthach, of Leinster, who is said to have been one of the most eminent poets in the reign of Loigaire. Tradition says that he became a Christian, and his pupil Fíacc, whom he had trained in the art of poetry, was consecrated a bishop by Patrick. Of the poets of Ireland at this early age we know nothing. One wonders what manner of poems were sung by that bard whose sepulchral stone, old but of unknown age, has preserved his bare name and calling, written in the character which the Irish of those days used to inscribe upon their tombstones : VELITAS LUGUTTI, "(This is the tomb) of the poet Lugut."[1] The poets were men of dignity and consequence in the society of their tribes and country. They were not only poets but judges, for they possessed the legal lore which was perhaps preserved in poetical form. The administration of justice depended on

[1] At Crag, in Co. Kerry.—Macalister, *Studies in Irish Epigraphy*, ii. p. 52.

their knowledge; their arbitrations were the substitute for a court of justice.   Such was the position
of Dubthach, lawyer at once and poet, like Charondas
of Catana, whose laws, cast in poetical form, were
sung, we are told, at banquets.   He was a native of
Leinster, and if he was one of the commission which
drew up the *Senchus Mór*, we may take it that he
represented that kingdom, for the name of the King
of Leinster, Loigaire's enemy, does not appear.

The legend of Patrick's visit to Tara, when he
entered through closed doors, relates that when he
appeared in the hall Dubthach alone of the company
rose from his seat to salute the stranger.   This
seems to be a genuine fragment of tradition.[1]   That
there had been a friendship between Patrick and
Dubthach was believed in later times at Sletty, in
Leinster, of which Fíacc, pupil of Dubthach, was the
first bishop.

## § 4. *Ecclesiastical Foundations in Meath*

The early traditions of Patrick's work in founding
new communities claim our notice, for though we
cannot control them in any particular case, the
probability is that many of them have a basis in
fact, and collectively they illustrate this side of his
activity.

Within Loigaire's own immediate kingdom not
a few churches claimed to have been founded by

---

[1] Cp. Appendix A, ii. 5.

Patrick, one or two of them in the neighbourhood
of the royal hill.    But though the names of the
places where these churches were built are recorded,
they are in most cases for us mere names; the sites
cannot be identified, or can only be guessed at.    In
a few places in the land of Meath we can localise
the literary traditions.    We may begin with a church
which was founded not by the bishop himself, but by
a disciple and, it was believed, a relative.    Not far
south from Tara lies Dunshaughlin, and the name,
which represents [1] Domnach Sechnaill, "the church
of Sechnall," is supposed to preserve the name of
Sechnall or Secundinus, said to have been Patrick's
nephew.    Here Secundinus is related to have composed the first Latin hymn that was composed in
Ireland, and the theme of the hymn was the apostolic
work of his master.    This hymn is undoubtedly contemporary, and there is no reason either to deny or
to assert the authenticity of the tradition which
ascribes it to Secundinus, but there are considerations which make it very difficult to accept his
alleged relationship to Patrick.[2]    It is composed in
trochaic rhythm, but with almost complete disregard
of metrical quantity,[3] and its twenty-three quatrains

---

[1] It should be Donagh-shaughlin, for Donagh is *domnach*, a church,
whereas *dún* is a fort.    There is no doubt that Dun here is a corruption, as
we get the form Donnaclsacheling in a document of A.D. 1216 (Reeves, *Eccl.
Ant.* p. 128).

[2] See Appendix B, note on cap. ii. p. 23.

[3] See Appendix A, i. 6.    One of the best quatrains is the fourth :

Dominus illum elegit ut doceret barbaras
nationes, ut piscaret per doctrinae retia,
ut de seculo credentes traheret ad gratiam
Dominumque sequerentur sedem ad etheriam.

begin with the successive letters of the alphabet. Literary merit it has none, and the historian deplores that, instead of singing the general praises of Patrick's virtues and weaving round him a mesh of religious phrases describing his work as pastor, messenger, and preacher, the author had thought well to mention some of his particular actions. But the hymn has its value. It is among the earliest memorials that we possess of his work; and if it was composed by Secundinus, it was written before Patrick had been fourteen years in Ireland, and is thus older than the greater memorial which he wrote himself before he died. And the writer may have derived his inspiration from Patrick's own impressions about his work. We may suspect that some of the verses echo words which had fallen from Patrick's lips in the hearing of his disciple, as when the master is compared to Paul,[1] or described as a fisherman setting his nets for the heathen, or called the light of the world, or a witness of God *in lege catholica.* But Secundinus, if he was the hymnographer, did not live to see the fuller realisation of Patrick's claims to the fulsome laudations of his hymn. The disciple died long before the master had finished his "perfect life."[2]

In another district of Meath, Donagh-Patrick, near the banks of the Blackwater, seems to mark a

---

[1] The *Confession* shows that this comparison was sometimes in Patrick's mind.

[2] Perfectam vitam, *Hymn* v. 4.   Secundinus died A.D. 447, acc. to *Ann. Ult.*

spot associated with an important success of the apostle. Here Conall, son of Niall, and brother of king Loigaire, had his dwelling, still marked by the foundations of an ancient fort, and he was less deaf than his greater brother to the persuasions of Patrick's teaching. He submitted to the rite of baptism, and he granted a place, close to his own house, for the building of a church. Patrick measured out the ground, and a church of unusual size arose, twenty yards from end to end, and it was known as the Great Church of Patrick. Such was the scale of the early houses of Christian worship in Ireland.

The conversion of Conall was an important achievement, but it is related that there were other sons of Niall, who were so bitterly adverse to the new doctrine, that they were fain to take the life of its teacher. Not far from the place where he won the friendship of Conall, Patrick had been in danger of his life at the hands of Coirpre, Conall's brother. At a little distance above the confluence of the Blackwater with the Boyne, the village of Telltown recalls the memory of Taillte,[1] a place of great note and fame in ancient Meath. Here a fair was held and a feast celebrated at the beginning of autumn, and people gathered together to witness the games which were held there, perhaps under the presidency of the High King. The record of the visit of

---

[1] Telltown comes by popular etymology from the genitive Taillteann. The site is marked by a round rath. O'Donovan said in 1856 that it had been in recent times a resort for the men of Meath for hurling, wrestling, and other sports (*Four Masters*, i. p. 22).

Patrick to Taillte mentions the games as the "royal agon," and the Greek word sends our thoughts to those more illustrious contests which were held at the same season of the year on the banks of the Alpheus in honour of Zeus. It is not clear whether Patrick is supposed to have timed his visit to see and denounce the heathen usages of the festival. Perhaps he would have avoided such an occasion with the same discretion which Otto, the apostle of the Pomeranians, exercised when he waited outside the town of Pyritz till the pagan folk had finished the celebration of a religious feast.[1] The story is that Coirpre, son of King Niall, wished to put Patrick to death at Taillte, and scourged his servants because they would not betray their master into his hands.

But if the bishop was in danger from a son of Niall at Taillte, he is said to have fared worse at the hands of a grandson of Niall[2] at another place of high repute in the kingdom of Meath. The hill of Uisnech, in south-western Meath, was believed to mark the centre of the island, and was a scene of pagan worship. Patrick visited the hill town, and a stone known as the "stone of Coithrige"—perhaps a sacred stone on which he inscribed a cross—commemorated his name and his visit. The stone has disappeared, but the traveller is reminded of it by

---

[1] Herbord, *Vit. Ott.* ii. 14. The silence of early authorities is decisive against the isolated statement that Patrick preached at Taillte against the "burning of the firstborn offspring." (See Appendix B, note.)

[2] Mac Fechach.—Tírechán, $310_{24}$.

*Curse*

the stone enclosure which is known as "St. Patrick's bed." While he was there, a grandson of Niall slew some of his foreign companions. Patrick cursed both this man and Coirpre, and foretold that no king should ever spring from their seed, but that their posterity would serve the posterity of their brethren. Tradition consistently represents Patrick as finding in malediction an instrument not to be disdained.

It is recorded that, proceeding from Donagh-Patrick up the Blackwater, he came to the Ford of the Quern,[1] and planted there another Christian settlement. This place was probably near the old town of Kells, then called Cenondae. Unlike Trim, Kells has some traces of the early age of Christian Ireland, though nothing that can claim association with the age of Patrick. The ancient stone house which is preserved there, is connected by tradition with the name of the great saint who a hundred years after Patrick's death went forth from Ireland to convert north Britain.[2]

Some churches are said to have been established by Patrick in the north-western region of Meath, which was known by a name, now obsolete, as the kingdom of the two Tethbias.[3] The river Ethne,

---

[1] Áth Brón.—Tír. 307₂₈.

[2] St. Colomb's House. For its description and measurements see Petrie (*Round Towers*, 430-31), who compares it with St. Kevin's House at Glendalough, and Dunraven's *Notes on Irish Architecture*, vol. ii. p. 50 (plans and photograph).

[3] Tírechán, 310-11.

which is now pronounced Inny, flows through this region to contribute its waters to a swelling of the Shannon, and divides it into two parts, the northern and the southern Tethbia.   Perhaps the only place here that we have any ground for associating with Patrick is Granard.   We are told that from the hill of Granard he pointed out to one of his followers the spot where a church should be founded.   This church, Cell Raithin, may have been the origin of the settlement which grew into the town of Granard. Among the inmates of the monastery established here is said to have been one who had a specially interesting connexion with Patrick's life.   Gosact, described as the son of his old master, was, according to the tradition, here ordained a priest by the captive stranger who had once kept his father's droves.   There cannot be any reasonable doubt that the tomb of Gosact was in later times to be seen at Granard,[1] and that the tradition of the place represented him as the son of Miliucc.   Nor should we have any good reason to question that Gosact, who was buried there, was a son of Miliucc.   But we have seen grounds for believing that the story of Patrick's servitude under Miliucc of Dalaradia was an error; and it would follow that Gosact, son of Miliucc, was not the son of Patrick's master. Nevertheless, Gosact may have been connected with the years of bondage, and may perhaps supply us with the clue which we desire for explaining how

[1] See Appendix C, 4, *ad fin.*

it came about that it ever occurred to any one to place the scene of the captivity in the land of Miliucc. In the earliest notice of Gosact that is preserved, he is said to have been fostered by Patrick during the servitude of seven years. This suggests the conjecture that, in conformity with a custom which prevailed in Ireland, Miliucc had sent his son from home to be brought up by Patrick's master in Connaught, and that through this accident, happening at the time of the captivity, Patrick had associated with Gosact. The record of this bond between Patrick and Miliucc's son might have originated the error that Miliucc was Patrick's master.

It is said that, having done what he could do towards planting his religion here and there in Tethbia, Patrick bent his steps northward to one of the chief strongholds and sanctuaries of pagan worship in Ireland.[1] In the plain of Slecht, in a region which belonged then to the kingdom of Connaught, but falls now within the province of Ulster, there was a famous idol. It was apparently a stone, covered with silver and gold, standing in a sacred circuit, surrounded by twelve pillar stones. This idol was known as Cenn Cruaich or Crom Cruaich, and it has been suggested that a fossilised memory of the same worship is found in a name among the British Celts beyond the sea, Pennicrucium. We may suspect that either later generations exalted unduly the importance of the precinct in

---

[1] See note, Appendix B.

Mag Slecht as a national centre of religion, or that
its importance had dwindled before the days of
Patrick.    It was told in later times that the firstlings,
even of human offspring, used to be offered to this
idol, in order to secure a plenteous yield of corn and
milk, and that the High Kings of Ireland themselves
used to come at the beginning of winter to do worship
in the plain of Slecht.    If the cult in that plain
possessed such national significance as was in later
times believed, it would have been one of Patrick's
greatest feats if he assaulted and conquered· the
power of heathendom in one of its chief fastnesses.
The story tells, with a simplicity which defeats
itself, that he came and struck down the idol with
his staff.    If this was done, if the golden pillar of
the older god was thus cast down by the servant
of the new divinity, it must have been done
with the consent of secular powers.    It would thus
have marked, perhaps more than any other single
event, the formal success of Christian aggression
against the pagan spirit of Ireland, and it would
inevitably have stood out in the earliest records as
one of the decisive victories, if not the supreme
triumph.    The blow struck by Patrick at the stone of
Mag Slecht would be as the stroke of Boniface at
the oak of Geismar.    The fall of Cenn Cruaich
should be as illustrious in the story of the spreading
of Christianity in the island of the Scots as was the
fall of the Irmin pillar on a Westphalian hill in
the advance of Christendom from the Rhine to the

Elbe, under the banner of Charles the Great. The apostle of the Irish might as justly and proudly have sent some fragment of the fallen image to the Roman pontiff, a trophy of the victory of their faith, as in a later age the apostle of the Baltic Slavs sent to Rome the three-headed god which he took from the temple of Stettin to show the head of the Church how a new land was being won for Christ. But the truth is that the episode of Cenn Cruaich, though the incident rests on an ancient tradition, held no prominent place in the oldest records. Perhaps we shall be near the mark if we infer that the story is based on a genuine fact, but that the later accounts impute to it a significance which it did not possess.[1] We may suppose that the worship of the idol was of interest only to the surrounding regions, and had no national import for the whole island. If Patrick went to the place and with the help of secular authority suppressed the worship and cast down the god, it was simply one of his local successes, one of many victories in his struggle with heathenism, not a crowning or typical triumph.

[1] It may be observed that if the idol of Mag Slecht had been eminently important for all Ireland, and had been destroyed at a period subsequent to St. Patrick, there could hardly fail to be a Christian record of its fall. In the *Annals of the Four Masters*, s.a. 464, it is said that Conall, son of Niall, ancestor of the lords of Tyrconnell, was done to death by the "old Folks" of Mag Slecht, who caught him unprotected. The thought occurs that Conall had supported the attack on the worship of Cenn Cruaich, and that his death was an act of vengeance wreaked by people of the plain who still clung to the old faith.

# CHAPTER VII

IT is uncertain how long Patrick had been in the
island before he set forth to accomplish the thing
which had been the dream of his life, the preaching
of his gospel in the western parts of Connaught,
*ubi nemo ultra erat*, by the utmost margin of
European land. We remember how the cry of the
children of Fochlad, heard in the visions of the
night, was the supreme call which he felt as
irresistible. And although his outlook must have
widened as he came face to face with facts, and
new tasks of great worth and moment, presenting
themselves, transformed and enlarged the conception of his work as he had originally grasped it,
we cannot doubt that to bear light to the forest
of Fochlad was the most cherished wish of his
heart. Nor is it likely that, however much he
found to do in Ulidia and Meath, he would
have deferred this purpose long, unless some
grave obstacle had constrained him to delay.
The necessary condition of success was the consent of the king of the land; the decisive

hindrance would have been his disapprobation and opposition.

Now there was one district close to the woods of Fochlad where Patrick was unable to fulfil his wishes till after the lapse of thirteen or fourteen years. This was the land of Amolngaid, in north Mayo, the land which is still called by that king's name—Tír Amolngid, which is pronounced Tirawley. It was not till after his death that the Christian bishop visited those regions, and it may be inferred, perhaps, that Amolngaid could not be persuaded to look with favour on the strange religion which his sons afterwards accepted. According to the common view, the forest of Fochlad was restricted to this corner of Connaught, and in that case Patrick's fulfilment of his original purpose would have been thus long delayed. But it has been pointed out in a previous chapter that Fochlad had possibly a wider compass, stretching across Mayo towards the neighbourhood of Murrisk, and that the scene of Patrick's bondage was in that neighbourhood. If so, our records allow us to suppose, though certainty cannot be attained, that he may have visited the southern limits of Fochlad at an earlier period. We are told that he crossed the Shannon and visited Connaught three times. One of these occasions was shortly after the death of king Amolngaid;[1] but one or both of the other visits may have been earlier, and on such an earlier

[1] Perhaps A.D. 444-5.  See Appendix C, 14.

occasion he may have made his way to the region
which he had known of old as a bondslave. In
our records, events which belong to different
journeys are thrown together, and it is not possible,
except at some particular points, to distinguish
them; but this chronological uncertainty will not
seriously affect the general view of Patrick's labours
in Connaught as remembered there. In the following account of some of his acts it is assumed that
his first two journeys were in the lifetime of
Amolngaid; but while this assumption is adopted
for the purpose of the narrative, it will be understood that it is only tentative.[1]

The field of Patrick's work in his first journey
beyond the Shannon seems to have been, partly,
in the land of the children of Ailill. Their country
covered a large part of the county of Sligo, and
perhaps extended southward into Roscommon to the
neighbourhood of Elphin. As in the case of other
Irish kingdoms, its memory is still preserved in
the name of a small portion of its original compass.
The barony of Tir-errill is a remnant of the land
of Ailill, son of king Eochaidh, and brother of
king Niall.

In the north of this kingdom, on the west side
of Lough Arrow, Patrick founded a church in a
district which still bears the old name of Aghanagh;
and east of the same lake, at the extreme border

---

[1] See Appendix C, 13, on Patrick in Connaught.

of Tirerrill, the parish of Shancoe enables us to
fix the whereabouts of another church which he
established at Senchua.   There is a curious piece
of evidence which suggests that Christianity had
already made an attempt to win a footing in these
regions.   When Patrick ordained[1] a certain Ailbe,
who belonged to the family of Ailill, to the rank of
priest, he told him of the existence of a " wonderful "
subterranean stone altar in the Mountain of the
Children of Ailill.   There were four glass chalices
at the four corners of the altar, and Patrick warned
Ailbe to beware of breaking the edges of the
excavation.   As Shancoe was Ailbe's church, we
are entitled to infer that the altar was somewhere
in the Bralieve hills, which are in that district.[2]   It
is clear that, if the tradition is genuine, Patrick had
seen the place himself, and the story implies that it
was not he who had set the altar in the lonely spot
on the mountains, but that it had been used in older
days and abandoned.

No commemorative name has survived to mark
the place of another church in the same regions
which owed its origin to Patrick, the Cell Angle ;[3]
but what seems to have been the most important
foundation of all was farther north, in the parish
of Tawnagh,[4] still called as it was called when he

[1] At Duma Graid, close to Lake Kilglass.   See Tírechán, 313, and *Vit.
Trip.* p. 94.
[2] Between Sligo and Leitrim.
[3] May the name be the same as that of the tribe of the Anghaile (Annaly),
who extended their power subsequently into Tethbia (cp. O'Donovan, *Book of
Rights*, p. 11, *note*)?                              [4] Tamnach.

first gave it a place on the ecclesiastical map of
Ireland.

It seems probable that in his first journey Patrick
also visited the north of Sligo, and consecrated
Brón bishop for a church founded at Caissel-ire.
This place was on the sea-shore, under the massive
hill of Knocknaree, which dominates on the west
the modern town of Sligo, and the name Kill-espug-
brone [1] still preserves the memory of the fifth-
century bishop.

He also worked in the regions south of Lake
Gara, where Sachall, whom we shall presently meet
as a bishop, became his pupil.[2]   Thence he may
have journeyed southward through the plains and
wilds of Kerry,[3] founding some churches on his
way, till he came to the lake country on the confines
of Mayo and Galway.   Then he turned westward
through Carra and founded the church of Achad-
fobuir.   The old name has clung to the place—
Aghagower, and in ancient times it had ecclesiastical importance.[4]   It marks clearly a stage in the
apostle's progress to the famous mountain to which
his visit gave a new name.

If we are right in supposing that this was the
region in which Patrick spent the years of his
captivity, that this was the home of the children of

---

[1] " Church of Bishop Brón."
[2] In Mag Airthic.   See Appendix C, 13.
[3] Ciarrigi.   Through the baronies of Costello, Clanmorris, and Kilmaine.
Possibly Aghamore, south of Kilkelly, may lie on the supposed route.   It has
been conjectured that the church *in campo Nairniu* (Tírechán, 321) was there.
[4] In quo fiunt episcopi.

Fochlad who called to him in his dreams, the church of Aghagower would possess a singular interest among all the churches which he founded in Ireland, as fulfilling the wish which had first impelled him to make the great resolve of his life. Here he revisited the scenes where he had herded his master's flocks and prayed at night in the woods in snow and rain. Here he climbed again the mountain which he mentions in his own description of the days of bondage, and which was always henceforward to be linked with his own name. Crochan Aigli rises high and prominent on the north shore of the wild desolate promontory, which is girt on three sides by the sea, and is known as the "sea-land."[1] To the summit of this peak Patrick is said to have retired for lonely contemplation and prayer. It is said that he remained there fasting forty days and forty nights, like the Jewish teachers, Moses, Elias, and Jesus. It may be thought that this report arose from the pious inclination of later admirers to seek in his life similitudes to the lives of Moses and other holy men of the Christian Scriptures. But it is conceivable that the similitude was designed by Patrick himself. It is not unlikely that, if he desired a season of isolation to commune with his own soul and meditate on things invisible, he should have fixed the term of his retreat by the

[1] Muiriscc (*Muir* = sea) Aigli. (The promontory dominated by Knocknaree in Sligo Bay was also called Muiriscc, Tír. 327.) The promontory was also known as Umail. This name is preserved in the *Owles*, designating the regions on both sides of Clew Bay, now the baronies of Murrisk and Burris-*hoole*; the latter word also contains the name Umail.

highest examples.   The forty days and forty nights may be the literal truth, and may have helped to move the imagination of his disciples to create a legend.   For in after days men pictured the saint encompassed by the company of the saints of Ireland.   God said to the souls of the saints, not only of the dead and living, but of the still unborn, " Go up, O ye saints, to the top of the mountain which is higher [1] than all the other mountains of the west, and bless the folks of Ireland."   Then the souls mounted, and they flitted round the lofty peak in the form of birds, darkening the air, so great was their multitude.   Thus God heartened Patrick by revealing to him the fruit of his labours.

Ever since, this western mount has been associated with the foreign teacher, not only bearing his name, but drawing to it multitudes of pilgrims, who every year, as the anniversary of his death comes round, toil up the steep ascent of Croagh Patrick, imbued still with the same superstitious feelings which moved the minds of Christian and heathen, of clerk and lay alike, in the days of Patrick.   The confined space of its summit is the one spot where we feel some assurance that we can stand literally in his footsteps and realise that, as we look southward over the desolate moors and tarns of Murrisk, northward across the bay to the hills of Burrishoole and Erris, and then westward beyond the islets to the spaces of the ocean, we are viewing a scene on

---

[1] Its height is 2510 feet.   Mount Nephin, close to Lake Conn, is higher.

which Patrick for many days looked forth with the bodily eye. But the spot has a greater interest if it is associated not only with the ground of solitary retreat in his later years, but with the servitude of his boyhood. For if this was so, the meditations on the mount were interfused with emotions intelligible to the children of reason, who do not understand the need of "saints" for fasting and prayer. It requires little imagination to realise in some sort what the man's feelings must have been when he returned to the places of his thraldom, conscious that he was now a "light among the Gentiles," and that his bitter captivity had led to such great results. It was a human as well as a saintly impulse to seek isolation on the mountain where he had first turned to thoughts of religion amidst the herds of his heathen lord.

In the case of what we may suppose to have been another and later journey in Connaught some genuine tradition of the line of advance appears to have been preserved. The bishop is said to have travelled westward through the southern corner of Leitrim to the banks of the Shannon. That river sweeps to the east below the town of the Rock,[1] and then, continuing its southward course, widens into a series of swellings, which, though small compared with the greater sheets of water into which it afterwards expands, are striking in their peculiar form. The stream flows through Lake Nanoge,

---

[1] Carrick-on-Shannon.

Lake Tap, Lake Boderg, and Lake Bofin, but the special feature is the long arm of water which it flings south-westward, known as Lake Kilglass. The effect of this is that the river seems to bifurcate, and a promontory is formed by the true stream and Lake Bofin on the east, and by the blind water passage of Lake Kilglass on the west. It was to these river-lakes that Patrick bent his way, and the place of his crossing, though not designated by any name that is still used, is yet so clearly defined that we cannot mistake it, and can hardly doubt that the tradition is true. He first crossed over a river-swelling, and then found a second swelling in front of him, which he also passed. The only place in the course of the Shannon which satisfies these conditions is the place which has been described. When he was rowed across Lake Bofin, Patrick found himself on the water-girt promontory which is washed on the west by Lake Kilglass. In order to reach the district of Moyglass, which was his first destination, he took the shortest and most direct way, and crossed this second lake (perhaps near the modern Carnado Bridge) instead of making half-a-day's journey round its shores.

On reaching the other bank he was in the plain of Glass,[1] and here again we find that the name of a large district has been preserved in the name of

---

[1] He first went to a place called Duma Graid, and ordained there the arch-presbyter Ailbe, who resided at Shancoe (as mentioned above). It may be suspected that the name Duma Graid (for which we expect a modern Doogary) is preserved in Dockery's Island, near the mouth of Lake Kilglass.

a small part.  The little townland of Moyglass is adjacent to Lake Tap, but the ancient plain of Glass extended, we may be confident, from the banks of the river Shannon to the foot of the western hills, which screen the river here from the great plain of Roscommon.  In this district the bishop established a Cell Mór or great church, and his visit gave the place its abiding name.  It can be inferred that Patrick's church was close to the village of Kilmore.

From the small plain of Glass Patrick made his way into the great plain, known as Mag Ai, which extends over the central part of the county of Roscommon.  It is divided from the Shannon by a screen of low hills, and only from some of the ridges in the south of it can one descry, shimmering far away, the waters of Lake Ree.  When he crossed that chain of hills, Patrick found himself in the land of the Corcu Ochland, and he was welcomed by a certain Hono, who is described as a Druid, and was evidently a man of wealth and influence.  There is good reason to believe that Hono was prepared for Patrick's coming, for two of Patrick's disciples, Assicus and his nephew Bitteus, along with Cipia, the mother of Bitteus, were already with Hono when Patrick arrived. We may probably infer that Christianity had already made some way here, and that, on Patrick's coming, no persuasions were necessary to induce Hono to co-operate in founding a church and monastery. They went together to the place which still bears the name of the White Rock—Ailfinn, and there founded together one of the most important of Patrick's ecclesiastical foundations, which in later times, when the great dioceses were formed, was to become the seat of a diocesan bishop. The community of Elphin was to be under the headship of Hono's descendants, but its first members were Assicus, Betheus, and Cipia. Bishop Assicus, whose name has not been forgotten at Elphin, was a skilful worker in bronze, and used to make for Patrick altars and cases for books. Square patens of his workmanship were long preserved as treasures at Armagh and at his own Elphin.

The next station of the bishop's journey was the seat of the kings of Connaught, the fortress of Crochan, famous in story. On one of the highest and broadest of the low ridges which mark the plain of Ái stood the royal palace, and though, as in the case of the other palaces of the kings of Ireland, no remains of the habitation survive except the earthen structure, it is something even to stand on the site of Rathcrochan, where queen Maeve and her lord lived—if they lived at all. Around the royal fort itself the ground is covered with other mounds and raths and memorials of ancient history, so that one can hardly fancy what appearance Crochan presented to Patrick. Near at hand was the place of sepulchres, to which the kings went down from their stronghold, as the kings of Mycenae went down from their citadel to the tombs

below. In that field of the dead one red stone
stands conspicuous to the present day, and the
ill-certified tradition is that it marks the tomb of
Dathi, the successor and nephew of Niall. If there
were any truth in that tradition, the pillar would be
an interesting link with the age of Patrick, for it
would have been set up not many years before he
visited the place.[1]

Imagination peopled many spots in Ireland with
supernatural beings—not only with fairies, but also
with an earthfolk[2] that was once at least human, a
conquered population who had formerly held the
island, and, driven by invaders from the surface of
the ground, had found new homes in chambered
mounds, where they practised their magic crafts.
But no spot was more closely associated with these
fabled beings than the hill of Rathcrochan. On
ground so alive with legend, in a place which stimulated fancy, it was hardly possible that the incident
of Patrick's visit should be handed down in the
sober colours of history or that it should escape
the meshes of fable. But the legend-shaping
instinct of some Christian poet wrought here with
signal grace, and the story must have been invented
not many decads of years after the visit to
Rathcrochan.

Patrick, the tale tells, and the bishops who

---

[1] See note, Appendix B.
[2] Tuatha De Danann, people of the goddess Danann. They are said, in
the mythical history of Ireland, to have colonised the country and to have
been conquered by the Milesians.

accompanied him, had assembled together at a fountain[1] near Rathcrochan to hold a council before sunrise, when two maidens came down, after the fashion of women, to wash at the fountain. They were the daughters of the High King of Ireland, and their names were Ethne the White and Fedelm the Red. They lived at Crochan, to be fostered and educated by two Druids, Mael and Caplait. These Druids had been deeply alarmed when they heard that Patrick was about to cross the Shannon, and by their sorceries they had brought down darkness and mist over the plain of Ai to hinder him from entering the land. The darkness of night prevailed for three days, but was dispelled by the saint's prayers.

When the princesses beheld the bishops and priests sitting round the fountain, they were amazed at their strange garb, and knew not what to think of them. Were they fairies—men of the *side*; or were they of the earth-folk—the Tuatha De Danann; or were they an illusion, an unreal vision? So they accosted and asked the strangers, "Whence have ye come, and where is your home?" And Patrick answered, "It were better for you to believe in the true God whom we worship than to ask questions about our race." Then the elder girl said, "Who is God, and where is God, and of whom is he God? Where is his dwelling? Has he sons and daughters, your God, and has he gold and silver? Is he immortal?

[1] Fountain of Clebach.

Is he fair? Has his Son been fostered by many? Are his daughters dear to the men of the world, and fair in their eyes? Is he in heaven or in earth? in the sea, in the rivers, in the hill places, in the valleys? Tell us how we may know him, in whatwise he will appear. How is he discovered? Is he found in youth or in old age?"

To these greetings Patrick replied: "Our God ✗ is the God of all men, the God of heaven and earth, of sea and rivers, of sun and moon and stars, of the lofty mountain and the lowly valleys, the God above heaven and in heaven, and under heaven; he has his dwelling around heaven and earth and sea and all that in them is. He inspires all, he quickens all, he dominates all, he supports all. He lights the light of the sun; he furnishes the light of the night; he has made springs in the dry land, and has set stars to minister to the greater lights. He has a Son co-eternal with himself, and like unto himself. The Son is not younger than the Father, nor the Father older than the Son. And the Holy Spirit breathes in them. The Father, the Son, and the Spirit are not divided. I wish to unite you with the heavenly King, as ye are daughters of an earthly king. Believe."

With one voice and with one heart the two king's daughters said, "Tell us with all diligence how we may believe in the heavenly King that we may see Him face to face, and we will do as thou sayest." Patrick said, " Do ye believe that by baptism ye

can cast away the sin of your father and mother?"
They said, "We believe." "Do ye believe in
repentance after sin?" "We believe." "Do ye
believe in life after death?" "We believe." "Do
ye believe in the resurrection in the day of Judgment?" "We believe." "Do ye believe in the
unity of the Church?" "We believe."

Then Patrick baptized them in the fountain and
placed a white veil on their heads, and they begged
that they might behold the face of Christ. And
Patrick said, "Until ye shall taste of death, ye
cannot see the face of Christ, and unless ye shall
receive the sacrifice." They answered, "Give us
the sacrifice that we may see the Son, our bridegroom." And they received the Eucharist, and fell
asleep in death. And they were placed in one bed,
and their friends mourned them.

Then Caplait the Druid came, and Patrick
preached to him, and he believed and became a
monk. His brother Mael was wroth at his falling
away, and hoped to recall him to the old faith, but
on hearing Patrick's teaching he too became a
Christian and his head was tonsured.

When the prescribed days of lamentation were
over, the maidens were buried in a round tomb near
the fountain. Their grave was dedicated to God
and to Patrick and his heirs after him, and he
constructed a church of earth in that place.

In this curious legend is embedded some matter
of historical significance. In the first place we

must treat the story of the brother Druids separately
from the story of the maidens, for they are bound
together only by an external link, and their motives
are distinct.   The motive of the legend of the two
virgins who died in the hour of their conversion
recurs in other tales,[1] and the solid basis of fact
was their tomb by the spring at Rathcrochan.   At
that tomb the story grew up that when they were
baptized, their desire for the heavenly vision was
fulfilled immediately by their death.   This legend
was then worked up artificially, and the dialogue was
composed and written down in Irish, partly in verse.[2]
The freshness and simplicity, which are so striking,
and some particular traits, justify us in surmising
that this happened at an early date, within the
first generation after the saint's death.   The naive
wonder of the maidens at the appearance of the
clerks, the brief view which Patrick unfolds of the
articles of his religion, the emphasis laid upon the
unity of the Church, point to the conclusion that
the story took shape when Patrick's ways of
teaching, and the first impressions made upon
pagans by the apostles of the new faith, were within
the memory of the Church.   The dialogue is
artificial, for the questions of the damsels are
arranged so as to lead up to the bishop's exposi-
tion of his creed.   And, on the other hand, the
baptismal questions of Patrick assume a knowledge

---

[1] See note, Appendix B.
[2] See Appendix A, ii. 1.

on the part of the princesses which is inconsistent with their previous ignorance.

Now if we are right in the view that the legend originated at an early date and was cast into literary shape—at least before the end of the fifth century— we can hardly escape the inference that the maidens whose memory was preserved at Crochan were in truth daughters of Loigaire. Such an identification was not at all likely to have been invented by popular legend, nor by any recorder of Patrick's acts, living within a generation of his death. In sending children to be brought up away from their home, king Loigaire would have followed the general practice of the country, and that he should send them to the royal residence of Connaught would have been natural enough. The fathers of king Amolngaid and king Loigaire were brothers, and it would not be surprising that Loigaire should send his daughters to Rathcrochan to be educated by the Druids of Amolngaid.

But the episode of these brethren has an independent motive of its own. One brother, Mael, has an Irish name, designating the native tonsure, by which only the front part of the head was shaven from ear to ear; while Caplait, his fellow, has a Latin name (*Capillatus*), which signifies the removal of all the hair in the fashion already largely adopted in the western Empire, and subsequently known as the Roman tonsure.[1] Both Druids alike were

---

[1] See Appendix A, i. 4, on the tonsure question.

tonsured by Patrick according to the story; both
alike, it is implied, wore the native tonsure before
they were converted.  The name *Caplait* could
not have been applied to either till after his
conversion.  But when they became monks it
applied equally to both, just as *Mael* was equally
applicable to both when they were still pagans.
Thus the story, taken literally, does not hang
together, and the transparent names suggest that it
arose from some circumstance connected with the
Christian tonsure.  Fortunately, the narrative
supplies us with the clue.  The writer who tells
the tale observes that the incident gave rise to an
Irish maxim, *cosmail Mael do Chaplait*, "Mael is
like unto Caplait."  It is manifest that here, as in
other cases of the same kind, the story originated
from the proverb, not the proverb from the story.
The story was told to explain the existence of the
proverb, but the existence of the proverb itself
is the ultimate fact.  It happens to be a fact of
historical significance.  We may infer that the
Christian tonsure had been introduced and enforced
by Patrick, but that his rule was relaxed and disregarded after his death, the native clergy adopting
the old native tonsure of the Druids.  The two
fashions subsisted for a time side by side, then
the Roman fell completely out of use till it was
restored in the seventh century.  But the proverb
"Mael is like unto Caplait" arose when the two
tonsures were in use together, and expressed the

claim that the native mode was as legitimate for a monk as the foreign.

From Rathcrochan, Patrick and his company proceeded westward and planted religious foundations in the region which is now most easily described as the barony of Castlereagh. A number of Gallic clergy were with him, and these he dispersed to found churches in various places. One of these places stands out in interest, though it is of small account now. Baslic survives as the name of a parish, and preserves the memory of the foreign clerks who thought of the greater *basilicae* of the Empire when they built their little sanctuary in the wilds of Connaught and gave it the high-sounding name of *Basilica sanctorum*. No place-name, due to Christianity, in Ireland has a greater interest than Basilica, west of Rathcrochan. Another church founded in this region, near the banks of the river Suck, was Cell Garad, which is perhaps to be sought at Oran, where an old burial-ground and the fragment of a belfry mark an ancient ecclesiastical site. Both Baslic and Cell Garad were the seats of bishops.

Patrick then went northward to Selce,[1] in the land of Brian. Here the sons of Brian welcomed him and were baptized, and he founded a church close to Lake Selce. On a hill hard by, where he and his companions encamped, a memorial of

---

[1] Selce has not been identified.

their visit was preserved for centuries. They
wrote upon some stones in the place, and it was
probably their own names that they recorded, so
that posterity knew who were of Patrick's company
when the sons of Brian were baptized at the hill
of Selce. Two bishops were with him, Bron,
whose home, as we saw, was in the north, on the
seashore under Knocknaree, and Sachall, bishop
of the new church of Baslic; eight priests, including
Benignus, his favourite pupil; and two women. It
may have been that the names of the company
were inscribed on three stones severally consecrated
by the names *Iesus, Christus, Soter.*

From here Patrick may have proceeded westward to Lake Tecet—Lake Tecet of Ireland,
bearing the same name as the more famous Lake
Tecet of Britain, which the stranger knows as the
Lake of Bala. The boggy soil makes the waters
dark, and if we look down from one of the hills
which partly gird it, the form of the lake, with its
many corners and inlets, eludes the eye. It was
probably near the western or northern shore that
Adrochta, who took the veil from Patrick's hand,
founded a church. Nor is she forgotten to-day,
for as we walk on the eastern bank of the lake, we
are in the parish of "Adrochta's Church."[1]

We now come to a journey of Patrick for which
we have a definite chronological indication, since we

[1] Kill-aragbt. From here Patrick may have revisited Mag Airthic and
the Kerries.

know that it was undertaken soon after the death
of king Amolngaid, and that king probably died
about thirteen years after Patrick's arrival in
Ireland. The story represents the land of
Amolngaid as the particular region of Fochlad
which had been the goal of Patrick's desires, and
describes the occasion of his setting forth as if it
had been brought about by a pure chance. Near
the palace of king Loigaire at Tara he overheard
a conversation between two noblemen, one of whom
informed the other that he was Endae, son of
Amolngaid, and had come from the far west, "from
Mag Domnon [1] and the wood of Fochlad." Then
Patrick, hearing the magic name of his dream, was
thrilled with joy, and, turning round, he cried to
Endae, "Thither I will go with thee, if I live, for
God bade me go." But Endae replied, "Thou
shalt not come with me, lest we be slain together."
"Yet," said the saint, "thou shalt never reach thy
home alive if I come not with thee, nor shalt
thou have eternal life. For it is on my account
that thou hast come hither." And Endae said,
"Baptize my son, for he is young. But I and
my brethren may not believe in thee till we come
to our own folk, lest they mock us." And Patrick
baptized his son Conall.

It appears that Endae and his six brethren had
come to Tara to invoke the judgment of the High

---

[1] *Irrus* Domnand, "the peninsula of Domnu"=barony of *Erris* in Mayo.
Cp. Rhŷs, "Studies in Early Irish History," p. 38.

King in a dispute about the inheritance of their father's property. The claim of Endae and his son was opposed to the claims of the other six. In giving judgment king Loigaire is said to have invited the aid of Patrick, and they decided that the inheritance should be divided among the claimants in seven parts. This doom was in favour of Endae's brethren, if, as we may suppose, Endae's claim was that the division of the property should be eightfold, his son Conall receiving a separate portion for himself. But however this may have been, Endae is said to have dedicated his seventh portion and his son Conall to Patrick and Patrick's God.

When the award was given, Patrick and a company of ecclesiastics prepared to set forth with Endae. But they took the precaution of making a formal agreement with Endae and his brothers, and we may be certain that whatever the other terms may have been, the bodily safety of the Christians was expressly ensured. The most significant circumstance concerning this treaty is that it was made under the warranty of king Loigaire. This is an important piece of evidence as to the attitude of that king to the Christian teachers. It exhibits his policy of enlightened toleration, and shows that, though personally he clung to the beliefs of his fathers, yet in his capacity of king of Ireland he was willing to assist the diffusion of a doctrine subversive of those beliefs.

Patrick set out with Endae and his brethren, and having crossed the river Moy, perhaps at a ford where the "town of the ford" stands to-day,[1] they entered the territory of Amolngaid, where were the woods of Fochlad, and beyond, to westward, the wild Mag Domnon. That the baptism of Conall and the coming of the Christian teacher in the company of the chiefs should arouse wrath and disgust among the Druids is not surprising, and there may be some historical foundation for the legend which tells how the chief Druid, Rechrad, sought to kill Patrick. Along with nine Druids, arrayed in white, he advanced to meet Endae and his company. When Endae saw them, he snatched up his arms to drive them off, but Patrick raised his left hand and cursed the wizard, and Rechrad fell dead, and was burned up before the eyes of all. The other Druids fled into Mag Domnon. And when the folk saw this miracle, many were baptized on that day.

It was in this way, according to the legend, that Christianity entered the northern regions of Fochlad. Near the forest, and close to the sea-shore, was founded a church,[2] and not far from it a cross was set up, of which the memory is preserved in the local name Crosspatrick.[3] The

---

[1] Ballina.

[2] It was one of the many Donaghmores, "great churches," which Patrick is said to have founded. He consigned it to the care of Mucneus.

[3] The name of a townland, in which there is an old churchyard and traces of ruins, to the right of the road from Ballina to Killala, a mile south of Killala. For Donaghmore and Mullaghfarry (*farry* = *forrach* = *foirrgea*, Tír. 327) see O'Donovan, *Hy Fiachrach*, pp. 466 and 467, notes.

church, built doubtless of timber, was afterwards to be overshadowed by the neighbouring foundation of Killala, conspicuous by its lofty belfry. Elsewhere Patrick caused a square church of earth to be constructed, at the gathering-place of the sons of Amolngaid, which has been identified with Mullaghfarry, "the hill of the meeting-place."

# CHAPTER VIII

## FOUNDATION OF ARMAGH AND ECCLESIASTICAL ORGANISATION

### § 1. *Visit to Rome* (*circa* A.D. 441-3)

It is possible that Patrick had intended in earlier years to visit Rome long before he began his labours in Ireland. If he entertained such a thought, it would seem that circumstances hindered him from realising it.[1] But it would not have been unnatural if he continued to cherish the idea of repairing to the centre of western Christendom; and we might expect that when he had spent some years in the toils, afflictions, and disappointments, the alternating hopes and fears, the successes and defeats, incident to missionary work in a barbarous land, he would have wished to receive some recognition of his work and sympathy with his efforts from the head of the western churches. He might count upon sympathy and encouragement; the interest which the Roman see was prepared to take in the remote island had been shown by the sending

---

[1] See Appendix C, 8.

*Evangelism + relics!*

of Palladius; whether Patrick had ever himself received a message from the successor of Celestine is unknown.

In addition to the object of directing the attention of the Roman bishop to the growth of the Church in Ireland—an object which would at that time appeal strongly to Patrick or to any one else in his place—there was another motive for visiting Rome, which, though subordinate, must not be passed over. Patrick was the son of his age, and it would display a complete ignorance of the spirit of the Church, in Gaul and elsewhere at that time, if we failed to recognise the high importance which he must have attributed to the relics of holy men, especially of the early apostles, and the value which he would have set on acquiring such parcels of matter for his new churches in Ireland. The religious estimation of relics had become general in the fourth century. Such a learned man as Gregory of Nyssa set great store by them. The subject might be illustrated at great length, but it will be enough to remind the reader of the excitement which was caused in the religious world in the year 386 A.D., when Ambrose of Milan discovered the tombs of St. Gervasius and St. Protasius. The bishops of the west vied for shares in the remains. In Gaul, three cities, Tours, Rouen, and Vienne, were fortunate enough to receive scraps of linen or particles of blood-stained dust which had touched the precious bodies. The estimation of relics in Gaul will be best understood by reading the work of Victricius, Bishop of Rouen and missionary of Belgica, "in praise of the saints." [1] It is certain that Patrick could not have helped sharing in this universal reverence for relics, and could not have failed to deem it an object of high importance to secure things of such value for his church. The hope of winning a fragment of a cerement cloth or some grains of dust—*pulvisculum nescio quod in modico vasculo pretioso linteamine circumdatum* [2]—would have been no small inducement to visit Rome, the city of many martyrs.

Patrick had been eight years in Ireland when a greater than Celestine or Xystus was elected to the see of Rome. [3] The pontificate of Leo the Great marks an eminent station in the progress of the Roman bishops to that commanding position which they were ultimately to occupy in Europe. His path had been prepared by his forerunners, but it is he who induces the Emperor to accord a formal and imperial sanction to the sovran authority of the Roman see in the west, [4] and he plays a more leading and decisive part than any of his predecessors in moulding Christian theology by his famous Epistle on the occasion of the Council of Chalcedon. That Leo should have taken as direct and energetic an interest in the extension of the borders of Christendom as the less eminent bishops before him is what we should expect.

---

[1] *De laude sanctorum* (Migne, *Patr. Lat.* xx.).
[2] Jerome, *Adversus Vigilantium*, c. 5.     [3] A.D. 440.
[4] See above, chap. iii. p. 64.

It was in the year after his elevation that Patrick, according to the conclusion to which our evidence points, betook himself to Rome.[1] No step could have been more natural, and none could have been more politic. It was equally wise whether he was assured of the goodwill of Leo or, as is possible, had reason to believe that his work had been misrepresented. To report the success of his labours to the head of the western churches, of which Ireland was the youngest, to enlist his personal sympathy, to gain his formal approbation, his moral support, and his advice, were objects which would well repay a visit to Rome, and an absence of some length from Ireland. It is indeed hardly too much to say that nothing was more likely to further his success than an express approbation of his work by the highest authority in Christendom.

But it is possible that he may have had a more particular motive, which may explain why he chose just this time for his visit. Hitherto, active in different parts of the island, he had established no central seat, no primatial or "metropolitan" church for the chief bishop. Not long after his return, he founded, as we shall see presently, the church of Armagh, fixing his own see there, and establishing it as the primatial church. This was a step of the highest importance in the progress of ecclesiastical organisation, and it is not a very daring conjecture to suppose that Patrick may have wished to consult

---

[1] For the evidence see Appendix C, 15.

the Roman bishop concerning this design and obtain his approbation.

The result of the visit to Rome is briefly stated in words which are probably a contemporary record, "he was approved in the Catholic faith." He may well have received practical advice from Leo—such advice as a later pontiff gave to Augustine for the conversion of the English. But Patrick bore back with him to Ireland visible and material proofs of the goodwill of Rome. He received gifts which, to Christians of his day, seemed the most precious of all gifts, relics not of any lesser martyrs, but of the apostles Peter and Paul. They were gifts particularly opportune for bestowing prestige upon the new church which he was about to found, and where they were afterwards preserved.

## § 2. *Foundation of Armagh* (A.D. 444)

No act of Patrick had more decisive consequences for the ecclesiastical history of the island than the foundation, soon after his return from Rome, of the church and monastery of Ardd Mache, in the kingdom of Oriel. King Daire, through whose goodwill this community was established, dwelled in the neighbourhood of the ancient fortress of Emain, which his own ancestors had destroyed a hundred years agone, when they had come from the south to wrest the land from the Ulidians and sack the palace of its lords. The conquerors did not set up their own abode in the stronghold of the old kings of Ulster; they burned the timber buildings and left the place desolate, as it were under a curse. The ample earth structures of this royal stronghold are still there, attesting that Emain, famous in legend, was a place of historical importance in the days when Ulster belonged to one of the elder peoples of the island.[1] Once and again, long after the days of St. Patrick, the Picts from their home in Dalaradia made vain attempts to recover their storied palace, but it was not destined to become a place of human habitation again until, more than a thousand years after its desolation, a house seems to have been built there by an Ulster king "for the entertainment of the learned men of Ireland."

The abode of king Daire was somewhere in the neighbourhood. It seems possible that he was the king of Oriel, though it may be held that he was only king of one of the tribes which belonged to the Oriel kingdom.[2] Daire was not ill disposed towards the foreign religion, and he was persuaded to grant Patrick a site for a monastic foundation not far from his own dwelling. Eastward from Emain, concealed from the eye by two high ridges, rises the hill known as Ardd Mache, "the height of Macha," bearing the name, it is said, of some heroine of legend. At the eastern foot of this hill, Daire apportioned a small tract of ground to Patrick, and

---

[1] It may be Ptolemy's *Regia* ('Ρηγία). Cp. Rhŷs, "Studies in Early Irish History," p. 49 (*Proc. of British Acad.* vol. i.).

[2] See note, Appendix B.

this was the beginning of what was to become the chief ecclesiastical city of Ireland. The simple houses which were needed for a small society of monks were built, and there is a record, which appears to be ancient and credible, concerning these primitive buildings. A circular space was marked out, one hundred and forty feet in diameter, and enclosed by a rampart of earth. Within this *less*, as it was called, were erected, doubtless of wood, a Great House to be the dwelling of the monks, a kitchen, and a small oratory.[1] This record has an interest beyond this particular monastery, as we may believe that it represents the typical scheme of the monastic establishments of Patrick and his companions.

We know not how long Patrick and his household abode under the hill of Macha, but this settlement was not to be final.[2] It seems that the bishop ultimately won great influence over the king, who evidently embraced the Christian faith; and then Daire resolved that the monastery should be

---

[1] The dimensions of these houses are given, *Vit. Trip.* p. 226:—"27 feet in the Great House, 17 feet in the kitchen, 7 feet in the oratory [*aregal*, supposed to be derived from *oraculum*]; and it was thus that he used always to found the *congbala*" [*i.e.* the sacred enclosures, or cloisters]. If these houses were circular, the numbers represent the diameters. For the topography of Armagh see the paper of Reeves, *The Ancient Churches of Armagh* (Lusk, 1860), with a plan. The locality of the first settlement, *ubi nunc est Fertae martyrum*, "the grave of the relics" (Muirchu, 290), he fixes, by means of the monastery of Temple-fertagh, which existed at the beginning of the seventeenth century, to the land south of Scotch St., near Scotch St. river (p. 10).

[2] The two stages, first below, and then on the hill, are doubtless historical. We may conjecture that the second and final foundation is that which is recorded in the Annals, and that the first settlement had been made before the visit to Rome.

raised from its lowly place to a loftier and safer site. A curious story, with the marks of antiquity about it, has come down, showing how all this befell, and it would be difficult to say how much is fable and what was the underlying fact. Patrick, so the tale relates, had from the very first cast his eyes upon the hill of Macha. But Daire refused to grant it, and gave him instead the land below. One day a squire of the king drove a horse to feed in a field of grass which belonged to the monastery. Patrick remonstrated, but the squire made no answer, and when he returned to the field on the morrow, he found the horse dead. He told his master that the Christian had killed the horse, and Daire said to his men, Go and kill him. But as the men were on their way to do his bidding, an illness unto death suddenly fell on Daire, and his wife said, " It is the sake of the Christian. Let some one go quickly, and let his blessing be brought to us, and thou shalt be well ; and let those who went to slay him be stopped." Then two men went to Patrick and told him that Daire was ill, and asked him for a remedy. Patrick gave him some water which he had consecrated. With this water they first sprinkled the dead horse, and it was restored to life ; and then, returning to Daire's house, they found it no less potent in restoring their lord to health.

Then Daire visited the monastery to pay respect to Patrick, and offered him a large bronze vessel, imported from over seas. The bishop acknowledged the gift by a simple "I thank thee," in Latin. The king looked for some more elaborate and impressive acknowledgment ; he was annoyed that the cauldron should be received with no greater sign of satisfaction than a *gratzacham*, as the Latin phrase *gratias agamus* sounded in rapid colloquial pronunciation. And on returning home he sent his servants to bring back the bronze, as a thing which the Christian was unable to appreciate. When they came back with the vessel, Daire asked them what Patrick said, and they replied, "He said *gratzacham*." "What," said Daire, "*gratzacham* when it was given, *gratzacham* when it was taken away! It is a good word, and for his *gratzacham* he shall have his cauldron." Then Daire went himself with the cauldron to Patrick, and said, "Keep thy cauldron, for thou art a steadfast and unchangeful man." And he gave him, besides, the land which he had before desired.

Whatever may be thought of the anecdotes of the horse and the cauldron, we may believe that Patrick won the respect of Daire as a man of firm character, and that for this reason Daire was induced to promote him to the higher site, granting him the land on the hill, with the usual reservation of the rights of the tribe.[1] So it came about that Patrick and his household went up from their home at the foot of the hill and made another home on its

---

[1] This is expressed by *quantum habeo*, "so far as it is mine," in Muirchu, 292$_{31}$.

summit.   The new settlement was probably constructed on the same plan, though the close may
have been larger, to suit the area of the hill-top.[1]
The old settlement below was perhaps devoted to
the uses of a graveyard,[2] and in later days a cloister
was to arise there, known as the Temple of the
Graveyard.

Such, according to ancient tradition, was the
founding of Armagh, which rose to be the supreme
ecclesiastical city in Ireland.   Though we have no
record of Patrick's own views, it is hardly possible
to escape the conclusion that he consciously and
deliberately laid the foundations of this pre-
eminence.   It is true that some of his successors
in the see supported and enhanced its claim to
supremacy and domination by misrepresentations
and forgeries, just as in a larger sphere the later
bishops of Rome made use of fabricated documents
and accepted falsifications of history in order to
establish their extravagant pretensions.   But as in
the case of Rome, so in the case of Armagh, misrepresentation of history could only avail to increase
or confirm an authority which was already acknowledged and to extend the limits of a power which
had been otherwise established.   If the church of
Armagh had been originally on the same footing as
any of the other churches which were founded by
Patrick, it is inconceivable that it could have
acquired the pre-eminence which it enjoyed in the

---

[1] See note, Appendix B.            [2] *Ib.*

seventh century merely by means of the false assertion that the founder had made it supreme over all his other churches. Now we know of no political circumstances or historical events between the age of Patrick and the seventh century which would have served to elevate the church of Armagh above the churches of northern Ireland and invest it with an authority and prestige which did not originally belong to it. The only tenable explanation of the commanding position which Armagh occupied is that the tradition is substantially true, and that Patrick made this foundation, near the derelict palace of the ancient Ulster kings, his own special seat and residence, from which he exercised, and intended that his successors should exercise, in Ireland an authority similar to that which a metropolitan bishop exercised in his province on the continent.[1] The choice of Armagh may seem strange. It may be said that if his "province" was conterminous with the whole island, the hill of Macha was hardly a well-chosen spot as an ecclesiastical centre. We might expect him to have sought a site somewhere in the kingdom of Meath, somewhere less distant from the hill of Uisnech, which the islanders regarded as the navel of their country. Trim, for instance, would seem to be a far more suitable seat for a bishop whose duties of supervision extended to Desmond as much as to Dalriada. There are two points here

---

[1] There can be little question that the (contemporary) expression *in provincia nostra* in *Ann. Ult.*, A.D. 443, means "in Ireland," conceived as a single ecclesiastical province, like the province of a metropolitan.

which may be taken into consideration. If we confine our view to the sphere of Patrick's own missionary activity, namely, northern Ireland, Armagh was a sufficiently convenient centre. Meath and Connaught and the kingdoms of Ulster, the lands in which Patrick had himself chiefly worked, might seem to require closer supervision, and it may have been a matter of policy not to attempt to press his authority too strictly over the churches of the south. We shall see presently that though he visited southern Ireland, his work there was relatively slight. The evidence suggests that while the whole island formed a single ecclesiastical province, in which Patrick occupied the position of " metropolitan," there was actually, though not officially, a province within a province. He exerted a more direct and minute control over the northern part of the island. But, in any case, the position of an ecclesiastical metropolis cannot be entirely determined by compasses ; geographical convenience cannot be always decisive. Here we come to a second consideration. The circumstance that king Loigaire was not a Christian may have weighed with Patrick against choosing a place in Meath. He may have thought it expedient to fix the chief seat of ecclesiastical authority in the territory and near the palace of a Christian king. If Daire was king of Oriel, his conversion to Christianity, in contrast with the obduracy of Loigaire, will go far to explain the choice of Armagh. It counted for

much to have a secure position near the gates of a
powerful king, and his conversion would have been
the greatest single triumph that Patrick had yet
achieved.

Our oldest records do not describe Patrick's work
in the kingdoms of Ulster with the same details or at
the same length as his work in Connaught. But
they indicate that he preached and founded churches
in the kingdoms of Ailech and Oriel, as well as in
Ulidia; and there is reason to believe that fuller
records existed at an early period and were used by
one of the later biographers. It may be noted that
he is said to have consecrated the site of a church at
Coleraine, and that a stone on which he sat was
shown at Dunseveric, on the shore of the northern
sea. In the land of the Condiri, who gave their name
to the diocese of Connor, many churches attributed
their origin to him, for instance, Glenavy,[1] near the
banks of Lake Neagh, and Glore, the church of
Glenarm.

## § 3. *In South Ireland*

While Patrick's sphere of immediate activity
seems to have been mainly the northern half of the
island, there is not much room for serious doubts
that he claimed to hold a position of ecclesiastical
authority over the southern provinces also. His
own description of himself not as bishop in a par-

---

[1] Láthrach Patricc (*Trip.* 349₈). Cp. Reeves, *Antiquities of Down and
Connor*, pp. 47 and 236; for Glore, *ib.* 87, 338; for Dunseveric, *ib.* 286.
For Clogher and Ard-Patrick (Louth) see note, Appendix B.

ticular province, but as bishop in Ireland generally,[1]
is sufficient to make this clear ; and there are not
wanting ancient records of his visits to Leinster and
Munster. He is said to have baptized the sons of
Dunlang, king of Leinster, and Crimthann, king of
the Hy Ceinselaich ; he is recorded to have visited
the royal palace at the hill of Cashel and baptized
the sons of Natfraich, king of Munster. It was
remembered that he had passed through Ossory,
and worked in the regions of Muskerry. If, as is
possible, Christianity had made greater way in the
southern kingdoms, he had less to do as a pioneer,
but the task of organisation must have devolved
upon him here as in the north. It is easy to understand why comparatively scanty traditions should
have been preserved of his work in the south. His
special association with the see of Armagh did not
dispose the communities of Munster and Leinster to
remember a connexion which supported the claims
of that see to a superior jurisdiction.

In Leinster, Patrick had two fellow-workers who
occupied a special position. Auxilius and Iserninus,
whom he had known at Auxerre, had been sent to
Ireland about six years after his own coming.[2] The
origin of Auxilius is unknown. His name is still
commemorated by a church which he founded,
Kill-ossy,[3] not far from Naas, one of the chief abodes
of the kings of Leinster. Iserninus was of Irish

---

[1] *Ep. against Corot.* 375.

[2] *Ann. Ult.*, A.D. 439.          [3] Or Killishea.

birth. His native name was Fith. He was born in the neighbourhood of Clonmore,[1] on the borders of Carlow and Wicklow. Here, in the land of his clan, he first set up a church, but his ultimate establishment was at Aghade,[2] on the Slaney. These regions formed part of a considerable kingdom which was at this time ruled over by Endae Cennsalach, who seems to have founded the political importance of his tribe, for the land came to be known by the name of the Children of Cennsalach. This king did what lay in his power to oppose the diffusion of the new faith, and Iserninus found it prudent to withdraw beyond the borders of his kingdom. Perhaps he found a refuge at Kilcullen,[3] close to Dún Aillinn, one of the strongholds of the kings of Leinster. But Crimthann, the son and successor of Endae, was converted and baptized by Patrick at his dwelling in Rathvilly, on the banks of the Slaney, where earthworks still mark a seat of the kings of the Children of Cennsalach. This case is similar to the case of the sons of Amolngaid, and illustrates the general fact that while the older generation was still, fervently or patiently, clinging to the old beliefs, the younger generation was steadily turning to the new. The conversion of Crimthann enabled Iserninus to return to his own land, and he established himself at Aghade, a crossing-place on the Slaney, about nine miles below Rathvilly.

[1] See note, Appendix B.  [2] Áth Fithot, south of Tallow.
[3] Old Kilcullen, south of (new) Kilcullen, in Co. Kildare.

Among the acts which are ascribed to Patrick in
Leinster, the consecration of Fíacc, the Fair, a pupil
of the poet Dubthach, and himself a poet, deserve
mention.[1] The conversion of the poet into the
Christian bishop reminds us of the more illustrious
contemporary case of Sidonius Apollinaris. There
seems no reason to doubt the truth of this tradition,
and perhaps the bell, the staff, the writing tablet, and
the cup and paten, which Patrick is said to have
given to Fíacc, were preserved at the church where
his memory was specially cherished. He was first
settled at a church which was called after himself,
Domnach Féicc, the situation of which is not im-
probably supposed to have been east of the Slaney,
not far from Tullow.[2] But he afterwards became
bishop of Slébte, on the western bank of the Barrow,
under the hills of Margy,[3] and ended his days there.
In the early middle ages Slébte was a notable place
on the ecclesiastical map, but the desolate site shows
no vestiges of its ancient importance. At the end
of the seventh century Slébte renewed the ties
which bound it to Armagh in the days of Fíacc and
Patrick, and we possess a monument of this reconciliation in the earliest biography of Patrick that has
come down to us, written by a clerk of Fíacc's
church.[4]

---

[1] See note, Appendix B.         [2] *Ib.*
[3] In barony of Slievemargy, in Queen's County, a mile or so north-west of
the town of Carlow.
[4] The *Life* by Muirchu, see Appendix A, ii. 3.

## § 4. *Church Discipline*

It is not clear whether Auxilius and Iserninus were already invested with episcopal rank when they left Gaul, or were consecrated in Leinster by Patrick.[1] But in any case, they seem, along with Secundinus, who came with them from Gaul, to have held an exceptional position of weight as counsellors and coadjutors. Coming, perhaps, from the episcopal city where Patrick himself had been trained, they corroborated the Gallic influence, we might say the influence of Auxerre, which presided at the organisation of the Church in Ireland. It was natural that Patrick should take special counsel with these men for laying down rules of ecclesiastical discipline, and, on the occasion, perhaps, of one of his visits to Leinster, a body of rules was drawn up in the form of a circular letter, addressed by Patrick, Auxilius, and Iserninus to all the clergy of Ireland.[2] The miscellaneous regulations are arranged in a haphazard manner, and were evidently prompted by abuses or practical difficulties which had come to the notice of the framers. Most of the rules deal with the discipline of the clergy. They testify to such irregularities as a bishop interfering in his neighbour's diocese; vagabond clerks going from place to place;

[1] See note, Appendix B.
[2] Generally described inaccurately as the Acts of a Synod. The genuineness of the document is vindicated in Appendix A, 4.

churches founded without the permission of the
bishop. It is ordained that no cleric from Britain
shall minister in Ireland, unless he has brought a
letter from his superior. All the clergy, from the
priest to the doorkeeper, are to wear the complete
Roman tonsure, and their wives are to veil their
heads. A monk and a consecrated virgin are not
to drive from house to house in the same car, or
indulge in protracted conversations. Provision is
made for the stringent enforcement of sentences of
excommunication. One of the most important
duties of Irish Christians at this period was the
redemption of Christian captives from slavery;[1]
and this furnished an opportunity for imposture
and deception. It is provided that no one shall
privately and without permission make a collection
for this purpose, and that, if there be any surplus
from a collection, it shall be placed on the altar
and kept for another's need.

It is interesting to observe a prohibition of the
acceptance of alms from pagans. It points to the
comprehensive religious view of some, perhaps
many, of the still unconverted—Loigaire himself
may have been an instance,—who, though not
prepared to abandon their own cults, were ready
to pay some homage to the new deity whose reality
and power they did not question.

In a church growing up in a heathen land, it

---

[1] For this sphere of Christian activity in the early Church see Harnack,
*Mission und Ausbreitung des Christentums*, p. 120.

seems to have been found inexpedient and impracticable to enforce long periods of penitence for transgressions which were regarded more lightly in Ireland than in the Roman Empire. Accordingly we find that only a year of penance is imposed on those who commit manslaughter or fornication or consult a soothsayer,[1] and only half a year for an act of theft.

The provisions contained in this circular letter cannot represent all the rules which Patrick, with his coadjutors, must have made for ecclesiastical order in Ireland. A number of other canons were ascribed to him, and though we cannot be sure that they are all authentic, it cannot be proved that they are all of later origin.[2] One of them, not the least important, is a provision which, without any express evidence, we might surmise that Patrick would have ordained. It required no special discernment to foresee that in a young church difficult questions would inevitably arise which might lead to grave controversy and dissension. How were such to be decided ? Could they safely be left to local councils, with no higher court of appeal? The obvious resource was to follow the common practice of other western churches and request the Bishop of Rome to lay down a ruling. For

[1] A Christian who believes in a supernatural female form (*lamia quae interpretatur striga*) seen in a mirror is to be anathematised. One is reminded of

Was seh' ich? Welch ein himmlisch Bild
Zeigt sich in diesem Zauberspiegel! (Goethe, *Faust*, Part I.)

[2] See Appendix A, i. 4.

Patrick, as for his contemporaries, this was simply
a matter of course. To consult the Roman see,
and obtain a ruling in the form of a decretal,
was the universally recognised means in the
western provinces of securing unity and uniformity
in the Church. The position which the Roman
see occupied, by common consent, in the days of
Patrick has been sufficiently explained in a previous
chapter;[1] and if this position is rightly understood,
it becomes evident that, when Ireland entered into
the ecclesiastical confederation of the west, it was
merely a direct and inevitable consequence that,
for the church in Ireland, just as for the churches
in Gaul or in Spain, the Roman see was both a
court of appeal, and also the one authority to which
recourse could be had, whenever recourse to an
authority beyond Ireland itself seemed desirable.
This was so axiomatic that, if we are told that
Patrick expressly prescribed resort to Rome in
case of necessity, the only thing which might
surprise us is that he should have thought it
needful to formulate it at all. But in a new
church, unfamiliar with the traditions of the older
churches within the Empire, it was clearly desirable
to define and enact some things which were
observed in Gaul and Spain and Italy without
express definition or enactment. We are therefore
fully entitled to accept as authentic the canon which
lays down, " If any questions (of difficulty) arise in

[1] Chap. iii. pp. 61 *sqq.*

this island, let them be referred to the apostolic seat."[1]   Not to have recognised the Roman see as the source of authoritative responses would have been almost equivalent to a repudiation of the unity of the Church.

That Patrick should have prescribed to Irish monks the form of tonsure which was usual in western monasteries was a matter of course.   It was more significant that he introduced, as seems to be the case, the Paschal reckoning which was at that time approved by Rome.   It would appear that an older system for the determination of Easter was in use among the Christian communities which existed in Ireland before his coming.   He brought with him a table of Easter days based on the system then accepted at Rome, so that in the celebration of this feast the new province might be in harmony with western Christendom.[2]

Though we have no direct testimony as to the liturgy which Patrick introduced, we cannot doubt that it was the Gallican.   The Gallican liturgy, which differs from the Roman by its oriental character, prevailed in Ireland and Britain up to the end of the seventh century; and we are entitled to conjecture, in the absence of evidence to the contrary, that Patrick, trained at Auxerre,

[1] Collection of Irish Canons, 20. 5. b (ed.[2] Wasserschleben, p. 61).   For the possible date of the canon, and for some further illustration of the subject, see Appendix C, 16.
[2] See Appendix C, 17.

introduced the usage to which he was accustomed in that church.

## § 5. *Ecclesiastical Organisation*

St. Patrick has himself briefly described some of the features of his work, and his description bears out and supplements the general impression which we derive from the details recorded by tradition. In the first place, he indicates the double character of his work. On the one hand he created an ecclesiastical organisation, he chose and ordained clergy, for a people which had been recently turning to the Christian faith.[1] On the other hand, he planted that faith in regions which were wholly heathen, in the extreme parts of the island, as he repeatedly insists.[2] He spread his nets that a large multitude "might be caught for God," and that there might be clergy everywhere to baptize and exhort a folk needing and craving their service.[3] He says that he baptized thousands, and this need not be a figure of hyperbole,[4] and ordained ministers of religion everywhere. The foundation of monastic communities is borne out by his incidental observation that young natives have become monks, and daughters of chieftains "virgins of Christ."[5] These maidens, he says, generally took their vows against

---

[1] *Confession*, 368$_9$.    [2] *Ib.* 372$_{17}$; cp. 367$_{13}$.    [3] *Ib.* 368$_{26}$.
[4] Otto of Bamberg is said to have baptized 22,156 converts in Pomerania during his first journey! Mon. Prieflingensis, *V. Ott.* ii. 20; Ebbo, *V. Ott.* ii. 11.
[5] *Confession*, 369$_{22}$.

the will of their fathers, and were ready to suffer persecution from their parents. He mentions especially a beautiful woman of noble birth whom he baptized. A few days after the ceremony she came to him and intimated that she had received a direct warning from God that she should become a "virgin of Christ." It is not suggested that the opposition of the parents was due to heathen obduracy; it would rather appear that, in the cases which are here contemplated, the parents themselves had likewise embraced Christianity. But they had a natural repugnance to seeing their children withdrawn from the claims of the family and the world. The triumph on which Patrick in this passage complacently dwells is not the triumph of Christian doctrine but of the monastic ideal.

Patrick refers to perils through which he passed in the prosecution of his work. He says that divine aid "delivered me often from bondage and from twelve dangers by which my life was endangered."[1] He mentions one occasion on which he and his companions were seized, and his captors wished to slay him. His belongings were taken from him and he was kept in fetters for a fortnight, but then, through the intervention of influential friends, he was set free and his property restored.[2]

Such experiences would probably have been more

---

[1] *Confession*, $367_{16}$.

[2] *Ib.* 372. It may be conjectured, from the context, that this happened in Connaught.

frequent if he had not resorted to a policy which stood him in good stead.   He used to purchase the goodwill and protection of the kings by giving them presents.[1]   In the same way he provided for the security of the clergy in those districts which he most frequently visited, by paying large sums to the judges or brehons.   It is easily conceived that their goodwill was of high importance for harmonising the new communities and their new ideal of life with the general conditions of society.   Patrick claims to have distributed among the judges at least "the value of fifteen men."   All these expenses were defrayed from his own purse.[2]

Another feature in his policy, on which he prided himself, was plain dealing and sincerity towards the Irish.   He never went back from his word, and never resorted to tricks, in order to win some advantage for "God and the Church."   He believed that by adhering strictly to this policy of straightforwardness he averted persecutions.[3]

While Patrick was assisted by many foreign fellow-workers, it was his aim to create a native clergy; and it was a matter of the utmost importance to find likely youths and educate them for ecclesiastical work.   Our records do not omit to illustrate this side of his policy.   Benignus, who afterwards succeeded him in Armagh, was said to have been

---

[1] So Otto of Bamberg used to distribute presents in Pomerania as a means of propagating Christianity, Herbord, _Dial._ 2. 7.

[2] The question arises, Where did Patrick get his money?   Did he inherit from his father?   It is useless to ask.

[3] _Confession_, 371₂₅.

adopted by him as a young boy soon after his coming to Ireland,[1] and Sachall, who accompanied him to Rome, was another instance. A similar policy was contemplated by Pope Gregory the Great for England. We have a letter which he wrote to a presbyter, bidding him purchase in Gaul English boy slaves of seventeen or eighteen years, for the purpose of educating them in monasteries.[2]

The churches and cloisters which were founded by Patrick and his companions seem in most cases to have been established on land which was devoted to the purpose by chieftains or nobles from their own private property. But the interests of the tribe to which the proprietor belonged, and the interests of the proprietor's descendants, had to be considered, and the consideration of these interests seems to have led to a peculiar system. We find that in some cases the proprietor did not make over all his rights to the ecclesiastical community which was founded on his estate, but retained, and transmitted to his descendants, a certain control over it, side by side with the control which the abbot, a spiritual head of the community, exercised. There were thus two lines of succession—the secular line, in which the descent was hereditary, and the ecclesiastical line, which was sometimes regularly connected by blood with the founder. This dual

[1] See the anecdote in Tírechán, p. 303.
[2] Epistles of Gregory, vi. 10 (A.D. 595), *M.G.H.* vol. i. p. 389.

system kept the ecclesiastical community in close
touch with the tribe, and it has been pointed out
that the tendency ultimately was "to throw the
ecclesiastical succession into the hands of the lay
succession, and so to defeat the object of the founder
by transferring the endowment to the laity."[1]
Armagh and Trim are conspicuous instances of this
dual succession.

In other cases the connexion of the monastery
with the tribe was secured, and the interests of the
proprietor's family were consulted by establishing
a family right of inheritance to the abbacy.   There
was only a spiritual succession ; the undivided
authority lay with the abbot ; but the abbots could
be chosen only from the founder's kin.[2]   Such a
provision might be made conditionally or unconditionally.   It might be provided that preference
should be given to members of the founder's family,
if a person suitable for such a spiritual office could
be found among them.   The monastery of Drumlease in Leitrim, which was founded by one Fethfió, furnishes an instructive example.[3]   Fethfió laid
down that the inheritance to Drumlease should
not be confined unconditionally to his own family.
His family should inherit the succession, if there
were any member pious and good and conscientious.

---

[1] Todd, *St. Patrick*, p. 154.

[2] The early abbots of Hi (Iona) were almost entirely chosen from a branch
of the family of Tirconnell (Reeves, *Adamnan*, genealogical table, p. 342).

[3] See the bequest of Fith Fio in *Lib. Arm.* (*Trip.* 338).   It is added that
if there be no suitable person in the community of Drumlease, some one from
Patrick's community (Armagh, or any Patrician community ?) should be chosen.

If not, the abbot should be chosen from the community or monks of Drumlease.

But in other cases the original proprietor seems to have alienated his land and placed it entirely in the hands of an ecclesiastical founder, who was either a member of another tribe or a foreigner. But the tribe within whose territory the land lay had a word to say. It seems to have been a general rule that the privilege of succession belonged to the founder's tribe, but that if no suitable successor could be found in that tribe, the abbacy should pass to the tribe within whose territory the monastery stood.[1]

In our earliest records we find some ecclesiastical foundations expressly distinguished as "free," which would seem to imply a release from restrictions and obligations which were usually imposed, and a greater measure of independence of the tribe.[2] Thus in Sligo a large district was offered by its owners "to God and Patrick," and we are told that the king, who seems to be acting as representative of the tribe, "made it free to God and Patrick."[3] But it is impossible to determine what were the limits of this immunity.

---

[1] *Corus Bescna*, p. 73 (*Ancient Laws of Ireland*, vol. iii.).

[2] Tírechán, $330_{29}$, *fecit alteram (aeclessiam) hi Tortena orientali in qua gens oThig Cirpani, sed libere semper.* Cp. $321_7$.

[3] *Additional Notices* in *Lib. Arm.* ($338_4$, *liberauit rex Deo et Patricio*). The exact boundaries of the land are given, as if from the original document. Two interests were concerned here, that of Caichán and that of MacCairthin, and the land is described as "Caichán's Fifth." The two men are designated as *flaith* (lord) and *aithech* (tenant-farmer ?), and they jointly devoted the land to ecclesiastical use.

The Church in the Roman Empire has been described as an *imperium in imperio*, and the typical ecclesiastical community in Ireland may be described as a tribe within a tribe. The abbot, or, where the dual system prevailed, his lay coadjutor, exercised over the lay folk settled on the lands of the community a control similar to that which the tribal king exercised over the tribe. But though the community was thus constituted as an independent body and formed a sort of tribe itself, not subject to the king, it was nevertheless bound by certain obligations to the tribe within whose borders it lay. We have seen that the right of eventual succession to the abbacy was often reserved to the tribe. But in general the monastery was bound not only to furnish the religious services which the tribe required, but to rear and educate without cost the offspring of any tribesman who chose to devote his son to a religious life.[1] The tribesman, on his part, was bound, when he had once consigned his child to the care of the monks, not to withdraw him, on pain of paying a forfeit.[2] A monastery might welcome novices from other tribes, if their parents chose to pay the cost of their education ; its attachment by a closer bond to what might be called its lay tribe was expressed in this right of the tribesmen to a free training for an ecclesiastical career.

It is also to be observed that the member of a religious house, though he belonged to a society

---

[1] *Corus Bescna*, p. 73.    [2] *Ib.* p. 71.

which managed its affairs independently of the tribe, did not altogether cease to be a tribesman.[1]   If he was slain, the compensation was due not to the church but to his tribe.   It is uncertain how far he continued to share any of the secular liabilities of his lay tribesmen.   On his father's death he inherited his portion of the family property, like any of his brethren ; but we cannot say how far, in early times, the tribe permitted a monastic community to exercise rights over land thus inherited by one of its members.   In later times the Church assumed possession, perhaps allowing the monk to hold his inheritance as a tenant, and furnishing him with stock.[2]   But this custom may not have been introduced until the Church had waxed in power and cupidity.   It is uncertain, too, what claims the new-born monasteries ventured to press, in their early years, upon the liberality of those who had permitted their foundation.   At a subsequent period they claimed[3] not only first-fruits and tithes and the firstlings of animals, but also first-born sons, and when a man had ten sons, another as well as the eldest.   We may doubt whether such claims, modelled on the law of Moses, and exceeding in audacity the claims of any other church, were often admitted[4] or seriously pressed ; but it is certain that rights of such a kind were not and could not have been sought by Patrick and his fellows.

[1] Cp. *Ancient Laws*, iii., Introd. p. lxxii.
[2] *Ib.* luii., *Corus B.* pp. 41, 43.     [3] *Ib.* pp. 39-43.
[4] Cp. Introd. pp. luiii. *sqq.*

This sketch of the conditions under which the new religious settlements were planted in Ireland is necessarily vague and slight, and is presented with the reserve which is due when the material for reconstruction is fragmentary and we have to argue back from circumstances which prevailed at a later period. But the evidence at least shows clearly that the organisation was conditioned and moulded by the nature of the secular society. On one hand there was a bond, of various degrees of intimacy, connecting the religious community with the tribe, in the midst of which it was established; and on the other hand, the community took upon itself the form and likeness of a tribe or clan, its members being regarded as the family or followers of its head.

There is no reason to suppose that all Patrick's ecclesiastical foundations took the shape of monastic societies. Many of the churches which he founded were served, doubtless, by only one or two clerics, and furnished with only enough land to support them. But the monastic foundations were a leading feature of the organisation. They were to be centres for propagating Christianity and schools for educating the clergy. But they also served the religious needs of the immediate district. A staff of clergy was attached, and the abbot was frequently also a bishop. It is not difficult to conjecture the reason and purpose of this remarkable union of the monastic institution with general church organisation. It was

probably due to the circumstance that there were no
cities in Ireland; centres had to be created for
ecclesiastical purposes, and it was almost a matter
of course that these ecclesiastical towns should be
constructed on the monastic principle. If towns had
existed, they would have been the ecclesiastical
centres, the seats of the bishops; the bishops would
not have been abbots or attached to monasteries.
The fact that the word *civitas*, " city," was used to
designate these double-sided communities illustrates
the motive of this singular organisation.

But the peculiarity must not mislead us into the
error of supposing that there was no diocesan
organisation, or that the bishops whom Patrick
ordained had not definite and distinct sees.[1] It is
inconceivable that in instituting bishops he should
not have been guided by geographical considerations, or that in organising a clerical body he should
not have submitted them to the jurisdiction of the
bishops whom he ordained. The limits of the
bishoprics would naturally have corresponded to
the limits of tribal territories; this was not only
the simplest scheme, but was also dictated by
obvious political expedience. The anomalous state
of things which presently arose, the multiplication
of bishops without sees, was assuredly never antici-
pated by Patrick. It was due to the extravagant
growth of monasticism. When new monasteries
were founded, they determined to have bishops of

[1] See Appendix C, 18.

their own, and to be quite independent of the
bishops of the dioceses in which they were situated.
This practice was not indeed confined to Ireland.
There are several notable instances in Gaul.[1] But
whereas elsewhere it was the exception, in Ireland
it seems to have become the rule. The desire of
new foundations to be self-sufficient and completely
independent of the diocesan bishop would not perhaps have been so strong if the diocesan bishop had
not usually been associated with one of the older
monasteries. But once the practice of bishops
without sees was introduced, bishops multiplied
like flies. A new and narrow conception of the
episcopal office prevailed, and when it was recognised that bishops need not have sees, there was
no reason to set a limit to their number. The
order of bishop became a dignity to which any man
of piety might aspire.

There is no evidence that Patrick consecrated
bishops without sees, and perhaps it would not be rash
to say that he never did so. It cannot be seriously
doubted that he established a diocesan organisation,
which, in the course of the subsequent development
of religious institutions, largely broke down. The
maintenance of the diocesan structure could not be
secured without control from above, and unless we
refuse to believe that Patrick attempted anything in
the way of organisation, it is evident that he must
have founded a superior archdiocesan or metropolitan

---

[1] Todd, *St. Patrick*, 51 *sqq.*

jurisdiction. He exercised this higher authority himself, and it is difficult to doubt that he attached it to the see which he occupied, the see of Armagh. The position of this see has already engaged our attention. But the centrifugal tendencies which marked the secular society of Ireland made themselves felt no less acutely in the Church; the ecclesiastical communities were animated by the same impulse to independence as the tribes; and it was hard for the Bishop of Armagh, as for the King of Ireland, to exert effectual authority. The independent tribal spirit was not flexible or readily obedient to the distant control of a prelate who was a member of another tribe; there was no secular power able or willing to enforce submission to the higher jurisdiction. Thus it was a continual struggle for the bishops of Armagh to maintain the position which Patrick had bequeathed to them; and the rise within their province, during the sixth century, of new and powerful communities, owing them no obedience, and outstripping their church in zeal, learning, and reputation, conduced to the decline of their influence. It was not till the end of the seventh century that the church of Armagh began to succeed in re-establishing its power. In the meantime the interests of religion had perhaps not suffered through the absence of ecclesiastical unity. At no time were the churchmen of Ireland more conspicuous, and famous in other lands, for learning and piety than in the sixth and seventh centuries.

The difficulties and errors which have arisen as to the spirit and principles of Patrick's ecclesiastical policy are due to the circumstance that after his death his work was partly undone, and the Irish Church developed on lines which were quite from the purpose of his design. The old Easter reckoning survived his reform and lasted till the seventh century.[1] Irish monks abandoned the recognised mode of shaving the head which he had enjoined, and adopted the native tonsure of the pagan Druids.[2] The central authority at Armagh could not maintain itself against the centrifugal spirit of the land or resist the love of local independence which operated in ecclesiastical exactly as in political affairs. Monasticism, an institution which appears to have been intensely attractive to the temper of the people, ran riot, we might say, at the expense of ecclesiastical organisation. Abbots became of more account than bishops. The political changes in Gaul and Italy, connected with the dismemberment of the Empire, tended to keep Ireland out of touch with the continental churches in the later part of the fifth and in the sixth century. The injunction to appeal to Rome, though no one would have thought of repudiating it, was a dead letter. Looking at Irish Christianity as it appears in the seventh century, when the movement set in to bring it into line with the rest of the western Church, students have been inclined to assume that Patrick in-

---

[1] See Appendix C, 17.      [2] See above, chap. vii. p. 143.

augurated the peculiar features which were really
alien to the spirit of his work.   Whatever con-
cessions and modifications he may have found it
necessary or politic to make in view of the social
conditions of Ireland, he certainly did not anticipate,
far less intend, such a development as that which
actually ensued.

But though his organisation partially collapsed,
and though the Irish Christians did not live up to
his ideal of the *unitas ecclesiae*, there was one feature
of his policy which was never undone.   He made
Latin the ecclesiastical language of Ireland.   The
significance of this will claim our consideration when
we come to examine his historical position.   It was
remembered in the traditions of his work that he
used to write alphabets for youths who were chosen
for a clerical career ; it was the first step in teaching
them Latin.

Some knowledge of the Latin alphabet must have
penetrated to Ireland at an earlier period.   It must
have been known in the scattered Christian communities, and it may have been known much more
widely.   It was not a new thing when Patrick
arrived, but his work seems to have secured it a new
position.   Yet we cannot say exactly what happened.
We cannot say whether the introduction of the Latin
script originated a written Irish literature, or only
displaced an older form of writing in which a literature already existed.   In the mist which rests over
the early history of Ireland this is one of the darkest

points.  It would be out of place to discuss the
question here at large, but one or two considerations
may be briefly noted.  The mode of writing which
the early Irish possessed—though how long before
the fifth century we know not—and seem to have
mainly used for engraving names on sepulchral
monuments, is alphabetic.  The characters, which
are called ogams, consisting of strokes and points,
were probably a native invention, since such inscriptions are found only in Ireland and in regions of the
British islands which came within the range of Irish
influence.  But it will not be maintained that the
alphabet itself was a native product, an independent
discovery.  It is simply the Latin alphabet,[1] with
the last three letters left out and two letters added.[2]
And a cipher representing the Latin alphabet can
hardly fail to imply that when it was invented the
Latin alphabet was in use.  No positive evidence
has yet been discovered to show that the Irish
ever employed, besides their monumental script, a
less cumbersome system of symbols, suitable for
literature and the business of life, other than the
Roman.  A few statements which may be gathered
from their own later traditions are not sufficiently

---

[1] It has twenty-one letters, a b c d e f g h i l m n o p q r s t u v, and ng (a
guttural nasal, which occurs in the name *Amolngaid*; cp. the Greek double
gamma).  If the Goidels had originally invented an alphabet to suit their
own language they would never have constructed this.  They had to resort to
various devices to represent their sounds by its means.  See further note,
Appendix B.

[2] More strictly, a new letter was added, and *u* was differentiated into two,
to represent its two sounds.  It is as well to say that in describing the ogams
as a cipher it is not intended to imply that they were cryptic, but only that
they were not an independent alphabet.

clear or authentic to carry much weight. The
absence of evidence, however, is not decisive. It
is to be remembered that writing was in use among
the Celtic Iberians of Spain and the Celts of Gaul
before the Roman Conquest. The Iberians had
their own script, and some of the Spanish peoples
had a considerable literature.[1] In Gaul, we are told
by Caesar, the lore of the Druids was not written
down, but Greek writing was used for public and
private purposes.[2] This means that the Gallic
tongue was written in Greek characters, and some
examples of such writing are preserved.[3] These
facts show at least that the art of writing might have
reached Ireland at an early period. But there is no
proof that it did. If any pre-Roman alphabet was
ever used it has left no traces of its presence. But
the Roman alphabet was introduced, perhaps much
sooner than is generally supposed, after the Roman
occupation of Britain. And from it some learned
man in Ireland constructed the ogam cipher for
sepulchral uses. The diffusion of Christianity tended,
doubtless, to diffuse the use of writing, but Latin
letters were a gift which the pagans of Ireland
received from the Empire, independently of the gift
of Christianity.

[1] For the Iberian alphabet see Hübner's *Monumenta linguae Ibericae* (1893).
Cp. Strabo, 3. 1. 6.
[2] *B.G.* vi. 14.
[3] Desjardins, *Géographie de la Gaule*, ii. 214, note 3.

# CHAPTER IX

WRITINGS OF PATRICK, AND HIS DEATH

## § 1. *The Denunciation of Coroticus*

CHRISTIANITY had been introduced among the Picts of Galloway at the beginning of the fifth century by the labours of a Briton, who is little more than a name. Ninian, educated at Rome, had probably come under the influence of St. Martin of Tours, and had then devoted himself to the task of preaching his faith in the wilds of Galloway, where, on the inner promontory which runs out towards the Isle of Man, he built a stone church. As the only stone building in this uncivilised land it became known as the White House (Candida Casa), and its place is marked by Whitern. An important monastic establishment grew around it, which enjoyed a high reputation in Ireland in the sixth century, and was known there as the "Great Monastery." The work of Ninian was, in one way, like the work of his contemporary Victricius in Gaul, being missionary work within the Roman Empire, if Galloway and its inhabitants belonged to the Roman province of

Valentia. The Roman power may the more easily have controlled these barbarous subjects since they were severed from their kinsmen, the Picts of the north beyond the Clyde, by the British population of Strathclyde.

After the Roman legions were withdrawn from Britain, and the island was cut off from the central control of the Empire, the task of maintaining order in the western part of the " province of Valentia " seems to have been undertaken by one of those rulers who sprang up in various parts of the island, and are variously styled as " kings " or " tyrants." A word must be said as to the condition of Britain in the fifth century, because it is very generally misunderstood.

There can be no greater error than to suppose that the withdrawal of the Roman legions from Britain in 407, and the rescript of the Emperor Honorius, three or four years later, permitting the citizens of Britain to arm themselves and provide for their own defence, meant the instant departure of all things Roman from British shores, the death of Roman traditions, the end of Roman civilisation. The idea that the island almost immediately relapsed into something resembling its pre-Roman condition is due partly to the scanty nature of our evidence, partly to a misreading of the famous work of Gildas " on the decline and fall of Britain," partly to a mistaken idea of the isolation of Britain from the continent, and largely to that anachronistic habit, into

which it is so easy to fall, of judging men's acts and
thoughts as if they could have foreseen the future.
It cannot be too strongly enforced that in those
years which mark *for us* the Roman surrender of
Britain, and for many years after, no man—emperor
or imperial minister or British provincial—could
have thought or realised that the events which they
were witnessing meant a final dismemberment of the
Empire in the west, that Britain was really cut off
for ever.  The Empire had weathered storms before,
and emerged stable and strong; to the contemporaries
of Honorius and Valentinian the Empire was part of
the established order of things, and a suspension of
its control in any particular portion of its dominion
was something temporary and passing.  The British
provincials did not and could not for a moment
regard themselves and their province as finally
severed from Rome ; they still considered themselves
part of the Empire ; for a hundred and fifty years
some of them at least considered themselves Roman
citizens.  From this point of view alone it is not
conceivable that the traditions and machinery of the
Roman administration should have disappeared at
once, the moment the central authorities ceased to
control it.  What could the provincials have deliberately put in its place ?  All the circumstances
seem to enforce the conclusion that the administration, in its general lines, continued, but was gradually
modified, and ultimately decayed, through three
main causes—financial necessities which must have

soon led to a reduction of the elaborate machinery
of administration, the organisation of new methods
of self-help, and the development of local interests
promoted by the ambition of private persons who
won power and supremacy in various districts. There
was doubtless a Celtic revival, but for many years
after the rescript of Honorius, Roman institutions
must have continued to exist alongside of, or controlled by, the local potentates, who are described
as "kings" or "tyrants." And in the later years of
the fifth century the great successes won by the
British against the English invaders were achieved
by generals—Ambrosius Aurelianus, and Arthur—
who were not "kings" or "tyrants," but rather, in
some sense, national leaders, and whose position can
be best explained by supposing that they represent
the traditions of Roman rule, and are, in fact,
successors of the Roman dukes and counts of
Britain. If in some cases the tyrants may have
combined their own irregular position with the title
of a Roman official it is what we should expect.

The man whom we find in the reign of Valentinian III. ruling in Strathclyde, and maintaining
such law and order as might be maintained, was
named Coroticus or Ceretic, and he founded a line
of kings who were still reigning at the end of the
following century. His seat was the Rock of Clyde.[1]
As the seat of a British ruler, amid surrounding
Scots and Picts, this stronghold came to be known

---

[1] Ail Clúade.

as Dún na m-Bretan, "the fort of the Britons," which was corrupted into the modern Dumbarton. The continuity of the rule of Coroticus with the military organisation of the Empire is strongly suggested by the circumstance that his power was maintained by "soldiers";[1] and his position seems thus marked as distinct from that of pre-Roman chiefs of British tribes. His soldiers may well be the successors of the Roman troops who defended the north. His position—whether he assumed any Roman military title or not—may be compared to that of the general Aegidius, who maintained the name of the Empire in north Gaul when it had been cut off from the rest of the Empire. Aegidius transmitted his authority to his son Syagrius, as Coroticus transmitted his to his son Cinuit; and if Syagrius had not been overthrown by the Franks, a state would have been formed in Belgica which would have resembled in origin the state which Coroticus formed in Strathclyde. Of course the Gallo-Roman generals Aegidius and Syagrius, while their authority was practically uncontrolled, were in touch with the Empire, maintained the Imperial machinery, and had a position totally different from the irregular position of the semi-barbarous Briton on his rock by the Clyde; but we may be sure that Coroticus was careful to make the most of his claim to represent the Imperial tradition and rule over Roman citizens. And while the contrast is obvious,

---

[1] *Milites.*

it is not uninstructive to observe the analogy, which is less obvious, between the position of Britain and its rulers, still attached in theory, name, and tradition to the Empire, though cut off from it, and the position of those parts of the Belgic and Lyonnese provinces, which, aloof from the rest of Imperial territory, maintained themselves under Aegidius and his son Syagrius for a few years amid the surrounding German kingdoms.

Coroticus, then, was the ruler of Strathclyde in the days of Patrick. We can easily understand that he may sometimes have found it difficult to pay his soldiers and retainers, and that for this purpose he may have been forced to plunder his neighbours. However this may be, he fitted out a marauding expedition; it does not appear that he led it himself, but it crossed the channel, and descended on the coast of Ireland, probably in Dalaradia or Dalriada. Perhaps it was an act of reprisal for raids which the Scots and Picts of these lands may have made upon his dominion; it may have been, for all we know, an episode in a regular war. At all events he was supported in his enterprise by the Picts of Galloway, who had relapsed into heathenism, and by some of those heathen Scots who had come over from Ireland and settled in the region northwest of the Clyde. In the course of their devastation these heathen allies of Coroticus appeared on the scene of a Christian ceremony. Neophytes, who had just been baptized and anointed with the baptismal chrism, were standing in white raiment; the sign of the cross was still "fragrant on their foreheads" when the heathen rushed upon them, put some to the sword and carried others captive. Patrick, whether he had himself performed the ceremony or not, must have been near the spot of this outrage, for he was informed of it so soon, that on the next day he despatched one of his most trusted priests—one whom he had trained from childhood —to the soldiers of Coroticus, requesting them to send back the booty and release the captives. The message, which must have reached them before they left Ireland, was received with mockery, though the soldiers of Coroticus were Christians and "Romans," and it was not they but their heathen allies who had massacred the defenceless Christians. It is not clear whether Coroticus himself was present when the message was delivered, but it is certain that Patrick regarded him as responsible, and we must suppose that he had declined to interfere before Patrick wrote the letter which is our record of this event. The only thing which the indignant bishop could do for the release of his "sons and daughters" was to bring the public opinion of the Christians in Strathclyde to bear upon Coroticus and his soldiers. He wrote a strong letter, addressing it apparently to the general Christian community in the dominion of Coroticus, and requiring them to have no dealings with the guilty "tyrant" and his soldiers, "not to take food or drink with them, not to receive **alms** from them, nor show respect to them, until they should repent in tears and make satisfaction to God by releasing the Christian captives." He asks that the letter should be read before all the people in the presence of Coroticus. The guilt of the outrage is laid, in this communication, entirely upon Coroticus; it is ascribed to his orders; he is called a betrayer of Christians into the hands of Scots and Picts. Apostrophising him the bishop writes: "It is the custom of Roman Christians in Gaul to send good men to the Franks and other heathens to redeem captives for so many thousand pieces of gold; you, on the contrary, slay Christians and sell them to a foreign nation that knows not God; you deliver members of Christ as it were into a house of ill fame."

The sequel of this episode is unknown. We have no record whether the letter of Patrick had any effect on the obstinate hearts of Coroticus and his soldiers, or whether those to whom it was addressed applied the pressure of excommunication, which he begged them to put in force. The Irish legend that the king was turned into a fox by the prayers of the saint is based on the idea that he declined to release the captives; but it may have no other foundation than the letter which we possess.

But this letter has an interest for the biographer of Patrick beyond the details of the occurrence which evoked it. Beside, and distinct from, the wrathful indignation which animates his language, there is a strain of bitterness which had another motive. He is clearly afraid that his message will not be received with friendship or sympathy by the British Christians to whom it is sent. He complains expressly that his work in Ireland is regarded in Britain—in his own country—with envy and uncharitableness. "If my own do not know me—well, 'a prophet has no honour in his own country.' We do not belong, peradventure, to one sheepfold, nor have we one God for our father." He refers to his own biography, to his birth as a Roman citizen, to his unselfish motives in undertaking the toil of a preacher of the Gospel in a barbarous land where he lives a stranger and exile; as if he had to justify himself against the envy and injustice of jealous detractors. "I am envied"; "some despise me." This bitterness is a note of the letter, and almost suggests that in Patrick's opinion the envy and dislike with which his successful work in Ireland was regarded in north Britain was partly responsible for the outrage itself.

There is no extant evidence to fix the date of this episode, but the dominance of the same bitter note in the other extant writing of Patrick, which was written in the author's old age, makes it not improbable that the letter belongs to the later rather than to the earlier period of his labours in Ireland. To that other document, the *Confession*, we may now pass.

## § 2. *The Confession*

Men of action who help to change the face of the world by impressing upon it ideas which others have originated, have seldom the time, and seldom, unless they have received in their youth a literary training, the inclination, to record their work in writing. The great apostles of Europe illustrate this fact. None of them, from Wulfilas to Otto of Bamberg, has left a relation of his own apostolic labours. We are lucky if a disciple took thought for posterity by writing a brief narrative of his master's acts. But in the case of the apostle of the Scots, as in the case of the apostles of the Slavs, no disciple wrote down what he could aver of his own certain knowledge. If Benignus, his pupil and successor, had done for Patrick what Auxentius did for Wulfilas, what Willibald did for Boniface, we should have certainty on many things where it is now only possible to note our ignorance. But although neither Patrick nor any of the other apostles who preached to Celt, German, or Slav wrote the story of his own life, some of them have left literary records which bear on their work. The most conspicuous example is the correspondence of our West-Saxon Boniface, the apostle of the Germans; but fortunately in Patrick's case, too, circumstances occasionally forced him to write. The *Confession* is of far greater interest and value than the letter against Coroticus; for, though not an autobiography, it contains highly important autobiographical passages, to which reference has been made in the foregoing pages.

This work was written in Patrick's old age, at a time when he felt that death might not be very far off. "This," he says, "is my confession before I die," and accordingly the work is known as the Confession. This title, however, might easily convey a false idea. The writer has occasion to confess certain sins, he has occasion also to make a brief confession of the articles of his faith, but it is in neither of these senses that he calls the work as a whole his Confession. Neither his sins nor his theological creed are his main theme, but the wonderful ways of God in dealing with his own life. "I must not hide the gift of God"; this is what he "confesses"; this is the refrain which pervades the *Confession* and emphatically marks its purpose.

Of miracles, in the sense of violations of natural laws, the *Confession* says nothing; but his own strange life seemed to Patrick more marvellous than any miracle in that special meaning of the word. The *Confession* reveals vividly his intense wondering consciousness of the fact that it had fallen just to him, out of the multitude of all his fellows who might have seemed fitter for the task, to carry out a great work for the extension of the borders of Christendom. As he looked back on his past life, it seemed unutterably strange that the careless boy in the British town should have shone forth as a

light to the Gentiles, and the ways by which this
strange thing had been compassed made it seem
more mysterious still.  But what impressed him
above all as a divine miracle was that he should
have felt assured of success beforehand.  What we,
in a matter-of-fact way, might describe as a man's
overruling imperative desire, accompanied by a
secret consciousness of his own capacity, to attempt
a great and difficult task seemed to Patrick a direct
revelation from one who had foreknowledge of the
future—*qui novit omnia etiam ante tempora secularia.*
The express motive of the *Confession* is to declare
the wonderful dealings of God with himself, as a
sort of repayment—*retributio*—or thanksgiving.[1]

But it would hardly have been necessary to make
such a declaration in writing if it had not seemed
to him that his life and work were partly misunderstood.  It was inevitable that a man of Patrick's
force of character and achievements should have
aroused some feelings of jealousy and voices of
detraction ; and the *Confession* is evidently a reply
to things that were said to belittle him.  One charge
that was brought against him was his lack of literary
education.  His deficiency in this respect was probably urged as a disqualification for the eminent
position of authority which he had won by his
practical labours.  Compared with most of the
many bishops in Gaul, compared perhaps with
most of the few bishops in Britain, Patrick might

[1] *Conf.* 360₈.

well have been described as illiterate. In the eyes
of his countryman, Faustus, in the eyes of Sidonius
Apollinaris, the Bishop of Armagh would have
seemed, so far as style is concerned, unworthy
to hold a pen. On this count Patrick disarms
criticism by a full admission of his *rusticitas*, his
lack of culture, and acknowledges that as he grows
old he feels his deficiency more and more. It was
even this consciousness of literary incompetence
that had hitherto withheld him from drawing up
the *Confession* which he has at length resolved to
write. Then he goes on to explain by passages
from his life how it was that, though he missed the
early training which is to be desired in a religious
apostle, he had nevertheless presumed to take in
hand the work of converting heathen lands. His
narrative is designed to show that it was entirely
God's doing, who singled him out, untrained and
unskilled though he was ; that there were no worldly
inducements to support the divine command, which
he obeyed simply without any ulterior motive, and
in opposition to the wish of his kinsfolk. Here he
is meeting another imputation, which stung him
more than the true taunt of illiteracy. His detractors must have hinted that it was not with
perfectly pure and unworldly motives that he had
gone forth to preach among the Scots. He does
not conceal that the island in which he had toiled
as a captive slave had no attraction for him ; he
implies that he always felt there as a stranger in a

strange land.[1] "I testify," he says, summing up,
"in truth and in exultation of heart, before God
and His holy angels, that I never had any motive
save the gospel and promises of God, to return at
any time to that people from which I had formerly
escaped."[2] He repudiates especially the imputation
that he won any personal profit in worldly goods
from those whom he converted, or that he sought
in any way to overreach the folk among whom he
lived. To show how discreetly he ordered his
ways, how careful he was to avoid all scandalous
suspicion, he mentions that when men and women
of his flock sent him gifts, or laid ornaments on
the altar, he always restored them, at the risk of
offending the givers.

It is easy enough to read between the lines the
kind of detraction that wounded St. Patrick; it
may seem less easy to determine in what quarter
the unfriendly voices were raised. But there are
certain indications which enable us to suspect that
it was in his own country and by his own countrymen that the charges to which he obliquely refers
were brought against him. At the end of the
composition he says that he wrote it "in Ireland";
and this gives us a reasonable ground for supposing
that it was addressed mainly to people outside
Ireland. When he speaks of "those peoples
amidst whom I dwell," when he mentions "women

---

[1] Cp. *Letter, ad init., inter barbaras itaque gentes habito proselitus et pro-
fuga.*
[2] *Conf.* 374₂₀. Compare 357₁₅.

of *our* race " (not " women of *my* race "), in contrast
with women of Scottish birth,[1] we can hardly be
wrong in thinking that he is addressing not his
Irish disciples, but some of his British fellow-
countrymen.    And we may well believe that if this
" apology " for his life had been meant in the first
place for Ireland, he would have taken some care
to veil his feeling of homelessness ; he would not
have shown so clearly that he felt as an alien on
outlandish soil, and that he was abiding there only
from a sense of duty, doing despite to the longings
of his heart.    This inference is borne out by the
writer's express statement that he wishes his
" brethren and kinsfolk " to know his character and
nature.[2]    Nor is it contradicted by the fact that
he closely associates those whom he addresses
with his own work.[3]    On the contrary, this enables
us to identify more precisely the origin of the
detraction which evoked the *Confession.*    The
unfriends who disparaged him were clearly some
of those British fellow-workers who had laboured
with him in propagating the Christian faith in
Ireland.    That jealousy and friction should occur
between the chief apostle and some of his helpers
is only what we might expect, as in any similar
case ; and it may be that some of those who felt
themselves aggrieved returned in disgust to Britain,

---

[1] *Conf.* 370₂.   The passage 373₅₋₉ also supports the view in the text.   In
that passage the oldest MS. has *ab aliquo uestro* ; and we should probably
read *uestrum* with the later MSS.

[2] *Ib.* 359₂.                [3] *Ib.* 372₃₁.

and indulged their ill-will by spreading evil reports about Patrick's conduct of the Irish mission. It was for the communities in Britain where such reports were circulated, it was to refute those who set them afloat, that the *Confession* was in the first instance intended.

But Patrick had been exposed to one direct attack, which seems to have caused him more distress and agitation of spirit than any experience during his work in Ireland. Before he was ordained deacon, he had confessed to a trusted friend a fault which he had committed at the age of fifteen. His friend evidently did not consider it an obstacle to ordination, and subsequently supported the proposal that Patrick should be consecrated bishop for Ireland.[1] But afterwards he betrayed the secret, and the youthful in-discretion came to the ears of persons whom we may perhaps identify with some of Patrick's foreign coadjutors.[2] "They came," he says in his rude style, "and urged my sins against my laborious episcopate." The words prove that he had already laboured for some years—other indications suggest fifteen or sixteen years[3]—when this attack was made. He does not tell us how he met or weathered the danger; he ascribes his escape from stain and opprobrium to Divine assistance. We can sympathise with him in his deep resentment

---

[1] See above, chap. iii. p. 53.       [2] But see note, Appendix B.
[3] See Appendix A, 5.

of an attack so manifestly unjust, of a friend's
treachery apparently so inexcusable ; but the incident clearly shows that there existed a party
distinctly hostile to him, men who were ready to
seize on any handle against him. His want of
culture had been hitherto the chief reproach which
they could fling ; when they discovered a moral
delinquency, though it was more than forty years
old, the opportunity was irresistible.

But while the vindication was addressed to an
audience beyond Ireland, it was intended also for
the Irish. It might almost be described as an
open letter to his brethren in Britain, published in
Ireland. He describes it himself as "a bequest
to my brethren, and to my children whom I
baptized," for the purpose of making known "the
gift of God," *donum Dei.*

The spirit and tone of this work are so consistently humble from first to last, that it almost
lends itself to a misconstruction, in the sense that
the measure of Patrick's achievements was smaller
and the sphere of his work more restricted than
our other sources give us to suppose. It has even
been said that the *Confession* is a confession of a
life's failure.[1] Any such interpretation misreads
the document entirely. On the contrary, the main
argument, as we have already seen, is that the
success which Patrick had been led to hope and
expect—through divine intimations as he believed

---

[1] This is the theory of Professor Zimmer.

—had been brought to pass. If success is not proved by vaunting, failure assuredly is not proved by the absence of boasts. But the proud consciousness of the writer that his life had been fruitful and prosperous comes out more subtly in the implied comparison which he suggests between himself and the first Apostle of the Gentiles, by quotations and echoes from Paul's epistles.[1]

It is pathetic to read how the exile would fain visit Britain, his home, and Gaul, where he had many friends, but feels himself bound by the spirit to spend the rest of his life (*residuum aetatis meae*) in his self-chosen banishment, to maintain his work, and especially to protect by his influence the Christians, whom dangers constantly threatened. His energy and undismayed perseverance had accomplished a great work, and he decided not to desert it till death compelled him.

His two writings furnish the only evidence we possess for forming an idea of his character. The other documents, on which we depend for the outline of his life and work, preserve genuine records of events, but reflect the picture of a man who must not be mistaken for the historical Patrick. The bishop, of British birth and Roman education, is gradually transformed into a typical Irish saint, dear to popular imagination, who curses men and even inanimate things which incur his displeasure.

---

[1] The Second Letter to the Corinthians seems to have been especially before him. This was natural. In it Paul was vindicating his character.

He arranges with the Deity that he shall be de-
puted to judge the Irish on the day of doom.
The forcefulness of the real Patrick's nature is
coarsened by degrees into caricature, until he
becomes the dictator who coerces an angel into
making a bargain with him on the Mount of
Murrisk.[1]   The stories of the Lives, so far as
they characterise Patrick, present the conception
which the Irish formed of a hero saint.   The
accounts of his acts were not written from any
historical interest, but simply for edification ; and
the monks, who dramatised both actual and
legendary incidents, were not concerned to regard,
even if they had known, what manner of man he
really was, but were guided by their knowledge of
what popular taste demanded.   The mediaeval
hagiographer may be compared to the modern
novelist ; he provided literary recreation for the
public, and he had to consider the public taste.
In regard to the process by which Patrick was
Hibernicised, or adapted to an Irish ideal, it is
significant that the earliest literature relating to
his life seems to have been written in Irish.   This
literature must have been current in the sixth
century, and on it the earliest Latin records are
largely based.

The writings of Patrick do not enable us to de-
lineate his character, but they reveal unmistakably
a strong personality and a spiritual nature.   The

---

[1] The legend will be found in *Vit. Trip.* pp. 112 *sqq.*

man who wrote the *Confession* and the *Letter* had strength of will, energy in action, resolution without over-confidence, and the capacity for resisting pressure from without. It might be inferred, too, that he was affectionate and sensitive; subtle analysis might disclose other traits. But it is probable that few readers will escape the impression that he possessed besides enthusiasm the practical qualities most essential for carrying through the task which he undertook in the belief that he had been divinely inspired to fulfil it. A rueful consciousness of the deficiencies of his education weighed upon him throughout his career; we can feel this in his almost wearisome insistence upon his *rusticitas*. Nor has he exaggerated the defects of his culture; he writes in the style of an ill-educated man. His Latin is as "rustic" as the Greek of St. Mark and St. Matthew. He was a *homo unius libri*; but with that book, the Christian Scriptures, he was extraordinarily familiar. His writings are crowded with Scriptural sentences and phrases, most of them probably quoted from memory.

## § 3. *Patrick's Death and Burial* (A.D. 461)

It would appear that some years before his death Patrick resigned his position as head of the church of Armagh, and was succeeded by his disciple Benignus.[1] If this is so, it seems probable

---

[1] The old lists of the Armagh succession agree in assigning to Benignus ten years as bishop, so that, as Benignus died in 467 (*Ann. Ult.*, *sub anno*), he would have succeeded in 457.

that he retired to Dalaradia, and spent the last three or four years of his life at Saul, in the Island-plain. Here he may possibly have written his *Confession*; here he certainly died. His death is encircled with legends which reflect the rival interests of Armagh and Downpatrick, but attest the fact that he died and was buried at the barn of Dichu. It was a disappointment to Armagh not to possess his body, and it was a stimulating motive for mythopoeic ingenuity to explain how this came to pass.

When the day of his death drew nigh, an angel came and warned him. Forthwith he made preparations, and started for Armagh, which he loved above all places. But as he went, a thorn-bush burst into flame on the wayside and was not consumed. And an angel spoke—not Victor, the angel who was accustomed to visit Patrick, but another sent by Victor—and turned him back, bidding him return to Saul, and granting him four petitions, as a consolation for the disappointment. Of these petitions two are significant. One was that the jurisdiction of his church should remain in Armagh; the other that the posterity of Dichu should not die out. The first represents the interests of Armagh; the second clearly originated in the Island-plain.

Patrick obeyed the command of the angel, who also predicted that his death would "set a boundary against night." The rite of the Eucharist was administered to him at Saul by Bishop Tassach of Raholp, and at Saul he died[1] and was buried. After his death there was no night for twelve days, and folk said that for a whole year the nights were less dark than usually. And other wonders were recorded. Men told how angels kept watch over his body and diffused, as they travelled back to heaven, sweet odours as of wine and honey.

But miracles of this kind were not the only legends which gathered round the passing of the saint whom Armagh and Ulidia were alike eager to appropriate. The old strife between the kingdom of Ulidia and the kingdom of Orior[2] blazed up anew, in story, over Patrick's grave. The men of Orior advanced into the island-plain, and blood would have been shed on the southern banks of Lake Strangford if a Divine interposition had not stirred the waves of the bay, which by a sudden inundation dispersed the hosts and prevented a battle.[3] This was before the burial; but after the coveted body had been entombed, the men of Orior came again, resolved to snatch it from the grave.[4] Finding a waggon drawn by two oxen, they imagined the body was inside, and drove off, to discover, when they were near Armagh, that no body was there, They had been the victims of an illusion, designed,

[1] March 17.

[2] Oirthir, not to be confounded with the kingdom of Oriel (Oirgéill), of which it formed the eastern portion.

[3] Inundations are a recurring motive in the legends of the Island-plain. See the salt-marsh stories, above, p. 91.

[4] This second incident can be shown to be a subsequent invention. See Appendix C, 19.

like the rising of the waters, to prevent the shedding
of blood.

From these two myths an inference of a negative
kind can be drawn with certainty.    It is plain
that, whatever controversy may have arisen concerning the burial of Patrick, there was no armed
conflict.    For the common motive of both legends
is to account for the circumstance that the event did
not lead to a war between the two peoples.    But it
would not be equally legitimate to draw the positive
inference that the stories preserve the memory of a
dispute, though not with arms, on the occasion of
the saint's death.    They point undoubtedly to a
controversy and dispute, but this controversy and
dispute may have arisen in subsequent years.    The
story of the angel's appearance reflects a conciliation
between the claims of Saul and the claims of
Armagh, and the two legends of the frustrated
attempts of the men of Orior embody the same
motive of peace and concord.    Armagh had to
acquiesce in the fact that Saul possessed Patrick's
body ; Saul acquiesced in the assertion that it was
Patrick's own wish to lie at Armagh.

But this was not the only rivalry aroused by the
desire of possessing the saint's mortal remains.
When in later years a church was founded on the
hill beside Dún Lethglasse, and overshadowed the
older foundations of the neighbourhood, it was
alleged that Patrick was buried in its precincts, and

that the church was founded on that account. The story was invented that the angel gave him directions as to the fashion of his sepulture. " Let two un-tamed oxen be chosen, and left to go where they will." This was done. The oxen, drawing the body in a waggon, rested at Dún Lethglasse, and there it was buried.[1]

It is clear that all these tales must have taken shape at a considerable time after the saint's death. If his burial had actually caused any such commotion as the legends suppose, his tomb would assuredly have been conspicuous or well known, and no doubt could have arisen as to the place where he was laid. There would have been no room for the double claim of Saul and Dún Lethglasse. But so great was the uncertainty that it suggested a resemblance with Moses, whose grave was unknown. It is recorded, though it is not a record which we can implicitly trust, that St. Columba investigated and discovered the place of Patrick's sepulchre at Saul. These doubts and uncertainties justify us in concluding that Patrick was buried quietly in an unmarked grave, and that the pious excitement about his bones

---

[1] This story is also told by Muirchu, but not in immediate connexion with the story of the waggon and oxen seized by the men of Orior. It seems probable that the latter was suggested by the former. We meet the duplicate waggon and oxen in the Life of St. Abban (Colgan, *Acta Sanctorum*, i. March 16, cc. 41 *sqq.*), where the account of that saint's death and burial and the struggle between the north and the south Leinster men is obviously borrowed from the stories about St. Patrick. Another story of wild bulls drawing a saint's body to its tomb will be found in the Life of St. Melorus of Cornwall, *Acta Sanctorum* (Boll.), Jan. 1, vol. i. p. 136.

arose long after his death.    And we can feel little
hesitation in deciding that the obscure grave was at
Saul.    Of the three places which come into the story
Saul alone needs no mythical support for its claim,
a claim in which Armagh itself acquiesces.    Legend
is called in to explain why the saint was not buried at
Armagh ; legend is called in to explain why he should
be buried at Downpatrick ; no legend is required to
account for his burial at Saul.

No visible memorial of Patrick has escaped the
chances of time, with one possible exception.    In
the Middle Ages the church of Armagh cherished
with superstitious veneration two treasures which
were believed to have belonged to him, a pastoral
staff and a hand-bell.    The crozier was deliberately
destroyed in the war of sixteenth-century zealots
against mediaeval superstition, but the four-sided
iron hand-bell still exists.[1]    Both relics were very
ancient, but to say that the bell was certainly
Patrick's would be to go beyond our evidence, which
only establishes a probability that it existed at
Armagh a hundred years or so after his death.

[1] It is to be seen in the National Museum at Dublin.    For the evidence
as to the bell and the staff, see notes, Appendix B.    For the copy of the gospels,
which used falsely to be supposed to be his, see note, Appendix B, on
chap. viii. p. 162.

# CHAPTER X

Two extreme and opposite views have been held
as to the scope and dimensions of St. Patrick's
work in Ireland. There is the old view that
he first introduced the Christian religion and converted the whole island, and there is the view,
propounded the other day, that the sphere of his
activity was merely a small district in Leinster.
The second opinion is refuted by a critical examination of the sources and by its own incapacity
to explain the facts,[1] while the first cannot be sustained because clear evidence exists that there were
Christian communities in Ireland before Patrick
arrived.

But the fact that foundations had been laid
sporadically here and there does not deprive Patrick
of his eminent significance. He did three things.
(1) He organised the Christianity which already existed;
(2) he converted kingdoms which were still pagan,
(3) especially in the west; and he brought Ireland into

[1] This theory of Professor Zimmer is examined at length in Appendix
C, 21.

connexion with the Church of the Empire, and made it formally part of universal Christendom.

These three aspects of his work have been illustrated in the foregoing pages. His achievements as organiser of a church and as propagator of his faith made Christianity a living force in Ireland which could never be extinguished. Before him, it might have been in danger of extinction through predominant paganism; after him, it became the religion of Ireland, though paganism did not disappear. He did not introduce Christianity, but he secured its permanence, shaped its course, and made it a power in the land.

Not less significant, though more easily overlooked, is the rôle which he played by bringing Ireland into a new connexion with Rome and the Empire. Ordinary intercourse, as we have seen, had been maintained for ages with Britain, Gaul, and Spain; but now the island was brought into a more direct and intimate association with western Europe by becoming an organised part of the Christian world. There had been constant contact before, but this was the first link.

The historical importance of this new bond, which marks an epoch in the history of Ireland as a European country, has been somewhat obscured through the circumstance that after Patrick's death the Irish Church, though it did not sever the link which he had forged, or dream of repudiating its incorporation as a part of Christendom, went a way of

its own and developed on eccentric lines.   Relations
with the centre were suspended, and this suspension
seems to have been due to two causes.   The instinct
of tribal independence, co-operating with the powerful attraction which the Irish found in monasticism,
promoted individualism and disorganisation ; monastic institutions tended to over-ride the episcopal
organisation founded by Patrick, and the resulting
lack of unity and general order was not favourable
to the practical maintenance of that solidarity with
Christendom which was inaugurated by the sending
of Palladius.   But it was not entirely due to the
self-will and self-confidence of the Irish themselves
that they drifted from his moorings.   The political
changes on the continent must also be taken into
account.   We can hardly doubt that but for the
decline of the Imperial power and the dismemberment of the Empire in western Europe, the isolation [1]
and eccentricity of the Irish Church in the sixth
century would not have been so marked.   The
bishops of Rome, between Leo I. and Gregory the
Great, were not in a position to concern themselves
with the drift of ecclesiastical affairs in the islands of
the north.   But no sooner has Gregory accomplished
his great revival and augmentation of the authority
of the Roman see in western lands than the movement begins which gradually brings Ireland back
within the confederation from which it had practically,

---

[1] Except in regard to Britain, and the British Church was similarly
isolated.

though never formally or intentionally, been severed. The renewal of the union with continental Christianity in the seventh century was simply a return to the system established by Patrick and his coadjutors, and it would not be surprising if, in that period, men looked back with intenser interest to his work and exalted his memory more than ever.

It seems probable, as we saw, that the tendencies which asserted themselves after Patrick's death were partly of the nature of a relapse. Men went back to some practices which had been adopted in the Christian communities existent before his arrival on the scene. An old Easter reckoning, which he had attempted to supersede, was resumed. Perhaps, too, the Druidical tonsure from ear to ear had been used by earlier Irish Christians, and when it afterwards prevailed over the continental tonsure which he introduced, this was also a reversion to a pre-Patrician practice.

The work of Patrick may be illustrated by comparing him with other bearers of the same religion to peoples of northern and central Europe. He did not go among a folk entirely heathen, like Willibrord among the Frisians, or Adalbert among the western Slavs, or Bruno of Querfurt among the Patzinaks. The circumstances of his mission have some resemblance to those of Columba's mission in Caledonia. Columba went to organise and maintain Christianity among the Irish Dalriadan settlers and to convert the neighbouring Pictish heathen, just as Patrick went to organise as well as to propagate his faith. But while the conditions of their tasks had this similarity, their works are contrasted. It was the aim of Patrick to draw Ireland into close intimacy with continental Christianity, but Columba, who represented in Ireland tendencies opposed to the Patrician tradition, had no such aim, and he established a church in north Britain which offered a strenuous, though not long-protracted, resistance to unity.

The nearest likeness to Patrick will perhaps be found in St. Boniface, the Saxon Winfrith. He, too, like Patrick and Columba, had both to order and further his faith in regions where it was not unknown, and to introduce it into regions where it had never penetrated. But, like Patrick, and unlike Columba, he was in touch with the rest of western Christendom. The political and geographical circumstances were indeed different. Boniface was backed by the Frank monarchy; he was nearer Rome, in frequent communication with the Popes, and the Popes of that day had an authority far greater than the Popes before Gregory the Great. If Patrick looked with reverence to Rome as the apostolic seat, Boniface looked to Rome far more intently. In Patrick's day the Roman Empire meant a great deal more than the Roman see; in the days of Boniface the Pope was still a subject of the Emperor, but the Emperor was far away in Constantinople, and to a bishop in Gaul or Britain it was the Bishop of Old Rome who, apart from the authority of his see, seemed to represent the traditions of Roman Christendom. But the work of Boniface and Patrick alike was to draw new lands within the pale of Christian unity, which was closely identified with the Roman name.

St. Patrick did not do for the Scots what Wulfilas did for the Goths, and the Slavonic apostles for the Slavs; he did not translate the sacred books of his religion into Irish or found a national church literature. It is upon their literary achievements, more than on their successes in converting barbarians, that the fame of Wulfilas rests, and the fame of Cyril. The Gothic Bible of Wulfilas was available for the Vandals and other Germans whose speech was closely akin to Gothic. The importance of the Slavonic apostles, Cyril and his brother Methodius, is due to the fact that the literature which they initiated was available, not for the lands in which they laboured—Moravia and Pannonia, which no longer know them—but for Bulgaria and Russia. What Patrick, on the other hand, and his foreign fellow-workers did was to diffuse a knowledge of Latin in Ireland. To the circumstance that he adopted this line of policy, and did not attempt to create a national ecclesiastical language, must be ascribed the rise of the schools of learning which distinguished Ireland in the sixth and seventh centuries. From a national point of

view the policy may be criticised; from a theo-
logian's point of view the advantage may be urged
of opening to the native clergy the whole body
of patristic literature, and saving the trouble of
translation and the chances of error.   But the
point is that the policy was entirely consonant
with the development of western, as contrasted
with eastern, Christianity.   In the time of Patrick
there was within the realm of the Emperor
Theodosius II. a Syrian, as well as a Greek,
ecclesiastical literature; in Armenia there was an
Armenian; even in Egypt there was a Coptic;
whereas in the realm of his cousin and colleague
Valentinian III. there was only one ecclesiastical
language, the speech of Rome itself.   The reason
was that Latin had become the universal language,
not a mere *lingua franca*, in the western provinces,
a fact which conditioned the whole growth of
western Christendom.   In the East, where this
unity of tongue did not exist, no policy was
adopted of imposing Greek on any new people
which might be brought into ecclesiastical connexion with the Church of Constantinople.   In the
West the ideal of a common church language was
formed, just because, within the Empire, there were
no rivals to Latin, and so it was a matter of course,
and not, at first, the result of a deliberate policy,
that the Latin language and literature should
accompany the Gospel.   And this community of
language powerfully conduced to the realisation of

the *unitas ecclesiae*.   The case of Ireland shows
how potent this influence was.   If Patrick had
called into being for the Scots a sacred literature
such as Cyril initiated for the Slavs, we may be
sure that the tendencies in the Irish Church to
strike out paths of development for itself, which
were so strongly marked in the sixth century,
would have been more effective and permanent in
promoting isolation and aloofness, and that the
successful movement of the following century which
drew Ireland back into outward harmony and more
active communion with the Western Church would
have been beset by far greater difficulties and
might have been a failure.   Even if the reform
movement had been carried through in such conditions, there would have been the danger of a
grave schism, like that which rent the Russian
world in the seventeenth century when the reforms
of Nicon the Patriarch were carried, but at the cost
of dividing the Church for ever by the great *raskol.*
The history of that episode illustrates the formidable resistance which a national sacred literature,
partly consisting of, partly based on, translations,
can offer to the ideal unity of a universal religion.
If Greek had been originally established as the
ecclesiastical language of Russia in the days of
Vladimir, we may surmise that in the days of
Alexius all national peculiarities and deviations
which had been introduced in the meantime could
have easily been corrected without causing the

great split. On the other hand, if Gaelic had been established by Patrick as the ecclesiastical tongue of Ireland, the reformers who in the seventh century sought to abolish idiosyncrasies and restore uniformity might have caused a rupture in the Irish Church, which would have needed long years to heal. The Latin language is one of the *arcana imperii* of the Catholic Church.

It is true that the Irish Church moved on certain lines which Patrick did not contemplate and would not have approved. The development of the organisation which it was his task to institute was largely modified in colouring and conformation by the *genius terrae*. But it would be untrue to say that his work was undone. The schools of learning, for which the Scots became famous a few generations after his death, learning which contrasts with his own illiterateness, owe their rise to the contact with Roman ideas and the acquaintance with Roman literature which his labours, more than anything else, lifted within the horizon of Ireland. It was not only the religion, but also the language which was attached to it, that inaugurated a new period of culture for the island, and opened a wider outlook on the universe. The Irish were soon busily engaged in trying to work their own past into the woof of ecumenical history, to synchronise their insular memories with the annals of Rome and Greece, and find a nook for their remote land in the story of the world.

These considerations may help to bring into
relief the place which Patrick holds in the history
of Europe. Judged by what he actually compassed,
he must be placed along with the most efficient of
those who took part in spreading the Christian faith
beyond the boundaries of the Roman Empire. He
was endowed in abundant measure with the quality
of enthusiasm, and stands in quite a different rank
from the apostle of England, in whom this victorious
energy of enthusiasm was lacking, Augustine, the
messenger and instrument of Gregory the Great.
Patrick was no mere messenger or instrument. He
had a strong personality and the power of initiative ;
he depended on himself, or, as he would have said,
on divine guidance. He was not in constant communication with Xystus, or Leo, or any superior ;
he was thrown upon the resources of his own judgment. Yet no less than Augustine, no less than
Boniface, he was the bearer of the *Roman idea.*
But we must remember that it was the Roman idea
of days when the Church was still closely bound up
in the Empire, and owed her high prestige to the
older institution which had served as the model for
her external organisation. The Pope had not yet
become a spiritual Caesar Augustus, as he is at the
present day. In the universal order, he was still
for generations to be overshadowed by the Emperor.
The Roman idea at this stage meant not the idea of
subjection to the Roman see, but of Christianity as
the religion of the Roman Empire. It was as im-

possible for Patrick as it was impossible for the High King of Ireland to divorce the idea of the Church from the idea of the Empire. Christianity was marked off from all other religions as the religion of the Romans in the wider political sense of that Imperial name. If Christianity aspired in theory to be ecumenical, Rome had aspired in theory to realise universal sway before Christianity appeared. The poet Claudian, in his brilliant sketch —written when Patrick was a boy—of the amazing career of Rome, expresses her ecumenical aspiration in the line—

Humanumque genus communi nomine fouit.[1]

That aspiration was destined to be fulfilled more completely in another sense after her political decline. The dismemberment of the Empire and the upgrowth of the German kingdoms brought about an evolution which enabled the elder Rome to reassert her influence in a new way and a new order. But it was the same idea, at different stages of development, which was borne by Patrick, by Augustine, by Boniface, and by Otto.

In this book an attempt has been made to complete the picture of the transformation which was wrought in Europe, during the century succeeding the death of the great Theodosius, by showing how, while the visible fabric of the Empire was being undermined and disjointed, one corner of Europe

[1] *De Cons. Stil. Lib.* iii. l. 151.

which its peace had never reached was brought within the invisible sway of its influence. We must remember that the phrase "dismemberment of the Empire" is far from embracing all the aspects of the momentous events which distinguish that eventful age. The process of Romanising was going foward actively at the same time. The German peoples who settled in the western provinces, at first as unwelcome subjects, soon to become independent nations, were submitted there to the influences of Roman culture, which were never more active and efficacious than when the political power of Rome was waning. As the Roman conquest of the Hellenic world had signified also that the Hellenic idea entered into a new phase of its influence, so the Teutonic occupation of western Europe meant a new sphere and a new mode of operation for the ideas which it was Rome's function and privilege to bestow upon mankind. And while Goths and Burgundians, and Franks and Suevians and Vandals, were passing on Roman soil, in greater or lesser degree, under the ascendency of an influence which was to be the making of some and perhaps the marring of others,—an influence which had begun before, but now became more intense,—the folks of Hiverne were reached by the same ineluctable force. But, while the Teutons came themselves into Rome's domain to claim and make good their rights in the imperial inheritance, the smaller share which was to fall to the Scots of Ireland was conveyed to their own gates. It was Patrick with his auxiliaries who bore to their shores the vessel of Rome's influence, along with the sacred mysteries of Rome's faith. No wonder that his labours should have been almost unobserved in the days of ecumenical stress and struggle, when the Germans by land and by sea were engaging the world's attention, and the Huns were rearing their vast though transient empire. But he was labouring for the Roman idea no less than the great Aetius himself, though in another way and on a smaller scene. He brought a new land into the spiritual federation which was so closely bound up with Rome, *nexuque pio longinqua reuinxit.*

# APPENDIX A

The most important sources for St. Patrick's Life are contained in a manuscript known as the *Liber Armachanus* (preserved in the library of Trinity College, Dublin), to which frequent reference will be made in Appendix A. For a full account of this Codex I must refer to the *Introduction* to Dr. Gwynn's definitive, "diplomatic" edition of all the documents which it contains. It is enough to say here that it was written in the first half of the ninth century, part of it at least before A.D. 807-8 by Ferdomnach, a scribe of Armagh, who died in A.D. 846. He wrote by the direction of the Abbot Torbach, and Dr. Gwynn has shown reasons for believing that the documents relating to Patrick were executed after Torbach's death (A.D. 807). These documents were printed by Dr. W. Stokes in the Rolls edition of *The Tripartite Life of St. Patrick*, Part ii. (1887); and I have given my references, for the most part, to the pages of this edition because it is the most convenient and accessible. The quotations, however, are always taken from Dr. Gwynn's reproduction of the text of the MS. Another edition of these Patrician documents by Dr. E. Hogan was published in vols. i. and ii. of the *Analecta Bollandiana*, 1882-3; see App. A, ii. 3, p. 263. The Irish parts, and the Latin passages containing Irish names, have been included in the *Thesaurus Palæohibernicus* of Dr. Stokes and Professor Strachan, vol. ii. 238 *sqq.*, 259 *sqq.*

## I

### 1. *The Confession*

Our most important sources, the only first-hand sources we possess, for the life of St. Patrick are his own writings, two in number, namely, the document which is fitly known as his *Confession* (from its last words, *haec est confessio mea antequam moriar*), and his *Letter* against Coroticus. The motive and contents of the *Confession* are dealt with in the text and in subsequent notes. Its tradition and genuineness may be considered here.

The *Confession* is preserved in the *Codex Armachanus* (ff. 22-24) along with other Patrician documents which will claim our attention. But the text is not complete. Considerable portions are missing, which are found in later MSS. There is nothing in these portions to excite suspicion of their genuineness ; in fact we have positive evidence that one of these missing parts was read in the text of the *Confession* in the seventh century, for Tírechán $(310_5)$ refers to a passage $(372_{33})$ which is not found in the Armagh MS., and on the other hand there is not the slightest reason to suppose that the text of these later MSS. does not represent the full extent of the original work.[1] The question arises, How are the omissions in the oldest MS. to be accounted for ? The theory that the scribe omitted passages which were illegible in his exemplar cannot be seriously entertained, as there are no proofs to support it. The statements made by Todd,[2] Haddan and Stubbs,[3] and Zimmer[4] as to the obscurity or defectiveness of the copy used by the Armagh scribe are not borne out by the alleged evidence.[5] The nature and subject of the omitted passages give us no clue, for, though it might be just conceivable that one passage was deliberately left out because it refers to a fault committed by Patrick in his boyhood, the omission of the other portions cannot be similarly explained ; and an explanation which does not apply to them all will carry no conviction. It seems that the imperfect state of this text of the *Confession* may be due to no more recondite cause than the haste and impatience of the scribe to finish his task. There may have been some external motive for such haste and carelessness ; and as a matter of fact there is positive evidence that he stopped before his proposed task was finished. The heading of the *Confession* is : *Incipiunt Libri Sancti Patricii Episcopi*. This shows, as has often been observed, that the scribe intended to copy both the *Confession* and the *Letter* against Coroticus. But he did not

[1] Zimmer put forward the theory that the original *Confession* contained more biographical details than our texts (*Celtic Church*, p. 50). See my criticism showing that his argument has no basis (*Eng. Hist. Review*, xviii., July 1903, pp. 544-6).

[2] *St. Patrick*, p. 347.

[3] *Councils*, ii. p. 296, note *a*.

[4] *Celtic Church*, *ib.*

[5] Bury, *ib.*

fulfil his purpose; he never copied the *Letter*. The *Confession* ends on f. 24 v° b; the second column is a blank; and therefore it is certain that the *Letter* was never included in this MS. Further, the paragraph [1] which the scribe has attached to the end of the *Confession* ought, possibly, to have followed the *Letter*, though of course the autograph volumen may have contained only the *Confession*. It seems then most simple to suppose that the scribe was hurried, and that in writing out the *Confession* he "scamped" his work for the same reason which impelled him to omit copying the *Letter*.

It is perhaps superfluous now to defend the genuineness of the *Confession*, especially as Professor Zimmer, the most important critic who impugned it, now admits it. Two considerations are decisive. (1) There is nothing in the shape of an anachronism in the document, nothing inconsistent with its composition about the middle of the fifth century. (2) As a forgery it would be unintelligible. Spurious documents in the Middle Ages were manufactured either to promote some interest, political, ecclesiastical, local, or simply as rhetorical exercises. But the *Confession* does not betray a vestige of any ulterior motive; there is no reference to Armagh, no reference to Rome, no implication of any interest which could prompt falsification. And what Irish writer in the sixth century [2] would have composed as a rhetorical exercise, and attributed to Patrick, a work written in such a rude style? But besides these considerations, which are decisive, the emotion of the writer is unmistakable; and I cannot imagine how any reader could fail to recognise its genuineness.[3]

A critical edition (the first accurate text) has been published by Rev. N. J. D. White in the *Proceedings of the Royal Irish Academy*, 1904), to which I may refer for an account of the MSS. and previous editions.

## 2. *The Letter against Coroticus*

The other extant work of St. Patrick is the *Letter*, which may be most conveniently called the "Letter against Coroticus." It

---

[1] Huc usque uolumen quod Patricius manu conscripsit sua: septima decima Martii die translatus est Patricius ad caelos.

[2] Sixth century or not much later, because the writings of Muirchu and Tírechán attest its existence in the second half of the seventh century.

[3] The attempt of Pflugk-Harttung (*Die Schriften S. Patricks*, in *Neue Heidelberger Jahrbücher*, p. 71 *sqq.*, 1893) to prove the *Confession* and *Letter* spurious is a piece of extraordinarily bad criticism. He designates the *Liber Armachanus* as " Irlands pseudoisidorische Fälschung."

is addressed to Christian subjects of Coroticus, a ruler in north Britain ; its motive and contents will be dealt with App. B, p. 316. It is not contained in the Armagh MS., but it was known to Muirchu in the seventh century ; and that the scribe of the Armagh MS. knew it and intended to copy it may (as pointed out above, p. 226) be justly inferred from the heading before the *Confession* : incipiunt libri sancti Patricii episcopi. The document is preserved in a St. Vaast MS., from which it was printed in the *Acta Sanctorum* (March 17) ; in two Fell MSS., which were collated for the edition of Haddan and Stubbs (*Councils*, ii. 314 *sqq.*) ; and in a Cottonian MS. (Nero EI), the text of which is given in Stokes's edition (*Trip.* vol. ii. 375 *sqq.*).

The genuineness of the document [1] seems to be written on its face, as in the case of the *Confession* ; that a falsification should have taken this form would be inexplicable. An analysis of the language and style points clearly to the same authorship as the *Confession* ; and the occurrence of such phrases in both documents as *certissime reor* or the favourite *utique* is characteristic of a writer who was *indoctus* and had no great command of language. It is noteworthy, and need not excite suspicion, that in both documents he uses the same formula in describing himself :—

*Confession*, 374₃₆, *Patricius peccator indoctus scilicet Hiberione* conscripsit.

*Letter*, 375₁₁, *Patricius peccator indoctus scilicet Hiberione* constitutus episcopum me esse fateor.

[Critical edition by Rev. N. J. D. White, in *Proc. of R.I.A.* 1904.]

### 3. *Dicta Patricii*

Besides these two works of St. Patrick, there is preserved (in the *Liber Armachanus*) a brief section entitled *Dicta Patricii*, consisting of the three following utterances :—

I. Timorem Dei habui ducem itineris [2] mei per Gallias atque Italiam etiam in insolis quae sunt in mari Tyrreno.[3]

II. De saeculo recessistis [4] ad paradisum,[5] Deo gratias.

III. Ecclesia [6] Scotorum, immo Romanorum, ut Christiani ita ut Romani sitis, ut decantetur uobiscum oportet, omni hora orationis,

---

[1] Now fully admitted by Zimmer, who formerly doubted it.
[2] iteneris A.          [3] terreno A.
[4] requissistis A (with sign of query, Z, in margin).
[5] paradissum A.          [6] aeclessia A.

uox illa laudabilis Cyrie[1] lession,[2] Christe lession.[3]  Omnis ecclesia[4] quae sequitur me cantet Cyrie lession, Christe lession.  Deo gratias.

In considering the question of the authenticity of these *dicta* we must take into account their position in the *Liber Armachanus*.  The section occurs between Muirchu's life and Tírechán's Memoir (see below), immediately before the beginning of the latter, and consequently I used to think that the scribe (Ferdomnach) had found them at the end of the book from which he copied Muirchu's Life.  This assumption, however, falls to the ground through a brilliant discovery of Dr. Gwynn.  Immediately before the *Dicta Patricii*, occupying the upper and middle part of the same column (fol. 9 r° a), is a paragraph (*Patricius uenit . . . aeclessiae uestrae*) describing acts of Patrick in Connaught.  Dr. Gwynn recognised this as a section belonging to Tírechán's Memoir (see below, p. 250), and drew the conclusion that it had been accidentally omitted from its context by the scribe of the exemplar of Tírechán which Ferdomnach used, and had been afterwards inserted by that scribe at the beginning of his MS., whence it was copied by Ferdomnach just as he found it.  The external indications fully confirm Dr. Gwynn's discovery.  (1) The text of the preceding column (fol. 8 v° b), containing the end of Muirchu's Life and some brief additions (obviously entered at the end of the Muirchu exemplar), terminates before the foot of the column, leaving seven lines blank.  (2) The first word, *Patricius*, in fol. 9 r° a, has an enormous initial (the type in Dr. Gwynn's edition fails to do justice to its size), evidently marking the commencement of a new document.

It follows that the section of the *Dicta Patricii* was copied into the *Liber Armachanus* from the Tírechán exemplar.  We must suppose it to have been written, in that exemplar, on the first page, in a blank space which still remained after the scribe had written the omitted paragraph of Tírechán.  Now the entry of these *Dicta* in the book containing Tírechán's Memoir may not be without significance, for a passage in this Memoir furnishes direct evidence bearing upon the first *Dictum*.

Tírechán (see below, Appendix A, ii. 1) consulted a book which was lent to him by Bishop Ultan of Ardbraccan, and from

---

[1] Curie A.           [2] $= \dot{\epsilon}\lambda\dot{\epsilon}\eta\sigma o\nu$.

[3] It may be well to translate this sentence.  "Church of the Scots, nay of the Romans, in order that ye may be Christians as well as Romans, it behoves that there should be chanted in your churches (*uobiscum*) at every hour of prayer the *Kyrie eleison, Christe eleison.*"  Compare Mr. Jenkinson in the *Academy*, Aug. 11, 1888.       [4] aeclessia A.

it he derived a number of details regarding Patrick's life before he came as a missionary to Ireland. We may refer to this book as the *Liber apud Ultanum*,[1] and its great importance lies in the fact that it is (after the *Confession*) the earliest work bearing on Patrick's life for which we have a direct testimony. In it Tírechán found Patrick's four names, and doubtless the summary sketch which he gives of his captivity and travels,[2] and probably the date of his death. This book existed in Ardbraccan in the first half of the seventh century.

The account of the captivity in this book depended partly on the *Confession*. The notice of Patrick's travels on the Continent is as follows :—

Uii aliis annis ambulauit et nauigauit in fluctibus et in campistribus locis et in conuallibus montanis *per Gallias atque Italiam totam atque in insolis quae sunt in mari Terreno*, ut ipse dixit in commemoratione laborum.

The italicised words are identical with words in the first of the *Dicta Patricii*; and the expression *ut ipse dixit* permits us to infer that this *Dictum Patricii* was accepted before the *Liber apud Ultanum* was written (latest date, first half of seventh century).

It has been suggested that the words *in commemoratione laborum* refer to some lost work of Patrick. Such an assumption is quite unnecessary. The words admit of two other explanations. (1) I formerly suggested [3] that in the *Liber apud Ultanum* the phrase *commemoratio laborum* occurred in reference to the autobiographical details in the *Confession*, and that Tírechán, not knowing the *Confession* at first hand, thought that all the biographical facts furnished by his source were derived from Patrick's own account. But (2) I now think that the words *ut ipse . . . laborum,* "as he said himself in describing his labours," merely refer to the utterance preserved in the *Dicta Patricii,* and that the first *Dictum* was the source of the compiler of the *Liber apud Ultanum.*

I think we may go a step farther, and attempt to answer the question, How did the *Dicta Patricii* get into the copy of Tírechán's Memoir ? It seems not unlikely that they were pre-

---

[1] See Tírechán, p. 302.

[2] The assumption that all these details are taken from the book is confirmed by the one explicit exception. The sojourn in the *insula Aralanensis* is given on the oral authority of Bishop Ultan ($302_{24}$). This was evidently Ultan's explanatory comment on the text *in insolis*, etc.

[3] In a paper on Muirchu in the *Guardian,* Nov. 27, 1901.

served in the very *Liber apud Ultanum* which Tírechán used. One would judge from Tírechán's extracts that it contained miscellaneous entries about Patrick's life, and it may well have contained the *Dicta Patricii*. If so, we can easily understand that they might have been copied at Ardbraccan from the Ardbraccan book into a MS. of Tírechán—possibly by Tírechán himself.

It is obvious that these *dicta* could in no case be correctly described as a work of Patrick. So far as they were genuine utterances they must have been remembered, and handed down, or put on paper, by one of his disciples. The second *dictum* is certainly Patrician, for it occurs in the *Letter* against Coroticus ($379_{22}$, *Deo gratias: creduli baptizati de seculo recessistis ad paradisum*). It may be said that it was simply transcribed from this context. But this assumption is in the highest degree improbable. If any one conceived the idea of making a collection of *dicta*, why should he have included only this particular excerpt?[1] It seems far more likely that these words were a favourite phrase of Patrick, and that he made use of his favourite phrase in the *Letter*.

The first *dictum* is, I have no doubt, genuine also. It is not at all the sort of thing that any one would think of inventing; there was no motive. And perhaps readers of the *Confession* and *Letter* will not think me fanciful if I detect a Patrician ring in the words *timorem Dei habui ducem itineris mei*.[2]

The third saying presents more difficulty. The genuineness of the first two does not establish any strong presumption in favour of the third; because if any one desired to father the introduction of a liturgical practice on Patrick, nothing would have been more natural than to attach it to the two genuine *dicta*. (In any case, we should be inclined to reject the second part of the *dictum*, which repeats the first; the expression *omnis aeclessia quae sequitur me* suggests a period when Patrician were strongly contrasted with non-Patrician communities.) The question turns on the date of the introduction of the *Kyrie eleison* into the liturgy. We know that it was not introduced into Gaul till not long before the Council of Vaison in 529. Its use is enacted by the third canon of this Council, where it is stated that the custom

---

[1] It may be pointed out that the small number of the *dicta*—three, or more probably two—is in favour of their genuineness.

[2] Since writing this, I observe that the same thing struck Loofs (*De ant. Brit. Scot.que eccl.* p. 50). He held the *Dicta* to be genuine, admitting the possibility of later additions. So too B. Robert, *Étude crit. sur la vie et l'œuvre de St-Patrick* (1883), p. 74.

of saying the *Kyrie* had been already introduced (*est intromissa*) *tam in sede apostolica quam etiam per totas orientales atque Italiae provincias.* This shows that if Patrick introduced it, he got it not from Gaul but from Rome.[1] Now M. Duchesne observes (*Origines du culte chrétien*, 3rd ed. p. 165, note 2) that the Council seems to regard the chant as having been *recently* introduced in Rome and Italy. "Recently" is vague, but the inference cannot be pressed, since the same phrase *est intromissa* embraces the Eastern Churches, where the *Kyrie* was in use before the end of the fourth century. The question of the introduction of the *Kyrie* in the west has been discussed by Mr. Edmund Bishop, in two papers in the *Downside Review* (December 1899, March 1900), to which Mr. Brightman kindly called my attention. His general conclusion is that "it spread to the west through Italy, its introduction into Italy falling in the fifth century at the earliest; probably in the second half rather than in the first." The truth is that there is no evidence what the Roman divine service was, in its details, in the fifth century; and therefore it is possible to hold that the *dictum* of Patrick may be genuine, and a testimony that the *Kyrie* was used at Rome in the first half of that century.

But while we admit this possibility, we can hardly build upon it. It must be acknowledged that the expression *aeclessia Scotorum immo Romanorum* suggests seventh or eighth century. If it is Patrician, *Romanorum* ought to mean the Church of the Roman Empire. For it is very difficult to conceive Patrick associating the Irish Church with Rome as opposed to Gaul and the rest of western Christendom. But in this context *Romanorum* (and *Romani*) supplies the ground for using the *Kyrie*, and would therefore logically stand in contradistinction to Gaul and other parts of the Empire where the *Kyrie* was not in use.

Again, the tenor of this *dictum* is in marked contrast to the other two. It is not an emotional expression of Patrick's experience, but an ecclesiastical injunction. The *Deo gratias* at the end is out of place.

On the whole I am strongly disposed to think that the third *dictum* is spurious and was added, perhaps, after A.D. 700, to the two genuine *dicta*.

I may refer in this connexion to the important discussion of

[1] This is also shown by the addition of *Christe eleison*, as Mr. Brightman has pointed out to me. Cp. Gregory the Great, *Ep.* ix. 12. Milan is also excluded; the Milanese only use *Kyrie*. I have had the advantage of communicating with Mr. Brightman on the subject; otherwise I should hardly have ventured to deal with it, as I have no liturgical knowledge.

the Stowe Missal by Dr. B. MacCarthy in the *Transactions of the Royal Irish Academy*, 1886, vol. xxvii. 135 *sqq.*, a paper which seems to have entirely escaped the notice of M. Duchesne. His general conclusion is that the mass, which is the oldest part of the MS.—and which he separates as Ba—is as old as the first half of the fifth century (pp. 164-5), and he considers it to be the mass introduced by Patrick. He dates the transcription to the seventh century (after A.D. 628).

### 4. *Ecclesiastical Canons of St. Patrick*

It would be strange if the organisers of the Church in Ireland in the fifth century had not held synods, or some substitute for synods, and committed their resolutions to writing;[1] and if so, there would be every probability that the *Acta* or canons would have been extant in the eighth century, and would have been perfectly well known to the bishops and clergy who sat in the synods of the seventh and eighth centuries; for it was not till the ninth century that the destruction of books began through the devastations of the Northmen.

It was clearly one of Patrick's duties to take measures to establish and secure harmony and unity of ecclesiastical administration between the north of Ireland, the special field of his own activity, and the south, which lay outside his immediate sphere of operations.

As a matter of fact, we possess evidence which, if it is genuine, records a " synod " or meeting in which Patrick was concerned; but it has been called in question, and is generally rejected. Nevertheless the last word has not been said.

The evidence is twofold.

(1) We have thirty canons preserved in a MS. which once belonged to the cathedral library of Worcester, and is now MS. 279 in the library of Corpus Christi College, Cambridge. It was written on the continent in the ninth or tenth century, and an account of it and its contents will be found in *The Early Collection of Canons known as the Hibernensis, two Unfinished Papers, by Henry Bradshaw*, 1893. These canons are usually described as the acts of a synod—Synodus I. Patricii—and were printed inaccurately in the collections of Spelman (i. 52 *sqq.*) and Wilkins (i. 2-3). An accurate text is given in Haddan and Stubbs, *Councils*, ii. 328-30.

---

[1] So the missionary Boniface insists on the necessity of synods and *canonica iura* in a letter to Pope Zacharias (Ep. 50, p. 299, ed. Duemmler in M.G.H. *Epp.* iii.).

The document begins thus :

Gratias agimus Deo patri et filio et spiritui sancto.  Presbiteris et diaconibus et omni clero Patricius Auxilius Isserninus episcopi salutem.

Satius nobis negligentes praemonere [quam] culpare que facta sunt, Solamone dicente, Melius est arguere quam irasci.  Exempla difinitionis nostrae inferius conscripta sunt et sic inchoant.

The canons follow.

Thus the document professes to be a circular letter addressed by Patricius, Auxilius, and Iserninus to the clergy, and embodying ecclesiastical rules and penalties on which the three bishops agreed.  It seems misleading to describe these rules as the canons of a synod ; they are canons laid down by a conclave of three bishops whose authority was acknowledged, and a conclave of three bishops is not a synod in the usual sense of the term.

It may be observed, before going farther, that the preface, instead of arousing suspicion, prepossesses us in favour of the genuineness of the document.  Conferences and co-operation between Patrick and the southern bishops Auxilius and Iserninus are, as I hinted above, just what we should expect ; and a forger who, say in the eighth century, desired to foist upon Patrick canons of later origin would have been much less likely to associate Patrick with these two bishops than with others, such as Benignus, who appeared more conspicuously in the story of his life.  We may fairly argue that, if the canons themselves should turn out to be spurious, at all events the forger must have founded his superscription on the fact that genuine canons had been issued by the three bishops.  Consequently, the superscription seems to me, in any case, to be evidence for the co-operation of Patricius, Auxilius, and Iserninus in organising the Church in Ireland.

The early date of the canons was rejected by Todd, who assigned them to the ninth or tenth century (pp. 486-8), by Haddan and Stubbs, who place their origin between A.D. 716 and A.D. 777 or 809 (ii. 331, z), and by Wasserschleben (*Die irische Kanonensammlung*, ed. 2, p. l.).  Todd brought forward three arguments : (1) the injunction in canon 6 that clergy should wear the Roman tonsure ; (2) the implication of "a more near approach to diocesan jurisdiction, as well as a more settled state of Christianity in the country than was possible in the days of St. Patrick"; (3) the reference in canon 25 to the offerings made to the bishop (*pontificialia dona*) as a *mos antiquus*.

Haddan and Stubbs add as another argument a point noticed by Todd, but not pressed by him as an objection, that (4) canon 33 must have been enacted "when the Britons and the Irish had become estranged, *scil.* by the adoption of Roman customs by the latter (north as well as south) while the former retained the Celtic ones"; and hence they derive their limits of date mentioned above.

Now, if we admit that all these objections are valid, it would not necessarily follow that the whole document is spurious. There is the alternative possibility that the document as a whole is genuine, but interpolated. The interpolations would amount to canons 25, 30, 33, 34, and a clause in canon 6.

Before I proceed to criticise the arguments of Todd, and Haddan and Stubbs against the genuineness of the document, it will be convenient to state the other evidence for Patrick's activity in the shaping of ecclesiastical canons, as it has a close and immediate bearing on the present question.

(2) The *Collectio Canonum Hibernensis*, which has been admirably edited by Wasserschleben (*Die irische Kanonen-sammlung*, ed. 2, 1885), was put together, it is generally agreed, at the end of the seventh or in the first years of the eighth century. The external evidence is that two of the thirteen manuscripts which contain the collection were written in the eighth century. The internal evidence is that the latest authors cited are Theodore of Tarsus (*ob.* 690) and Adamnan (*ob.* 704);[1] none of Bede's works are cited. As for the place of its origin, Wasserschleben and Bradshaw, though they differed otherwise, agreed that it originated in Ireland, while Loofs (*De antiqua Britonum Scotorumque ecclesia*, p. 76) argued for Northumbria on the insufficient grounds that the headings *Hibernenses, Synodus Hibernensis*, implied an origin outside Ireland, and that an Irish compiler would hardly have been acquainted with the *Penitential* of Theodore. A rubric in a Paris MS. (which came from Corbie and was written in Brittany) may contain a clue :

Hucusq ; Nuben et cv. cuiminiae & du rinis.

Bradshaw infers that the collection was compiled by "an Irish monk or abbot of Dairinis" near Youghal. Dr. W. Stokes

---

[1] Bradshaw has clearly distinguished two recensions of the collection, which he designates as the A-text and the B-text. Theodore's *Penitential* is the latest work quoted in the A-text, Adamnan's *Canons* the latest in the B-text. See Bradshaw's letter to Wasserschleben in Wasserschleben's edition of the Canons, p. lxx.

acutely saw that the name of Cucummne, a learned ecclesiastic (*ob.* 742 or 747, *Ann. Ult.*) is concealed in the corruption; and also amended *Ruben* (*Academy*, July 14, 1888). Mr. Nicholson, in an ingenious article in the *Zeitschr. für kelt. Philologie*, iii. 99 *sqq.* (1899), amends thus:

> Hucusq; Ruben et cucuimini iae et durinis,

and finds the names of Rubin (*ob.* 725) and "Cucuimne of Ia" (Hy). He concludes that the collection was compiled in Hy and probably by Adamnan. The question need not be discussed here, since for the present purpose it is indifferent whether the compilation was made in Ireland or in Hy.

The Collection has been characterised by Bradshaw as "an attempt, and there seems good ground for looking upon it as a first attempt, to form a digest of all available authorities, from Holy Scripture, from the decisions of Councils, native and foreign, and from Church writers, native and foreign, arranged methodically under sixty-five several titles; though the method has not been carried out so fully as to produce an arrangement of the titles themselves in any but the most accidental sequence" (*Early Collection of Canons*, p. 6).

A survey of the sources will be found in Wasserschleben's Introduction. Native sources are referred to under the headings *Hibernenses, Sinodus Hibernensis, Patricius,* and also with other superscriptions which will be mentioned below.

Among the canons attributed to *Patricius* we find fourteen items which are contained in the circular epistle of Patricius, Auxilius, and Iserninus:

| Patr., Aux., Is. | Hibernensis. | Patr., Aux., Is. | Hibernensis. |
|---|---|---|---|
| Preface | 66. 18. a, b | 12 | 40. 8 |
| 1 | 42. 25. c | 14 | 28. 10. c |
| 4 | 42. 26. a | 20 | 33. 1. e |
| 5 | 42. 26. a | 24 | 43. 4 |
| 6 b | 52. 7 | 28 | 40. 9 |
| 8 | 34. 2. b | 31 | 10. x |
| 11 | 39. 10. b | 34 b (cp. 3) | 39. 11 |

It is to be observed that 43. 4 = 24 is quoted as from *Sinodus Patricii*. Another canon of the Patrician conclave is also cited in the Hibernensis, but under a different title, which will be noticed below.

Thus the evidence of the Hibernensis establishes that a considerable portion of the matter in the circular letter of the three bishops was held to be of Patrician origin (*c.* A.D. 700), and consequently it would be impossible to accept the date assigned by Haddan and Stubbs for the circular letter except in the sense that some interpolations might have been introduced in the course of the eighth century.

The question now arises as to how far we can, *prima facie*, trust the compiler of the Hibernensis as to the Patrician origin of the canons which he labels Patrician, and which are also found in the circular letter. In estimating the value of his evidence, one consideration, it seems to me, is very important. There is another set of canons (extant in more than one MS.) ascribed to Patrick, and generally referred to as *Synodus II. Patricii*.[1] Of these thirty-one canons, nine are quoted in the Hibernensis, but in no case attributed to Patrick ; three others are quoted in one MS. of the later recension (B-text) of the Hibernensis, namely, in the Valicellanus (tenth century), and one of them is there ascribed to Patrick. The correspondence is shown in the following table :—[2]

| Syn. II. Patricii. | Hibernensis. | Syn. II. Patricii. | Hibernensis. |
|---|---|---|---|
| 2 | 2. 23 : Sinodus Romana | 14 | 12. 15. c : Sinodus |
| 3 | 47. 8. d : Romani | [17 | 47. 20 : Paterius (Patricius)] |
| 4 | 40. 1. c : Sinodus Romana | 23 | 35. 3 : Dominus in evangelio |
| 8 | 28. 14. d : Sinodus Romanorum | 24 | 16. 4 : Sinodus Romana |
| [10 | 11. 1. b : Sinodus] | 25 | 46. 35. b : Romani |
| [11 | 47. 20 : Sinodus Romana] | 30 | 36. 8 : Sinodus |

The circumstance that the Hibernensis ascribes to Patricius the canons (with one exception) which it quotes from "Synodus I.," and does not ascribe to him the canons which it quotes from "Synodus II.," is a fact which places the two "Synods" on a different footing, and furnishes a certain *prima facie* evidence in favour of the circular letter known as Synodus I. For the claim of Synodus II. to authenticity is invalidated by the fact that one canon (27) is in direct contradiction with a passage in Patrick's *Confession*.[3]

It will be observed that most of the quotations in the Hibernensis which correspond to canons of Synodus II. are ascribed to *Romani* or *Sinodus Romana*. These headings are frequent in the

---

[1] Spelman 1. 59 *sq.*, Haddan and Stubbs, ii. 333 *sqq.*

[2] The canons which are cited in the Valicellane only are marked by square brackets. The list of correspondences in Haddan and Stubbs, ii. 333, *a*, is incomplete.

[3] See Haddan and Stubbs, ii. 333, a.

Hibernensis, and it is important to determine what they mean. There are, I think, twelve quotations of this kind[1] which have been identified in non-Irish sources, mostly in the *Statuta ecclesiae antiqua*. There are, as shown in the above table, six quotations corresponding to canons of Irish origin included in Synodus II. There is one quotation under *Sinodus Romana*, 33. 1. e, which is found in the circular letter of the three bishops. There are twenty-two (25) quotations which cannot be controlled.[2] There seems to be no case in which a canon referred to as *Sinodus Romana* can be discovered in the Acts of a synod held at Rome.

Thus out of forty-two (45) "Roman" headings, it is remarkable that only twelve can be identified in non-Irish sources, and of these four are from non-Roman councils, six from the *Statuta eccl. ant.*, two from the decrees of a bishop of Rome. Seven others are from Irish sources. It seems, on the face of it, much more likely that most of the remaining quotations which have not been identified were derived from native sources, seeing that the Acts of the Irish synods before A.D. 700 have not been preserved; it is hardly likely that so many as twenty-two (25) citations of this kind from foreign sources would remain unidentified.

There is a particular indication which seems to me of some significance; 33. 1. e cites a canon found in the circular letter of the three bishops (can. 20), as from *Sinodus Romana*. 33. 1. f follows with a quotation, evidently from the same context and under the heading *item*, but not found in the circular letter.[3] The inference, I submit, is that both sections are quoted from

---

[1] 1. 8. b; 5. 2; 6. 2. b (two MSS. give *Sin. Rom.*, one *Sin. Rom. siue Kartagin.*, the rest *Sin. Kartagin.*); 7. 3. a; 20. 3. b; 40. 13. a; 46. 35. c; 46. 38. a, b; 47. 12. b; 47. 12. c; 47. 20; 66. 19. a. There is another case of *Syn. Rom. uel Kart.* in one MS.; 9. 1. a. The quotation from Pope Symmachus, *Ep. ad Caes. ep. Arel.* c. 1, under the title *Regula canonica Romana* in 17. 8 may stand on a different footing.

[2] 14. 2. c; 17. 7. b; 17. 9. b; 18. 2. a; 20. 3. a; 20. 3. c; 20. 5. a; 21. 2; 33. 1. f; 35. 4. c; 41. 6. a and b; 42. 7; 42. 25. a; 45. 13; 45. 14; 46. 29; 52. 2; 52. 3; 52. 6; 56. 4. a; 66. 16. To these may be added three other items: 20. 6. a, *institutio Romana*; 28. 5. b and 33. 4, *disputatio Romana*. Also 42. 23 *Sinodus Romana*, but the chapter is found only in one MS.; and in 3. 4 one MS. has an additional quotation from *Synodus Romanorum*. I do not include 42. 24, because the heading *eadem sinodus* may be referred to the heading of c. 22 *Sinodus Hibernensis*, and not to the heading of 23 *Sinodus Romana*, which, as I have mentioned, is found in only one MS. (Sangallensis).

[3] Here are the two sections :—

e. *Sinodus Romana* : Omnis qui fraudat debitum fratris ritu gentilium excommunis sit donec reddiderit. f. *Item* : Qua fronte rogas a Deo debitum tibi dimitti cum debitum proximi tui non reddidisti?

the Acts of an Irish synod, in which the canon found in the circular letter was adopted, but without a reference to its origin.

The only theory which seems to me to cover all the facts is that in the Hibernensis, *Sinodus Romana* (or *Romani*) designates synods held in Ireland[1] in the seventh century in the interest of Roman reform, and under the influence of its advocates. This view will explain the two categories of canons which can be identified as of Irish origin, and canons which are unidentified. It is also perfectly consistent with the fact that twelve canons have been identified in foreign sources, only that we have to suppose that the compiler took them, not from the original sources, but from the Acts of Irish synods at which they were adopted.

We may infer that the document known as *Synodus II. Patricii* was taken from the Acts of an Irish synod of the seventh century.

Before we leave the Hibernensis, it must be mentioned that it contains a number of other canons ascribed to Patrick which do not appear in the circular letter. They are fourteen in number,[2] besides two which are found only in one or two MSS.[3] The two most remarkable of these quotations (chapters entitled *de eo quod malorum regum opera destruantur* and *de eo quod bonorum regum opera aedificent*)[4] are found in the pseudo-Patrician treatise *De Abusionibus Saeculi*, c. 9.[5] The most important is 20. 5. b, ordaining an appeal to Rome (cp. chap. iii. § A, and App. C, 16).

The question has now to be considered whether the objections which have been urged against the circular letter of Patricius, Auxilius, and Iserninus amount to a valid proof that it is spurious or has been interpolated.

(1) The sixth canon of this letter enjoins, under penalty of separation from the Church, that the tonsure of clerics be *more*

---

[1] It may be observed that in the Valicellane MS. we find some instances of *Hibernensis uel Romana*; 33. 4, 6, and 9.

[2] 11. 1. b; 20. 5. b; 21. 12; 21. 6. b; 25. 3; 25. 4; 29. 7; 37. 27; 37. 29; 42. 26. b; 44. 9; 46. 32. b; 47. 11. b; 67. 2. d. Of these 37. 29 has the curious heading *Sinodus totius mundi et Patricius decreuit* (with the variants *Sinodus Hibernensis et Pat. decr.*, and simply *Sinodus Hibernensis*).

[3] 21. 25 occurs only in one MS., 37. 6 in two.

[4] 25. 3 and 4.

[5] In Ware's *S. Patricio . . . adscripta Opuscula* (London, 1656, a rare little volume), pp. 85-7. See below, p. 245.

*Romano.* We know that in the seventh century the Celtic tonsure *de aure ad aurem* prevailed in the Irish, as in the British, Church, and this was one of the chief questions in the Roman controversy. The conclusion has been generally drawn that this was the tonsure of Irish clerics in the fifth century, and that the Roman tonsure, the *corona* (supposed to be an imitation of the *spinea Christi corona*), was not known in Ireland until the victory of the Roman party in the seventh century. This conclusion relies on the support of a text in the *Catalogus Sanctorum Hiberniae*, where it is said that in the first period of the Irish Church, including the time of Patrick, one tonsure *ab aure usque ad aurem* was worn (H. and S., *Councils*, ii. p. 292). The particular statements, however, of this document are not decisive. If this statement were entirely true, it would follow that Patrick permitted or acquiesced in the native form of tonsure, and cannot have promulgated the canon in question.

Another possibility, however, must be considered. It is equally conceivable that (as Ussher held)[1] the native tonsure might have been condemned by Patrick, Auxilius, and Iserninus —men who had been trained on the continent, under Gallic and Roman influences—and that after their time the prepossession of the Irish in favour of the native pagan tonsure prevailed, and the prohibition of the three bishops became a dead letter.

It might therefore be argued that, if no other evidence is forthcoming, and if there are no other insuperable objections to the circular letter, the canon concerning the tonsure cannot be declared non-Patrician, but that, on the contrary, we are entitled to appeal to it as a proof that the foreign tonsure was introduced in the days of Patrick.

There is, however, a striking and interesting piece of positive evidence which has been quite overlooked because it requires some interpretation. It occurs in the Memoir of Tírechán, who, it is to be remembered, belonged to the north of Ireland, and wrote before that part of the island adopted Roman usages (see below, p. 248). The passage occurs in *Lib. Arm.* f. 12 rᵒ a (Rolls ed. p. 317). The conversion and tonsure of the two brothers Caplait and Mael is there recounted. Caplait believed first, *et capilli eius ablati sunt.* Then Mael was converted:

Et ablati sunt capilli capitis illius id norma magica in capite uidebatur airbacc ut dicitur giunnae.

---

[1] "Brit. ecc. ant.," in *Opera*, vol. vi. p. 491. The same view was urged by Varin. But neither Ussher nor Varin gave positive proof.

This passage seems slightly corrupt, and it is not known what exactly the *norma magica,* called in Irish *airbacc giunne,* was. This, however, does not concern our present purpose. Mael, like Caplait, was shorn of his hair. As both Mael and Caplait were magicians or Druids, they already bore the native tonsure from ear to ear (the name Mael, tonsured one, implies this), and the Christian tonsuring must evidently have removed the hair from the back part of their head. Thus the story as told by Tírechán and his source implies the tradition of a distinction between the native and the Christian tonsure of Ireland in the time of St. Patrick.

But the explanatory remark which Tírechán adds to his story throws new light on the whole matter. He says :

De hoc est uerbum quod clarius est omnib[us] uerbis Scoticis : similis est caluus contra caplit.

The *Tripartite Life* (Rolls ed. 104$_6$) gives the proverb in the Irish form : " cosmail Mael do Chaplait."

A moment's consideration will show that Tírechán cannot be right in supposing that this saw " Mael is like to Caplait " arose out of the story which he tells. Both Mael and Caplait were magicians converted to Christianity and tonsured under Patrick's direction ; in this they resembled each other ; but how could such a resemblance become enshrined in a popular saying, unless there were some typical contrast to give it a point ? There is, however, no contrast in the story, except that Mael was more obstinate and aggressive, and was converted subsequently to his brother. We cannot hesitate to conclude that the saying did not arise from the story, but, as we should *a priori* expect, the story was invented (or adapted) to account for the saying. What was the origin of the saying ?

The clue lies in our hands. *Caplait* is a loan word from the Latin *capillatus* " de-capillated, shorn " ; and a proverb declaring that the *mael* is like to the *caplait* proves that the two were not the same. The *mael* being the man with the native tonsure, the *caplait* was the man with a foreign tonsure, as his foreign name implies. This proverb, which was current in the seventh century, preserves the memory of a Christian tonsure (distinct from the native) formerly used in Ireland.

But the proverb gives us still more information than this. It directly confirms the view, which I suggested above as possible, that the foreign tonsure was at first (in Patrick's time) enforced, and afterwards yielded to the native one. The proverb is evidently a surviving witness of the struggle (probably in the latter part of the fifth century) between the two forms of tonsure. The clerics who clung to native customs cried : There is no distinction between a *mael* and a *caplait*—that is, the old national tonsure is as good a mark of his calling for the Christian cleric as the foreign tonsure which removes all the hair from the crown.

The story of the conversion of the two magicians, as told by Tírechán, was evidently designed to illustrate this proverb, but without any comprehension of the proverb's real significance. In other words, it was invented, or reshaped, at a time when the native tonsure had so completely ousted its rival that men almost forgot that there had been a rival. The story indeed bears upon it an obvious mark of manufacture, in that it represents one of the Druids as named Caplait. He could not have borne this name till after his conversion. That the story was entirely invented for the purpose of explaining the proverb is extremely unlikely. I suggest as probable that in the original story there was only one Druid, who on his conversion received the Christian tonsure, and thus from being *Mael* became *Caplait*. The proverb suggested the duplication of Mael-Caplait into two brethren.

It is another question—and for the present purpose does not matter—whether the Christian tonsure of the fifth century was the tonsure of the seventh century, the *corona*, or not. It may have been a total shaving of the head, no fringe being left. The earliest mention of the *corona* seems to occur in Gregory of Tours, *Liber Vitae Patrum*, xvii. 1 (p. 728, ed. M.G.H.), and it may not have become general before the sixth century. We have no particulars as to the exact nature of the tonsure referred to in Socrates, *H.E.*, 3. 1. 9, or in Salvian, *De gub. Dei*, 8. 21. Once the coronal tonsure was introduced in the west,[1] the total tonsure was distinguished as the Greek or St. Paul's tonsure (see Bede, *H.E.*, iv. 1) ; but it seems not improbable that the total tonsure was universal in the early part, at all events, of the fifth century. There is a passage in Tírechán which seems to me to preserve the memory of the practice of total tonsure in the days of St. Patrick. It is the name of Patrick's charioteer, fol. 13 v° b (322)[26] :

Et sepiliuit illum aurigam totum id totmael caluum.

---

[1] It is officially recognised in the 40th canon of the Fourth Council of Toledo, A.D. 633.

The hybrid name *Tot-mael* contrasts the Christian tonsure with the native semi-tonsure, but it suggests total rather than coronal tonsure. It is, in any case, another undesigned testimony to the difference between the ecclesiastical and the native tonsures in Patrick's time; while it possibly indicates that the *mos Romanus* introduced into Ireland in the fifth century may have been partially different from the *mos Romanus* which was reintroduced in the seventh.

But the passage in Tírechán on which I have commented appears to me to demonstrate that the foreign tonsure had at one time been customary for clerics in Ireland; and therefore the objection to the genuineness of the circular letter, which has been founded on the inclusion of a canon on this subject, falls to the ground.

(2) The second objection urged by Todd is that some of the canons imply a nearer approach to diocesan jurisdiction, and a more settled state of Christianity, than was possible in the days of St. Patrick. (So far as a relatively settled state of Christianity is concerned, it must be remembered that Todd did not realise how far Christianity had spread in Ireland before St. Patrick; and if we take into account that the letter of the three bishops is designed both for those parts of the island where Christian communities had existed many years before, as well as for those (like Connaught) where churches had only recently been planted, there is nothing in the canons that need surprise us on this head).

The canons which imply spheres of ecclesiastical jurisdiction are 30 and 34 :—

30. Aepiscopus quislib*et* qui de sua in alteram progreditur parruchia*m* nec ordinare p*rae*sumat nisi p*er*missionem acceperit ab eo qui in suo principatu[m] e*st*; die dominica offerat tantum susceptione et obsequi hic contentus sit.

34. Diaconus nobiscu*m* similiter qui inconsulto suo abbate sine litteris in aliam parruchiam absentat [MS. adsentiat] nec cibum ministrare dec*et* et a suo p*re*sbitero quem contempsit per penitentiam uindic*et*ur.

The first of these canons implies that a bishop has a defined *paruchia* and that he cannot perform episcopal acts in another *paruchia* without the permission of its *princeps*. The second deals with the case of a deacon belonging to a monastic community, the head of which is not a bishop but a presbyter; he is forbidden to betake himself to another district without a letter from his abbot.

Canon 30 corresponds to the 22nd canon of the Council of Antioch (A.D. 341, Mansi, *Conc.*, ii. 649), ἐπίσκοπον μὴ ἐπιβαίνειν ἀλλοτρίᾳ πόλει . . . εἰ μὴ ἄρα μετὰ γνώμης τοῦ οἰκείου τῆς χώρας ἐπισκόπου.[1] *Paruchia* means an episcopal diocese[2] as in Eusebius, *Hist. ecc.* v. 33, 1 and 3. For the considerations which show that Patrick must have defined spheres of episcopal jurisdiction, I must refer to Excursus 18 in Appendix C on the Patrician Episcopate.

In canon 34 *paruchia* seems to have a different meaning, and refer to the district which the church of the abbot's monastery served. It is the district of a presbyter, not of a bishop. This ambiguity would not be fatal to the genuineness of the canon. In the passage of Eusebius, cited above, παροικίαι also occurs in the sense of rural districts, several of which were under one bishop, as Duchesne has pointed out.[3] But the canon may well be a later addition to the genuine document, belonging to an age when the monastic communities had acquired greater importance.

(3) The *mos antiquus* of canon 25 may refer not to Ireland but to the Christian Church generally.

(4) Another objection is founded on canon 33, which enjoins :

Clericus qui de Britanis ad nos ueniat sine epistola etsi habit*et* in plebe non licitum ministrare.

It is suggested that this must belong to a period when the British and Irish churches were estranged by the latter's adoption of Roman customs, that is, not earlier than A.D. 716. I cannot see the cogency of this argument. The canon does not seem to me to imply hostility to the British Church, but to be a natural precaution and safeguard against unauthorised and possibly heretical clerics coming over from Britain. It is an application to Irish circumstances of the 7th canon of the Council of Antioch (Mansi, ii. 644), μηδένα ἄνευ εἰρηνικῶν δέχεσθαι τῶν ξένων.[4] In Patrick's time, when there was Pelagianism in Britain, some such precaution may have been specially necessary ; and it is conceivable that a case of a heretic coming over to Ireland and attempting to propagate his views may have occurred and called forth this ordinance. The words *sine epistola* (ἄνευ εἰρηνικῶν) show that no hostility to the British Church is implied.

---

[1] Cp. the 15th canon of Nicaea, Mansi, ii. 200.
[2] So too in the *Hibernensis*, i. 22, a and c.
[3] *Fastes épiscopaux de l'ancienne Gaule*, vol. i. p. 41.
[4] Cp. also canon 27 of the Council of Hippo, A.D. 393 (Mansi, iii. 923) : ut episcopi non proficiscantur trans mare nisi consulto primae sedis episcopo suae cuiusque prouinciae, ut ab eo praecipue possint formatas sumere.

The outcome of this investigation is that the case for rejecting the circular letter of the three bishops on internal evidence breaks down ; and otherwise an early date is suggested, as Todd admits when he says that some of the canons "were certainly written during the predominance of paganism in the country." Hence, the external evidence being in its favour, we need not hesitate to accept the document as authentic.

### [Note on the *Liber de Abusionibus Saeculi*]

This treatise [1] is ascribed to Patrick in some MSS., but the authorship has been generally rejected, on account of the Latin style, which is very different from that of the *Confession* and the *Letter*, and on account of the Scriptural quotations, which are taken from St. Jerome's version. In itself, the difference in the quality of the Latin might not be decisive, for we have a conspicuous example of similar difference in style between the *Historia Francorum* and the *Gloria Martyrum* of Gregory of Tours.

In MSS. this treatise is variously ascribed to Cyprian and Augustine. The external evidence for Cyprian is best, because Jonas of Orleans, who lived in the first half of the ninth century, quotes it as Cyprian's : *De institutione regia*, c. 3, Migne, *P.L.* 106, 288-9. This testimony and the testimonies of the MSS. are directly contradicted by the internal evidence, namely, by the Scriptural citations from the Vulgate, which render the authorship of Cyprian or Augustine untenable.

There is earlier evidence which points in a different direction. In the eighth century the tract was regarded as the work of Patrick both in Ireland and in Gaul. (1) The ninth Abuse is quoted almost entirely in the *Hibernensis* (above, p. 239) and ascribed to Patricius. (2) Extracts from the same section are quoted in a letter of Cathuulfus (apparently otherwise unknown), addressed *c.* A.D. 775 to King Charles the Great, and preserved in a ninth-century MS. (*Epp. Karolini Aevi*, ii. p. 503. The editor, E. Dümmler, leaves the quotation unidentified).

This evidence proves that the treatise is older than A.D., 700, and strongly suggests that its origin is Irish, that it was ascribed in Ireland to Patrick, and travelled to Gaul under his name. The twelfth Abuse, *populus sine lege*, is consonant with the origin of the work outside the Roman Empire.

---

[1] Printed by Pamelius in his edition of Cyprian ; by Ware in his *Opuscula* of St. Patrick (1656) ; by Migne, *P.L.* 40, 649 *sqq.*

### 5. *Irish Hymn ascribed to Patrick*

The LORICA of St. Patrick is an unmetrical quasi-poetical composition of great antiquity. It is called the *Faeth Fiada*, interpreted the "Deer's Cry," and hence the Preface in the *Liber Hymnorum* connects the hymn with the story of the deer metamorphosis in Muirchu (p. 282). But it seems (cp. Atkinson, *Lib. Hymn.* ii. 209) that the phrase really meant 'a spell or charm which had the power of rendering invisible, and that the story of the deer arose from a popular etymology.

We need not hesitate to identify this work with the *canticum Scotticum* which was current before the ninth century under Patrick's name, as we learn from a note in the *Liber Armachanus* (p. $333_{10}$). Whether Patrick was really the author was another question. The verdict of Professor Atkinson is as follows :—

"It is probably a genuine relic of St. Patrick. Its uncouthness of grammatical forms is in favour of its antiquity. We know that Patrick used very strange Irish, some of which has been preserved ; and the historians who handed down *mudebroth* as an ejaculation of his would probably take care to copy as faithfully as they could the other curious Irish forms which the saint had consecrated by his use" (*Lib. Hymn.* ii. p. lviii).

If it can be proved that some of the forms in the *Lorica* could not have been used by a native Irish writer, this would be a very strong argument for its composition by Patrick. It seems possible that Patrick's expression *mudebroth* was remembered as the solecism of a foreigner. "The oath *dar mo De broth* is mere jargon ; *De broth* ought to mean something like 'God's doom-day' ; but even then there would be a difficulty, because the genitive *Dé* could not precede its governing noun" (Atkinson, *ib.* ii. 179).

It may be said, then, that the Lorica *may* have been composed by Patrick ; but in any case it is an interesting document for the spirit of early Christianity in Ireland.

The latest editions are Atkinson's in the *Liber Hymnorum* (i. 133 *sqq.*) with translation (ii. 49 *sqq.*), and that of Stokes and Strachan in *Thesaurus Palaeo-hibernicus*, vol. ii. 353 *sqq.*

### 6. *Hymn of St. Sechnall*

The Latin HYMN of St. Sechnall or Secundinus, the coadjutor of Patrick,[1] preserved in the MSS. of the *Liber Hymnorum*, is certainly very ancient. It might be rash to affirm that its ascrip-

---

[1] For his alleged relationship see below, p. 292.

tion to Secundinus is correct; but Patrick is spoken of throughout as if he were alive, and the absence of all references to
particular acts of the saint or episodes in his life confirms the
view that it was composed before his death; hymnographers of
later times would hardly have omitted such references. There is
no mention of miracles. As the author thus confined himself to
generalities, the hymn supplies no material for Patrick's biography.
It is worth while noticing that, if the hymn is contemporary, as
it seems to be, the verse

> Testis Domini fidelis in lege Catholica

may be allusive to the event commemorated in *Ann. Ult. s.a.*
441 (see below, p. 367).

The hymn, in trochaic metre, is unrhymed, and does not
exhibit the characteristics of later Latin hymns composed in
Ireland. It takes no account of elision, or quantity, except in
the penultimate syllable of the verse, which is always short.[1]

The best text will be found in Bernard and Atkinson, *Liber
Hymnorum*, i. 3 *sqq.* On the metre see Atkinson, *ib.* xiii., xiv.

## 7. *Life of Germanus, by Constantius*

Constantius, who wrote the Life of Germanus of Auxerre, has
a place in literary history, for Sidonius Apollinaris published his
Letters at his suggestion and dedicated them to him. Constantius (for whose character see Sidonius, iii. 2) composed the
Life at the wish of Patiens, Bishop of Lyons (who also appears
in the correspondence of Sidonius), and one of the two letters
which are prefixed to the Life is addressed to Patiens. The
other is addressed to a Bishop Censurius (see Sidonius, vi. 10).
The episcopate of Patiens gives the years 450 and *c.* 490 as the
limits for the composition of the work, but the author implies in
the first prefatory letter that some time had elapsed since the
death of Germanus. W. Levison (*Neues Archiv* 29, pp. 97 *sqq.*
1903) suggests (p. 112) *c.* 480 or some years later as the
probable date.

The editions of the Life in the collection of Surius (iv. 405
*sqq.*, ed. 1573) and the *Acta Sanctorum* (July 7, p. 200 *sqq.*) do
not represent the original work, but a text with extensive additions.

---

[1] To this rule the MSS. present two exceptions, which should be
corrected : v. 70, *praeuidit*, which has been corrected to *praeuidet* (cp. Atkinson, *Lib. Hymn.* ii. 13), and v. 66, *qui ornatur uestimento nuptiale indūtus*,
where we ought evidently to read *inclŭtus*.

The older text of Mombritius (*Sanctuarium*, i. 319 *sqq.* 1480) comes much nearer to the original (Levison, p. 101). The original work is preserved, without the later interpolations, in various MSS., and its extent was recently defined by the Bollandists, *Bibl. hagiographica Latina*, i. 515, *n.* 3453, cp. ii. 1354. A critical edition is promised in the last volume of the *Scriptores rerum Merovingicarum* (M.G.H.), but in the meantime Dr. Levison has given not only the results of his researches on the MSS., but also a study of the Life in the important monograph cited above. The compass of the original work, and the subsequent additions, are set out clearly in tabular form on p. 113.

The motive of the Life—its main interest for its author—was to represent Germanus as a miracle-worker; he states as his object (in the letter to Patiens) *profectui omnium mirabilium exempla largiri.* The Life accordingly is full of miracles, and largely of typical miracles, some of which have a pronounced family likeness to some recorded in the Life of St. Martin by Sulpicius Severus (Levison, pp. 114 *sqq.*). Constantius forms no exception to the general rule that authors of hagiographies did not condescend to trouble themselves with chronology; there is not a single date in the book. But the main outline of the biography—though there may be inaccuracies in detail (cp. note, p. 297)—seems to be trustworthy, and has sustained the detailed criticism to which it has been subjected by Levison.

## II

### 1. *Memoir of Patrick, by Tírechán*

The earliest extant document that gives an account of St. Patrick's life is a memoir written in the second half of the seventh century by Tírechán, a bishop, who had been the alumnus or disciple of Bishop Ultan of Ardbraccan in Meath. He speaks of Ultan as no longer living,[1] so that his work was compiled after A.D. 657, the year of Ultan's death.[2] The mention of the recent plague (*mortalitates novissimae*) suggests that Tírechán was engaged on his memoir soon after the disastrous years A.D. 664-668.[3] The presumption is that it was compiled in the late sixties or the seventies; and as there is a presumption that Muirchu's biography (see below) was composed in the eighties or nineties, there is a presumption that Tírechán's

---

[1] 311₂₉, Rolls ed.	[2] *Ann. Ult. s.a.*
[3] 314₂₈ ; *Ann. Ult. s.aa.*

work is earlier than Muirchu's. At all events, we may take it as highly probable that it was not later.

Tírechán was attached to some community in north Connaught, probably in Tirawley.[1] His memoir, which is incomplete,[2] is divided into two books, of which the first (after a preliminary summary of Patrick's early life) deals with the saint's work in Meath, the second mainly with his work in Connaught.

The first was probably compiled in Meath, the second certainly in Connaught.[3] The author wrote in the interests of the *paruchia Patricii* (diocese of Patrician communities), of which Armagh claimed to be the head. He speaks of attacks and encroachments made upon that paruchia, and asserts the theory that by divine donation almost the whole island belongs to it.[4] The object of his work is to set forth the circumstances of the foundations of communities of Patrician origin, and for this purpose he collected material. Much of it he may have collected "on the spot," and he may have travelled to gather local traditions with a view to his work.[5] We know from his own statements that he had visited Armagh, Tara, Alofind, Saeoli, L. Selce, Baslick.[6] We know that he derived information not only from Bishop Ultan but from many *seniores*,[7] whom he consulted, presumably, in different places.

But he used written sources as well as oral traditions.

1. For his prefatory account of Patrick's early life he refers to a book in the possession of Bishop Ultan,[8] of which I have spoken above (p. 229). It is uncertain whether his reference to the *Confession* in another place ($310_5$, *in scriptione sua*) implies a first-hand acquaintance with that document; the reference might have been derived from the book of Ultan, which contained matter based on the *Confession*.

2. Certain passages in Tírechán are based on common sources with corresponding passages in Muirchu.[9] These sources were in Irish (see below, p. 258).

---

[1] See Bury, *Tírechán's Memoir of St. Patrick* (*Eng. Hist. Rev.* April 1902), p. 255.

[2] *Ib.* pp. 237, 238, 260.

[3] $311_{23-25}$. Cp. Bury, *ib.* 261.

[4] 311-312.

[5] Bury, *ib.* 258. "His whole book is a practical service to the cause of the claims of Armagh. It is virtually a list of the churches which claimed to have been founded by Patrick. If it had been completed, it would have exhibited the full extent of the *paruchia Patricii*."

[6] $313_{27}$, $307_7$, $313_{28}$, $313_{29}$, $319_5$, $318_{25} \times 301_9$.

[7] $311_{28}$.

[8] *In libro apud Ultanum*, $302_3$.

[9] Bury, *Tírechán's Memoir*, 248-250.

3. Two chronological passages imply written sources.[1]

4. Epigraphic source : inscribed stones near L. Selce.[2]

5. The confusion which I have traced in Tírechán (see Appendix C, 13) between different journeys of Patrick in Connaught can be most easily explained by assuming that he had some older written notes before him.

6. In the same paper in which I pointed out the use of Irish poetical sources by Muirchu ("Sources of the Early Patrician Documents," *E.H.R.*, July 1904) I showed that the story of the conversion of Loigaire's daughters is a Latin reproduction of an Irish poetical source, the evidence being of the same nature as in the case of the Muirchu passages, namely, graphic indications in the *Liber Armachanus*, combined with the rhythmic, assonant, quasi-poetical character of the Latin. There is perhaps some room for doubt whether it was Latinised by Tírechán himself or by an intervener.

7. Written sources are implied by the author's uncertainty as to numerals in three passages ($302_{30}$, $321_1$, $300_{27}$ [see next paragraph]).

The work of Tírechán stops abruptly, and is almost certainly incomplete—that is, it was left unfinished by the author.[3] But it has recently received a new accession by the convincing discovery of Dr. Gwynn that an isolated anonymous paragraph which precedes the Memoir in the *Lib. Arm.* (f. 9, r⁰ a, Patricius uenit—aeclessiae uestrae) is really part of the Memoir. Its place in the text can be approximately determined (it must come in f. 12, u⁰ 2, before the arrival at Selce). For proof and details I must refer to Dr. Gwynn's *Introduction* to *Book of Armagh*, chap. iii. (and see above, p. 229).

The Memoir was put together without any regard to literary style. In this respect it contrasts with the *Life* by Muirchu, as also by the fact that Tírechán supplies a number of chronological indications, while Muirchu's work furnishes no dates. In regard to contents, while the two works have a few incidents in common, Tírechán is mainly concerned with Patrick's work in parts of Ireland, especially Connaught, on which Muirchu does not touch at all. It is also to be observed (a point first emphasised by Dr. Gwynn) that Tírechán assumes on the part of his readers familiarity with

---

[1] Bury, *Tírechán's Memoir*, 239.

[2] $319_4$. Bury, "Supplementary Notes" (*Eng. Hist. Rev.* Oct. 1902), 702-703.

[3] It stops at p. 331, l. 9, in the Rolls ed. See my paper in *E.H.R. ut cit.* p. 237.

the general story of the saint's life. For instance, he refers to the call of the children of Fochlad as a familiar fact. We infer that the outline of the Patrician story was current in north Ireland in the time of Tírechán.

Though Tírechán had little idea of literary form, he has endeavoured to string together his information as to Patrick's activity in various places on a geographical thread. Critical examination shows (as I pointed out in a paper on Patrick's *Itinerary*,[1] and show more fully in a separate note, Appendix C, 13) that he has thrown the events of several journeys into one *circulus* or circular journey (setting out from Tara and returning to Meath) through Meath, Connaught, and Ulster.[2] It may be noted that Tírechán conceives all the events related in his Memoir as having happened during the year or two immediately following Patrick's arrival in Ireland, long before the foundation of Armagh;[3] and the fact that he makes Patrick, starting from Tara, return *finito circulo* to Loigaire and Conall seems to show that he conceived the bishop making his central quarters in Meath before he set up in Armagh.

An analysis, as well as criticism, of the Memoir will be found in Dr. Gwynn's *Introduction*, c. iii.

*Additions to Tírechán.*—In the *Lib. Arm.* a few notices are appended to the Memoir of Tírechán (ff. 15 vᵒ 2, 16 rᵒ a). They are the subject of a minute and careful discussion in Dr. Gwynn's *Introduction*, chap. vi. The first, on the three Petitions, was probably found in the MS. from which Ferdomnach copied the Memoir. It is separated by the word *Dairenne*, which has not been explained, from a number of notices which are probably (as Dr. Gwynn shows) due to Ferdomnach himself: (1) Patrick's age and the periods of his life; (2) comparison with Moses; (3) the contest for his body and Colombcille's discovery of his grave; (4) Patrick's mission by Celestine; Palladius also called Patricius; (5) Patrick's fourfold honour in Ireland; (6) a table of contents to "this *breviarium*" (I pointed out that this table refers not only to Tírechán's Memoir, but also to Muirchu's Life, *Eng. Hist. Rev.* April 1902, p. 237). Dr. Gwynn has shown in detail that these notes were suggested by passages in the preceding documents in the MS. (Muirchu and Tírechán), to which they may be regarded as editorial observations.

[1] *Proc. of R.I.A.* (xxiv. sect. C, 3), 1903, p. 164 *sqq.*
[2] This has been fully recognised by Dr. Gwynn, *loc. cit.*
[3] *Machia* (330₂₂) probably means Domnach Maigen, not Armagh (Gwynn, *loc. cit.*).

## 2. *Additional Notices in the "Liber Armachanus"*

These notices (ff. 16-19) are described by Ferdomnach as *serotinis temporibus inuenta,* and collected "by the diligence of the heirs"—that is, of Patrick's successors at Armagh. First comes the foundation of the Church of Trim, in Latin, but with Irish names and phrases ; then a few notices, chiefly of grants to Patrick in Connaught, Sligo, and Leitrim, also in Latin strewn with Irish forms ; then the text suddenly changes into Irish ($338_5$), diversified here and there by a Latin sentence, describing ecclesiastical grants, and acts of Patrick, in Connaught and Leinster. Then the scribe concludes with this apology :—

Finiunt haec pauca per Scotticam imperfecte scripta, non quod ego non potuissem Romana condere lingua, sed quod uix in sua Scotia hae fabulae agnosci possunt. Sin autem alias per Latinam degestae fuissent, non tam incertus fuisset aliquis in eis quam imperitus quid legisset aut quam linguam sonasset pro habundantia Scotaicorum nominum non habentium qualitatem.

He adds four Latin hexameters (with several false quantities), evidently of his own composition, formally declaring the completion of his task, and asking his readers to pray for him.

The scribe's explanation as to the language of his material is worthy of attention. It is clear that he had Irish material before him. Part of this material he translated into Latin, including the foundation of Trim, and the following notices up to $338_5$; but at this point, coming to a passage in which there were so many irreducible Irish words that there seemed little use in translating the few that could be translated, he simply transcribed his original. And he continued to do this to the end, although the same consideration does not apply to all the remaining text, with the exception of one or two passages which he turned into Latin ($340_{2-10}, 342_{1-11}$).

The importance of this lies in the fact that it reflects light on Tírechán. The similarity in character between these notices and those which Tírechán has wrought into his *Itinerary* is unmistakable, and points to the conclusion that he made use of Irish material, resembling in form and style that which the Armagh scribe partly translated and partly transcribed. The scribe, in fact, performed, though more slavishly, a task similar to that of Tírechán.

The scribe's own description of his additional material as

*serotinis temporibus inuenta,* "discovered in late times," naturally suggests a doubt whether these notices were not *inuenta* in a more pregnant sense than he intended to convey. We cannot control their antiquity, but their character is quite consistent with the supposition that they had escaped Tírechán when he was collecting local material, and had more recently been brought to the knowledge of Armagh, or collected by the care of the abbots. One passage ($337_{22}$) shows Armagh editing, and the whole collection is, like Tírechán's Memoir, in the interest of the Paruchia Patricii. But it is wholly different in character from the Armagh (eighth century) fiction, the *Liber Angueli*, and we can hardly be mistaken in supposing that genuine local records are here transcribed or translated.

(1) The Trim narrative is evidently translated from an Irish document. It contains a list of the lay succession at Trim from Fergus, grandson of Loigaire, and the last name is Sechnassach, tenth in succession from Loigaire. This, Dr. Gwynn observes, points to the later part of the eighth century as the date of Sechnassach, so that "this record was written at (or up to) a date which was almost recent when Ferdomnach used it." Probably the date of Sechnassach represents the time at which the record was obtained from Trim by an abbot of Armagh.

(2) The series of Connaught records and copies of grants begins a new leaf in the MS., and are evidently copied from a distinct batch of documents. An analysis of them will be found in Dr. Gwynn's *Introduction*, chap. vi.

(3) The Leinster records also begin a new leaf, the second half column of the preceding page being left blank. It may be conjectured that these notices were communicated to Armagh by Bishop Aed of Slébte (cp. below, p. 255) towards the close of the seventh century. This is strongly suggested by the circumstance that a notice of Aed's visit to Armagh immediately follows ($346_{21}$). The juxtaposition is almost irresistible. Dr. Gwynn (*Introduction*, chap. vi.) arrived independently at the same conclusion.

It would seem that after finishing his work the Armagh scribe gained access to a collection of Irish material describing St. Patrick's acts. He did not undertake the task of transcribing or translating it, but simply indexed it. This long list of abbreviated memoranda, which he has appended in small script, consists of names of places and people, associated with acts of St. Patrick, not recorded in the preceding documents. The traditions which these headings represent—they are almost entirely in Irish—are

for the most part found in the *Vita Tripartita* (see below, p. 272);
and Dr. Gwynn, who has made a careful study of the material,
has pointed out that it is disposed in groups corresponding more
or less to geographical regions (see his *Introduction*, chap. vi.).

Probably, however, he did not index the whole of his document. It may be shown, I think, that the scribe had before him
part of the same material which Tírechán used, and that the
object was to note those parts of it which Tírechán had not
incorporated in his Memoir. The ground for this conclusion is
that he has, through inadvertence, inserted references to a few
acts which are found in Tírechán. Thus the first two jottings [1]
correspond to Tírechán $31 3_4$ and $31 4_{13-22}$. Dr. Gwynn, however, has made (*ib.*) the important suggestion that Ferdomnach
simply transcribed memoranda which were left among the papers
of the Abbot Torbach, under whose direction he undertook the
task of copying and putting together the Patrician documents.
If he completed the MS., as is probable, after his master's death,
he would feel bound to include the matter, collected by Torbach,
as he found it, however obscure. This hypothesis seems very
probable. If it is true, my view would still hold, with the
substitution of Torbach for Ferdomnach.

An interesting proof of the antiquity of this material has been
discovered by the acuteness of Dr. MacCarthy. Patrick's dealings with the sons of Forat in Múscraige Tíre are described in
*Vit. Trip.* 210, and indicated in *Lib. Arm.* f. 19 r° b ($351_3$:
Fuirg Muindech Mechar, f. Forat). Patrick is alleged to have
given a lasting blessing to Mechar, who believed, whereas Fuirg,
who did not believe in him, is "to be in misery till doom."
Dr. MacCarthy has pointed out that these prophecies are
inconsistent with the history of the descendants of both brothers.
The seed of Mechar did not survive. We learn this from the
Genealogy of Múscraige Tíre (in *Book of Ballymote*, 141 b, and
*Book of Leinster*, 323 f.; extracts in MacCarthy's paper).[2] Dr.
MacCarthy thinks that the extinction of the line is to be placed
about the middle of the sixth century. On the other hand, the
descendants of Fuirg prospered; they were a distinguished and

---

[1] $348_{18}$, d.g. [ = *Duma Graid*, Reeves, but this is far from certain]; Ailbe
i Senchui altáre; and Machet Cetchen Rodán Mathona. Compare also $350_8$
with $331_4$.

[2] The credibility of the Genealogy, as an independent record, is particularly
strong; the Ballymote scribe was acquainted with the *Tripartite*, and quotes
from it *à propos* of the sons of Forat, notwithstanding the contradiction. The
discrepancy with the Patrician tradition is, in fact, a guarantee that the record
is trustworthy.

important clan in the ninth and tenth centuries (see the evidence which Dr. MacCarthy has collected from the *Annals*, Note D.).

The inference is that the record of Patrick's dealings with the sons of Forat had taken shape before the respective destinies of the posterities of Mechar and Fuirg could be foreseen.

### 3. *Life of Patrick, by Muirchu*

The first formal biography that we possess, perhaps the first formal biography that was written, was composed by MUIRCHU towards the end of the seventh century. Muirchu is designated as *maccu Machtheni*, son or descendant of Machthene. He refers to his father Coguitosus,[1] and there may be room for doubt whether a natural or spiritual father is meant. If the suggestion [2] that Coguitosus is a Latin rendering of Machthene (as connected with *machtnaigim*, "I consider with wonder") is correct, Cogitosus was Muirchu's father in the flesh.

There can be no doubt that Muirchu lived in North Laigin, and perhaps he may be specially associated with Co. Wicklow. The evidence is (1) his close association with Bishop Aed of Slébte (on the borders of Co. Carlow), to whom he dedicated his book, addressing him *mi domine Aido*, and from whom he derived material for it; (2) the existence of Kilmurchon "Church of Muirchu" in Co. Wicklow;[3] and, we may add (3), the connexion of Muirchu's "father" Cogitosus with this part of Ireland, a connexion fairly to be inferred from his writing a Life of Brigit of Kildare.

The fact that Muirchu lived and wrote in the latter part of the seventh century is established by the date of his friend Bishop Aed's death, which is recorded in the *Annals* as A.D. 700,[4] and by the circumstance that he as well as Aed attended the Synod known as " Adamnan's," which met shortly before that date (A.D. 697, *Ann. Ult.*).[5] As Muirchu's book is dedicated to

---

[1] P. 269₁₃ Rolls ed.: *patris mei Coguitosi*, the brilliant correction of Bishop Graves for the corrupt *cognito si* in A. On the passage, and on Cogitosus, see his paper in the *Proceedings R.I.A.* viii. 269 *sqq.*

[2] See Graves, *ib.* The conjecture is accepted by Dr. Stokes (*Trip. Life*, 269, note 2).

[3] Colgan, *Acta SS.* p. 465 and *n.* 31.      [4] *Ann. Ult. s.a.*

[5] See Reeves, *Adamnan*, pp. l. li. Professor Kuno Meyer has just published an old Irish treatise on the " Law of Adamnan " passed at this synod (" Cáin Adamnáin," in *Anecdota Oxoniensia*, 1905). The document contains a list of the bishops, abbots, and kings present at the synod which was held at Birr. Muirchu appears (p. 18): Murchu maccúi Machthéine. Muirchu appears in the Martyrologies under June 8 (see *Calendar of Oengus*, ed. Stokes, p. xciii.).

Aed (as still living), A.D. 699 is the lower limit for its composition.

Or perhaps more strictly for the composition of Book I. For Muirchu has divided his work into two Books. The ground of the division is not quite evident. One might have thought that Book I. would naturally have terminated with the episode of Loigaire, where the chronological order ceases. Now at the end of the Table of Contents to Book I. there occurs a notice (of which more will be said below) that Aed helped him; and it might be held that the distinction between Book I. and Book II. was based on the fact that he had Aed's co-operation in Book I. and not in Book II. In that case Book I. might have been composed before, and Book II. after, Aed's death.[1] If so, the Preface was written before Book II.

In this interesting dedicatory preface, written in a most turgid style, and partly modelled on the opening verses of St. Luke's Gospel, Muirchu declares, or seems to declare, that he is venturing upon a novel experiment, which had been tried before (in Ireland) only by his father Cogitosus. It is of considerable importance to know on Muirchu's authority that the Life of Brigit by Cogitosus[2] was a new departure in hagiography in Ireland. As Cogitosus must have written in the seventh century, it follows that before the seventh century hagiographical literature in Ireland must have differed materially in character from the works of Cogitosus and his son. One difference possibly was that the earlier writings, some of which Muirchu used (see below), consisted of *acta* and *memorabilia*, and were not regular biographies; but there are grounds, as will be shown, for inferring a more important difference, namely, that they were written in Irish.

Muirchu aspired to do for Patrick what his father had done for Brigit. But in venturing into what he calls the "deep and perilous sea of sacred story," he may have been helped by Aed. From the lemma[3] which is found at the end of the Table of Contents to Book I., one might think that Aed has even more claim to be considered the author than Muirchu. *Haec... Muirchu... dictante Aiduo... conscripsit.* Taken by itself, this might almost suggest that Muirchu's share in the work was little more than that of a scribe. But such an inference is completely contradicted by the dedicatory preface, in which Muirchu takes upon himself the

---

[1] I suggested this in the *Guardian*, Nov. 20, 1901, p. 1615, c. 2.

[2] Muirchu does not name his father's work, but his expression *ingenioli mei* ($269_{14}$) may be an echo of the *rusticus sermo ingenioli mei* in the prologue to the *Vita Brigidae*.     [3] $271_{17}$.

whole responsibility, though he acknowledges that he had undertaken the work in obedience to a wish of Aed.[1] If, then, the
lemma has any good authority,—it may be doubted whether it
is due to the author himself,[2]—we must interpret it to mean that
Aed furnished Muirchu with some of the material. But it is
possible that the note has no good authority, and merely
expresses the misconception of a copyist.

Muirchu used written sources. He refers to them in his
Preface in the phrase *incertis auctoribus*, which seems rather to
imply that the documents were anonymous than that he was
sceptical about their statements. In regard to the character of
the sources, it is important to observe that there is a strongly
marked contrast between the early portion of the biography up to
Patrick's arrival in Ireland and the rest of the book. The early
portion is free from the mythical element; whereas the narrative
of Patrick's work in Ireland is characterised by its legendary
setting. These two parts must therefore be carefully distinguished.

In the first part, the best of all authorities, the *Confession*, is
followed (though not without errors in interpretation[3]) so far as
it goes; then another source succeeds, dealing with Patrick's
studies on the Continent and his ordination, and including a
notice of Palladius. It seems, however, not unlikely that for
Muirchu these two sources may have been one; that he may
not have used the *Confession* itself, but a document in which the
*Confession* and the other source had been already condensed. In
any case, that other source is marked by the absence of mythical
elements and stamps itself as dependent on early and credible
records.[4] Nor are other possible traces of this source entirely
lacking. It may well be that it was also utilised by the author
of the *liber apud Ultanum* which was consulted by Tírechán.

But when Muirchu's story passes to Ireland it assumes a
different complexion. We enter a world beset by legends. But
here too Muirchu used written sources. A legendary narrative
had been shaped and written down before his time. The evidence
that he used written material here is as follows :—

(1) He refers to writings himself ($295_{16}$): *miracula tanta quae*

---

[1] $269_{19}$.

[2] This is suggested by the use of the third person. In the Preface
Muirchu writes in the first person. The note is similar to the note which is
prefixed to the memoir of Tírechán and is obviously due to a copyist.

[3] See $495_3$ Rolls ed. (ad Britanias nauigauit), and $495_{26}-$ (the second
captivity).

[4] Some mistakes have occurred in the course of compilation and transmission: see below, p. 348.

*alibi scripta sunt et quae ore fideli mundus celebrat.* This seems to imply some stories that were known to him only by oral tradition.

(2) The accounts given by Muirchu and Tírechán of the destruction of the magician who was shot into the air depend on a common written source;[1] and their notices of the angel's foot-steps at Scirte point in the same direction.[2] A comparison of these passages suggests that they are independent translations of a common Irish original.

(3) I have shown[3] that the Lives which are known as *Vita Secunda* and *Vita Quarta* depend on a document (W), whose compiler probably used not only Muirchu but Muirchu's source, which must have been written in Irish.

(4) This conclusion is confirmed by the evidence which I collected in a paper on "Sources of the Early Patrician Documents" (*Eng. Hist. Review*, July 1904). It is there shown that (*a*) the prophecy of the magicians (p. 274), and (*b*) the description of MacCuil's character (p. 286) reproduce Irish poetical sources. The proof lies in the tabular (columnar) arrangement of these passages in the *Liber Armachanus*, combined with their rhythmic and assonant character. In that article I also pointed out that the Irish material used by Muirchu began with the account of Patrick's ordination (if not at an earlier point), the proof being the form *Amathorege* for Amator of Auxerre. "Muirchu's *Amatorege* represents *Amathorig* and betrays that his source was in Irish." (On the form compare Zimmer, *Nennius Vindicatus*, p. 123 *note*).

The question arises whether part of the written material used by Muirchu, under Aed's guidance, originated at Sletty (Slébte). There is nothing decisive on this point in the text of Muirchu; for the notice of Fíacc's presence at Tara may have been inserted by him, from Sletty tradition, in a narrative which did not otherwise depend on Sletty tradition. That this was really the case seems to me to be shown by the fact that (as mentioned above) Tírechán used the same source as Muirchu for an incident in the Tara episode. This fact makes it difficult to suppose that Muirchu's account of that episode was based on Sletty tradition derived from Fíacc. The legend naturally arose in the regions of Tara and Slane.

[1] See Bury, *Tírechán's Memoir of St. Patrick*, p. 16; but I did not see then that the source was probably Irish.

[2] Tírechán, $330_{15-19}$: Muirchu, $276_{11-14}$, and $300_{10-13}$: Bury, *ib.* p. 14.

[3] "The Tradition of Muirchu's Text," in *Hermathena*, xxviii. pp. 199 *sqq.*

There is, however, another fact which must be considered. There is a presumption that the hymn *Genair Patraicc*, ascribed to Fíacc, was composed at Sletty, and this presumption is strengthened by the remarkable correspondence of the argument of the hymn with the argument of Muirchu's biography. The hymn will be discussed below, and it will be pointed out that its author used either Muirchu or (part of) Muirchu's material. In the latter case it would follow that this material existed at Sletty. But even then it need not have been derived from Fíacc or Sletty traditions contemporary with Patrick. Sletty might in the meantime have obtained copies of records existing at Armagh or elsewhere.

For these reasons I do not feel able to speak of a Sletty tradition with as much confidence as Dr. Gwynn. He traces this, or at least Leinster, tradition, not only in the narrative of Slane and Tara, but also in the Gallic portion.[1]

On the other hand, there can be no doubt that the Ulidian portions of Muirchu depend on a Ulidian or Down tradition. This has been set forth fully and lucidly by Dr. Gwynn. I think, however, that it must remain an open question whether Muirchu, as Dr. Gwynn is disposed to believe, visited Down and collected information on the spot. The local colouring might have been taken from a written source. In any case he used a written source (also used by Tírechán) for the Slemish episode.

For a full running analysis of Muirchu's work I may refer to Dr. Gwynn's *Introduction* (chaps. ii. and iii.) ; but I must indicate the remarkable construction of Book II., which he was the first to explain. The theme with which it opens is Patrick's diligence in prayer (sect. 1), which is illustrated (sect. 2) by the story of the dead man and the cross, which leads to another story (sect. 3) told on the authority of the auriga of Patrick. Then the narrative passes to the circumstances connected with Patrick's death and burial; after which there is a final section in which the author (with the words *Iterum recurrat oratio*) recurs to the initial subject, *De diligentia orationis*.[2] The sections which recount the

---

[1] On account of the notice of Auxilius (of Killossy) and Iserninus (of Kilcullen). It seems very probable that the notice of Iserninus in the *Liber Arm.* (f. 18) may have been derived from information furnished by Bishop Aed on the occasion of his visit to Armagh. See above p. 253.

[2] In the Table of Contents to Book II. this is the title of the first and the last section alike ; but the last item in the table was wrongly taken to be a heading of sect. 1 (though there are no other headings to the sections), until the true explanation was pointed out by Dr. Gwynn.

saint's death and burial form a separate unity within the framework, and there is external evidence which Dr. Gwynn has with
great probability interpreted as showing that this narrative was a
distinct document which Muirchu incorporated. The evidence
consists in two numerals (ui and uiii) which occur in the MS.
(fol. 8, r⁰ b), and must be explained as two of an original series
of numbers which occurred in the exemplar which the scribe
Ferdomnach had before him. These numbers could not have
represented the numbers of the sections of the whole Book (as
given in the Table of Contents), but they correspond exactly to
the sections of the narrative of the death and burial. This will
be best shown by a tabular arrangement.

Sections of Book II.

| | | | | | | |
|---|---|---|---|---|---|---|
| De Patr. delig. orationis | . | . | . | . | 1 | |
| De mortuo ad se loquente | . | . | . | . | 2 | |
| De inluminata dom. nocte, etc. | . | . | . | 3 | | |

Sections of incor-
porated document.

| | | | | | | | |
|---|---|---|---|---|---|---|---|
| De eo quod anguelus, etc. | . | . | . | . | 4 | = | [i] |
| De rubo ardente, etc. | . | . | . | . | 5 | = | [ii] |
| De quatuor Patr. petitionibus | . | . | , | 6 | = | [iii] | |
| De die mortis, etc. | . | . | . | . | 7 | = | [iiii] |
| De termino contra noctem possito ⎫ De caligine xii. noctium abstersa ⎭ | . | . | 8 | = | [u] | | |
| [De sacrificio accepto] . | . | . | . | . | 9 | = | ui |
| De vigilis primae noctis, etc. | . | . | . | 10 | = | [uii] | |
| De consilio sepulturae, etc. | . | . | . | 11 | = | uiii | |
| De igne de sepulchro, etc. | . | . | . | 12 | = | [ix] | |
| De freto sussum surgente, etc. | . | . | 13 | = | [x] | | |
| De felici seductione populorum | . | . | 14 | = | [xi] | | |

| | | | | | | |
|---|---|---|---|---|---|---|
| De diligentia orationis . | . | . | . | . | 15 | |

This incorporated document, however, with its signs of a
distinct numbering of its chapters, was composed (as the style
testifies) by Muirchu himself; it was not a mere transcription.
I therefore think that the sectional numberings did not belong to
Muirchu's source; but rather that this narrative was compiled
first by Muirchu with the intention that it should form Book II.
and that he numbered its sections accordingly; so that its
opening words, *Post uero miracula tanta*, etc., were the transition
from Book I. to Book II. Afterwards he changed his arrangement, by the introduction of the three chapters, which he made
the beginning of Book II.; this altered the numbering of the
chapters, and in transcribing his narrative of the death and burial
he was obliged to leave out the numbers; but he transcribed

two of them by inadvertence, and they were faithfully retranscribed by Ferdomnach.

In regard to the Tables of Contents, it might perhaps be suggested that they may have been added by an editor, and not drawn up by Muirchu himself. It is important to show that such a suggestion is untenable. A definite proof that Muirchu is responsible may be found in the last heading of the Table of Book I. There we read *aduersum Coirthech regem Aloo*, whereas in the text of the corresponding section, though the Irish form of the name Coroticus (MS. *Corictic*) occurs, he is not described as *rex Aloo*. Obviously the title is not due to an editor summarising the contents of the Latin text, but to Muirchu himself, who had before him an Irish document containing the legend of the metamorphosis of Coroticus. This is sufficient to establish Muirchu's authorship for the Tables.

Muirchu belonged to that part of Ireland which had conformed to Roman usage since c. A.D. 634, and in this interest he took part in Adamnan's Synod which brought about the conformity of the north. It would indeed be erroneous to suppose that these facts are required to explain the expression which he uses of the Roman see (*caput omnium ecclesiarum totius mundi*)—an expression which he might readily have used even if he had been an adherent of the Celtic celebration of Easter. But it may be asked whether the Life which Muirchu wrote at the wish of Aed had any tendency beyond its mere hagiographical interest. There is, I think, some reason for supposing that it had a particular motive. When Muirchu wrote, the church of Slébte had just been brought into close connexion with Armagh. The record stands thus in the *Liber Armachanus* (fol. 18, r° b ; p. 346 Rolls ed.), as translated by Stokes :—

Bishop Aed was in Slébte. He went to Armagh. He brought a bequest to Segéne of Armagh. Segéne gave another bequest to Aed, and Aed offered a bequest and his kin and his church to Patrick for ever.

We cannot hesitate to bring this visit of Aed to Armagh, and his dedication of Slébte to Patrick, into connexion with the interest which he evinced in Patrick's life, when he stimulated Muirchu to undertake the biography. So much seems clear. It is another question what was the motive of policy which drew

Aed so closely to Armagh; and it is yet another whether we can discover any reflexion of such a motive in Muirchu's work. Segéne, the abbot of Armagh, died in A.D. 688,[1] so that Aed's visit must have occurred before that date. During the penultimate decade of the century many must have been trying to prepare the way for bringing about uniformity between northern and southern Ireland, by inducing the north to accept the Roman usages which had, more than a generation ago, been accepted by the south. It is a reasonable conjecture that Aed, who took part in the Synod which afterwards brought about this result, was working towards it in his dealings with Armagh. And it certainly is not impossible that, in giving such a prominent place in his narrative to the legend of Patrick's first Easter in Ireland, Muirchu was thinking of the Easter controversy.[2]

In any case, it is significant that just at the time, or just on the eve, of the reconciliation of north and south, an ecclesiastic of south Ireland, whose name is associated with that reconciliation, should have given to the world a Life of Patrick, which, if it had come down to us anonymously, we should assuredly suppose to have been written in the north, and perhaps guess to have emanated from Armagh. No mention is made of traditions connecting Patrick with south-eastern Ireland—with the country of Muirchu—though such traditions existed. The notice of Fíacc's relics at Slébte is indeed a local touch, but one which could never have suggested a clew, since there is a precisely similar notice of Ercc's relics at Slane. Muirchu was eclectic; he had much more material than he used; so he expressly tells us, *pauca haec de multis sancti Patricii gestis*. It is to be noticed that apart from the events connected with the celebration of the first Easter, and apart from a number of unlocalised miracles, the *gesta* of Patrick which Muirchu describes are entirely laid in Ulster—at Armagh and in Ulidia. The tradition of Daire was, of course, preserved at Armagh; and the legend of the appearance of the angel to Patrick before his death bears on the face of it its Armagh origin. It seems probable, therefore, that some of Muirchu's written material was derived directly from Armagh; and we can hardly be charged with going beyond our data if we regard Muirchu's biography as setting a seal upon the new relation which had been established between Slébte and St. Patrick's church.

Muirchu's Life had a marked influence on all subsequent

---

[1] *Ann. Ult. s.a.*
[2] This is the conjecture of Zimmer, *Celtic Church*, p. 81.

Patrician biographies. It established a framework of narrative which later compilers adopted, fitting in material from other sources.

The text of Muirchu is preserved incompletely in A, the missing parts are supplied by a late MS. preserved at Brussels;[1] and later compilations (*Vita Secunda*, *Vita Quarta*, *Probus*) furnish help for criticising the text. See Bury, "The Tradition of Muirchu's Text," *cit. supra.*

## (4) *Hymn Genair Patraicc*

An Irish hymn on the life of St. Patrick, generally known as the HYMN OF FÍACC, or (from its first words) the hymn GENAIR PATRAICC, is included in the collections of Irish hymns preserved in two MSS. of the eleventh (Trinity College, Dublin, E, 4, 2) and eleventh or twelfth (Library of Franciscan Convent, Dublin) century. The MSS. ascribe the authorship to the poet Fíacc, who lived in the time of Patrick and became bishop of Slébte (Muirchu, 283₃); but this ascription is clearly false, not only from philological considerations, since the language points to a date which could not be much anterior to A.D. 800, but also from the evidence of the first verse—

Patrick was born in Nemthur, this is what he *narrates in stories*,

and the 12th verse—

He read the Canon with Germanus, this is what *writings narrate*,

expressions which show that the sources of the author were written documents, and that he could not have been a contemporary. There is also in v. 44 a reference to an event which occurred in A.D. 561, the abandonment of Tara, but this (see below) was probably not part of the original poem.[2]

The hymn was acutely analysed by Professor Zimmer in his *Keltische Studien*, ii. 162 *sqq.*,[3] and more soberly and judiciously by Professor Atkinson in the Introduction to the *Liber Hymnorum* (ed. Bernard and Atkinson, vol. ii.), pp. xl. *sqq.*

---

[1] These parts were first published by Rev. E. Hogan, *Anal. Boll.* vol. i. I have had the advantage of using a photograph of the MS., kindly given me by Dr. Gwynn.

[2] See also Todd, *St. Patrick*, 489; Stokes, Intr. to *Tripartite*, cxi. *sq.*; Bernard and Atkinson, *Liber Hymnorum*, ii. 175-6.

[3] Criticised by Thurneysen, *Revue celtique*, 6, 326 *sqq.*, who rejects the theory of interpolation except in the case of stanza 17. So too Stokes and Strachan.

Professor Atkinson submits it to a careful criticism from the metrical side, dealing also with linguistic points and the literary construction, and his analysis leads to the same general conclusion as Professor Zimmer's, namely, that the hymn has been largely interpolated, and that its original compass was very much smaller. I examined the work independently, from the literary side, and found that most of the stanzas which from this point of view arouse suspicion are those which Professor Atkinson, applying his objective metrical tests, branded as interpolations. It may be useful to give here the original uninterpolated hymn, as it emerges from these criticisms. It contained 15, instead of 34, stanzas.[1] I have adopted Professor Atkinson's translation, but with some changes, using the new lights furnished in the version of Dr. Stokes and Professor Strachan.

### Hymn Genair Patraicc

1. Patrick was born in Nemthur, this is what he narrates in stories ;
   A youth of sixteen years, when he was brought under tears.

2. [Sucat his name, it was said; what his father was, were worth knowing;
   Son of Calpurn, son of Potid, *grandson of deacon Odisse.*]

3. He was six years in bondage ; *men's good cheer he shared not.*
   *Many were they whom he served, Cothraige* (servant) *of four households.*

4. Said Victor to Milchu's bondsman, that he should go over the waves ;
   He struck his foot on the stone, its trace remains, it fades not.

5. (The angel) sent him *across all Britain*—great God, it was a marvel of a course !
   So that he left him with Germanus in the south, in the southern part of Letha.

6. *In the isles of the Tyrrhene Sea he fasted, in them he computed,*
   He read the Canon with Germanus, that is what writings narrate.

7. A help to Ireland was Patrick's coming, which was expected ;
   Far away was heard the sound of the call of the children of Fochlad wood.

---

[1] The stanzas which are abnormal, or defective, in metre, assonance, etc., are—2, 7, 9, 12, 14, 15, 17, 24, 26, 27, 29, 30, 31, 33 (for criticisms on their subject-matter see Atkinson, *ib.* xliii. *sqq.*). Stanza 16 has a " glossatorial " character (*ib.* xlviii.). The ejection of 10 on ground of subject-matter may be confirmed by the abnormal endings (*nua* and *tua*, cp. Atkinson, xlii.). 18 (rejected by Zimmer and Atkinson) is clearly an imitation of 18, and this is indicated by the repetition of the rhymes. The rejection of 19 and 20 depends on the subject-matter, and 21 repeats 19. The irrelevance of 22 is obvious. I leave the second stanza as doubtful, for though there is a metrical anomaly (*daec* a disyllable), there is no objection on the ground of the subject-matter ; but it could be dispensed with.

8. His druids from Loigaire hid not Patrick's coming ;
   The prophecy was fulfilled of the prince of which they spoke.

9. Hymns and Apocalypse, the Three Fifties, he used to sing them ;
   He preached, baptized, prayed ; from God's praise he ceased not.

10. Patrick preached to the Scots, he suffered great labour widely.
    That around him they may come to Judgement, every one whom he
    brought to life.[1]

11. When Patrick was ailing, he longed to go to Armagh :
    An angel went to meet him on the road at mid-day.

12. He said, "(Leave thy) dignity to Armagh, to Christ give thanks ;
    To heaven thou shalt soon go : thy prayers have been granted thee."

13. (Patrick) set a boundary against night that no light might be wasted
    with him :
    Up to the end of a year there was light ; that was a long day of peace !

14. Patrick's soul from his body after labours was severed ;
    God's angels on the first night kept watch thereon unceasingly.

15. Patrick, without sign of pride, much good he meditated ;
    To be in the service of Mary's son, it was a pious fortune to which he
    was born.

It has been supposed that the author of the hymn made use
of Muirchu's Life. This was suggested by Loofs (*Ant. Britonum
Scotorumque Ecclesiae*, 42 *sqq.*), and seems plausible not only
on account of the resemblances, but also because Muirchu
was connected with Aed of Slébte, and the attribution of the
hymn to Fíacc of Slébte suggests that it was composed there.
But there are some statements which are not found in Muirchu
(I have indicated them by italics in the foregoing text), so that
Muirchu's Life cannot, in any case, have been the only source.
There is no reason why the author might not have used some of
the documents which supplied Muirchu himself with information.[2]
If so, the hymn would be an independent testimony for that lost
material (whereas if it is based on Muirchu it has no historical
importance whatever, except in so far as the few statements not
found in Muirchu might depend on an older source than any
that we possess). In support of this view it may be urged
that, if the writer's main source was Muirchu, it is strange that
he has not embodied any of the portions of Muirchu which rest
on Ulidian tradition. This circumstance suggests that he used the
documents on which the other parts of Muirchu's Life were based.
It is perhaps significant that the statements concerning Cothraige

---

[1] Cp. Muirchu, 296₁₂.
[2] See Bury, *Guardian*, Nov. 27, 1901, p. 1647.

in 3 and the Tyrrhene islands in 6 are found in Tírechán, in connexion with the fact that one source of Muirchu had also been used by Tírechán.

[It may be noted that, in the interpolated stanza 26, the hymn, which is to be a *lorica* (lurech) to every one, is not the Hymn of Secundinus, as has been generally held, but, as Professor Atkinson has pointed out (*Lib. Hymn.* ii. xliv.) the "lorica" of Patrick.]

The most recent editions of the Hymn with the glosses are that of Atkinson (*Liber Hymnorum*, i. 96 *sqq.* ; English version in ii. 31 *sqq.*), and that of Stokes and Strachan (*Thesaurus Palaeohibernicus*, ii. 307 *sqq.*), who date the hymn about A.D. 800.

## 5. *Early Acts in Irish*

It has appeared in the foregoing pages that an analysis of Tírechán, Muirchu, and the Additional Notices discloses the existence of an early Patrician literature in Irish, of which a writer in the seventh century could avail himself; and it may be useful to emphasise this important conclusion by stating it under a distinct heading.

The Preface to Muirchu's Life is weighty in this connexion. The novel movement of which he designates his father Cogitosus and himself as pioneers was the writing of hagiography (*narratio sancta*) *in Latin.* Hagiography already existed in Ireland ; he implies, and refers to, written documents ; and analysis shows that he used Irish documents. Thus before the seventh century the hagiographical literature which entertained the pious in Ireland was composed in their own language ; and it was not till the age of Cogitosus and Tírechán that a new departure was made, and men began to write Latin works on Irish saints. But the demand for Irish Lives, for the mass of the folk who could not understand Latin, continued ; and the *Vita Tripartita* (see below) may be regarded as a descendant from the early Irish *acta*.

Some of these *acta*, such as the account of the episode of Slane and Tara, may have had wide circulation in different kingdoms; and there may have been different versions. Others may have had only local circulation, such as the Ulidian stories garnered by Muirchu, and the Connaught traditions collected by Tírechán. Besides, many communities which ascribed their foundation to Patrick seem to have preserved written records of grants, which, whether genuine or not, were old and drafted in Irish.

The Acts of Patrick which circulated in the sixth century

supplied the public with what they liked—miraculous legends in a historical setting. But the legends which Muirchu derived from this source differ strikingly from the ordinary apparatus of the hagiographer—from the miracles, for instance, so colourless and monotonous which Adamnan has strung together in his wearisome Life of Columba. The Patrician legends, to which I refer, were worked up in the cells of ecclesiastics ; but the arguments of the stories, which they moulded, were created by popular imagination, and suggested by the motives of "folklore." Such, for instance, is the story of the first Easter, inspired by a transference of Beltane customs to Easter Eve. Such are the Ulidian stories associated with the salt marshes at Lake Strangford. Such, we may con-jecture, is the story of the ogre MacCuill, who tempts Patrick, is converted, and then, sent to drift in a boat of skin, without oar or helm, reaches the Isle of Man, of which he becomes bishop. Some old legend, connecting Man with the coast of Dalaradia, seems here to have been hooked on to Patrick ; and perhaps MacCuill, of Cyclopean type, may be the mythical MacCuill, "son of hazel," husband of Banba. But in any case we may take it that the name of a mythical ogre, familiar in the folklore of the regions of Lake Strangford, supplied popular imagination with a motif for a story of Patrick's power.

But historical tradition was also present, determining and contributing. The Ulidian legends were determined by the memory of Patrick's actual and close association with Ulidia ; the legend of his appearance at Tara, by the memory of an actual visit ; the whole story of his relations with Loigaire, by Loigaire's loyalty to paganism. And we can detect genuine details, handed down by tradition, and embedded, like metallic particles, in the myth. Such is the notice of the presence of the poet Dubthach at Tara, when Patrick was there. It has all the appearance of being a true historical tradition, like the incident of Simon of Cyrene in the story of the Crucifixion of Jesus.

The character as well as the language of the hagiographical stories, which were doubtless read aloud in the pulpit, was deter-mined by the needs of the public for which they were intended. The excellent remarks of Professor W. Meyer, in the introduction to *Die Legende des h. Albanus* (1904), apply here. The chief object in these compositions was to produce "a strong impression" on the faithful (*ein starker Eindruck auf die Glaubensgenossen*). "Die Legenden wurden christliche Unterhaltungsliteratur. Solche Literatur schmiegt sich dem Empfinden des Volkes an und das Volk schafft selbst dabei mit. Die glänzenden Gedanken und die glänzende Darstellung der Caecilialegende entspricht der feinen Kultur Roms im 5. Jahrhundert; die phrasenhafte oder die unbeholfene Darstellung, mit welcher die so verschiedenen Freunde Fortunat und Gregor von Tours platte Kleinigkeiten umhüllen, entspricht ihrer Zeit, wo der Massstab des Schönen gänzlich fehlte " (p. 5).

### 6. *Vita Secunda* ($V_2$) *and Vita Quarta* ($V_4$)

The two anonymous Lives, most conveniently distinguished by their order in the *Trias Thaumaturga* of Colgan, who first published them,[1] are closely related, and taken together have considerable importance for the criticism of Muirchu's Life. A full comparison between the two documents will be found in my paper on the " Tradition of Muirchu's Text " (*Hermathena*, 1902, 186 *sqq.*). Both follow the order of Muirchu up to the end of the Tara episode, and at this point our text of $V_2$ stops abruptly. There is a close parallelism throughout. $V_4$ is rather more prolix, and has some notices which are not in $V_2$; but $V_2$ has also notices which are not in $V_4$, and has some Irish sentences which do not appear, or appear in a Latin equivalent, in $V_4$.[2] In the parts dependent on Muirchu, $V_2$ is closer to Muirchu. The comparison shows that neither document depends on the other, but both on a common source which I have designated W, the tenor of which can be, almost mechanically, reconstructed. It can then be shown that W was not simply a MS. of Muirchu, but " a document which was sometimes a free paraphrase, sometimes a close copy " of Muirchu (but derived from a MS. of Muirchu of different lineage from that contained in the *Lib. Arm.*). But it must have been something more. For there are a number of passages in $V_2$ and $V_4$ which are not in Muirchu, and " the close parallelism between $V_2$ and $V_4$ throughout, and not merely in the Muirchu portions, makes it practically certain that, in the other portions too, they were both following " the same source, namely W. Thus W was a compilation based on Muirchu and some other source (or sources).

The antiquity of this source is proved by the following facts : (1) Cothraige, the Goidelic form of Patricius, appears in an older form with initial *q* (*Quadriga, Quotirche*), which points to a document older than the seventh century (since Tírechán

---

[1] There is no other edition.

[2] I have shown, from misunderstandings in $V_4$ that its author was ignorant of Irish, while the author of $V_2$ was an Irishman (*op. cit.* 197).

has initial *c*); (2) this Goidelic name, not Patricius, appears in the part of W which related Patrick's dealings with Miliucc; (3) the name Succet takes the place of "Quadriga" where his sister Lupita recognises him, as it is the name by which she would have known him : such traits of verisimilitude are not likely to have been introduced by late compilers. It is probable that this source was in Irish. This would account for the Irish bits in W preserved in $V_2$. And the Irish source, from which W supplemented Muirchu, probably resembled (being based on the same material) the Irish source which Muirchu used for his Life. In this connexion it is to be observed that W and Muirchu give variant renderings of the prophecy of the Druids, pointing to variant versions of the Irish original.

As for the latter part of $V_4$, where $V_2$ fails us, it seems probable that W was also a source, though there may have been other sources (cp. Bury, *Tradition*, etc., p. 195).[1]

### 7. *Vita Tripartita*

A Life of Patrick written in Irish (but largely interspersed with Latin passages and clauses) is extant. A Latin translation of it was published by Colgan, who named it the *Vita Tripartita* because it is divided into three parts. This translation represents a different text from that preserved in the two existing MSS. from which Dr. Stokes published the *editio princeps* of the Irish text (Rolls Series, 1887). This edition can hardly claim to be critical, as no attempt whatever is made to establish the mutual relations of the MSS.[2] It is clear, even on a superficial examination, that the two extant MSS. imply an archetype representing a tradition different from the text which Colgan followed.

A study of the language of the Life, which is full of "Middle-Irish" forms, led Dr. Stokes to conclude that it was compiled in the eleventh century (*Introd.* pp. lxiv *sqq.*). The text contains several references to events of the ninth century (*ib.* p. lxiii);

---

[1] Dr. W. Levison of Bonn kindly called my attention to a *Vita* preserved at St. Omer which proves to be a copy of the *Vita Secunda* different from that used by Colgan. It is contained in Cod. 716 (*Legendarium beatae Mariae de Claromarisco*), a book of the thirteenth century, vol. ii. ff. 155-9. For the text of *Vita Quarta*, the Stowe MS. 105A (Brit. Mus.) is important (see my *Tradition*, etc., p. 186 *note*).

[2] Except so far as to show that neither of the two existing MSS. was used by Colgan. The text is based on Rawlinson B. 512, but it is not explained why this was chosen as the basis in preference to Egerton 93 (which—I speak under correction—does not seem inferior).

and Joseph, bishop of Armagh, who is mentioned at the end of Part III. (p. 266), is evidently identified rightly by Stokes with the bishop who died A.D. 936.[1] But this passage has further significance. The writer, having enumerated the members of Patrick's household, says : " and that is the number that should be in Joseph's company." It is a clear inference that he was a contemporary of Joseph, and that this appendix (found in the Egerton MS. and in Colgan's version) was written in the first half of the tenth century. This consideration suggests that, if the linguistic forms prove that the Life *could not* have assumed its present shape before A.D. 1000, then the work of the eleventh-century compiler was practically confined to "modernising" an older compilation and substituting new for ancient forms. In its older shape the Life existed in the time of Bishop Joseph, when the enumeration of Patrick's household was appended. But there is nothing to show that the Life as a whole was not put together at an earlier period. The references to events and persons of the ninth century may be significant. There is one passage which especially suggests the second half of the ninth century. " Quod probavimus : Connacán son of Colmán came into the land with a host " (p. 174). Connacán's death fell in A.D. 855 ; he was killed in Ulster.[2] The expression *quod probavimus*, instead of "which was fulfilled," suggests that the event was within the recollection of the writer. This, taken along with the reference to Cenngecán, king of Cashel (*ob.* 897), may raise a presumption that the Life took shape in the latter part of the ninth century. It may, of course, be argued by those who would ascribe greater antiquity to the work that these references were posterior insertions, not due to the original compiler. I am inclined to think, however, that this involves an unnecessary multiplication of hypotheses. The material used by the compiler was older than the ninth century, but there is no positive indication to suggest that the compilation was older.

The tendency of the work is strongly marked. Like Tírechán's Memoir, it is intended to support the claims of Armagh. Dr. M'Carthy even describes it as, in its present form, "rather a plea for the privileges of the primatial See than a eulogy of the apostle of Ireland."[3]

It is to be observed, indeed, that the tendency is entirely absent from Part I. This, however, would hardly justify us in assuming a different authorship or date for the composition of

---

[1] *Ann. Ult. s.a.*                    [2] *Ib.*
[3] *The Tripartite Life of St. Patrick*, in *Trans. of R.I.A.*, xxix. Pt. vi. 1889.

Part I.; inasmuch as the subject matter of this part (Patrick's childhood, youth, arrival in Ireland, and the Tara legend) did not offer opportunities for urging the Armagh claims. It may also be observed that all the references to events later than A.D. 800 occur in Parts II. and III.

The last paragraphs of Part I. (pp. 60-62), which are omitted in the Rawlinson MS., have clearly been inserted here from the end of Part III. (pp. 256-8). The motive of this repetition is, doubtless, supplied by a remark of Dr. M'Carthy: "That upon the recurrence of his festival a sketch of the life and labours of St. Patrick should be delivered in the churches of Ireland would be a procedure in mere conformity with ecclesiastical usage." The *Tripartite Life* was practically used as material for sermons, though we may not feel warranted to go so far as to say that it represents sermons reduced to literary form. The particular paragraphs in question were added to Part I. as a "wind-up" for pulpit purposes. There is a similar but shorter wind-up to Part II.

Among these added paragraphs (p. 60 = p. 256) occurs a bibliographical notice:—

"These are the miracles which the elders of Ireland declared and connected with a thread of narration. Colombcille, son of Fedlimid, first declared Patrick's miracles and composed them. Then Ultan, son of Conchobar's descendant; Adamnan, grandson of Tinne; Eleran of the wisdom; Ciaran of Belach Duin; Bishop Ermedach of Clochar; Colman Uamach;[1] presbyter Collait of Druim Roilgech" (trans. Stokes).

Of these works we know nothing, though we may suspect that "Ultan" may refer either to the memoir of Tírechán (cp. the lemma in the *Lib. Arm.*) or to the book which Ultan lent to Tírechán. Observe that no mention is made of Muirchu's Life. But Muirchu was certainly a source of the *Tripartite*. If, therefore, this list represents the works which were used in the compilation, the compiler did not use Muirchu's Life directly, but some later work in which it had been wholly or partly incorporated. This agrees with a conclusion which I had entertained on other grounds, namely, that the compiler used W (the common source of $V_2$ and $V_4$) in which the Muirchu narrative had been incorporated with non-Muirchu material. The inference would be that the author of W is to be sought in the list. For instance, Ciarán of Belach Duin, who died A.D. 775,[2] would suit chronologically.

---

[1] A scribe of Armagh, *ob.* 725 (*Ann. Ult.*).    [2] *Ann. Ult. s.a.*

The material of Tírechán appears almost entirely in Parts II. and III. But there are considerations which suggest that it was not derived merely from Tírechán, but from the older written material from which Tírechán himself selected the memoranda which he has recorded. The compiler certainly used Tírechán's memoir, which was accessible to him if he wrote at Armagh; but he has added supplements which produce the impression of having belonged to the original records and not of being later interpolations. (Cp., for example, the account of the altar in Sliab Húa-n-Ailella, p. 94, and of the inscriptions at Selce, p. 106.) It would, perhaps, be impossible to prove this directly, but there is another fact connected with the sources of the Life which enables us to establish the probability indirectly.

The Life contains a great number of notices of acts of Patrick in various parts of Ireland which are not recorded by Tírechán, but which are closely similar in character and style to the acts which he records. Now we know that this material existed in the eighth century. For in the *Additional Notices* in the *Liber Armachanus* (ff. 18 v° b, 19 r°), as we have already seen (above, p. 254), we find the greater part of it indicated by a series of memorial words (names of men and places), most of which (not all) are explained in the *Tripartite Life*, Parts II. and III.

The *Tripartite Life*, therefore, contains a considerable body of ancient material, homogeneous with the material which Tírechán worked into his memoir, and not to be found elsewhere. We have a means for controlling it in the collection of jottings in the *Liber Armachanus*; and an attempt to discriminate later accretions might be successful within certain limits.

For an analysis of the *Tripartite Life* in connexion with the jottings, see Dr. Gwynn's *Introduction*, chap. vi., with *Appendix*.

### 8. *Vita Tertia*

An anonymous *Life of Patrick*, dating perhaps from the ninth century, is preserved in MSS. representing two different recensions, which I have investigated and attempted to reconstruct in "A Life of St. Patrick" (*Transactions of R.I.A.* xxxii. C, Part iii.) 1903. A corrupt text, with large accretions at beginning and end, was published by Colgan in the *Trias Thaum.* as his "Tertia Vita," and this designation may be conveniently retained. The Life was written in Ireland by an Irishman, but the archetype of our MSS. was written in West Britain, as is shown by Brythonic (Welsh or Cornish) interpolations. One interpolation, which has led to vain speculation, must be noticed here. The passage in c. 21, alleging a visit of Patrick to Martin, can be shown to have been intruded into the context (which otherwise depends on Muirchu) and caused confusion in the sense. The interpolator states that an angel told *Martin* to go to the *insula Tamarensis*; modern biographers have supposed that the command was given to Patrick, though it can hardly be held that there is any ambiguity in the Latin, and have conjectured many things about the mysterious island. The island is St. Nicholas at the mouth of the Tamar in Plymouth Sound, as Mr. C. J. Bates discerned. St. Martin was popular in south-west Britain; and this interpolation enables us to connect the archetype specially with south-west Britain. From it was derived a lost Glastonbury copy which is the parent of two of our existing MSS., which contain an interpolation claiming Glastonbury as Patrick's burial-place.

The author of the *Life* used the *Confession*, Muirchu, Tírechán; but he also incorporated a number of stories and incidents not found in any of the documents in the *Liber Armachanus*. Some of these stories are also found in the *Vita Tripartita* or the *Vita Quarta*, but others are not found elsewhere (see my enumeration, *op. cit.* 221-2).

[The *Vita Patricii*, in the *Sanctilogium* of John of Tinmouth (see Text in Horstman's *Nova Legenda Anglie*, vol. ii.) is an abridgment of the *Vita Tertia*; cp. Bury, *op. cit.* 223-4.]

## 9. *Life by Probus*

A Life of St. Patrick, published in the Basel edition of Bede's works 1563, and reprinted by Colgan as the *Vita Quinta*, has for author a certain Probus, who compiled the work at the request of a certain Paulinus (*Ecce habes, frater Pauline, a me humili Probo*, etc. ii. 41). Of Probus we know nothing otherwise. Colgan (p. 219) conjectures that he is to be identified with Cœnachair of Slane, whose death by the Northmen is noticed in the *Annals* of the Four Masters, *sub a.* 948. Paulinus, he suggests (p. 64), may be the Mael Póil who is described in the same chronicle as bishop, anchorite, scribe, and abbot of Indedhnen (near Slane), *sub a.* 920, where his obit is noticed. If these conjectures were right the date of the Life would be prior to 920. But the conjectures have no basis, the identification of Probus resting merely on the possibility that this name might have been chosen as a Latin equivalent of Cœnachair. There is internal evidence that the author was Irish (see Colgan's note, p. 61), but the only indication of date is the prophecy that Patrick should baptize *Scotiam atque Britaniam, Angliam et Normanniam caeterasque gentes insulanorum* (i. 10). Colgan supposes that Gallic Normandy is meant, and if so the Life could hardly be much earlier than the middle of the tenth century.

Probus made use of Muirchu's Life, but reconstructed certain parts of it, introducing matter from other sources. Thus he adopts the two captivities in Ireland from Muirchu, but while he identifies the first with the captivity of the *Confession*, he connects Miliucc with the second. His story of the second captivity is that Patrick's parents and family were in Armorica when it was devastated by the sons of Rethmitus (read *Sethmiti*) king of Britain. Patrick, his brother Ructi, and a sister were carried captive to Ireland, where Patrick served Miliucc. [Ructi was married by another chief to his sister. This incident is obviously the same as Miliucc's attempt to marry Patrick to his sister, as recounted in the W document ($V_2$ and $V_4$); so it may be inferred that Ructi is an error for Sucti, and that Sucat-Patrick has been split by Probus or his source into two brothers.] But Miliucc's abode is placed near Mount Egli (instead of Mount Miss). On escaping Patrick is taken to Gaul by a man who sells him there into slavery,[1] but at "Trajectus" he is redeemed by Christians.

The story of the fictitious second captivity is thus composed of (1) matter derived from the true story of the first captivity, as told in Muirchu and the *Confession*; (2) the Armoric legend; (3) the story of the marriage of the brother and sister; and (4) the escape to *Gaul*, with the mention of two towns: *Venit cum Gallis ad Brotgalum, inde Trajectum*. Brotgalum, Colgan suggests, is meant to represent *Burdigalam*, Bordeaux (cp. Appendix C, 6).

After this Patrick goes through a number of experiences before he comes to sit at the feet of Germanus; or, in other words, Probus, before he resumes the narrative of Muirchu, interjects material derived from other sources. Patrick goes

(1) to St. Martin of Tours, who tonsures him;
(2) to the *plebs Dei*, who are barefooted hermits;
(3) to an "island between mountains and sea" where a great beast infested a fountain;
(4) to St. Senior, bishop, *in monte Hermon in dextro latere maris Oceani et vallata est civitas eius septem muris*; this bishop

---

[1] The narrative here (c. 14) is very confused, and perhaps there is interpolation.

ordained Patrick *in sacerdotem,* and he read with him for a long time; here Patrick heard in a vision the voice of children summoning him to Ireland; then he went with nine men, and held converse with the Lord, who made him three promises;

(5) to Ireland, where he is unsuccessful;

(6) to Rome; whence having received the apostolic blessing *reversus est itinere quo venerat illuc* (c. 20).

At this point the narrative of Muirchu is resumed most awkwardly. The author might have made Patrick visit Germanus on his way back through Gaul, but, instead, he proceeds: *transnavigato vero mari Britannico,* following Muirchu literally, without any attempt to make the extraneous matter fit in speciously to Muirchu's story.

Some of these incidents are also found in the *Vita Tertia,* namely, the visit to Martin, the visit to Rome, and the visit to *Mons Arnon*; besides which the visit to a hermit who gives Patrick the staff of Jesus is recorded.

Now the author of the *Vita Tertia* and Probus undertook the same problem of working these incidents into the main thread of the Muirchu story, and they solved it in different ways. Probus solved it by a single interpolation, grouping all the new matter together and finding a place for it before the sojourn with Germanus. In the *Vita Tertia* there are three distinct interpolations arranged as follows :—

(Muirchu) Reads with Germanus.

(Interp.) Sojourns with Martin.

(Muirchu) Germanus sends Segitius with him to Rome.

(Interp.) Visits a hermit in *quodam loco* and receives staff of Jesus.

(Muirchu) Is ordained bishop by Amator.

(Interp.) Visits Rome, and goes thence *ad montem Arnon* when he salutes the Lord.

It is difficult to say which of the arrangements is the more unskilful. The same matter is found in a more expanded and "advanced" form in the *Tripartite Life,* where the arrangement is as follows (Rolls ed. p. 25 *sqq.*) :—

(1) Patrick reads with Germanus; (2) is tonsured by Martin; (3) visits a cave, in the Tyrrhenian sea, "between mountain and sea," where there were three other Patricks, and a beast infested a fountain; (4) Victor bids him go to Ireland, and Germanus sends Segitius with him; (5) Patrick goes to sea, with nine, and visits an island, where he found a young married couple who had lived there since the time of Christ; and (6) goes thence to Mount

Hermon, near the island, where the Lord gives him the staff of Jesus and grants him three requests; (7) goes to Rome.

In these three documents we have the same matter differently combined, variously modified and augmented. Probus presents it in a more advanced stage than the *Vita Tertia*, the *Tripartite* in a more advanced stage than Probus. The matter, however, is not homogenous. The visit to Pope Celestine at Rome has no legendary superstructure, and is found in the W document ($V_2$ and $V_4$) which does not contain any of the other incidents. The rest of the common material depends on three motives: (1) the association of Patrick with Martin; (2) the staff of Jesus; (3) converse with the Lord. The *Vita Tertia* presents these motives in their simplest form: (1) it is not stated that Patrick was tonsured by Martin; (2) the staff of Jesus is received from a hermit, not from the Lord; (3) there is no account of the conversation, we are simply told *salutavit Dominum ut Moyses*. The *Tripartite Life* brings the second and third motives into the same setting.

In this legendary material the only thing which, for our purpose, requires investigation is the description of the place in or near which Patrick saluted the Lord. In the *Vita Tertia* it is designated: *montem Arnon ar mair Lethe supra petram maris Tyrreni in civitate quae vocatur Capua*, where the Irish words, *ar mair Lethe* are equivalent to *super mare Latinum*, that is, *super mare Tyrrhenum*. Probus has *in monte Hermon in dextro latere maris Oceani et vallata est civitas septem muris*. The *Tripartite* has *hisliab Hermóin*, "to mount Hermon."

What was the name of the mountain? The MSS. of the *Vita Tertia* give *Arnon*, Probus and *Trip. Hermon*. As the form Hermon may well have had a scriptural motive, we might suppose that the original name was Arnon. But the description in the *Vita Tertia* points in another direction. *Supra petram maris Tyrrheni* is clearly intended to represent the Irish words preceding. But why *petram*? It points to *montem ar maen ar mair Lethe*. And so, in view of *Hermon, Hermóin* in the other sources, it looks as if *Arnon* is a corruption of *Armóin* or *Armain*, which the writer took to mean the Irish *ar maen = supra petram*.[1]

The account in Probus of Patrick's visit to this place deserves attention. The city on the mountain is the seat of a bishop, who ordains Patrick priest. While he is there he hears the voices of children in a vision, and the angel bids him go to Ireland. Now

---

[1] I observe that Lanigan wished to derive *Hermon* from *her*, "great," and *maen*, "rock."—Todd, *St. Patrick*, 337 note.

here we have happening in the city of the bishop on Mount Hermon exactly what, according to the narrative of Muirchu (271-2), happened at Auxerre, the city of Germanus.

The conclusion is strongly suggested that the *sanctus senior episcopus* of Mount Hermon is simply a double of Germanus. In the transference of Germanus from Auxerre to the shores of the Mediterranean we have a step in the *Tripartite Life* where he instructs Patrick in the *Aralanensis insula* (p. 26 Rolls ed.). That, however, is a conscious combination of known sources; but, if the bishop of Mount Hermon masks Germanus, we have the Germanus episode coming down to us through a different channel of tradition.

Is it possible that this channel was British? There is a place, Llanarman in Wales, which means the church of Germanus. "Pen-arman" would mean the mountain of Germanus; and it is worth considering whether the presumable *mons Armain* of *Vita Tertia*, and *mons Hermon* of Probus, may not be explained as the "mountain of Germanus," being derived from a British source.

The rest of the work of Probus is based, entirely or almost entirely, on Muirchu and Tírechán.

### 10. *Notice of Patrick in the Historia Brittonum*

It is unnecessary to discuss here the complicated question of the gradual evolution of the *Historia Brittonum* through successive recensions. In its oldest form it seems to have been mainly founded on a lost legendary Life of Germanus of Auxerre, in which the British chief Vortigern played a prominent part. This, the oldest form to which we can get back, though there may have been a still older text behind it, can be fixed to the year 679, and there can be no doubt that it contained the Arthurian chapter (c. 56).[1] In the course of the following

[1] The literature which I have used in working through the Nennian problem is as follows:—Zimmer, *Nennius Vindicatus*, a brilliant and indispensable book, but too ingenious, and full of wiredrawn arguments; many of the conclusions have been upset by the Chartres text (Mommsen's Z) which Zimmer left out of consideration. This text was published by Duchesne, *Nennius retractatus*, in *Revue celtique*, xv. 174 *sqq.*; and was used by Mommsen for his authoritative edition of the work in *Chronica Minora*, vol. iii. (it is much to be regretted that he did not devote a separate column to printing the text of Z in full). New light was then thrown on the problem by Thurneysen, *Ztsch. f. deutsche Philologie*, xxviii. 80 *sqq.* His interpretation of *exberta* in the title in the Chartres MS. as a mistake for *excerpta* (*Incipiunt excerpta filii Urbagen*) seems probable (Dr. Traube's emendation *experta* has not convinced me); his identification of this son of

century a recension of this, with some additions, was executed, and we possess it in an incomplete form in a MS. preserved at Chartres. Then towards the year 800 the work was rehandled and considerable additions were made to it by Nennius, a native of Wales. All our MSS., except that of Chartres, are derived from the compilation of Nennius, but represent different recensions.

Among the other additions which Nennius, pupil of Elbodug, Bishop of Bangor,[1] made to the *Historia Brittonum*, was a sketch of the life of St. Patrick (caps. 50-55). It is to be observed that in another interpolation concerning the migrations of the Scotti (c. 15) Nennius refers to oral information which he received from Irish scholars (*sic mihi peritissimi Scottorum nuntiauerunt*), and it is possible that for the Patrician section also he may have received help from the same source. (1) The account of the mission of Palladius, the ordination of Patrick, and his departure for Ireland, is derived directly from Muirchu, but with some additions.[2] (2) The description of Patrick's experience on "Cruachan Eile" seems not to be derived directly from Tírechán, but to depend on another source, in which the words *ut uideret fructum sui laboris* occurred (*Hist. Britt.* $197_{18}$, Tírechán, $323_5$), and some other expressions common to both.

Urbagen with Run map Urbgen, who baptized the Northumbrians in 627 (*Hist. Britt.* c. 63), though plausible, cannot be considered certain. Duchesne, in a judicious and instructive criticism with reference to Mommsen's edition and Thurneysen's article, has summed up the conclusions which may safely be drawn from the data: *Revue celtique*, xvii. 1 *sqq.* Mr. E. W. B. Nicholson, who had reached several of Professor Thurneysen's conclusions independently, published his views in *Ztsch. f. celtische Philologie*, iii. 104 *sqq.* The most important point in this paper is that the true reading of the important words in the title of the Chartres MS. is: *exberta fili vrba gen.* See also L. Traube in *Neues Archiv*, xxiv. 721 *sqq.*

[1] Nennius, *Preface*, ed. Momms., p. 143; Elbodug died A.D. 809, Zimmer, *Nenn. Vind.* 51.

[2] (1) Noteworthy is the explanation of *sed prohibuit illum Deus quia nemo* etc. (Muirchu $272_{20}$) by the insertion of *per quasdam tempestates* after *Deus.* In the context this is incongruous, and it can hardly have been originated by Nennius. Had he a MS. of Muirchu containing additions inserted from Muirchu's source? [*Deus* is in the Bruxellensis, but omitted in the Armachanus.] (2) He changes Muirchu's *Victoricus* into *Victor angelus Dei.* (3) He says that Patrick's first name was *Maun* (*Magonus*, Tírechán, $302_5$). (4) It is to be observed that while Muirchu mentions two views as to the duration of Patrick's sojourn with Germanus, namely, forty or thirty years, Nennius gives a much smaller period, *per annos septem.* Thus Muirchu's *Life* does not explain Nennius, c. 52; he had some additional material. Nennius agrees with Brux. and $V_2$ $V_4$ in recording that Palladius died *in terra Pictorum.*

The date of the fifth year of Loigaire ($196_6$) might have been, but need not have been, taken from Tírechán. (3) The three petitions of Patrick (197) are identical with and correspond verbally to those which are added in the *Liber Armachanus* to the incomplete text of Tírechán (331); and the four points of comparison with Moses (198) are also found in the same order among these *Additions* to Tírechán (332).

The dates in c. 55 do not correspond to the dates in the *Additions* to Tírechán. The statement that he was ordained in his twenty-fifth year seems to stand alone. But the period of eighty-five years assigned to his preaching in Ireland has arisen, we may surmise, from a confusion of numerals (lxxii. and lxxxu.).

It is unnecessary to deal here with the notices of Patrick in the Chronicles of Marianus Scotus (*ob.* A.D. 1083 : text in Pertz, M.G.H., V., and Migne, P. L. 107, but these are superseded by MacCarthy's *Codex Palatino-Vaticanus*, No. 830, 1892 [Todd Lecture Series III.], to which I may refer for a discussion of the dates). Nor need I speak of Jocelin's biography (twelfth cent.) since it is founded on sources which we possess, and the only value which it may have for Patrician researches is that a minute examination might conceivably show that Jocelin used different recensions of some of our documents. For the purpose of the present biography, such pieces as the Homily on St. Patrick in the Lebar Brecc (printed by Stokes in *Vit. Trip.* vol. ii.), or the prefaces to the Hymns of Sechnall and Fíacc, do not demand particular notice.

## III

### 1. *The Irish Annals*

The extant chronicles which supply material for the history in the fifth century are : (1) Annales Ultonienses, or Annals of Ulster, compiled by Cathal MacManus of the island of Shanad (Bellisle) in Lough Erne, who died 1498. The chronicle begins at A.D. 431, and comes down to the compiler's own time (continued to 1504). For the early Middle Age, at least, it is the most valuable of the extant Irish Annals. Its greatest merit consists in the fact that the compiler did not attempt to solve chronological difficulties, but copied the data which he found. In his introduction to the Rolls series ed. of the work (vol. iv. p. ix.) Dr. MacCarthy says : "The sustained similarity between these and the other native Annals proves that the work of MacManus consisted in selection, mainly with reference to Ulster events, from the chronicles he had collected. . . . Unlike O'Clery and his associates [the 'Four Masters'], he neither tampered with the text, vitiated the dating, nor omitted the solar and lunar notation, but, side by side with the chronological errors he was unable to correct, preserved the criteria whereby they can with certainty be rectified."

The years are distinguished by the ferial incidence, and the lunar epact, of January 1, as well as by the A.D. and the Annus Mundi. Up to the year 486 the A.D. corresponds correctly to the other criteria, but from this point on up to A.D. 1014, it lags one year behind. Dr. MacCarthy was the first to fix the precise point at which the error arises and to explain its cause. It was due to the accidental omission of a blank year, corresponding to A.D. 486, before the A.D. numeration was inserted. The *Kal.* which represented 486 having fallen out, 486 was annexed to the *Kal.* which really represented 487 (*Introduction*, pp. xcvi.-ix.). Thus it is only the A.D. data that are wrong ; the ferial, lunar, and mundane data are right.

(2) Annals of Inisfallen (in Kerry). The entries in this chronicle are much fewer than in the *Ann. Ult.*, and the ferial and lunar data have been very imperfectly preserved in the only extant copy. Dr. MacCarthy, who has shown how the fifth-century portion can be reconstructed (*Cod. Pal.-Vat.* 830, pp. 352-3), regards it as "the most ancient body of chronicles we possess" (p. 369). He has shown that the early part was based on the Victorian cycle.

(3) Tigernach (*ob.* 1088) composed a chronicle at Clonmacnois, beginning in the remotest ages, of which only portions are preserved. They have been published by Dr. W. Stokes in the *Revue celtique* (vols. v. and vi.). The second fragment ends at A.D. 361, and the third begins at A.D. 489, so that his record of the Patrician period is lost. His incompetence in chronology has been shown by Dr. MacCarthy.[1] He drew mainly from the same sources as the compiler of *Ann. Ult.*, but as he was not influenced in his selection by the same Ultonian interest, his work contains many additional records.

(a) The *Chronicon Scotorum* is an abridgment of Tigernach. This was disputed by its editor (Hennessy, Rolls series), but has been established by Dr. MacCarthy,[2] who has at the same time shown the incompetence of the abbreviator (MacFirbis).

---

[1] Todd Lecture, Series iii. The *Codex Palatino-Vaticanus*, 830, p. 354 *sqq.*, cp. 252 *sqq.*    [2] *Ib.* 247 *sqq.*

For the fifth century its value consists in showing what entries were to be found in Tigernach.

(4) The *Annals of the Four Masters*, a chronicle in Irish from the earliest times, compiled in Donegal by O'Clery and three others in the seventeenth century, has some value for the early Middle Ages, because it preserves notices derived from older chronicles that are not extant. But its dates are untrustworthy because the compilers had no skill in chronological computation. This has been shown by Dr. MacCarthy (*op. cit.* p. 370 *sqq.*). One of their sources was the *Annals of Ulster*, which supplies a means of correcting their mistakes. Among their other authorities were the *Book of Clonmacnois* (Tigernach?) and the *Book of the Island of Saints* (in Lake Ree).

From these compilations it might be possible to reconstruct the common annalistic structure on which they are based; with the help of the chronological tracts and poems which are contained in the *Book of Leinster*, the *Book of Ballymote*, etc. It is clear that for such a reconstruction the *Annals of Ulster* would supply the clearest traces of the plan.

The Irish seem to have had a special taste and faculty for chronological computations,[1] and in the early part of the seventh century, if not sooner, they were laying the foundations for national Annals on the model of the Roman Annals. In the *Annals of Ulster* a number of entries, ranging from A.D. 467 to A.D. 628, are justified by references to the *Liber Cuanach*. Zimmer, with great probability, identifies Cuana, the author of this lost work, with Cuana mac Ailcene, a king of Fermoy, whose death is noted in *Chron. Scot.* and in *Annals of F. M.* under A.D. 640.[2] The references under the year 482 show that the *Book of Cuana* dealt with (the chronology at least of) the pre-Christian period. The authorship of a south Irish prince is consistent with the circumstance that many of the entries in question relate to the affairs of South Ireland.[3] For chronological studies I may refer also to the evidence of

---

[1] Cp. Columbanus, *Epist.* (M.G.H., Epp. iii.) 157, and the notice in the Würzburg MS. of St. Matthew, quoted by Zimmer, *Nenn. Vind.* 252, note (Scheps, *Die ältesten Evangelienhandschriften der Würzburger Bibliothek*, 27).

[2] A genealogy of Brito is ascribed by Gilla Coemgin to *senior nobilis Guanach*, and Todd pointed out that the reference was to the *Liber Cuanach* (Zimmer, *Nenn. Vind.* 250-1). Calling attention to the notice in *Ann. Ult. s.a.* 616, *usque hunc annum scripsit Isidorus cronicon suum*, Zimmer observes that the old recension (up to 616) of Isidore's chronicle was known in Ireland, and conjectures that its arrival may have been the stimulus which prompted the work of Cuana.

[3] An older authority, Maucteus, was quoted by Cuana (*Ann. Ult. s.a.* 471).

Tírechán, on which I have dwelt in *Eng. Hist. Rev.* April 1902, 244-5.

The *Annals of Ulster* (and Tigernach) have some entries in Latin and others in Irish. Of the Latin entries, some relate to Roman history, others to native history. So far as the fifth and sixth centuries are concerned, it is reasonable to conjecture that the Latin entries represent an early and generally accepted synchronistic reconstruction, which had been made with the help of Roman annals, and especially the Chronicle of Marcellinus. It has been proved by Dr. MacCarthy, from the synchronistic treatises which he has studied in connexion with Tigernach, that the chronology of pre-Patrician history was based on Jerome's edition of the Chronicle of Eusebius. For the fifth and sixth centuries Isidore and Bede are referred to, as well as Marcellinus; but most of the foreign entries are taken verbally from Marcellinus. The difficulties and uncertainties of the synchronisers seem to be reflected in the alternative dates of the *Annals of Ulster*, where an event given under one year often appears in another place, with the addition *hic alii dicunt*, or something of the kind.

In regard to the few and brief entries relating to Patrick, the internal evidence testifies to the antiquity of the tradition, and excludes any suspicion of fabrication on the part of the annalistic compilers. While the legendary date of Patrick's death, which had become vulgar in the seventh century, was admitted and emphasised, the true date, notwithstanding the inconsistency, was allowed to remain; and in the second place, not a single notice based on the assumption that Patrick was still alive appears in the interval between the true date and the false date. A fabricator who was concerned to invent notices about Patrick would not have been likely to leave thirty years a complete blank. Thus if the few Patrician entries prior to A.D. 461 were fabrications, it would seem that they must have been invented before the legendary date of his death in A.D. 493 had become current. This consideration establishes a strong presumption of their antiquity; if they are not genuine, they must have been very early inventions. But intrinsically they offer nothing to arouse suspicion; on the contrary, it is incredible that a fabricator, producing annalistic records in the interest of a "Patrician legend," would have confined himself to the interpolation of just these slender notices. These entries will be found under the years 432, 439, 441, 443, 444, 461; the notices of the deaths of Secundinus, 447 (*Ann. Inisf.* 448), and Auxilius, 459, may perhaps be added.

Dr. MacCarthy has made it highly probable that the Paschal Table formed the nucleus or framework of the early (from A.D. 432) portion of the original Annals (*loc. cit.* p. c. *sqq*). On this hypothesis he is able to give so satisfactory an explanation of the notice of Patrick's advent, that the truth of the hypothesis may almost be said to be demonstrated. The mission of Palladius is recorded, in the words of Prosper, under A.D. 431, with which the Inisfallen and Ulster Annals begin. But it is assigned to the wrong consuls in *Ann. Ult.*; A.D. 431 was the year of Bassus and Antiochus; but it is here described as the year of Aetius and Valerius, who were consuls in A.D. 432. Obviously, therefore, the words *Aetio et Valerio consulibus* have been erroneously transferred from the notice *s.a.* 432 to the preceding year; as is borne out by a passage in a chronological tract in the *Book of Ballymote*, where we read: "The year after that [the sending of Palladius], Patrick went to preach the gospel to Ireland. Etius and Valerianus were the two consuls of that year" (*loc. cit.* p. cix. *note*). Now, seeing that the advent of Patrick is not recorded in any Roman chronicle, and that Irish events are not dated in the Irish Annals by consular years, the question arises how the advent of Patrick came to be associated with the consuls of the year. Dr. MacCarthy solves the problem, simply and I think convincingly, by pointing out that Patrick drew up (before he left Gaul) and took with him to Ireland a prospective Paschal Table, which, like other western Paschal tables, would have had its initial year distinguished by the consuls. Even if we had no definite testimony that Patrick took with him a Paschal Table, we could have no doubt that he must have done so;[1] it was an inevitable precaution. But we have the definite testimony of Cummian, who mentions the 84 Paschal cycle, "quem sanctus Patricius, papa noster, *tulit* et fecit."[2] The initial year in this table would naturally be the year in which Patrick started for Ireland, A.D. 432; and thus the year of his advent was recorded with a consular date.

As for the other Patrician notices in the Annals enumerated above, the most probable origin seems to be that they were derived from brief entries made in the margin of this or another

[1] Dr. MacCarthy quotes appropriately the 20th canon of the Council of Milevi, A.D. 416.

[2] See Migne, P.L. 87, 969.

Paschal Table dating from the fifth century.[1] This view best accords with the paucity and the nature of the notices, which were certainly not composed by any one wishing to work the incidents of St. Patrick's life into existing Annals.

The old Welsh Annals (*Annales Cambriae* : the edition in the Rolls series has been superseded by that of Mr. E. Phillimore in *Y Cymmrodor*, ix. p. 141 *sqq.* 1888) contain a few notices of Irish ecclesiastical history. This chronicle extends from A.D. 444 to 977, but the first entry is under 453 and the last under 954, the preceding and the following years being respectively blank. Mr. Phillimore gives reasons for supposing that the Annals in their present form were finished in 954 or 955 (p. 144).

Now it is to be observed that before the year 516 (to which the battle of Badon is falsely assigned) there is no entry bearing on British history. Before this year there are only five entries, of which four relate to Ireland, and the fifth to the celebration of Easter. They are as follows :—

an' [A.D. 453] Pasca commutatur super diem dominicum cum[2] papa leone episcopo rome.

an' [A.D. 454] Brigida sancta nascitur.

an' [A.D. 457] Sanctus Patricius ad dominum migratur.

an' [A.D. 468] quies benigni episcopi.

an' [A.D. 501] Episcopus ebur pausat in christo anno. cccl. etatis suae.

The Irish dates do not coincide exactly with those of the Irish Annals. In *Ann. Ult.* 452 and 456 are given as alternative dates for the birth of Brigit; 467 for the death of Benignus; and the death of Ibar appears under three years, 500, 501, and 504. Tigernach gives 502, and adds the legendary age (cuius etas ccciii. annorum erat). The date of Patrick's death corresponds to the entry in *Ann. Ult.* A.D. 457. *Quies senis Patricii ut alii libri dicunt.*

In these (and one or two other Irish dates in the sixth century) there is nothing to suggest a British chronological tradition independent of the Irish Annals. The dates were clearly taken from Irish books, just like the Irish dates in the

---

[1] For such entries in the blank spaces of a Paschal Table, compare, *e.g.* the *Paschale Campanum* (*Chron. Min.*, ed. Mommsen, i. 745 *sqq.*).

[2] Mr. Phillimore's suggestion that *cum* is a misrendering of the Old-Welsh *cant* = by, seems improbable, as the notice is not likely to be a translation. I should say that *cum* is simply a dittogram of the last syllable of *dominicum*, and has ousted *a*.

*Historia Brittanum*; and throw no additional light on the chronology.[1]

Leaving out the Irish dates, which were certainly inserted at a late period in the growth of the chronicle,[2] we have a long and empty enumeration of years, unrelieved except by the notice of Pope Leo's decision as to the celebration of Easter in 455. This notice, which appears under 453, properly belongs either to 454 or 455. (It might appear under 454, because in that year Leo notified his decision to the bishops of the west).[3] This blank table of years, with one Paschal notice, seems a confirmation of Dr. MacCarthy's theory, and suggests that the original basis of the Cambrian Annals was a Paschal Table.

If this be so, the circumstance that the initial year is A.D. 444 should have some significance. I hazard the guess that it may have some connexion with the second visit of Germanus to Britain. In A.D. 444 Germanus was at Arles, where he took part in the deposition of Bishop Celidonius.[4] The investigation of Levison shows that the second visit probably occurred between this year and the death of Germanus, which happened before A.D. 450.[5] If, as is possible, 445 is the date, a Paschal Table with 444 as initial year might have been brought to Britain by Germanus.

## 2. *The Catalogus Sanctorum*

The *Catalogus sanctorum Hiberniae secundum diversa tempora* is a very brief sketch of the ecclesiastical history of Ireland from the time of St. Patrick to the year 665 A.D. Its composition may belong to the first half of the eighth century, but is generally admitted not to be later. The text has been printed by Ussher, *Brit. Eccl. Ant.*, 913 *sqq.* ed. 1639 = Works, vi. 477 *sqq.* (from two MSS.), and by Fleming, *Collectanea*, 430-1 (from a MS. which is supposed to be a Codex Salmanticensis at Brussels). From these two texts it has been printed by Haddan and Stubbs, *Councils*, ii. 292-4. There is a translation in Todd's *St. Patrick*, 88-9.

The framework of this sketch is patently artificial. Three

---

[1] We are indeed enabled to infer that before the tenth century A.D. 457 had been maintained by some to be the date of Patrick's death.

[2] An examination of the dates in the sixth century suggests that the entries of contemporary events did not begin before the seventh. Certainly the erroneous date of the battle of Mons Badonis was a late insertion.

[3] For references see Tillemont, *Mémoires*, xv. 769. Leo had taken the step of writing to the Emperor Marcian on the matter in 453.

[4] *Vit. Hilarii. Arel.* 16. See Levison, *Neues Archiv*, xxix. p. 99.

[5] Levison, *loc. cit.* pp. 125 *sqq.*

definite periods are distinguished, and to each is assigned a different category of saints. The chronology is marked by the reigns of the kings of Ireland, and the three periods are as follows :—(1) 432-544 A.D. *ordo sanctissimus* ; (2) 544-598 A.D. *ordo sanctior* or *sanctus sanctorum* ; (3) 598-665 A.D. *ordo sanctus*. There is thus a decline in saintliness in the second order of saints, and a further decline in the third.

The distinctive features of the first period, which includes the time of St. Patrick, are noted as follows :—(1) All the saints were bishops ; (2) There was unity in the Church, one liturgy, one tonsure (the Celtic), one mode of observing Easter, and all obeyed the guidance of Patrick ; (3) The saints did not disdain the ministration and society of women.

The second period differed in all three respects from the first : (1) This order of saints consisted chiefly of presbyters, there were few bishops ; (2) The unity of the Church was not wholly maintained ; it was maintained in regard to the tonsure and the Paschal cycle, but different liturgies were introduced, and different monastic rules ; it could no longer be said that *unum ducem Patricium habebant* ; (3) Women were separated from the monasteries.

The third order consisted of presbyters and only few bishops. The conversion of the south of Ireland to Roman usages falls into this period, so that it is marked by still more diversity than the second, since two different modes of tonsure and of the determination of Easter prevailed in Ireland. There was, moreover, a tendency among the saints to betake themselves to the solitary life of hermits.

The artificiality of this arrangement is emphasised by the circumstance that the author conceives each period to be coincident with exactly four reigns. This is contrary to fact in the case of periods 1 and 3. In period 1 the reign of Muirchertach, which lasted twenty years, is omitted ; in period 3, three reigns are omitted.

Thus historical accuracy has been sacrificed to symmetry. But there is also a fundamental chronological error. The author's date for the beginning of his second period is too late, for the activity of some of the leading saints whom he places in it, such as Ciarán of Clonmacnois and Finian of Clonard, began earlier than A.D. 544.[1]

These examples of looseness do not predispose us to accept the author's particular statements without further evidence. But

---

[1] Compare Zimmer's criticism, *Celtic Church*, 64-5.

the most important point in his conception of the development, namely, the decline from uniformity and the rise of individualism after the Patrician period (though he puts the beginning of this movement too late), is in consonance with probability and with other evidence.

### 3. *Liber Angueli*

This document, contained in the *Liber Armachanus* (printed in Rolls ed., 352 *sqq.*), is a clumsy invention, fabricated at Armagh, probably early in the eighth century, in the interests of the Armagh jurisdiction. It has importance for the ecclesiastical history of Ireland, but none for the acts of Patrick. Its motive, however, illustrates the confessed motive of Tírechán's *Memoir*, the interest of the *Paruchia Patricii*. It has been, for the first time, critically treated by Dr. Gwynn, who makes it highly probable that it consists of two different compositions: (1) the *Colloquy* with the angel, and (2) *Decrees* concerning the rights of Armagh. These parts are separated by a space in the MS. at the top of fol. 21 r° a (Part ii. begins *de speciali reuerantia*), and Dr. Gwynn shows by a careful comparison that they are probably of distinct origin, the *Decrees* being the older, and the *Colloquy* being composed as a sort of introduction to them with the view of supporting their validity by divine authority (see Gwynn, *Introduction* to the *Book of Armagh*, chap. vi.).

For the mention of the appeal to the Roman see in last instance, see App. C, 16.

# APPENDIX B

## NOTES

### CHAPTER I

P. 12.—The intercourse of Ireland with the Roman provinces is illustrated by coins found in the island. See *Proceedings of Royal Irish Academy*, ii. 184-8 (1843), on a find of coins (early imperial, from Vespasian to the Antonines) in Faugh Mountain, near Pleaskin, Giant's Causeway, Co. Antrim; cp. also *ib.* 186-7; *ib.* vi. 441 *sqq.* (1856), a paper by Petrie on coins of the Republic found near Rathfarnham, Co. Dublin; *ib.* 525, on eight coins (imperial, from Tiberius to Constantine) found near Downpatrick; *Proc. of Royal Soc. of Antiquaries of Ireland*, xxx. p. 176 (1900), fifteen coins (Constantine) at Tara.

P. 14.—Gaelic settlements in S.-W. Britain. Sources: Cormac's *Glossary*, s.v. mogeime (ed. Stokes); the text (of which an extract was printed by Zimmer in *Nennius Vindicatus*, p. 85) from Bodleian MSS. Rawlinson, B. 502 f. 72 c., and Laud 610 f. 100 a. 1, edited with translation by Kuno Meyer (*Y Cymmrodor*, 14, 101, *sqq.*). Cp. also *Historia Brittonum*, § 14, p. 156, ed. Mommsen. See Zimmer, *ib.* on these settlements. He determines the date of the composition of the Rawlinson-Laud document as about A.D. 750. The question as to the survival in West Britain of the descendants of an ancient pre-British Goidelic population (maintained by Professor Rhŷs, combated by Professor K. Meyer, see *Transactions of Hon. Soc. of Cymmrodorion*, 1895-6, p. 55 *sqq.*) does not affect the reality of a later Goidelic settlement in historical times. On the Dessi cp. Rhŷs, *Studies in Early Irish History*, p. 56; *Origin of Welsh Englyn*, pp. 26, 73, 179 (in *Y Cymmrodor* xviii. 1905); *Celtic Britain* (ed. 3), p. 247 *sqq.*

P. 10.—The statement that Man was never conquered by

Rome might have to be modified if, as has occurred to me, the words of Tacitus at the beginning of *Agricola* 24, *naue prima transgressus ignotas ad id tempus gentes crebris simul ac praeliis domuit*, record a descent of Agricola on that island. In the context an expedition to Caledonia seems excluded. [*Prima* is unintelligible. It may be an instance of the common confusion of *un* with *im, ima* (for *una*) having been taken as an abbreviation of *prima*.]

P. 14.—" Perhaps were conditions of military service." A stone of Killorglin (now in the Dublin Museum) bears the ogam inscription GALEATOS, which Professor Rhŷs explains as genitive of Latin *galeatus*, a helmed soldier. He thinks that it was a name " first given to a Goidel who had worn the Roman *galea*, that is one who had served in the Roman army. For one cannot help comparing it with *Qoeddoran-i* as connected with *Petrianæ*, and the name *Sagittarius*, of which the genitive *Saggitari* was found in ogam on a stone discovered at Burnfort, in the neighbourhood of Mallow, in Co. Cork. All three names are presumably to be explained on the supposition of Goidelic touch with Roman institutions, especially the military system ; not to mention such Latin names as *Marianus, Latinus*, and *Columbanus*, or their significance, so to say, in this context" (reprint from *Proceedings of Royal Society of Antiquaries of Ireland*, Part i. vol. xxxii. 1902, p. 16).


## CHAPTER II

P. 16.—Calpurnius : *Confession*, 357₄ (Armagh MS. has *Calpornum* ; Cotton MS. *Calpornium* ; Brussels MS. of Muirchu, *Cualfarni*, 495₇). Properly a *nomen*, but, like other *nomina*, adopted as a *cognomen*. As such, however, it does not seem to occur often. Cp. *C.I.L.* xiv. 570 ; iii. Suppl. Pars post. 14354²⁸ ; viii. 9157.

*Ib.*—Potitus : *Confession*, 357₅ (Armagh MS. *Potiti presbyteri*, and in the margin *filii Odissi* added in the same hand. It is to be noted that the copy of the *Confession* used by Muirchu seems to have had simply *Potiti presbyteri*, 494₇. Hence the inference is suggested that *filii Odissi* was not in the original text of St. Patrick's work, but was added in the margin from some other source, and inserted by the scribe of the Cotton MS. in the wrong place—before, instead of after, *presbyteri*. Potitus, not Odissus, was the presbyter. In the hymn *Genair Patraicc*, l. 4, Odissus is described as a deacon). Potitus was a common cognomen in the Roman empire; examples will be found in almost any volume of the *C.I.L.* (*e.g.* v. 834, 970, 6125, 7436; ii. 1172, 3799, 4006; xiv. 1332$_{11, 7}$, 3964, etc.).

P. 16.—Calpurnius a decurion : *Corot.* 377$_{20}$ decorione patre nascor. That Patrick's family were British provincials and lived in Britain there can be no question : *Confession,* 370$_{10, 12}$, and 364$_{1, 2}$ (cp. *Corot.* 375$_{23}$), passages which prove that Patrick regarded Britain as his native land, and that his family lived there continuously from the time of his captivity till his old age. There is no evidence whatever that they had come and settled in Britain during his boyhood, and his biographer in the seventh century writes unhesitatingly that he was *Brito natione, in Britannis natus* (Muirchu, 494, 6). Patrick does not say himself that he was of British descent, but the presumption that his family was British is confirmed by his Celtic name Sucat (see below, 291).

P. 17.—Decurions in smaller towns. The evidence is collected in Kübler's article *Decurio* in Pauly-Wissowa, *Real-Encyclopädie der classischen Altertumswissenschaft.* The *canabae* which grew up at military stations sometimes received self-governing privileges and had decurions (the evidence is for Apulum in Dacia, Moguntiacum, and Brigetio). There is also evidence for decurions in *pagi*, but only for Africa. *Vici* and *castella* were attributed to the larger towns near which they were situated, and had no *ordo decurionum* (see *Cod. Just.* 5. 27. 3. 1 ; 10. 19. 8). We can therefore infer that Calpurnius was a member of the municipal senate of some town in the neighbourhood of the *vicus* Bannaventa.

*Ib.*—The condition of decurions or *curiales* in the fourth and fifth centuries. Chief source : *Codex Theodosianus,* esp. xii. 1. The subject is well treated and elucidated in Professor Dill's *Roman Society in the Last Century of the Western Empire,* Bk. iii. chap. 2 (On the Decay of the Middle Class).

P. 18.—"Sixteen acres or upwards" : *ultra uiginti quinque iugera priuato dominio possidens, Cod. Th.* xii. 1, 33.

*Ib.*—"Sinews of the republic" : *nerui reipublicae, Novell. Maioriani,* vii. 1.

P. 19.—Curials who took orders. Julian's rescript : *Cod. Th.* xii. i, 50. Enactments of Theodosius I., *ib.* 121 (A.D. 390); 123 (A.D. 391 ; cp. esp. § 5).

P. 20.—Married clergy. Calpurnius and his father are instances of married clergy, belonging to the period of transition, before the principle of celibacy had been generally recognised. Enjoined by the Spanish Council of Elvira in A.D. 305, this principle had not been universally accepted even in Spain, for it was in answer to an appeal from a Spanish bishop that Pope Siricius wrote his Decretal of A.D. 385, laying down the necessity of celibacy. This ruling expressed the rapidly growing tendency in the western churches, yet at a much later time Gallic councils found it necessary to legislate against married clergy. There is therefore nothing surprising in finding married deacons and presbyters in Britain in the fourth century. It is open to any one who chooses to *believe* that Calpurnius and Potitus gave up family ties before they took orders ; but such a belief would be a pure act of faith, superfluous and ungrounded.

P. 23.—The names *Patricius* and *Sucat*. The statement of medieval biographers that the name *Patricius* was first assumed on the occasion of ordination must be regarded as a conjecture to explain the tradition that he had four names. The earliest mention of the four names (Sucat, Magonus, Cothrige, and Patricius) is in Tírechán (p. 302), who found them in a written source. There is no difficulty about Cothrige ; it has been recognised (by Todd, Rhŷs, Thurneysen, Zimmer) that it is simply an Irish equivalent for Patricius, with the regular mutation of *p* to *c*, which we find in early loan words from the British language (*e.g. casc = pascha, cruimthir = premter* for *presbyter*, cp. Zimmer, *Early Celtic Church*, p. 25). I have pointed out traces of an older (labio-velar) form : *Qatrige* ("Tradition of Muirchu's Text," p. 200). I have also shown (*ib.* p. 201) that, in early tradition, this name was specially connected with Patrick's captivity, and this supports the view that he was named Patricius as a child (his Irish captors rendered it *Qatrige* or *Qotrige*). The genuineness of the name Sucatus (also recorded by Muirchu, *Sochet*, p. 494), which corresponds to the modern Welsh *hygad*, "warlike" (cp. Stokes, *Trip.* p. 616, and the explanation in the scholia on the hymn *Genair Patraicc*, l. 3), is generally admitted and derives some support from a similar consideration (Bury, *ib.* p. 201). It is probable that when Patricius went to Ireland as a bishop his name was generally rendered Patraicc (with *p*), because it now came in its Latin form, and not as a Brythonic word (Patric ?). But we have traces of the use of the other form in *petra Coithrigi* at Uisnech (Tír. $310_{25}$) and *petra Coithirgi* at Cashel (*ib.* 331). Before the seventh century, the *Sprachgefühl* for the mutation of foreign *p* to *c* had so completely disappeared that the equation *Cothrige = Patricius* was not recognised, and an absurd derivation for

*Cothrige* was invented (Tír. 302); but it is significant that this etymology was connected with the captivity.

The fourth name *Magonus* (Tír.: *Magonius* in later documents) appears in the *Historia Brittonum* as *Maun*. It seems to me to be simply the Roman cognomen Magonus (see *C.I.L.* v. 4609; viii. 9515).[1]

P. 23.—Concessa. There is no reason to doubt the tradition (Muirchu, p. 494) that this was the name of Patrick's mother. No credit can be attached to the names or existence of numerous sisters (Lupita, etc.) mentioned in later documents. The tradition that Secundinus (Sechnall) was his sister's son might be regarded as a ground for assuming that he had at least one sister. But it is to be observed that the tradition appears in an extremely suspicious form. In the preface to the *Hymn* which is called by his name (*Lib. Hymnorum*, i. p. 3), Secundinus is described as "son of Restitutus of the Lombards of Letha and of Darerca, Patrick's sister." But a woman named Dar-erca must have been an Irishwoman, not a Briton; and the expression "Lombards of Letha" for Italy suggests that the statement was not derived from a very ancient source. Secundinus does not appear in Muirchu; in Tírechán he is only mentioned in a list of bishops ordained by Patrick; and in the *Additional Notices* (p. 346), where he occurs once, nothing is said of kinship. But he is mentioned twice in the Annals.[2] In A.D. 439 (*Ann. Ult.*) he arrives in Ireland, already a bishop, to help Patrick; and this record must be preferred to Tírechán's statement that Patrick ordained him. Under A.D. 447 his death is recorded (*Ann. Ult.* A.D. 448, *Ann. Inisf.*), in the seventy-fifth year of his age. At that time Patrick cannot have been much more than fifty-eight (see Appendix C, 3), so that he would have been about seventeen years younger than his nephew. This is impossible, except on the supposition that the mother of Secundinus was half-sister of Patrick, daughter of a former wife of Calpurnius.

In *Add. Notices* Lomman (p. 335) is described as his sister's son, and four brothers of Lomman are named as bishops in Ireland; and (p. 340) a brother of Patrick is mentioned as father of Náo and Naí. It is to be observed that none of the names are Latin. Does Patrick's statement in the *Letter against Corot.* 377₁₅ (quis me compulit—alligatus spiritu—ut non uideam

---

[1] Stokes (*Urkeltischer Sprachschatz*, 198) and Rhŷs seek a Celtic etymology for Magonus. Rhŷs treats it as a derivation from Goidelic *magus* (whence the Irish *mug*, "servant"), meaning perhaps originally a "boy."

[2] His day was Nov. 27; *Mart. of Donegal*, p. 319.

aliquem de cognatione mea?) justify the inference that none of his *cognati* were in Ireland?

[The story which places Patrick's capture in Armorica (*Vit. Trip.* p. 16; *Probus*, i. 12; Schol. on hymn *Gen. P.*, etc.) has obviously no historical value, being clearly prompted by the motive of connecting Patrick with Brittany. It has an interest, however, in preserving the name "Sechtmaide, king of the Britons"—a reminiscence apparently of the Emperor Septimius Severus.]

P. 26.—Men-servants and maid-servants. This addition to the data of the *Confession* comes from the *Letter against Coroticus*, 377$_{19}$.

P. 31.—Port to which Patrick escaped. He mentions the distance himself: *ducenta milia passus* (*Conf.* 361$_{33}$). Wicklow would suit either theory of the place of captivity. Of course the distance must not be pressed too closely, but it is to be remembered that Patrick wrote when he had fuller knowledge of the geography than he can have had at the time of his escape. The reason for conjecturing Wicklow is that it seems to have been a port where foreign ships might be looked for; both Palladius and Patrick landed there. Muirchu calls it *portum apud nos clarum* (275$_{12}$).

P. 32.—Suck their breasts: *sugere mammellas eorum, Conf.* 362$_{18}$. I conjecture that the origin of this remarkable phrase, which clearly means to enter into a close intimacy, was a primitive ceremony of adoption. Among some peoples, when a child is adopted, a rite of mock-birth is performed; for instance, the child is placed under the dress of the adoptive mother, and creeps out. For the custom of mock-suckling see Frazer's *Golden Bough*,[2] vol. iii. p. 380, *note*. The make-believe suckling is analogous to, and has the same emblematic meaning as, a make-believe parturition; and it will be admitted that this explanation satisfies perfectly the present context: "I declined to let myself be adopted by them." It is not necessary to infer that a literal adoption was proposed to Patrick by any of the crew; the expression is merely figurative for a close and abiding intimacy (just as we use colloquially the phrase "to be adopted").

It has been thought that the expression is taken from the Vulgate rendering of Isaiah lx. 16: *suges lac gentium et mamilla regum lactaberis*. Even if it were so, the point of the phrase would not be explained, but Mr. White has shown on other grounds the improbability of such a reference. There are no other vestiges of the use of the Vulgate in Patrick's citations from the O.T., whereas there is unmistakable evidence of his use of an Old-Latin version (see White, *Proc. of R.I.A.* 1905, p. 231, and the note on the passage).

P. 34.—They came to the habitations of men: *Conf.* 36331, 34 *ad homines.* This is certainly the right reading, and stood in the MS. used by Muirchu (49532). The *Cod. Arm.* gives *omnes*, which is unsuitable in the context.

*Ib.*—"Thou shalt remain with them two months." Patrick refers here to a second captivity (36325), and his words (which are not lucid) misled his biographers (beginning with Muirchu) into supposing that he was captured on some later occasion. But I cannot think that his words: *et iterum post annos multos adhuc capturam dedi*, refer to the two months which he spent with the traders. They come in curiously after the incident of the dream, and before the mention of the two months. *Post annos multos* cannot naturally be taken of the six years of his captivity in Ireland, but must mean a term of years after his escape. I believe that the sentence is a parenthetical reference to his lifework in Ireland, conceived as a second captivity. "And again, after many years, my captivity was continued." The motive of this abrupt observation was the preceding dream, to which he attributes great significance; it furnishes, in fact, the interpretation of the dream. The second banishment to Ireland is prefigured by the great stone which lay upon his body, and which he could not resist; the sun which lightened its weight is the divine guiding which made that banishment endurable.

### CHAPTER III

P. 37.—Patrick at Lérins. *Dictum Patricii*, see above, App. A, i. 3; Tírechán, 30228 *erat hautem in una ex insolis quae dicitur Aralanensis annis xxx, mihi testante Ultano episcopo.* It seems obvious that the Bollandists and Todd were right in supposing that *Aralanensis* arose from *Lerinensis*. The more recent view that Arelate is meant seems very improbable; though the name Arelate may conceivably have influenced the corruption (cp. App. C, 6 *ad fin.*).

P. 38.—Island monasteries: Gallinaria, Gorgon, Capraria, Palmaria. See Ambrose, *Hexaem.* 3, c. 5, *insulas uelut monilia*; Jerome, *Epist.* 73 § 6 (Migne, 22, 694) [c. 400 A.D.]; Sulp. Severus, *V. Mart.* 6, 5 (*Gallinaria*). For Capraria, see Rutilius Namatianus, *De reditu suo* [c. A.D. 417], i., 439 *sqq.*—

squalet lucifugis insula plena uiris,

and for Gorgon *ib.* 517 *sqq.* For cloisters in the Dalmatian Islands see Jerome, *Epist.* 92. For the Stoechades : Cassian, *Coll.* 18, Praef. (Migne, 49, p. 1089) ; Ennodius, v. *Epiphanii,* 93, *medianas insulas Stoechadas* (so Sirmond and Vogel ; *cycladas,* MSS.) *Lerum ipsamque nutricem summorum montium planam Lerinum,* described as *sanctarum habitationum loca.*

P. 38.—Monastery of Lérins. For the names Lero, Lerina (Lirinus is the form in the best MSS. of Sidonius), see Pliny, *Nat. Hist.* 3, 5. Strabo, 4, 1, 10 gives the names Planasia and Leron.

The exact date of the foundation of the monastery by Honoratus is unknown, but it cannot have been later than the first years of the fifth century. The earliest reference seems to be in a letter of Paulinus of Nola in A.D. 410, or a few years later (*Ep.* 51 to Eucherius and Galla in island of Lero ; this letter seems to show that the foundation was recent). Tillemont in his note on the question (*Mém. ecc.* xii. p. 675) quotes and contests the statement of Baronius and Barralis, that the monastery was founded in A.D. 375 (so Alliez), but he does not give the source for this statement. So far as I can discover, the only foundation for it is indicated by Barralis (*Chronologia sanctorum . . . monasterii sacrae insulae Lerinensis,* 1613), p. 190, where he says he found it *in quodam membr. codice perantiquo Lerin. MS.* We cannot attach any importance to this. Tillemont points out the objections to this date, and founds one of his arguments on the age of Saint Caprasius.

The chief sources for the history of the monastery during the first forty years of its existence are : Hilary, *Sermo de vita s. Honorati* ; Eucherius, *De laude eremi,* cp. also his other writings ; Vincentius, *Commonitorium primum et secundum* ; Honoratus, *Vita s. Hilarii.* All these works will be found in Migne, *P.L.* vol. l. Further information is to be gathered in Paulinus, *Ep.* 51 ; Faustus, *Epp.* ed. Krusch (M.G.H.), and ed. Engelbrecht (*Vienna Corp. Scr. Ecc.*) ; *Homilia de S. Maximo in Eusebii Emiseni ep. homeliae,* p. 84, vº *sqq.* (ed. Gagneius, 1589) ; Sidonius Apollinaris, *Carmen,* 16.

Consult Barralis, *op. cit.* ; Silfverberg, *Hist. Mon. Lerinensis usque ad ann.* 731 (Copenhagen, 1834) ; Tillemont, *Mém. eccl.* (xii. art. on Saint Honoratus, with notes ; *ib.* xv. arts. on Hilary, Eucherius, Vincentius, Maximus of Riez ; *ib.* xvi. art. on Faustus) ; Alliez, *Les îles de Lérins, Cannes, et rivages* (1860), and *Histoire du monastère de Lérins,* vol. i. 1862 ; the articles on Honoratus, Hilary, etc. in the *Dict. of Christian Biography* ;

Krusch's and Engelbrecht's prefaces to their editions of Faustus.

Pp. 38-9.—Snakes at Lerinus: Hilary, *Sermo*, c. 3 (1257, ed. Migne).—Fresh water flows *in media maris amaritudine*, *ib.* 1258. —*In mare magnum recedentia*: Eucherius, *De laude eremi*, c. 1 (701 ed. Migne).—Vines, etc., *ib.* c. 42.—Anecdote of the tablet of Honoratus: Hilary, *Sermo*, c. 4, 1261 (*mel suum ceris reddidisti*).—"Break through the wall of the passions," etc. : Eucherius, *Hom.* ii. 836.—*Venire ad eremum*, etc., *Id.*, *Hom.* iv. 842.—Manual work was practised at Lérins, Gennadius, *de scr. ecc.* lxix.

P. 40.—Faustus. Engelbrecht (preface to his ed.) gives reasons for placing the birth of Faustus *not long* before 410; but they are not absolutely decisive.

P. 47.—Semi-Pelagianism at Lerinus.—Vincentius, author of the *Commonitorium* (which Neander justly describes as "ein für die Geschichte des Begriffs von der Tradition epochemachendes Buch," *Kirchengeschichte*, iii. 262), held semi-Pelagian views (cp. *ib.* iv. 405). Faustus was also a strong exponent of modified Pelagianism, though severe in condemnation of Pelagianism; his work, *De gratia dei et libero arbitrio*, is extant (*Opp.* ed Engelbrecht; Migne, 58, 783 *sqq.*). On the other hand, Hilary of Arles was a follower of Augustine, and Lupus a decided anti-Pelagian. Cp. Duchesne, *Fastes épiscopaux de l'ancienne Gaule*, pp. 129-30.

P. 42.—Victoricus: appears transformed into an angel in Muirchu; and in later biographers the name is changed to Victor. In Tírechán (330₂₂) we meet a Victoricus whom Patrick ordained bishop for Domnach Maigen.

P. 43.—Pelagius, a Scot, but probably born in Britain. See Bury, "The Origin of Pelagius," in *Hermathena*, xxx. p. 26 *sqq.*, where the evidence is set out. Zimmer holds that he was born in Ireland (*Pelagius in Ireland*, pp. 18-20). For a general account of the Pelagian theory and the course of the controversy, see Harnack, *History of Dogma*, vol. x.

P. 47.—Patrick's reluctance to go to Ireland: cp. esp. *Conf.* 365₁₉, contra, *Hiberione non sponte pergebam donec prope deficiebam* (cp. *Ps.* 18.37, White).

P. 49.—Autissiodorum.—For the connexion of Patrick with Auxerre see Muirchu, pp. 496, 272 ; cp. Hymn *Gen. Patr.* 19, 20 (p. 98, *Lib. Hymn.* vol. i.). The authenticity of the record that Patrick received his theological training in Gaul is borne out by the desire to visit the brethren in Gaul which he expresses in the *Confession*, 370₁₂.—For Amator, see Appendix C, 9. For Iserninus and Auxilius: Muirchu, p. 273; *Add. Notices*, p. 342 (*Patricius et Isserninus*, 1. *epscop Fith, cum Germano fuerunt in Olsiodra ciuitate*, etc., a passage which shows that Iserninus was an Irishman); and Appendix C, 9. The notice in *Ann. Ult. s.a.* 439 might seem to imply that Iserninus was already a bishop when he went to Ireland in that year; but Tírechán says that Patrick ordained Eserninus at Killcullen. See below, p. 310.

Pp. 49-50.—Patrick ordained *deacon*: *Confession*, 365₁₂ (see Appendix C, 9). Patrick discouraged in his enterprise: *Conf.* 371₁₁, *multi hanc legationem prohibebant*, etc.

P. 50.—Germanus: see Appendix A, i. 7, on the *Vita Germani* of Constantius, and W. Levison's monograph there cited. On the apparent inconsistency of the statement that he held a military command with the fact of his civil career (see Levison, *op. cit.* p. 117).

P. 51.—Germanus in Britain: Prosper, *Chron. s.a.* 429—the source for the fact that Germanus was sent by Celestine as his representative *ad insinuationem Palladii diaconi*. We are not told whether Palladius was a deacon of Rome or of Auxerre. It is to be observed that this notice is strictly contemporary; the first edition of the Chronicle was published only four years later. Constantius, in the *V. Germani*, does not mention the part played by Celestine. He represents the mission of Germanus, with whom Lupus of Troyes was associated, as decided by a synod of Gallic bishops which assembled in response to an appeal from Britain (c. 12). It is difficult to say how far we should be justified in accepting the statement of Constantius and reconciling it with Prosper's, in the sense that a Gallic synod decreed the mission and Celestine sanctioned and approved it (so Tillemont, *Mém. ecc.* xv. 15, and others). But it may be so far correct, that an appeal was made from Britain to Gaul, probably to Auxerre, and that Auxerre enlisted the intervention of Rome. The question is discussed in Levison, *op. cit.* pp. 120-2.

*Ib.*—British Pelagians: Agricola was prominent. Writings of a British Pelagian are edited by Caspari, *Briefe, Abhandlungen und Predigten aus den zwei letzten Jahrhunderten des kirchlichen Alterthums* (1890), who ascribes them to Agricola. For Fastidius cp. Tillemont, xv. 16, 17; but Mr. H. Williams seeks to defend him against the charge of heresy (*Transactions of Society of Cymmrodorion*, 1893-4, p. 71 *sqq.*).

P. 52.—Pelagianism in Ireland: see Zimmer, *Pelagius in Ireland*, 22-24.

*Ib.*—Patrick's false friend: *Confession*, p. 365, 366: esp. 366$_{13}$, et comperi ab aliquantis fratribus ante defensionem illam [see below, note on p. 202], quod ego non interfui nec in Brittanniis eram, nec a me orietur [I would read *oriebatur*: "without any prompting from me"], ut et ille in mea absentia pro me pulsaret.

P. 54.—Mission of Palladius: Prosper, *Epit. s.a.* 431, *ad Scottos in Christum credentes ordinatus a papa Celestino Palladius primus episcopus mittitur*. It has been pointed out by Zimmer that this notice probably owes its insertion in the Chronicle to the circumstance that Prosper was at Rome in this year (*Celtic Church*, p. 32). The mission of Palladius is also referred to rhetorically by Prosper in his *Contra Coll.* c. xxi.; Migne, *P.L.* li. p. 271: *ordinato Scotis episcopo dum Romanam insulam studet seruare catholicam, fecit etiam barbaram Christianam* (sc. *Caelestinus*).

P. 56.—Churches said to have been founded by Palladius: See $V_2 24 = V_4 28$ (= W source) = *V. Trip.* p. 30. In Cell Fine "he left his books and the casket with relics of Paul and Peter, and the board on which he used to write" (*V. Trip.* trans. Stokes). In Donard were preserved the relics of "Sylvester and Solinus" ($V_4$; Solonius, *V. Trip.*). Acc. to $V_4$ the Tech na Romhan was founded by the disciples of Palladius. For the identification of this name with *Tigroney*, see Shearman, *Loca Patriciana*, p. 27. Shearman has attempted to identify the site of Cell Fine with the ancient cemetery of Killeen Cormac (near Colbinstown in Kildare on the borders of Wicklow). He supposed that Killeen has not here its usual sense of "little church," but stands for "Kill Fhine," so that the name would mean "the church of the clan of Cormac"; and he supposes that the saint Abbán maccu Cormaic was buried here. It cannot be said that he has made out his case. His argument largely depends on his view that the remarkable bilingual inscription preserved in the graveyard is connected with the poet Dubthach maccu Lugair—a view which must be rejected (see below, p. 305). The same sources mention the landing-place of Palladius. Muirchu (p. 272) has no local details, and only notes his failure in general terms. The *feri et inmites homines*, who would not receive his doctrine, evidently mean especially Nathi son of Garrchu, who is mentioned in other sources as opposing Palladius.

P. 59.—Patrick's preparations. Cp. Muirchu, 275$_{10}$.

P. 59.—Companions of Palladius: *Augustinus et Benedictus*, Muirchu, 272₃₁. The thought strikes one that they might have brought some intimation from Ireland that Patrick would be acceptable as successor to Palladius. If Palladius died in Dalaradia, and these companions came with a message from Dalaradian Christians, this might have been a motive for Patrick's special connexion with that region of Ireland.

Pp. 61 *sqq.*—Position of the Roman see. For what I have said on this subject I must acknowledge my particular obligations to the important study of M. E.-Ch. Babut, *Le Concile de Turin*, 1904. His chief object is to determine the date and circumstances of the Council of Turin (Sept. 417), but the book is of much wider scope. For the position of the apostolic see in the latter half of the fourth century, Rade's *Damasus, Bischof von Rom*, 1882, is important.

## Chapter IV

P. 70.—Kingdom of Cashel. Cp. the remarks of Rhŷs, *Studies in Early Irish History*, p. 31.

P. 74.—Solar worship. Patrick, *Confession*, p. 374. Cormac's *Glossary*, *s.v.* indelba. It has been suggested that a circle on an inscribed (ogam) stone, which seems to be oriented, at Drumlusk, near Kenmare, is connected with solar worship (Macalister, *Studies in Irish Epigraphy*, ii. 116-7). Cp. H. Gaidoz, "Le dieu gaulois du soleil et le symbolisme de la roue," *Rev. arch.* 1884 and 1885.

*Ib.*—Pillar worship. Patrick, *ib.* p. 369. For the idol Cromm Cruach, see p. 306. Cp. the stone of worship (*ail adrada*) in *Ancient Laws*, iv. 142.

P. 76.—For white dress of Druids, see Tírechán, p. 325-6. For their tonsure see Appendix A, i. 4.

P. 79.—Muirchu, 273-4. "Adzehead" was evidently meant as a nickname for the tonsured monk. I have given the oracle as it is found in Muirchu's Latin rendering. He must have known the prophecy in a different form from the Irish version which is preserved in the glosses on the Hymn *Genair Patraicc* (*Liber Hymnorum*, i. p. 100): "Adzehead will come, over the mad-crested sea, his cloak hole-head, his staff crook-head, his table in the west of his house; all his household will answer Amen, Amen." See Atkinson, *ib.* ii. 181-2, and my article on the "Tradition of Muirchu's Text," p. 203 (in *Hermathena*, 28, 1902).

CHAPTER V

P. 81.—Patrick's landing-place in Ireland. Muirchu, p. 275. Palladius had landed at the same place (*Vit. Trip.* p. 30 ; V₂, 24 and 25). Todd (*St. Patrick*, 338 *sqq.*) thought that the circumstances of the landing of Palladius were transferred to Patrick, it being unreasonable to suppose that both missionaries should have landed at the same place. This is a bad argument. For, in the first place, Inber Dee may have been the usual port for ships from South Britain ; and, in the second place, nothing was more natural than that Patrick should first go to the region in which his predecessor had been active. And if this is admitted there is nothing unreasonable (Todd's second objection) in supposing that the chieftain Nathi MacGarrchon, who (according to *Vit. Trip.* p. 30, V₂, 24) opposed Palladius, should also have opposed Patrick (V₂, 25). It is more to the purpose that Muirchu says nothing of Nathi, but it may be observed that his opposition might help to explain why both bishops remained such a short time in Wicklow.

P. 83.—Sea-journey from Wicklow to Ulidia. Dr. Gwynn suggests that Muirchu (who seems to have visited Ulidia, see Appendix A, ii. 3) made this journey himself. Patrick's visit to Inis Patrick is also mentioned by Tírechán (p. 303), who seems almost to imply that it was the first place he visited in Ireland. According to Tírechán's account he proceeded from the islands off Skerries directly to the plain of Breg (the visit to Ulidia is not mentioned). Here we have a Meath tradition, at variance with the Ulidian tradition reproduced by Muirchu. It is perhaps impossible to decide between them. There can be no doubt that Patrick was active both in Down and in Meath ; the question at issue is only one of chronological order. Muirchu worked the Ulidian episode into a narrative which originated in Meath, but this proves nothing for the superior authenticity of either. And on the other hand, the motive which probably influenced Muirchu in accepting the Down tradition that Mag Inis in Ulidia was the first field of Patrick's labours—namely the bishop's desire to visit and convert his old master, and pay him the price of his freedom—cannot have very much weight, even if we accept the tradition that Patrick was a captive in north Dalaradia. In my narrative I have adopted Muirchu's order, but without any decided opinion that it is right. If, as I think, Dalaradia was the destination of Palladius when he left Wicklow, there may have been a good reason for Patrick's proceeding thither first.   If the tradition that his first Easter in Ireland A.D. 433 was celebrated at Slane is accepted, very little time is left for his labours in Ulidia.

P. 84.—Patrick's landing-place in Dalaradia.   Muirchu, p. 275.   The *ostium Slain* was identified by J. W. Hanna in a rare tract, *An Enquiry into the True Landing-place of St. Patrick in Ulster*, printed at Downpatrick in 1858.   The river flows into the lake at Ringban, about two miles from Saul, dividing the townlands of Ringban and Ballintogher (see Ordnance Map). Mr. Hanna discovered that the name Slaney was still in use for the river, and this furnished him with the identification.   Since he wrote, the name has been forgotten.   The church of Ballintogher is called the church of Bally-*bren* in the Taxation of Pope Nicholas ; offering the same word by which the mouth of Strangford Lough, *fretum quod est Brene*, was known to Muirchu (see further on the locality, O'Laverty, *Diocese of Down and Connor*, i. 216 *sqq.*).

*Ib.*—Dún Lethglasse.   For the striking remains of the fort, also called Rathceltchair, see Mr. Westropp's valuable study on the forts of Ireland in *Transactions of R.I.A.* vol. xxxi. p. 586, where it is cited as an instance of the mote type of fort.   It has a platform separate from the central mound, and the mound is surrounded by three ramparts thirty feet wide.

*Ib.* — Dichu.   The proof of Dichu's reality[1] is supplied by the petition (Muirchu $296_{10}$) *ut nepotes Dichon qui te benigne susceperunt misericordiam mereantur et non pereant.   Nepotes Dichon* means the Hy Dichon, Dichu's tribe ; and, though *susceperunt* may be an error for *suscepit*, the text is not inconsistent with the story.   There is further confirmation in the independent testimony to the existence of Rus or Ros, son of Trechim, said to have been Dichu's brother.   (See Appendix, C, 12 ; on the *Senchus Mór*.)   Rus is said to have lived at Derlus ($V_2$ c. 31 = $V_4$ c. 37, *Vit. Trip.* p. 38, cp. $V_3$ c. 33), which was at Mrechtan, now Bright.   It has been conjectured that the Castle of Bright stands on the site of Derlus (O'Laverty, *op. cit.* i. p. 148), and the Protestant church is supposed to be on the site of the ancient church (*ib.* 147).

P. 86.—For Skerry, cp. Reeves, *Eccl. Ant.* pp. 83-4.

P. 87.—Sabul, Saul (see Reeves, *op. cit.* pp. 220 *sqq.*).

P. 90.—Tassach at Raholp.   That he was stationed in the neighbourhood of Saul is implied in Muirchu $297_{10}$.   For his

---

[1] Dichu of Saul appears in the *Martyrology* of Donegal under April 29 (p. 114).

connexion with Rathcolpa see *Mart. Dung.* April 14; schol. on *Genair Patraicc* hymn, l. 53 (*Lib. Hymn.* i. p. 102). There are ruins of an ancient church, known as Church-Moyley, described in Reeves, *Eccl. Antiq.* p. 39.

P. 90.—Loarn at Bright. *V. Trip.* p. 38, $V_4$ c. 37, $V_2$ c. 31. It was recorded in a common source of *V. Trip.* (p. 40) and $V_2$ (c. 32) that near Bright Patrick converted Mochae, who afterwards founded a church at Noendrum, now Mahee island in L. Strangford (*ob.* 497, *Ann. Ult.* and Tigernach). O'Laverty has much to say on this, *op. cit.* i. 143-4. For Bright, cp. Reeves, *op. cit.* p. 35; for Noendrum, *ib.* pp. 10, 148 *sqq.*, 187 *sqq.* It is a legitimate inference from the silence of our authorities, that no church at Dún Lethglasse was founded by Patrick. For its history see Reeves, *op. cit.* 141 *sqq.*, 220 *sqq.* The first bishop recorded is Fergus, whose death is placed in *Ann. Ult.* at A.D. 584 or 590.

P. 91.—*Mudebroth.* Dr. W. Stokes interprets *Dei mei iudicium* (*Trip.* p. 289), but cp. Atkinson, *Lib. Hymn.* ii. p. 179.

*Ib.*—Druimbo, *Collum bouis.* Cp. O'Laverty, *op. cit.* p. 228 *note.*

## CHAPTER VI

P. 102.—Foundation of Trim. *Additional Notes,* 334-6 (translation with notes in Todd's *St. Patrick,* 257 *sqq.*). The name of the wife of Fedilmid is given as Scoth Noe ( = *flos recens*). Lomman is said to have been a son of a sister of Patrick ($335_{13}$). The legendary character of the story is obvious; but there seems no reason to doubt the Trim traditions which it involves—the co-operation of the Briton Lomman with Fedilmid and his British wife and their son Fortchernn. Lomman's name appears in the *Martyrologies* (Tallaght and Donegal) under October 11.

P. 104.—The legend of the Easter fire at Slane and Patrick's visit to Tara is told in the text after Muirchu, who used an older (probably Irish) source. It is very briefly summarised in Tírechán (p. 306); he differs from Muirchu as to the number and names of the Druids. Todd has the merit of having seen that the whole story is unhistorical and that it is absurd to draw any chronological inferences or treat seriously its chronological implications. On the other hand, historical motives clearly underlie the story, as I have sought to show in the text. It may be said that the celebration of Patrick's first Easter at Slane *may be* a historical fact. It is evident that this was a tradition at

Slane ; and it is quite possible that Patrick may have spent his first Easter there for the purpose of baptizing converts, as Easter was at that time one of the chief occasions for that ceremony. We may regard this as a possibility ; but we are only entitled to say that there must have been some motive for the location of the fire at Slane. It is a nice problem whether the scriptural parallels (the contest between Moses and the magicians, and the Book of Daniel), which pervade Muirchu's account, were first introduced by Muirchu himself, or presided at the original composition of the legend. I am inclined to adopt the second alternative ; and to hold, with Todd (though he does not clearly distinguish Muirchu from Muirchu's source), that Patrick's contest with the Druids took place "at the first Christian passover or Easter celebrated by him in Ireland," because the similar contest of Moses occurred shortly before the first passover of the children of Israel, in the land of Goshen (as Muirchu— following his source?—points out). Zimmer's view, that the motive of Muirchu in giving prominence to the story of Patrick's first Easter was connected with the Easter controversy in the seventh century (*Celtic Church*, p. 81), has been noticed above, Appendix A, ii. 3 ; but if Muirchu was specially interested in it on that account, the Easter question had certainly nothing to do with the origin of the legend, which must be far older than the seventh century. For Beltane fires cp. Frazer, *Golden Bough*, iii. 259 *sqq.*; for fires on Easter Eve, *ib.* 247 *sqq.*

[There is a remarkable notice in the *Calendar* of Oengus that on April 5 "on the great feast of Beccan MacCula, with a victory of piety excellent Patrick's baptism was kindled in Ireland" (transl. Stokes, p. lxvii.). This obviously refers to the Slane legend, but the date April 5 must have a different origin, as Easter did not fall on that day in 433. During Patrick's episcopate it fell only once on April 5, viz., in A.D. 459, whether on the 84 or 84 (12) cycle. The notice therefore suggests that in that year there was a baptismal ceremony which was remembered ; and it might be conjectured that it was the occasion of the raid of Coroticus, which probably occurred towards the end of Patrick's life. See cap. ix. and notes.]

P. 104.—High festival at Tara (*Feis Temrach*). The holding of such an assemblage by Loigaire is recorded in *Ann. Ult. s.a.* 454 (cp. *s.a.* 461), and by his successor Ailill Molt, *s.a.* 467 (alternative dates 469, 470). According to the *Book of Rights* (p. 7), such conventions were held every seventh year ; other traditions represent them as triennial (cp. Todd, *St. Patrick*, p.

416). But these notices in the *Annals* suggest that they were not held at stated periods in the fifth century, but were summoned at the pleasure of the High King for special purposes. This is especially suggested by the notice (*Ann. Ult. s.a.* 461) that Loigaire lived seven years and seven months after the Feast of Tara, as if it were a unique, not a recurring, event in his reign ; and the statement is inconsistent with a septennial as well as with a triennial period. The periodic convention contemplated by the *Book of Rights* was held at Samhain (Nov. 1).

P. 105.—The company driving over the plain of Breg might possibly contain a reminiscence of the custom of a *Flurumritt*, as described by Mannhardt, *Der Baumkultus der Germanen und ihrer Nachbarstämme*, 397 *sqq.* In the Archduchy of Austria it was the custom for the sons and servants of the house to ride round the fields at Easter, *vor Sonnenaufgang im schnellsten Laufe.* Other instances of such early processions are cited. The custom of proceeding *ad laevam* against the sun with malicious intent, seems still to exist near Lough Case in Mayo. There is a pile of stones near the lake "round which stations are made *desiul* [rightward], except in the case of maliciously disposed persons, who occasionally come on the sly in the dead of night, and go round widdershins in order to raise storms to destroy crops and kill cattle" (Professor Rhŷs, *Proceedings of Royal Society of Antiquaries of Ireland*, Part iii. vol. viii. 5th series, 1898, p. 233).

P. 110.—The *Burg* in Eiffel district (on first Sunday in Lent): Mannhardt, *Baumkultus*, p. 501. Compare also the practice of the Gallic Druids described by Caesar, *B.G.* vi. 16, and the material collected by Mr. Frazer, *Golden Bough*, iii. 319 *sqq.*

P. 111.—Burning of Sandan. Cp. Frazer, *Golden Bough*, iii. 168 *sqq.*

P. 112.—Mode of burial of Loigaire. Tírechán, 308₄ : the text should be read as follows :—

"Nam Neel pater meus non siniuit mihi credere sed ut sepeliar in cacuminibus Temro" (quasi uiris consistentibus in bello, quia utuntur gentiles, etc.), "ego filius Neill, et filius Dunlinge [*sc.* sepeliatur] im Maistin in campo Liphi pro duritate odi[u]i."

Dr. Gwynn saw that *ego* is to be construed with *sepeliar.* It seems best to suppose that *quasi—bello* is not part of Loigaire's declaration. As Mr. Stokes points out, *odiui* can be translated as a perfect (the relative being omitted), but *odii* proposed by Todd furnishes better sense. The two foes were still to face each other in their tombs, standing in their armour, Loigaire looking southward and the King of Laigin northward.

P. 115.—Dubthach.  Muirchu 283₂, *Dubthoch maccu-Lugil poetam optimum*; *Add. Notices* 344, *Dubthach maccu-Lugair.* Material about the Hy Lugair of Leinster is collected in Shearman's *Loca Patriciana.* Shearman's theory that the Killeen Cormac bilingual stone commemorates Dubthach and three of his sons cannot be maintained.  The ogam inscription means "(monument) of Ovanus, descendant of Ivacattus," and the Latin inscription reads Ivvere Drvvides, which Professor Rhŷs interprets "of the Druid of Ivvera ( = Ireland)."  Thus the stone would commemorate one Ovanus, a Druid.  It certainly belongs to the Christian period, and may probably be dated to the sixth century.  Professor Rhŷs thinks it is by no means impossible that this Druid was of the race of Dubthach maccu-Lugair (*Studies in Early Irish History*, p. 7).  But there can hardly be much ground for such a supposition, especially as Dubthach was a poet, not a Druid.  The inscription illustrates the survival of Druidism.

The presence of Dubthach, a Leinster poet, at Tara, in the legend, is remarkable.  Was the incident inserted by Muirchu himself, from Slébte tradition, or is Muirchu only responsible for the reference to Fíacc, Dubthach's pupil?  It seems probable that Dubthach's presence appeared in the legend in its original form, and was a genuine reminiscence (cp. Appendix A, ii. 5), and if so, it betrays that Patrick's legendary appearance at Tara was suggested by an actual visit, in very different circumstances, for the purpose of consulting with Loigaire and representatives from various parts of Ireland, one of whom would have been Dubthach, about the status, etc., of Christian communities.  For the *file*, poet and lawyer, cp. D'Arbois de Jubainville, *Droit celtique*, i. 321 *sqq.*

P. 117.—For the foundations in Meath, see Tírechán, 307 *sqq.*

P. 118.—Donaghpatrick.  The place is marked by a fine earth-fort of the mote type, with a crescent platform, separated from the mound by a ditch.  See Westropp, *Trans. of R.I.A.* xxxi. p. 714.

P. 119.—Taillte: burning of the first-born offspring.  Cp. *Book of Leinster*, 201 a. 15, and O'Curry, *Manners and Customs*, vol. i. p. dcxl.

P. 120.—Uisnech.  For the plan of this hill-town, see Westropp, *ib.* p. 688.

P. 123.—The account of Patrick's visit to Mag Slecht (which

was near Ballymagauran in Co. Cavan) is found in later lives (*Vita Tertia*, c. 46, and *Tripartite*, p. 90). But there is reason to suppose that an account of the visit has fallen out of Tírechán's text (p. 311): see Bury, *Itinerary of Patrick in Connaught*, pp. 154-6.

P. 123.—Cend Cruaich, *Tripart.*; ceneroth or cencroth (corruption of cencroch?), *Vit. Tert.*; Cromm Cruach, *Book of Leinster*, 16 b. 30, and cp. 213 b. 38 *sqq.*; Crom Cróich, *Rennes Dindsenchas* (ed. Stokes), in *Rev. Celt.* 16, 35-6. See Rhŷs, *Celtic Religion*, pp. 200 *sqq.* In the *Vita Tertia*, c. 46, it is said that Loigaire used to adore in Mag Slecht; but we cannot attribute much importance to this statement.

CHAPTER VII

P. 127.—Amolngaid. The name occurs on a gravestone at Breastagh, north of Killala, in King Amolngaid's country: maq(i) Corrbri maq(i) Ammllongatt— "(monument of . . .) of the son of Corpri, son of Amolngaid" (Rhŷs, *Proceedings* of *R.S.A.I.* Part iii. vol. vii. 5th series, p. 235, 1898). The *Genealogy of the Hy Fiachrach* (ed. O'Donovan, p. 11) gives Coirpre as the name of a son of King Amolngaid; likewise a notice in the *Book of Lecan* (fol. 46, see O'Donovan, *ib.* p. 12, *note* a). There is thus ground for supposing that the person commemorated was a descendant of the king.

P. 129.—Mathona was connected with Tamnach. Tírechán calls her sister of Benignus, Patrick's successor. He probably confounded the famous Benignus with an obscure namesake whom he mentions in another place ($319_{15}$): *Benignus frater Cethiaci de genere Ailello.* We should expect Mathona, in Tirerrill, to be *de genere Ailello.*

P. 134.—For the place of crossing the Shannon (Sinona) indicated by Tírechán, see my *Itinerary of Patrick in Connaught*, where it is shown that the view which placed it near Clonmacnois is untenable.

P. 136.—On Rathcrochan and the various mounds around it, see O'Donovan's long note, *Annals of Four Masters, s.a.* 1223, vol. iii. pp. 204-6; and cp. Westropp, *Trans. of R.I.A.* xxxi. p. 687. On the red stone: O'Donovan, *Hy Fiachrach*, pp. 24-5, *note* (no mention of this stone is found before the seventeenth century).

P. 139.—Baptismal queries. Three questions were put in the Roman usage :—

Credis in Deum Patrem omnipotentem?

Credis et in Iesum Christum, Filium eius unicum, dominum nostrum, natum et passum?

Credis et in Spiritum sanctum, sanctam ecclesiam, remissionem peccatorum, carnis resurrectionem?

(Duchesne, *Origines du culte chrétien*, p. 313.)

P. 140.—Death of Ethne and Fedelm after their baptism. The same thing is told in Muirchu's story *de Morte Moneisen Saxonissae* (p. 496). Monesan, daughter of a king in Britain, cannot be induced by her parents to marry, but persists in asking her mother and her nurse cosmic questions. Her parents, hearing that Patrick received weekly visits from God, took her to Ireland, and besought the saint to allow their daughter to see God. He baptized her, and she immediately committed her spirit to the hands of the angels: *moritur ibi et adunatur*. She was buried at a church which Muirchu does not name, but her relics were venerated there in his time. Compare also the story of Ros, brother of Dichu, and the instance in the life of St. Brendan, cited by Todd (*St. Patrick*, p. 459 and note). The other cases which he quotes (p. 125 and note 2) are not so closely parallel.

P. 145.—Inscription at Selce. Tírechán, p. 319; Bury, "Supplementary Notes" in *Eng. Hist. Review*, October 1902. Bishop Brón MacIcni was consecrated by Patrick (Tír. 305₁₀), and his name appeared as bishop on the Selce inscription (319₇). The inference is that Patrick's visit to Killespugbrone (327₁₉) was on the first journey; but of course he may have been there twice. Brón is commemorated in the Martyrologies of Tallaght and Donegal at June 8, and in the latter his death is assigned to A.D. 511.

P. 148.—Patrick's foundations in Tirawley. I may refer to two papers by Bishop Healy in the *Irish Eccl. Record*, 1889 (673 *sqq.* and 906 *sqq.*), giving an account of an antiquarian visit which he made to the neighbourhood of Killala.

## CHAPTER VIII

P. 151.—Relics. For the notices in Tírechán see App. C, 16. The relics at Armagh are also mentioned in *Liber Angueli*, 354. A ridiculous story was afterwards invented that Patrick threw all the inhabitants of Rome into a miraculous sleep, and then plundered the city of its most precious relics (*Vit. Trip.* p. 238). It illustrates the moral ideals of medieval Irish ecclesiastics, but hardly proves, as Todd suggests (p. 481), "the unscrupulous manner in which the lives were interpolated to prop up later superstitions." For the extension of the cult of relics from the seventh century forward see Zimmer, *Celtic Church*, pp. 119 *sqq.*; but his thesis that relics were unknown before in Ireland is highly improbable.

P. 155.—Emain, Navan. For a description and plan of the remains see M. d'Arbois de Jubainville, *Rev. Celt.* xvi. p. 1 *sqq.*; and cp. Westropp, *Trans. of R.I.A.* xxxi. p. 684.

*Ib.*—House of entertainment at Navan : *Ann. of Four Masters*, *s.a.* 1387.

*Ib.*—If Daire was King of Oriel, one is surprised at the way he is introduced by Muirchu (290) as *quidam homo dives et honorabilis in regionibus Orientalium* (*i.e.* in Orior = Airthir, the eastern part of Oriel = Oirgialla. This passage proves that Orior extended further westward than the regions comprised in the two modern baronies of Orior). This looks as if he were only an under-king, perhaps King of the Hy-Nialláin (O'Neill-land) cp. *Book of Rights*, p. 146, for he was a descendant of Niallán, cp. *Trip.* p. 228, and Todd, p. 481. On the other hand, if the tradition that Daire co-operated with Loigaire and Corc in initiating the Senchus Mór is correct, it looks as if he may have been King of Oriel. In a tract in the *Lebor na hUidre* (edited by Stokes in his *Tripartite Life*, pp. 562 *sqq.*) he is called *rí Ulad* (p. 564) by an anachronism. It seems that he was in any case chief of the Hy-Nialláin, and probable that he was also King of Oriel. The mere fact that Armagh was chosen by Patrick as his chief seat seems to me (as I have indicated in the text) an argument in favour of this conclusion.

P. 156.—Date of foundation of Armagh, A.D. 444. We must here follow the Annals (see Appendix A, iii. 1). In the story of the foundation of Trim in the *Additional Notices*, it is stated that Trim was founded immediately on Patrick's arrival in Ireland, *i.e.* A.D. 432, "in the twenty-fifth year before the foundation of Armagh." This would place the foundation of Armagh in 457— a date which is obviously too late, and has been rightly rejected by Todd (*St. P.* p. 470). Is it possible that there had been a pre-Patrician foundation at Trim, twenty-four years older than Armagh, and that the statement is due to a confusion between this and Patrick's second founding ?

P. 159.—Northern Church at Armagh. The church which Patrick founded on the hill is called by Muirchu "northern church," *sinistralis aeclessia* ; hence Reeves supposes it "to have stood somewhere near the extremity of the north transept of the present cathedral" (p. 15). On the other hand, it has been suggested that the adjective means that the church was built *north and south* (cp. Todd, *St. P.* p. 412, and Stokes, note on Muirchu, p. 292). The argument for this interpretation is that the church was called the *sabhall*, and that the other church which bore the same name (at Saul) lay north and south (*transverse*) according to the *Vita Tertia*, c. 31 ; hence it is suggested that churches with this peculiarity were called *sabhalls*. Reeves had taken this view in an earlier work, *Antiquities of Down and Connor*, pp. 220-1.

P. 159.—Graveyard. *Vit. Trip.* 228, "the place where is the *ferta* to-day" (Stokes), *not* as Colgan (so Reeves and Todd), "the place where are the two graves, *da ferta*."

P. 162.—Clogher (in Tyrone). No connexion of Patrick with Clochar is mentioned in the *Lib. Arm.*, but there is a good deal about it in the *Vit. Trip.* 174 *sqq.* The Bishop of Clochar, macc Cairthinn, is described as Patrick's champion. (It is not clear that he is the same as *filius Cairthin* in *Add. Notices*, 338₃). The *Domnach Airgit* was preserved at Clochar, at the time when the Part III. of the *Vit. Trip.* was compiled (p. 176), and afterwards transferred to Clones. It is now in the Dublin Museum, and its history will be found in the papers of Dr. Petrie (*Trans. of R.I.A.* vol. xviii. 1838), and Dr. Bernard (*ib.* vol. xxx. Pt. vii., 1893). An inner box of yew is protected by a silver-plated copper cover, which is enclosed in an outer case of gold-plated silver, richly ornamented. It contained, but not originally, a copy of the Latin gospels, of which mutilated fragments are preserved. It used to be thought that this MS. dated from the fifth century, and belonged to Patrick, but Dr. Bernard's careful examination proves that it can hardly be earlier than the eighth century. As for the box, which was probably meant for relics, not for a MS., it may be identified with the *Domnach Airgit* of the *Vita Trip.*, and is therefore at least as old as the tenth century ; but more cannot be said.

It may be observed that Clochar is called *Clochar macc nDoimni* (*Vit. Trip.* p. 178), and one of the bishops whose consecration Tírechán notices (304) is Iustianus mac hu Daiméne.

*Ib.*—Ardpatrick. The tradition that Patrick founded Ard Patric east of Louth, though not in the *Lib. Arm.*, deserves mention, because Mochtae, whom Patrick established there according to *Vit. Trip.* 226-8, is mentioned in Adamnan's

*Vita Columbae* in the only passage where Adamnan refers to Patrick (*Preface*):—

quidam proselytus Brito, homo sanctus, sancti Patricii episcopi discipulus, Maucteus nomine.

According to *Ann. Ult.* Maucteus died in A.D. 535 or 537. If he was a pupil of Patrick, he must have been very old when he died. A work by Mochtae was quoted in the *Liber Cuanach: Ann. Ult.*, *s.a.* 471; and the opening words of a letter of his are given *s.a.* 535: *Maucteus peccator prespiter sancti Patricii discipulus in Domino salutem.*

P. 163.—Patrick in Leinster. Sources: Tírechán 330-1; *Add. Notices*, 342-6 and 349-50 (with corresponding passages in *Vit. Trip.*). For Munster and Ossory, see Tír. 331. The Muskerry of Co. Cork is indicated in *Add. Notices*, p. $351_2 = Vit. Trip.$ 220. For North Munster (Thomond) see $350_{31} = Vit. Trip.$ 200. Tírechán notices the foundation of Domus Martyrum (Martortech) at Druimm Urchaille (in Co. Kildare). For its site compare Shearman's conjectures, *Loc. Patr.* p. 112.

*Ib.*—Consecration of Auxilius and Iserninus.—The evidence for their consecration by Patrick is Tírechán, $331_3$: *et ordinavit Auxilium puerum Patricii exorcistam et Eserninum et Mactaleum in Cellola Cuilinn.* It may be questioned whether the text is sound; there is certainly some mistake about Auxilius, who could not be described as *puer Patricii exorcista*, and it is not stated to what order they were ordained. In Tírechán's list of bishops ordained by Patrick (304), Auxilius and Mactaleus appear, but not Iserninus. In the corresponding passage in the *Vit. Trip.* (186) nothing is said of ordaining ("he *left* Auxilius in Killossy, and Iserninus and MaccTail in Kilcullen"). In the Add. Notices in *Lib. Arm.* (p. 342) it seems to be implied that Iserninus was already a bishop. See above, p. 310.

P. 164.—Birth of Iserninus in Cliu (*Add. Notices*, p. 342). For the locality see Shearman, *Loca Patriciana*, p. 141 *note*.

P. 165.—Fíacc. Memoranda in *Lib. Arm.* (*Trip.* 344); cp. Muirchu, 283. The story represents Fíacc as consecrated bishop *per saltum*. This may be an error. It is possible that he did not become a bishop till he went to Slébte, and that at Domnach Féicc he was in inferior orders.

*Ib.*—Domnach Féicc. Shearman, 186-8; the argument is at least plausible, that it lay in the region between Clonmore and Aghowle. He would fix it more precisely in the townland of Kilabeg.

P. 170.—The liturgy used by Patrick. Compare Duchesne, *Origines du culte chrétien*, 3rd ed. (1903), chap. iii. p. 88 *sqq.* The *Antiphonary* of Bangor is an example of a Gallican liturgy unmodified by Roman influence, and according to Dr. MacCarthy we have another in the oldest part of the Stowe missal (see above Appendix A, i. 3, *ad fin.*). For Celtic liturgies see Warren, *Liturgy and Ritual of the Celtic Church* (1881), the chief book on the subject. A *missa Patricii* (mass of Patrick) is mentioned in Tírechán ($322_{19}$). I cannot say what attention should be paid to the statements about the Scottic liturgy in the *Cursus Romanus* printed in Warren 77 *sqq.* (Haddan and Stubbs, *Councils*, i. 138). Cp. Ussher, *Brit. eccl. ant.* (*Works*, vi. p. 480).

P. 176.—It is worth while to collect the notices of grants to Patrick and *free* churches mentioned in the *Liber Armachanus.* Muirchu, $291_{31}$, (Armagh) partem illam agri—do tibi nunc quantum habeo.

Tírechán, $320_{21}$ (Drummut Cerrigi) immolauerunt agrum et bona patris eorum Patricio. *Ib.* $309_{30}$ (Endeus).

*Ib.* $321_7$, aeclessiam liberam ; $330_{29}$, sed libere semper.

*Add. Notices* 338 (offering of Caichán's fifth : note *liberauit* Deo et Patricio).

*Ib.* 337, (sons of Conlaid offered) octo campi pondera id est uaccas campi octo (8 ballyboes) in hereditate sua … Deo et Patricio in sempiterna saecula.

*Ib.* $340_{3-10}$ ; $344_1$.

*Ib.* $335_{2-6}$ (Trim.).

P. 184.—Alphabets (*abgitoria* or *elementa*) : Tír. $308_{13}$, $320_{28}$, $322_{15}$, $326_{30}$, $327_{20}$, $328_{28}$. The suggestion that these were figurative alphabets, "the A B C of the Christian doctrine" (tentatively put forward by Stokes, *Vit. Trip.* p. cliii.), can hardly be entertained, unless it is shown that *abgitir* was used in this sense without the addition of *crabaith* ( = *fidei*). Tírechán saw a psalter written by Patrick for Sachall—doubtless at Baslick ($301_8$). Justus, a deacon of Patrick, is said to have possessed a baptismal liturgy which Patrick gave him, *libros baptismatis* (*ib.* 318). He gave Mucneus *libros legis septem*, which seems to mean the Heptateuch ? *ib.* $326_{17}$.

Tírechán has a story that in a district of Connaught Patrick and his companions had tablets, written *more Mosaico*, in their hands, and that pagans took them for swords, saying that they seemed to be wooden in the day-time, but were really of iron for shedding blood. It is inferred that these tablets were wooden staves, roughly resembling in shape the short swords of the ancient Irish: compare Graves, *Hermathena*, iii. 237 and 228 *sqq.*, and Todd, *St. Patrick*, 509. [It may be noted that in this passage of Tírechán *cum uiii aut uiiii uiris* points to the use of a written source; the numeral was not clear in the MS.]

P. 185.—The ogam alphabet. A word must be said on its structure, as it bears upon my contention that Latin letters must have been used in Ireland before the fifth century. The twenty-one ogam scores form four groups of five, with one letter (p) as a supernumerary. The vowels form one group; the other groups are (2) h d t c q; (3) b l v s n; (4) m g ng f r. It has been suggested with great probability that the elements of the second group were selected as being the initials of the first five Irish numerals; but the principle of arrangement in groups 3 and 4 has not been discovered. The choice of *p* as the letter to be excluded from the groups and treated separately must have depended on that principle. The supposition that the inventor of the cipher contemplated only twenty symbols, and that the symbol for *p* was subsequently added when found indispensable, is in itself unlikely (for why should he have fixed the number twenty?), and breaks down on the fact that, while *ng* might have been treated by a shift, *p* was required for the archaic word *poi*, which occurs on several of the extant sepulchral inscriptions.[1] Including *p*, and excluding *ng*, which was clearly a native invention, we have simply a cipher of the Latin alphabet up to *u*, with a single modification. The symbol *u*, which did double duty in Latin as both consonant and vowel, is represented by two symbols, one for each function. The fact that only the last three letters (x y z) of the Latin alphabet are discarded, and that all the others are represented, renders this explanation of the ogam cipher very much simpler than a derivation from Greek or Iberian (or Runic, which has been suggested).

That the cipher implies that the alphabet for which its symbols are substituted was in use can hardly be questioned. As the date of the oldest ogam stones cannot be determined, we cannot fix a date for the introduction of Roman writing. But there can be no question that the older stones are pagan, and the inference is clear that this writing was introduced independently of Christianity.

[1] Instances are collected by Professor Rhŷs in *Proceedings of R.S.A.I.* Pt. i. vol. xxxii. p. 5; to which add the Donard stone (*ib.* Pt. ii. vol. xxxiii. p. 114).

P. 187.—Bishop Nynias, generally called Ninian, see Bede, *H. E.* iii. 4. This passage in Bede furnishes the only trustworthy tradition about Nynias. His expression *ut perhibent* shows that his information was oral. Bede does not fix the date of Nynias further than by the vague *multo tempore* before St. Columba, and by the statement that the church which Nynias built was dedicated to St. Martin. The usually accepted date, *c.* 400 A.D., depends on the statement in Ailred's *Vita Niniani*, c. 2, that Nynias visited St. Martin (and obtained at Tours masons to build his stone church). There is no evidence that the *Life* composed by Ailred, abbot of Rievaulx in the twelfth century, was based on any ancient documents unknown to Bede ; Ailred seems to have drawn his material, mainly legendary, from traditions in Galloway, and, with the exception of the visit to Martin, he adds nothing that can pretend to be a historical fact to the brief notice of Bede. The personal contact of Nynias with Martin, however, may be a genuine tradition ; and it furnishes the most probable explanation of the connexion of Martin's name with Candida Casa. But we have an independent testimony that the conversion of the Picts of Galloway must have been at least early in the fifth century—namely, their description as *apostatae* in Patrick's *Letter against Coroticus*, which shows that they had been converted and fallen away before the middle of the fifth century. [The fullest collection of everything bearing on Nynias is Forbes's *Lives of St. Ninian and St. Kentigern*, 1874. A more recent edition of Ailred's *Vita* will be found in Pinkerton's *Lives of the Scottish Saints*, revised by W. M. Metcalfe, vol. i. 1889. For a criticism on Ailred, see J. Mackinnon, *Ninian und sein Einfluss auf die Ausbreitung des Christenthums in Nord-Britannien*, 1891. See also Plummer's note on Bede, *H.E.* iii. 4.]

*Ib.*—Candida Casa, Whitern, was known in Ireland in the sixth century as Magnum Monasterium or Rosnat, and had a high reputation as a monastic school : see passages in Colgan, *Acta Sanctorum Hib.* i. p. 438). This reputation led to the rise of a legend that Nynias founded a church in Ireland and died there. A lost Irish life, known to Ussher (*Brit. Eccl.* vi. 209) contained this story, and Nynias appears in Irish Martyrologies under the name of Moinenn "my Nynias" (*Mart. of Tallaght*, ed. Kelly, p. xxxiv. ; *Mart. Dung.* ed. Todd, p. 249).

P. 190.—Ceretic or Coroticus. The only source for the

following events is Patrick's *Letter* (see below); but the identification of Coroticus, who is the subject of the *Letter*, depends on other considerations which seem quite conclusive. The Table of Contents to Muirchu's Life describes the section which Muirchu devoted to him as *de conflictu sancti Patricii adversum Coirthech regem Aloo*[1] (p. 271 ; in Muirchu's text he is simply described as *cuiusdam regis Britannici*, p. 498). *Aloo* at once suggests the Rock (*Ail*) of Clyde, Bede's *Alcluith* (ciuitas Brettonum munitissima usque hodie quae uocatur Alcluith, *H.E.* i. 1), Adamnan's *Petra Cloithe*; and this identification agrees with the close association of Patrick's Coroticus with the Picts and Scots, which shows that he must have ruled in Northern Britain. But the determination of Coroticus as ruling at Alcluith is demonstrated (as has been most clearly shown by Zimmer, *Celtic Church*, p. 54, cp. Skene, *Celtic Scotland*, i. 158, note) by a genealogy of the kings of that place, preserved in a Welsh source. In the last quarter of the sixth century, in the time of Columba, Rodercus, or Rhydderch, reigned at Alcluith (Adamnan, *V. Col.* i. 15 : Rodercus filius Tothail qui in petra Cloithe regnavit), and we find him also as Riderch hen (Rhydderch the Old) in the *Historia Brittonum* (ed. Mommsen, p. 206). Now the pedigree of this Rhydderch is found in a Welsh genealogy (ed. Phillimore, in *Y Cymmrodor*, 9, 173) : he was son of Tutagual (cp. Adamnan, *filius Tothail*), who was son of Clinoch, who was son of Dumngnal, who was son of Cinuit, who was son of Ceretic *guletic*. It is evident that Ceretic, from whom Rhydderch was sixth, corresponds chronologically to Coroticus, the contemporary of St. Patrick, reckoning a generation—thirty years—to each king. The identification so completely fits with all the data that we can have no doubt of its truth. Thus Zimmer fixes the date of Ceretic or Coroticus as 420-450 A.D. But it is better to say that the reigns of Ceretic and his son Cinuit probably fell more or less between 420 and 480.

Zimmer thinks that the description of Ceretic as *guletic* in the Welsh source points to his position as claiming to be a successor of the Roman *dux Britanniarum*. I do not feel certain that we can go so far, but I have no doubt that Ceretic and his *milites* represented the Roman defence of North Britain. That these *milites* were Roman citizens is clear from Patrick's words (*Letter*, p. 375₂₃, *militibus—non dico ciuibus meis atque ciuibus sanctorum Romanorum sed ciuibus demoniorum*—the sting of

---

[1] This comes from Muirchu's Irish source for the legend. See above, App. A, ii. 3.

this reproach is that they professed to be Roman). Coroticus was a *tyrannus* for Patrick (*per tirannidem Corotici*, p. 376₁₉). It is not clear whether the *reges* and *tyranni* who arose in various parts of Britain in the fifth century (for example, Vortigern) bore Roman official titles : the fact that there were also generals who were not *reges* and who seem to correspond to the Roman commanders (Ambrosius Aurelianus ; Arthurius) cannot be considered decisive. For the continuance of Roman civilisation in Britain after the rescript of Honorius (A.D. 410), see Mr. Haverfield's observations in "Early British Christianity" in *Eng. Hist. Rev.*, July 1896, pp. 428-30 ; and on the other hand for a Celtic revival, his paper on "The Last Days of Silchester," *ib.* Oct. 1904, pp. 628-9).

[It is hardly necessary to mention the old view in Rees, *Welsh Saints*, p. 135, followed by Todd, *St. Patrick*, p. 352, that Coroticus was Caredig, of Cardigan, son of the Welsh chief Cynedda.]

P. 192.—That the scene of the outrage was in North Ireland, in Down or Antrim, is only a probable conjecture : (1) these coasts were the most likely destination of an expedition from Strathclyde ; and (2) the circumstance that Patrick *happened* at the time to be close to the place suggests Ulster. Zimmer says nothing as to this ; but his theory would evidently compel him to assume that the outrage was committed in South Ireland, for otherwise the *Letter* of St. Patrick would imply that his activity was not confined, as Zimmer contends that it was, to North Leinster. For a conjecture that the date may have been A.D. 459, see above, App. B, p. 303.

*Ib.*—Heathen Scots. *Scottorum atque Pictorum apostatarum* (Patrick, *Letter*, p. 375₂₆). The Picts, not the Scots, are apostates (cp. p. 379₇) ; the natural inference is that the Scots (of Britain) were still heathen. Zimmer's inference that they were Christians (p. 55) seems extraordinarily perverse. He asks us to observe that the Scots "are not reproached with paganism." The implication is inadmissible. Their paganism is taken for granted ; in fact, it is their excuse. If they had been professing Christians their guilt would have been greater even than that of the Picts, who had fallen away from Christianity. The fact that it is on the Picts, not on the Scots, that Patrick's reproaches fell, proves that the Scots were heathen and therefore might not be expected to know better.

The mention of the Scots in this document is important, because it proves that Scottish settlements in North-Western

Britain had begun before the middle of the fifth century. This must be taken into account in criticising the notice in Bede, *H.E.* i. 1, of the origin of the British Dalriada.

P. 193.—The outrage on the neophytes : *Letter against Coroticus*, 375₂₂₋₃₂. The language of Patrick implies that it was the Scots and Picts, not the *milites Corotici*, who slaughtered some of the Christians :

socii Scottorum atque Pictorum apostatarum quasi sanguine uolentes saginari [see White's ed.] sanguine innocentium Christianorum quos ego innumerum [? *leg.* innumerum numerum ; *Boll.* innumeros] Deo genui atque in Christo confirmaui.

The text of the *Letter* is full of corruptions, some of which may be easily corrected. In the following sentence we should perhaps read :

Postera die <quam> qua crismati neophiti in ueste candida, dum flagrabat in fronte ipsorum <crux>, crudeliter trucidati atque mactati gladio <a> supradictis, < * * > et misi epistolam, etc.

*Crux* or *crucis signum* may have fallen out before *crudeliter.* For the sign of the cross and white chrism at baptism, see Warren, *Liturgy and Ritual of the Celtic Church*, p. 65 ; cp. p. 217. It was laid down by Innocent I. (*Ep.* xxv., Migne, *P.L.* xx. 555) that chrism *in pectore* might be performed by presbyters, chrism *in fronte* only by bishops. For the Roman and Gallican baptismal ceremonies see Duchesne, *Origines du culte chrétien*, cap. ix.

P. 194.—There is a difficulty, perhaps only superficial, in Patrick's narrative in his *Letter*. He makes Coroticus fully responsible for the outrage, but his language suggests that the message which he had sent to demand the captives before the plunderers left Ireland was not addressed to Coroticus personally ; the ruler's name is not mentioned, and the plural is used (*cachinnos fecerunt de illis*, 376₄). It is possible, however, that something has fallen out (see last note) before the words *et misi epistolam*.

*Ib.*—The persons in Strathclyde to whom the *Letter against Coroticus* was transmitted and who were asked to excommunicate the tyrant are not designated by a more precise expression than *sancti et humiles corde* (376₂₈). They were, no doubt, the whole Christian community ; but there is no indication who was to receive the letter in the first instance. There is apparently a reference to the contemplated transmission of the letter from one place to another in Britain (certainly from Ireland to Britain) by the hands of some *famulus Dei* in $380_{19}$, and the writer is afraid that it might possibly be abstracted. The inference seems to be that it was not to go direct to Alcluith, but to some other place (could it possibly have been Whitern ?).

P. 194.—The reference to the redemption of captives from the Franks is an illustration from Patrick's own writings of his knowledge of Gaul. An untenable inference has been drawn from this passage by Sir S. Ferguson and Dr. Stokes, namely, that it must have been written before the Franks "crossed the Rhine and settled in Gaul, *i.e.* before A.D 428 " (Introduction to *Tripartite Life*, p. ci). The argument is based on ignorance of Frank history. The Salian Franks in question had been settled west of the Rhine since the time of Julian. Consequently if there was any validity in the argument it would prove that the *Letter* must have been written before 358 A.D. But the reasoning is invalid. It is not clear whether the Salians are meant; but if they are meant, as they well may be, there is no reason in the world why they should not have carried off captives to their territory in Lower Germany, on the Gallic side of the Rhine, early in the fifth century, whether in the days of Chlojo or before ; in fact it is what we should expect in those troubled years from 407 to the campaigns of Aetius in the late twenties. The argument that the Franks must have carried their captives *beyond the Rhine* is to me unintelligible.

*Ib.*—Legend of the transformation of Ceretic into a fox : Muirchu, p. 498 : *ilico uulpeculi* (sic legendum) *miserabiliter arrepta forma.* The curious expression (*ib.*$_{19}$), *ex illo die illaque hora uelut fluxus aquae transiens nusquam comparuit*, may possibly have been suggested by the words in the *Letter* $380_7$ referring to Coroticus : *miserum regnum temporale quod utique in momento transeat sicut nubes uel fumus qui utique uento dispergitur : ita peccatores et fraudulenti a facie Domini peribunt.* Muirchu found that story in an Irish written source (see above, App. A, ii. 3).

P. 195.—Bitter phrases and self-justification in the *Letter* : see $375_{20-21}$ ; $376_{16}$ (*non usurpo aliena*) ; $377_{14}$-$378_2$ : $379_{12-18}$. For similar phrases in the *Confession* and the *Letter*, cp. Mr. White's list of recurrent phrases (*Proc. of R.I.A.* 1905, p. 299), to which may be added the use of *utique*.

P. 197.—"Confession." What Patrick meant by *confessio* is made clear by the last sentences of the work ($374_{28}$-$375_5$), and borne out by the general tenor. Compare esp. $358_{4-10}$ (*confiteremur*), $361_{17}$, $366_{20}$, $370_{34}$.

P. 202.—The attack on Patrick, on account of the youthful fault (*Conf.* $365_2$, etc.):

et quando temptatus sum ab aliquantis senioribus meis qui uenerunt et peccata mea contra laboriosum episcopatum meum< ·· >, utique in illo die fortiter impulsus sum ut caderem [cp. Ps. 118, 38] hic et in aeternum, sed Dominus pepercit proselito et peregrino, etc.

It is clear that the attack was made in Ireland (cp. App. C, 5). It seems probable that the persons described as *seniores mei* were ecclesiastics in Ireland, and this view has been adopted in the text. But in another passage we read that *aliquanti de senioribus meis* were offended by his persistence in the determination to go to Ireland ($367_{29}$), and this might suggest the view that they came from Britain (*uenerunt*) for the purpose of attacking him. It seems impossible to decide. The vision which Patrick saw the night after an interview with the *seniores* has caused some difficulty; he tells it so badly. "That night I saw in a vision of the night a writing which had been written against me,[1] dishonouring me.[2] And at the same time I heard the answer of God saying to me, 'We have seen with displeasure the face of' the person aforesaid [viz. the friend], revealing his name."[3] The passage immediately following deserves attention. The writer gives thanks for two things:

[1] ut non me (sc. Deus) inpediret a profectione quam statueram, et [2] de mea quoque opera quod a Christo Domino meo dedicaram, sed magis ex eo sensi in me uirtutem non paruam.

Here he designates as two great crises the attempts to dissuade him from his missionary purpose, and the attack afterwards made upon him, to which *ex eo* refers.

P. 206.—Patrick regrets his want of education (*Conf.* $359_{26}$):

quatinus modo ipse adpeto in senectute mea quod in iuuentute non conparaui; quod obstiterunt peccata mea ut confirmarem quod antea perlegeram (*sc.* the rudiments he had learned before his captivity).

---

[1] For *scriptum erat* I would read *scriptum quod scriptum erat*.

[2] *sine honore*, supposed to mean "without recognition of my episcopal title."

[3] *male uidimus faciem designati nudato nomine* ($365_{29}$). This gives much better sense than the ordinary rendering, which refers *designati* to Patrick, and *nud. nom.* to the suppression of the episcopal title. I observe that Mr. White, though he does not adopt it in his translation, gives it as an alternative interpretation in his note.

P. 206.—Scriptural quotations in the *Confession* and *Letter*.
A full conspectus of these has been furnished by Rev. N. J. D.
White in his edition. His results as to the text used by Patrick
may be summed up as follows. For the Old Testament there is
no evidence that he used the Vulgate (cp. above, p. 293 *ad fin.*),
while there are distinctively Old Latin citations. The New
Testament citations are not so clear : some passages seem certainly
to imply the Vulgate ; others have Old Latin support. As there
can be little doubt that Patrick quoted largely from memory, I
am inclined to conjecture that he had been trained on an Old
Latin version in Gaul, but that he possessed in Ireland a copy of
the New Testament Vulgate, in which he looked up some of his
references. This would explain the twofold character of the
New Testament quotations, but I put forward the conjecture with
great diffidence.

*Ib.*—Succession of Armagh bishops. See the four lists in
Todd, *St. Patrick*, p. 174 *sqq.* All these lists interpolate Sechnall, and three of them the fictitious Sen Patraic, between Patrick
and Benignus. But the breviarium in the Book of Leinster
(f. 12, v° A ; see my paper in *E.H.R.*, October 1902) recognises
that Iarlathus (the successor of Benignus) was the third bishop.
I cannot, however, consider it certain that Benignus succeeded
Patrick before his death in 461, because the ten years which the
lists assign to Benignus may have been based on the Sen Patraic
interpolation, "Sen Patraic" being supposed to have died
in 457, and ten years (467-457) being thus obtained for
Benignus.

P. 207.—Day of St. Patrick's death. It is recorded in the
Calendar of Luxeuil (Martene et Durand, *Thesaurus Novus
Anecdotorum*, iii. c. 1592 (1717) ; Stokes, *Tripartite Life*, ii.
493).

*Ib.*—Two distinct sets of *petitiones* granted to Patrick are
recorded, one in Muirchu, the other in the *Lib. Arm.* at the end
of Tírechán's Memoir. (1) Of the four petitions mentioned by
Muirchu as granted by the angel before Patrick's death, two
have obvious motives : one (*a*) is of Ulidian origin, and the other
(*b*) is in the interest of Armagh (see above, p. 207). The other
two are : (*c*) that whoever sings the hymn concerning St. Patrick
(Sechnall's hymn) on the day of his death shall be saved ; and
(*d*) that Patrick shall himself judge all the Irish on the day of
judgment. One wonders what Patrick would have thought of
such petitions, especially of the latter. It seems clear that (*c*)
and (*d*) were first invented, and had become current before (*a*)

and (*b*) were added.[1] (2) The other set consists of three (*tres petitiones ut nobis traditae sunt Hibernensibus*, p. 331, Rolls ed.), and the *Vita Tertia* (c. 85) connects them with the sojourn for prayer on Mount Crochan. They are (*a*) that none of the Irish who repents, even on his death-bed, shall be shut up in hell; (*b*) that barbarous peoples shall not rule the Irish for ever; (*c*) that seven years before the last day Ireland shall be overwhelmed by the sea, and none of the Irish survive. These petitions are given in the *Historia Brittonum*, and must have been current in the eighth century.[2] The point of the second petition is not clear. Possibly it refers to invasions from Britain.

We may conjecture that the stories of the petitions grew out of an early legend that, through their saint's intercession, the men of Ireland were to have a privileged position at the Last Judgment.

P. 211.—St. Patrick's crozier. The history of the crozier known as *baculus Iesu*, which existed in Armagh in the eleventh century (see the obscure notices in Tighernach, *s.a.* 1027 and 1030), was transferred in the latter half of the twelfth century to the Cathedral Church of Dublin, and was publicly burnt as an object of superstition in 1538, will be found set out in Todd's *Introduction* (pp. viii. *sqq.*) to the *Book of Obits and Martyrology of the Cathedral Church of the Holy Trinity, Dublin*, ed. by J. C. Crosthwaite, 1844. The veneration with which it was regarded in the eleventh century shows that it was an ancient relic, and it can hardly be doubted that it was the existence of this relic at Armagh which occasioned the story that Jesus gave a staff to Patrick. This story occurs in the *Vita Tertia*, c. 23, which probably goes back to the ninth century; and even if the story was not invented till that period, the object which suggested it must have been older. It seems very probable that the staff was one of the *insignia consecrata* mentioned in the *Liber Angueli* (355$_{29}$, 356$_4$), and this would take us back to the eighth century. There is therefore reason for thinking that the crozier which perished in 1538 may have been extremely ancient, but there is no positive proof that the tradition which assigned it to Patrick is correct, or that it was as old as the fifth century.

*Ib.*—St. Patrick's bell. In *Ann. Ult. s.a.* 553, there is a notice, derived from the Book of Cuana, to the effect that in

---

[1] Another petition (which in *V. Trip.*, p. 116, appears in connexion with Mount Crochan) is added in V$_3$, c. 88. See Bury, *Trans. of R.I.A.* xxxii. C. Part iii. p. 223.

[2] I retract the date "*c.* A.D. 850" in my note †, *op. cit.* p. 218. I have abandoned a view of the relations of the Nennian MSS. which prompted me to assign this date.

that year St. Columba placed the relics of Patrick in a shrine.
Three relics had been found in Patrick's tomb, "the cup, the
gospel of the angel, and the bell of the will," and an angel
instructed Columba how to distribute them : the cup was to go
to Down, the bell to Armagh, and he was to keep the gospel
himself.[1] If this notice stood in the Book of Cuana, it would
show that early in the seventh century the "bell of the will"
existed at Armagh, and was believed to belong to Patrick. The
bell has been described, and its history traced, by Bishop Reeves
in *Transactions of the R.I.A.* xxvii. pp. 1 *sqq.* (1877). It is a
four-sided bell, weighing 3 lbs. 8 oz., made "of two plates of
sheet-iron, which are bent over so as to meet, and are fastened by
large-headed iron rivets." The handle is of iron. A shrine,
which is also preserved in the Dublin Museum, was made for it,
*c.* A.D. 1100. Bishop Reeves believed that the tradition which
ascribed the bell to Patrick is sound. He seems to have thought
that there is no room for reasonable doubt. But it is to be
observed that the statement cited from the *Liber Cuana* opens
the door to possibilities of fraud. We may infer from it with
certainty that for nearly a century after Patrick's death this bell
was not at Armagh. Its genuineness therefore depends on the
truth of the story of the opening of Patrick's tomb (at Saul), and
the discovery of the bell in the tomb. But if the relic was a
forgery, just such a story might have been invented.

## CHAPTER X

P. 218.—Latin the ecclesiastical language in the west. Since
these remarks were written, I came across two short but valuable
papers on the subject : P. Frédéricq, "Les conséquences de
l'évangélisation par Rome et par Byzance sur le développement
de la langue maternelle des peuples convertis" in the *Bull. de
l'Académie royale de Belgique*, Classe des lettres, 1903, n. 11,
738-751 ; F. Cumont, "Pourquoi le latin fut la seule langue
liturgique de l'occident ?" in *Mélanges Paul Frédéricq*, 1904,
63-66.

[1] The Armagh tradition, connecting Columba with St. Patrick's tomb, is
referred to in the *Additions to Tírechán* (see Appendix C, 19).

# APPENDIX C

## EXCURSUS

### 1. *The Home of St. Patrick* (*Bannauenta*)

CONFESSION, 357₅: *qui* (may refer either to Calpurnius or to Potitus) *fuit* [*in*] *uico Bannauem taberniae. uillulam enim prope habuit, ubi ego capturam dedi.* We are justified in inferring that the *uillula* or farmhouse was on the estate of Calpurnius, and that he resided permanently here or in the neighbourhood. The analysis and identification of *Bannauemtaberniae* (or *Bannauemtaburniae*[1]) have caused great difficulty. In the first place, the question arises whether it represents the name of the *vicus*, or is the name of the *vicus* (in the ablative) followed by a genitive representing the region or district. Now it has been observed (by Mr. Haverfield, *Eng. Historical Review*, v. 711, and Mr. Nicholson, *Academy*, May 11, 1895) that in the *Itinerarium Antonini* Bannaventa appears as the name of a station on Watling Street, probably three or four miles from Daventry. The idea that this Bannaventa is the place designated by Patrick has one considerable difficulty. For the only early evidence we have as to the situation of *Bannauemtaberniae* is inconsistent with it. Muirchu states that *Bannauemtaberniae* was *haut*[2] *procul a mari nostro* (495₉), and his next words show that in his time a distinct view was current as to its identification: *quem uicum constanter indubitanterque comperimus esse uentre.*[3] Muirchu's indication that the place was near the Irish Channel is the less lightly

---

[1] I have shown that this was possibly the original corruption, "Tradition of Muirchu's Text," p. 196.

[2] *haut* has been restored for -cha *ut* of the Brussels MS. The restoration, obviously right, is borne out by Probus (Colgan, *Trias Thaum.* 47), who here transcribes Muirchu. See Stokes, *ad loc.*

[3] Probus here, using another but related MS. of Muirchu, gives *Nentriae prouinciae.*

to be neglected, since it would best accord with the circumstances of the capture of Patrick, though of course it is not impossible that the Irish invaders might have penetrated to Northamptonshire. I therefore think that probabilities are distinctly against the Daventry theory unless it can be shown to involve a satisfactory explanation of the mysterious *bernie* or *burnie*.[1] But that Bannaventa is the name there can, I think, be no doubt,[2] and there is no objection to supposing that there was another Bannaventa near the sea-coast. The recurrence of place-names needs no illustration. Of the two parts of this compound name, we have more than one Venta in Britain ; and Mr. Haverfield has drawn attention to Banna (*loc. cit.*), "an unidentified spot in the north, probably a dozen miles east of Carlisle, near the Wall." *berniae*, however, remains unexplained. It must represent the name of a district (or perhaps river), added to distinguish Bannaventa from other places of the same name.

Muirchu's statement that the *vicus* was in or at Nentria (if this is the authentic reading) does not help us. But we can hardly doubt that he means by Nentria the same place which the Hymn of Fiacc means by *Nemthur*: l. 1, "Patrick was born in Nemthur." This name might correspond to an old Celtic *Nemetoduron* (a name preserved in *Nanterre* near Paris).[3] This British Nemetodurum was, we may presume, in the same region as Bannaventa.

The glossator in the oldest (eleventh century) MS. of the Hymn of Fiacc identified Nemthur with Ail Clúade, the Rock of Clyde, at Dumbarton. We are ignorant of his authority for this statement, which does not appear in any earlier source. The fact, however, that it is not inconsistent with the direct statements of earlier sources has procured credence for it. But it is inconsistent with the probabilities of the case. Patrick's father was a decurion, and he must have lived in civilised Britain. We have no evidence that there were Roman towns with municipal constitutions in Strathclyde. The truth is that north Britain was little more than a large military frontier. It is generally supposed

---

[1] Mr. Nicholson's explanation that it is a corruption of *Britanniae* will hardly be accepted. Palaeographically it has no probability ; it was hardly necessary, and we should rather expect *Britanniarum*.

[2] It is obvious how readily the corruption rose from *bannauētabernie* or *-urnie*.

[3] Stokes, *Tripartite*, Introduction, p. cxxxvii. He refers to Gregory of Tours, *Hist. Franc.* x. 28, *in uico Nemptudoro*. Skene (*Celtic Scotland*, ii. 436, n.) identifies Nemthur with *Neutur* in the Black Book of Caermarthen (*Four Ancient Books of Wales*, vol. ii. p. 3).

that Theodosius in A.D. 369 restored Roman rule, which had fallen back in the north as far as the Wall of Antoninus, and that the district which he recovered (recuperata provincia, Ammianus, 28, 3, 7), and which was renamed Valentia (by Valentinian, in compliment to his brother Valens), included the country between the Walls of Hadrian and Antonine. There is, strictly speaking, no direct authority for this conclusion; Ammianus does not indicate the position of Valentia. The supposition that it was in the north, and that Theodosius restored fortresses as far as the line of the northern wall, is, however, not improbable. But there is no probability that it was colonised[1] or became in the last half century of Roman rule anything more than a military district. The Rock of Clyde, at the extreme end of the Northern Wall, is the last place we should expect to find the *uillula* of a Roman decurion; and the opinion that the home of Calpurnius was in that remote spot cannot be accepted without better evidence than an anonymous statement which we cannot trace to any trustworthy source.

But it is not likely that the identification offered by the glossator was his own invention; it is much more probable that it was an idea of considerably older date, and we cannot avoid asking the question how it could have arisen. It might be conjectured that the idea of connecting Patrick personally with north Britain arose there, naturally enough, as a consequence of the influence of the Irish Church on north Britain. But whether the idea first arose there or in Ireland, a delusive support for it might have been found in *Corot.* 375$_{23}$. Patrick's expression there, *civibus meis*, in speaking of the soldiers of Coroticus, might have suggested that he belonged to the same place as Coroticus, and it was known that Coroticus was King of Ail (Clúade). Hence a narrow interpretation of Patrick's expression *civibus meis* was sufficient to generate the theory that Patrick's British home was there, and that Nemthur was identical with Ail Clúade.

This is the case against the vulgar view. On the other hand it might be argued that some things in the *Letter* of Patrick against Coroticus—especially his quotation "a prophet has no honour in his own country"—have more point if he was a native of that part of Britain which the letter concerns, namely, Strathclyde. It might be said that the existence of some small towns, *fora* or *conciliabula*, with municipal councils, in the province

---

[1] It is perhaps hardly necessary to observe that Ammianus when he says that Theodosius *instaurabat urbes* does not refer to Valentia (which he has not yet mentioned) in particular, but to Britain in general.

# APPENDIX

assumed to be Valentia, is not impossible, and that the existence
of "Roman citizens" and Christian communities in Strathclyde
is proved by Patrick's *Letter* for the middle of the fifth century.
And it might be suggested that *bernie* could be readily explained
as a corruption of *Berni<ci>e* (remembering Bede's description
of Whitern in Galloway as *ad provinciam Berniciam pertinens*, iii.
4, which, though referring to the political geography of his own
time, may correspond to the original extension of this obscure
name).

Nevertheless, in the absence of any trace of a Bannaventa (or
a Nemthur) in north British regions, we must, I think, give decisive
weight to the general probabilities of the case and suppose that
Bannaventa was south of the Wall of Hadrian, somewhere in
western Britain, not very far from the coast. See further, Preface.

## 2. *Irish Invasions of Britain*

(1) Pacification and fortification of Britain by Theodosius, A.D.
368, 369. Chief source: Ammianus, 27, 8, and 28, 3, who
mentions five enemies; Picti and Attacotti; Scotti; Franci and
Saxones (27, 8, 5). Two passages in Claudian illustrate the
campaigns of Theodosius. In the *Panegyric* on the Third Consulship of Honorius (A.D. 395) we read, vv. 54-6 :—

> Ille leues Mauros nec falso nomine Pictos
> Edomuit Scottumque uago mucrone secutus
> Fregit Hyperboreas remis audacibus undas,

and in the *Panegyric* on the Fourth Consulship (A.D. 397), vv. 28
*sqq.*:—

> debellatorque Britanni
> Litoris ac pariter Boreae uastator et Austri.
> Quid rigor aeternus, caeli quid frigora prosunt
> Ignotumque fretum? maduerunt Saxone fuso
> Orcades; incaluit Pictorum sanguine Thyle;
> Scottorum cumulos fleuit glacialis Hiuerne.

The first of these passages suggests that Theodosius pursued the
Scots across the sea, or at least made a naval demonstration in
the Irish Channel, and this is perhaps supported by the passage
in Pacatus, *Panegyric*, c. 5 : attritam pedestribus praeliis Britanniam
referam? Saxo consumptus bellis naualibus offeretur. redactum
ad paludes suas Scotum loquar?

(2) Troubles brought on Britain through the revolt of Maximus,
and pacification by Stilicho. Zosimus (source: doubtless

Eunapius), 4, 35 : the soldiers, having crowned Maximus, παρα-χρῆμα τὸν Ὠκεανὸν ναυσὶ διαβάντες landed at the mouth of the Rhine. Cp. Orosius 7, 34, 9. (While Zosimus imputes the blame of the insurrection to Maximus, Orosius says that he was created Emperor *inuitus propemodum.*) The rebellion was brought to an end by the death of Maximus in A.D. 388 (Idatius and Prosper Tiro, *ad ann.*), so that it cannot have been before that year that the Britannic legions returned to Britain.

Now the only contemporary evidence as to the fortunes of Britain during the fifteen years which followed the revolt of Maximus consists of two passages of Claudian : (1) *In Eutropium*, i. 393 (composed A.D. 399, June to Sept.)—

> fracto secura Britannia Picto,

where the context implies that this was accomplished during the reign of Honorius (*te principe*, 391) ; (2) *De Consulatu Stilichonis*, ii. 247 *sqq.* (composed end of A.D. 399) :—

> Inde Caledonio uelata Britannia monstro,
> Ferro picta genas, cuius uestigia uerrit
> Caerulus Oceanique aestum mentitur amictus :
> " Me quoque uicinis pereuntem gentibus " inquit
> " Muniuit Stilicho, totam cum Scottus Hiuernen
> Mouit et infesto spumauit remige Tethys.
> Illius effectum curis ne tela timerem
> Scottica, ne Pictum tremerem, ne litore toto
> Prospicerem dubiis uenturum Saxona uentis."

The second passage evidently suits the situation in which Britain would have almost inevitably found herself on the departure of Maximus with the legions. Two questions arise. In what year did Stilicho take measures for the defence of Britain? and did he visit the island in person? Keller supposes that the date was A.D. 385 and denies that he went to Britain (*Stilicho*, p. 17). As to the latter point it is possible that Keller may be right. The phrase *illius effectum curis* suggests this conclusion ; if Stilicho had visited Britain and provided for its security on the spot, Claudian would perhaps have used some more vivid and graphic phrase, leaving the reader in no doubt that his hero had appeared on the scene of danger.

Before criticising Keller's date, A.D. 385, it will be well to define the reference in the other passage, which distinctly states that the defeat of the Picts which is mentioned, was accomplished while Honorius was Emperor. This might mean one of two things. It might mean : since Honorius succeeded his father as sole Augustus in the west (Jan. A.D. 395); or it might mean : since

Honorius was created Augustus (Jan. A.D. 393). The words cannot assuredly be interpreted of the Caesarship of Honorius (he appears with the title Caesar in his first consulship, A.D. 386). In the absence of any other counter-indication, we are, I think, fully entitled to assume that *te principe* bears its most obvious and natural meaning, and that the defeat of the Picts occurred while Honorius (and not his father Theodosius) was solely responsible for the government of the west. We may therefore assign as limits to the date of this event, Jan. 395-June 399 A.D.).

Now Keller has made the mistake of associating these two passages of Claudian closely together. While the first emphasises a defeat of the Picts and does not refer to the other foes of Britain, the second describes the serious dangers which beset the island on three sides, and states that measures of defence were taken by Stilicho, but makes no mention of an actual defeat of the Picts, or indeed of any other enemy. There is therefore no reason for supposing that both passages refer precisely to the same events; and it may be argued with some force that if Claudian was thinking of the same achievements he would not have omitted, in rehearsing the military successes in the reign of Honorius, to mention the Scot and the Saxon as well as the Pict, especially as his description in the second passage conveys the idea that the Scot and the Saxon were the most formidable.

We may therefore refer the events mentioned in the poem " On Stilicho's Second Consulship " to a date prior to A.D. 395, and may return to consider and reject Keller's suggestion of A.D. 385. It does not need much consideration, for it is wholly inconsistent with the political situation. After Gratian's death in A.D. 383 Maximus was recognised as Augustus by Theodosius (A.D. 384 or 385, cp. Schiller, *Gesch. der röm. Kaiserzeit*, ii. 405), who was not then in a position to advance against the usurper (Zosimus, 4, 37). From that time until he marched upon Italy in A.D. 387, there were no hostile dealings between Maximus and Theodosius. Maximus ruled over Britain, Gaul, and Spain from his headquarters at Trier, and it cannot for a moment be supposed that Theodosius or any general of his interfered in the administration of those provinces. Stilicho was a general of Theodosius,[1] and he cannot possibly have had to do with Britain till after Theodosius came to the rescue of the young Valentinian in A.D. 388. Thus Keller's date is excluded.

[1] In A.D. 383 he was sent on an embassy to the Persians (whom Keller calls " Parthians," p. 15), and married Serena soon after (384 or 385). In A.D. 386 he was engaged in the campaign with the Gruthungi.

The true date can easily be surmised. After the execution of Maximus in summer A.D. 388 Theodosius remained in Italy, ordering the affairs of the west for the young Valentinian, and did not return to Constantinople till summer A.D. 391. No part of the Gallic Prefecture probably demanded his attention more than Britain, and we cannot be far wrong in supposing that the measures of Stilicho, recorded by Claudian, belong to these three years. As was observed, the words of Claudian rather suggest that Stilicho did not himself pass into Britain. But we may assume that Theodosius sent him into Gaul, and that from there he ordered what was necessary to be done.

It seems probable that Maximus retained in Gaul a considerable part of the Britannic army ; and if so, it was doubtless one of the cares of Stilicho to restore to Britain these contingents. We may assume that from A.D. 390 two legions (IInd and VIth), if not the XXth also, were in Britain.

(3) At the end of 401 Alaric entered Italy (for the chronology see Appendix 17 to Bury's edition of Gibbon, vol. iii.), and a legion was summoned for the defence of Italy. Claudian is again our source, *De Bello Gothico*, 416-8 :—

> Venit et extremis legio praetenta Britannis
> Quae Scotto dat frena truci ferroque notatas
> Perlegit exanimes Picto moriente figuras.

This description of a legion which might be called upon to act against both Irish and Pict certainly suggests the legion which was stationed in the northern military district, of which the headquarters was York.[1] Now in the *Notitia Dignitatum*, which represents the state of the civil and military service in the Empire in the first years of the fifth century, we find two legions in Britain, the VIth in the northern districts under the *dux Britanniarum*, the IInd in the south-eastern district under the *comes litoris Saxonici per Britannias*. No legion appears in the western district under the *comes Britanniae*. It has therefore been supposed that it was the XXth legion, stationed in the west, which was summoned to Italy ; and the fact that this legion does not appear in the *Notitia* at all has suggested that this document was drawn up after it had left Britain, but before it had been permanently assigned to any other station. Claudian's words need not be fatal to this theory, for the legion whose headquarters was at Chester would have to defend Britain against the Scots, and

---

[1] This seems to me a just remark of Mr. Hodgkin, *Italy and her Invaders*, vol. i. (2nd ed.), p. 716.

might have to defend it against Picts if they broke through the wall; and in any case the words of the poet in such a matter could not be precisely pressed. But the argument cannot be regarded as conclusive. It is perfectly possible that the XXth legion had been broken up before this time, that there were only two legions in Britain, and that it was the VIth which went to Italy. Its departure, it should be remembered, did not leave north Britain defenceless; there were large forces, cohorts, and alae, distinct from the legion. It is, moreover, possible that the British section of the *Not.* is of much older date.

(4) The elevation of the tyrant Constantine and his crossing into Gaul would seem to have happened in the first half of A.D. 407. This seems to follow from the account in Olympiodorus (fr. 12, ed. Müller). The second half of A.D. 406 is filled by the episodes of Constantine's predecessors, Marcus and Gratian. Zosimus (who, in regard to the dating, misunderstood Olympiodorus, as was pointed out by Freeman[1]) says that the invasion of Gaul by the Vandals and their fellows was one of the causes of the rebellion in Britain (vi. 3, 1). This cannot be true, if the text is sound in the entry of Prosper Tiro, which states that the Vandals and Alans crossed the Rhine at the end of December A.D. 406.[2] On the other hand, two considerations might tempt us to suspect this notice, namely, the unlikelihood of a migration in the middle of winter, and the existence of two edicts for a levée of provincials *contra hostiles impetus* dated April 18 and 20 at Ravenna (cp. Hodgkin, i. 739). But neither of these considerations is weighty enough to justify us in assuming without further evidence anything inconsistent with the testimony of Prosper's MSS. In any case, the crossing of Constantine into Gaul will fall in the year A.D. 407.[3] We can have no doubt that most of the soldiers in Britain accompanied Constantine when he departed to secure Gaul. But he must have left garrisons; it was important for him to retain his hold on the island if, as is probable, his corn supply depended on it. Mr. Freeman has summed up the event thus in its consequences for Britain: " Britain might be saved by a campaign in Gaul. But if this was the motive, the thought of saving Britain must soon have passed away from the minds of Constantine and his soldiers. Whether they cared for such an

---

[1] " Tyrants of Britain, Gaul, and Spain," *Eng. Hist. Review*, 1886, i. 55, note 3. This is the chief study on the subject (republished in *Western Europe in the Fifth Century*, 1905, chaps. ii., iii.). Cp. App. 20 to Bury's edition of Gibbon, vol. iii.

[2] II. k. Jan. ed. Mommsen, p. 465.

[3] Prosper's notice, *sub ann.* 407, agrees with the implication in Olympiodorus.

object or not, the course of things on the mainland soon made it hopeless for them to think of keeping up any relations with the great island. The crossing of Constantine into Gaul thus became the end of the Roman power in Britain " (p. 56).

It is possible that Constantine, before he departed, may have set up a colleague, named Carausius, to safeguard his interests in Britain. This at least is the inference drawn by Mr. A. J. Evans from a coin found at Richborough (see *Numismatic Chronicle*, third series, vii. 191 *sqq.* 1887, and App. 19 to Bury's edition of Gibbon, vol. iii.).

(5) We may now briefly consider the account of this last period of Roman domination which is given in the Epistle of Gildas, *De excidio et conquestu Britanniae*. Gildas, a native of west Britain, wrote in the first half of the sixth century, and his description in cc. 13-20 represents the confused memories of that troubled time, surviving in his own day. As Mommsen [1] says : " haec ut in universum rerum statum in Britannia qui tum fuit recte repraesentare videntur, sic ut narrantur magis famam incertam reddunt quam sinceram rerum gestarum narrationem."

In this account three great devastations are distinguished, and each is attributed to the withdrawal of the Roman garrison. The first was caused by the revolt of Maximus (cc. 13, 14); the island was devastated by Scots and Picts ; [2] and it was not until the islanders sent an embassy with letters to Rome that "a legion," *praeteriti mali* (the disloyalty of Britain) *immemor*, was sent to Britain, defeated the enemy, and built a wall across the island. The details are of course inaccurate, but the general fact that the rebellion of Maximus brought invasion upon Britain, and after his fall measures were taken (by Stilicho) for fortifying it, is correct.

But Gildas conceived that the "legion" when it had done its work did not remain in the island, but returned triumphantly to Rome ; and then the old foes began their ravages anew (c. 16). Again an embassy repairs to Rome and begs aid ; aid is again given, and the invaders are punished. The soldiers, having given good advice to the timid natives and erected new fortifications, *valedicunt tamquam ultra non reversuri*. Then follows the third devastation, and the famous futile message of the "groans of the Britons " is sent to Aetius.

Now this narrative does not correspond to the course of

---

[1] Preface to edition of Gildas (*Chron. Min.* iii. 1), p. 7.
[2] The Picts are described as a *gens transmarina* (the Picts of Dalaradia ?).

events as we gather it from the scanty contemporary sources, but we can see how it is based on actual occurrences. The third devastation, from A.D. 407, when the army finally departed, to A.D. 446 (the third consulship of Aetius), must represent truly enough the situation of Britain in those years. The circumstance that one legion was withdrawn in A.D. 402, and that the rest departed five years later, in A.D. 407, may have been the historical motive for distinguishing a second period of devastation, which would have to fall before A.D. 407.

But a further fact may underlie this tradition of a second devastation. There is no reason to reject the statement in the Irish Annals that King Niall was slain by the Ictian Sea (Sea of Wight), that is, the English Channel, while he was invading Britain, nor is there any reason to question the date assigned to his death, A.D. 405. And if the date is right, even within a year or so, then his last incursion into Britain may be regarded as the historical foundation of the "second devastation" of Gildas.

For the legend of the Slaying of Niall of the Nine Hostages (*orcuin Néill nóigiallaig*) see the version edited by Professor Kuno Meyer (in *Otia Merseiana*, ii. 84 *sqq.*).

The High Kings of Ireland who may have been concerned in the "Scotic" invasions of Britain from the middle of the fourth century to the year A.D. 427 were as follows, according to the Irish tradition :—

Eochaidh Muighmeadhoin, A.D. 358-366.

Crimthann, A.D. 366-379.

Niall (son of Eochaidh), A.D. 379-405.

Dathi (nephew of Niall). A.D. 405-428.


### 3. *The Dates of Patrick's Birth and Captivity*

The chronological framework of Patrick's life is determined by two certain dates : the year of his coming to Ireland, which rests upon clear and unvarying tradition, A.D. 432, and the year of his death, A.D. 461. This last date is supplied by the earliest source we have (excepting Patrick's own writings), Tírechán ($302_{29}$), and it is supported by the independent evidence of the Annals. For although the false, vulgar date (A.D. 493) established itself in the Annals, the true date remained inconsistently side by side with it. I must refer the reader to my discussion of the passage of Tírechán in the *English Historical Review*, xvii. p. 239 *sqq.* (1902), where I have shown that the date there given, A.D. 461, is supported by the Annals of Ulster,[1] the Annals of Inisfallen,[2] and probably by a chronological notice in the *Historia Brittonum*.[3]

But though these data are decisive, the vulgar date 493 has become so generally current that it may not be amiss to point to one or two further considerations which make against it ; especially as it is possible to dissociate it from the tradition that Patrick died at an age which is, to use a moderate expression, unusual—120, by supposing that he was born in the first years of the fifth century, was ordained bishop at the age of 30, and lived to the age of 90. This view would involve a forced explanation of the dates (see below) supplied by the *Confession*. It is to be observed (1) that the Annals and older sources do not furnish a single notice of any event in Patrick's life between 461 and 493 ; these thirty-two years are a blank. (2) Negative evidence is also furnished by the oldest *Life of St. Brigit* (by Cogitosus), which does not mention Patrick, or make any attempt to bring Brigit into connexion with him (as the latter Lives do, on the ground of the supposed date of his death in 493). Further (3), Benignus, Patrick's successor at Armagh, died in 467 (*Ann. Ult. sub a.* ; Annals in the *Book of Leinster*, f. 12, v⁰ A, see my extract in *English Historical Review*, xvii. pp. 700-1, 1902) ; and it will be allowed to be supremely improbable that Patrick should have resigned his bishopric when he was 60 years old or thereabouts, and survived his resignation 30 years. The question of the origin of the date 493, and of the two fabulous ages of Patrick (120 and 132) are treated in a separate Excursus.

Our other data depend upon the *Confession*. He had committed some fault when he was about 15 years old ;[4] he had confessed it to a friend before he was ordained deacon ;[5] and through the treachery of his friend[6] it was afterwards urged against him. These machinations against him occurred *post annos triginta*,[7] which has been generally interpreted to mean 30 years after the commission of the fault.[8] It is also generally assumed that the hostile machinations of which Patrick complains occurred in connexion with his consecration as bishop. I will show that the first of these two assumptions is not certain, and that the

---

[1] *Ann. Ult. sub a.* 461.

[2] *Ann. Inisf.* ed. O'Conor *sub a.* (" 488 " = ) 493 : *anno ccccxxxii a passione Domini.*          [3] Ed. Mommsen, p. 158-9.

[4] Rolls ed. p. 365₁₅, *nescio, Deus scit, si habebam tunc annos quindecim.*

[5] *Ib.*₁₁.          [6] 366₁₀.          [7] 365₁₀.

[8] So it is interpreted by Todd, *St. Patrick*, p. 392 ; by Neander, *Allg. Geschichte der christlichen Religion u. Kirche*, iii. 185, note ; by Zimmer, *Celtic Church*, p. 43.

second is erroneous; but, as they are usually accepted, I may first explain the chronological reconstruction which could be based on them. If Patrick's fault committed at the age of 15 was urged against him 30 years later when he was consecrated bishop in A.D. 432, we at once get his age in that year as 45, and the date of his birth as A.D. 387, and the date of his captivity ( = 387 + 16/17) as A.D. 403/4. This would follow, if we took the two numbers mentioned by Patrick as strictly precise. But it is to be observed that he gives the number 15 as approximate (*nescio, Deus scit, si habebam tunc annos quindecim*), and that 30 may be a round number. When he says that he does not think he was more than 15 when the delinquency was committed, we may presume that he was at least 15; on the other hand, we may take it that the number 30 is more likely to be slightly an overstatement than an under-statement. We should have, therefore, to consider it quite possible that the two numbers taken together might represent a period of somewhat less than 45 years—43 or 44; and it would not be safe to draw a more precise inference than that the birth date fell between 387 and 390, and the captivity between 403/4 and 406/7.

But the basis on which this reconstruction is built is unsound. (1) So far from its being clear that the 30 years are reckoned from the date of the fault, the words suggest a different view. *Occasionem post annos triginta inuenerunt*[1] *et aduersus uerbum quod confessus fueram antequam essem diaconus.* These words seem naturally to imply 30 years, not after the fault (which has not been yet mentioned), but after the confession of the fault.[2]  (2) It is quite clear that the occasion on which the fault was urged against him by *aliquanti seniores* was not the occasion of his consecration, but later, probably much later. The writer's language so obviously implies this that I find it difficult to conceive how it could have been otherwise interpreted. He says :—

Et quando temptatus sum ab aliquantis senioribus meis qui uenerunt et peccata mea contra *laboriosum* episcopatum meum, etc. . . . sed Dominus pepercit *proselito et peregrino* ($36_{2-7}$).

The significant word *laboriosum* shows conclusively that the

---

[1] I adopt the admirable correction of Dr. N. J. D. White for *occasionum— inuenerunt me* (MSS.).

[2] The truth is that the length of time which elapsed since the wrongdoing is not pertinent. The point is the interval between the confession of it to his friend, who offered no obstacle to his ordination as deacon (nor later to his ordination as bishop), and the occasion on which it was used against him. It is this lapse of 30 years which makes his friend's conduct so unaccountable.

intervention of the seniores did not occur till Patrick had already been working in Ireland long enough to describe his bishopric as "laborious"; and the words *proselito et peregrino*, describing his position in Ireland, manifestly confirm this interpretation. If the seniores had intervened at the time of his consecration, it would be quite inappropriate and pointless to describe their action as aimed *contra laboriosum episcopatum meum*.

Hence the chronological reconstruction falls to the ground, being based on an erroneous determination of the limits of the period of 30 years. The anterior limit most probably corresponds to the date of the confession of the fault before ordination, while the posterior limit is certainly subsequent to A.D. 432.

It follows that these data of the *Confession* furnish us with no precise dates, as we have no fixed year to reckon from. They may, however, give an approximate indication. The words *quod confessus fueram antequam essem diaconus* strongly suggest that the confession was made not long before Patrick's ordination as deacon. In another Excursus (9) it is shown that he was probably ordained before A.D. 418. Hence we should infer that the intervention of the seniores occurred before the year A.D. 448. More than this we are not entitled to infer. We have no means of determining precisely Patrick's age at the date of his consecration.

There are nevertheless two indications which suggest that 389 may have been the year of Patrick's birth : (1) the conjecture that he was taken captive on the occasion of King Niall's invasion in A.D. 405 is in harmony with our data ; it is a value of $x$ which satisfies our indeterminate equation, though it is not the only value. It implies A.D. 389 as the birth date. (2) I show in another Excursus (20) that one of the traditions as to Patrick's age at his death can be accounted for by supposing that he died at the age of 72 ; but $461 - 72 = 389$.

Speaking, then, with every reserve, I think we may say that 389 is the only year which is particularly indicated by any data we possess, and that if we assume it hypothetically as our starting-point we obtain a framework into which our data fit consistently, and without constraint. More than this cannot be said.

### 4. *The Place of Patrick's Captivity*

*Confession*, $367_{24}$, *in siluis et monte* ; $362_3$, *inter-missi* hominem cum quo fueram ui annis ; $364_{10-13}$, *putabam — audire uocem ipsorum qui erant iuxta siluam Focluti quae est prope mare occidentale, et sic exclamauerunt quasi ex uno ore Rogamus te, sancte puer, ut uenias et* adhuc *ambulas inter nos.* The last passage shows indisputably that Patrick, during his captivity, had "walked" near the wood of Fochlad; and otherwise it would be difficult to understand why he should have been so specially moved by thoughts of the people of Fochlad if he had known nothing of them personally. The obvious conclusion from the *Confession*, if we had no other data, would be that he spent six years of captivity with the master to whom he refers in western Connaught.

The authorities for the association of Patrick's captivity with north Dalaradia and Mount Miss are Tírechán, $329_{28}$-$330_{19}$, $311_{1, 2}$, and Muirchu, $275_{15-19}$, $276_6$-$277_6$, $300_{10-13}$. I have pointed out that parts of these passages of Tírechán and Muirchu depend on a common source (see above, p. 258). It is to be observed that, in these our earliest sources (1), the identification of Patrick's master with Miliucc of Mount Miss is introduced, not in connexion with the story of the captivity, but *à propos* of visits to that region after he had come as a missionary; and (2) the notices in both writers are characterised by legends—Miliucc's self-immolation, the footsteps of the angel, the flames from Patrick's mouth.

The rejection of Mount Miss as the scene of Patrick's servitude involves the rejection of Miliucc as his master; for the passage in Tírechán makes it clear that Miliucc was really connected with that region (*ascendit autem ad montem Miss Boonrigi quia nutriuit ibi filium Milcon Maccu-Buain*, $329_{28}$; the region was called from the name of Búan, Miliucc's ancestor).

That the forest of Fochlad was not confined to north-western Mayo, the barony of Tirawley, but extended southward to Murrisk, is, I think, a probable conclusion from the passage in Tírechán, $310_{3-12}$, where Crochan Aigli (Croagh Patrick) is closely connected with the *Silua Fochlithi*. It seems highly probable that Crochan Aigli, which has always been associated with Patrick in living tradition, is the mountain of the *Confession*. And in one document we have a distinct statement that this was so. It is remarkable that Probus, though he follows the narrative of Muirchu, nevertheless substitutes Crochan Aigli for Mount Miss (see above, p. 274). He must have had some motive for doing so; he must have had another tradition before him.

The question arises, what was the origin of the error (which evidently prevailed before the seventh century) that Patrick spent his captivity in north Dalaradia. Tírechán has a notice that a certain Gosactus (Guasacht),[1] whom Patrick ordained near Granard, was son of Miliucc (311), and his tomb was shown at Granard in later days, *Vita Secunda*, c. 15. This seems to bring Miliucc into touch with reality. He further states that Patrick, when a captive, had "nurtured Gosactus." Our first idea would be that this was an inference from the Miliucc legend; but it seems just possible that it might account for the rise of the legend, in the way explained above, p. 123 (cap. vi.).

There are two ways in which an attempt might be made to reconcile the tradition of the captivity near Mount Miss with the passage in the *Confession*. (1) It might be held that Patrick changed masters, and served as a slave in both regions. But the passage in which he describes his captivity seems incompatible with such a conjecture. He says that he had been six years with the man from whom he escaped, and his narrative distinctly conveys the impression that he had been in the same place since his arrival in Ireland. (2) It might be suggested that he escaped from Antrim to a port in Mayo, near the wood of Fochlad, and thus became acquainted with that district, though he could not have been very long there (cp. White, *Proc. of R.I.A.* 1905, p. 224). But the words of the dream *et adhuc*[2] *ambulas inter nos* are not satisfied by this hypothesis. "We beg you to come and continue to walk amongst us"; this implies a previous sojourning far more protracted than the day or two spent at the port in waiting for the vessel to sail. It may be added that a flight from the west to an eastern port is what we should rather expect than a flight from the east coast to a western harbour.

### 5. *Tentative Chronology from the Escape to the Consecration as Bishop*

[The following discussion is founded on the working hypothesis (see Excursus 3) that Patrick was born *c.* A.D. 389, and carried captive *c.* A.D. 405.]

In the twenty years intervening between Patrick's escape, *c.* A.D. 411-412, and his consecration as bishop, A.D. 432, we

---

[1] It is interesting to note that this name is found on three ogam stones, in the genitive forms *Gosoctas*, *Gossucttias*, and *Gosocteas* (see Rhŷs, *Ogam-inscribed Stones*, in reprint from *Proc. of Royal Soc. of Antiquaries of Ireland*, Part i. vol. xxxii. 1902, p. 24).

[2] The force of *adhuc* here (not synonymous with *iterum*) is exactly like its force in *adhuc capturam dedi*. See above, Appendix B, note on p. 34.

know that he visited Britain, that he was attached to the church of Auxerre and studied there, and that he sojourned for some time in the monastery of Lérins.   But our data do not permit us to arrange this part of his life with certainty, and various reconstructions are possible.   The two indications which we possess are :—

(1) His own statement that he was again in Britain, *post paucos annos* (after his escape), *Confession*, 364$_1$.

(2) His association with Bishop Amator of Auxerre, who probably ordained him deacon (the grounds of this probability will be shown in Excursus 9) ; the death of Amator probably happened in A.D. 418.

Our view will partly depend on the latitude we may feel justified in giving to the expression *post paucos annos.*   It might be held that his ordination by Amator preceded his return to Britain ; or it might be held that he was not ordained at Auxerre till after his visit to Britain, so that he would have returned to Gaul before A.D. 418.   The second alternative seems the more probable,[1] and it agrees with the tradition (Muirchu) that he went to Auxerre to study *after* his visit to Britain.   His choice of Auxerre, combined with the circumstance that it was a bishop of Auxerre who afterwards took a prominent part in helping the orthodox British against Pelagianism, suggests that relations of some intimacy were maintained between Auxerre and some of the British sees.   When Patrick, in Britain, made up his mind as to the destination of his life, he would have gone to Auxerre with recommendations from his friends.   It seems most likely that his connexion with Auxerre should have originated in this way.

The tradition as embodied in Muirchu represents him as remaining at Auxerre till his departure for Ireland, and though it might easily be erroneous, it is, so far as it goes, against the possible theory that Patrick's sojourn at Lérins is to be placed after his visit to Britain.   But we have another piece of evidence which seems to me decisive, namely, one of the so-called *Dicta Patricii.* See Excursus 6, *ad fin.*

The argument for placing the sojourn at Lérins before the return to Britain may be summed up thus : (1) the reminiscence of Patrick's wanderings almost certainly refers to his wanderings after his escape, and there can hardly be any doubt that the "islands in the Tyrrhenian Sea" mean the islands of Lérins, in

---

[1] Muirchu's *et erat annorum triginta* (496$_1$) must not be alleged ; it is based on a misconception of the *annos triginta* of the *Confession* (365$_{10}$), and influenced by the Scriptural parallel to which Muirchu refers.

view of the definite tradition (Tírechán, 302$_{24}$) that he stayed in the *insola Aralanensis*; (2) this date for the retreat to Lérins supplies the much-needed explanation of his delay in returning home.

The following chronology, then, may be a rough approximation :—

A.D. 411/2 escape from his ship-companions ;

A.D. 411/2-414/5 at Lérins ;

A.D. 414/5 returns to Britain ;

A.D. 415/6 goes to Auxerre ;

A.D. 416-8 is ordained by Amator ;

A.D. 418 death of Amator, who is succeeded by Germanus ;

A.D. 418-432 Patrick remains at Auxerre, as deacon ;

A.D. 429 Germanus goes to Britain to suppress the Pelagian heresy ;

A.D. 431 Palladius consecrated bishop for the Irish Church ;

A.D. 432 Patrick consecrated bishop by Germanus.

### 6. *The Escape to Gaul.   The State of Gaul, A.D. 409-416*

The Vandals, Sueves, and Alans, who entered Gaul at the end of A.D. 406, remained in the land, devastating, slaying, and burning until A.D. 409, in which year they crossed the Pyrenees, to find homes in Spain.   The extent of their ravages is indicated by Jerome, in a letter of A.D. 411, in which he mentions the devastation of Aquitania, Lugdunensis, and Narbonensis, and the destruction of Mainz, Rheims, and Speyer.[1]   It is also described by Salvian, writing at a much later date,[2] in the *De Gubernatione Dei*, who tells[3] how the Vandals, *gens ignavissima, de loco ad locum pergens de urbe in urbem transiens* laid all things waste.   *Arsit regio Belgarum deinde opes Aquitanorum luxuriantium et posthaec corpus omnium Galliarum.*   But more valuable as genuine pictures by eye-witnesses, men who had themselves suffered with the sufferings of Gaul, are the *Commonitorium* of Orientius, and an anonymous poem entitled *De Providentia Divina*.   Both these poems can be approximately dated to A.D. 415-416, and they describe the condition of the country at the time, enabling us to realise the long misery and desolation produced by the scourge of the years A.D. 407-409 Nor had Gaul, at least southern Gaul, been allowed a respite of

---

[1] Jerome, Ep. cxxiii. (*ad Ageruchiam*), Migne's ed. vol. i. 1057-8.

[2] After A.D. 439.

[3] vii. § 50.   Orosius, vii. 38 and 40, gives no details of the devastations.

peace to recover from the effects of that scourge, for the provincials had hardly become conscious that the Vandals had passed into Spain when Athaulf and his Visigoths entered Gaul. Moreover, a large body of Alans had remained behind, instead of accompanying their fellows across the Pyrenees. We derive a vivid picture of the unsettled state of Aquitaine from the *Eucharisticon* of Paulinus of Pella.[2]

Some passages in Orientius, the *De Providentia Divina*, and another anonymous poem *Ad Uxorem*, of the same period, illustrate the condition of the Gallic provinces.[5]

(1) Orientius (ed. Ellis, in the *Corpus Scriptorum Ecclesiasticorum*), ii. 165 *sqq.* :—

> Non castella locis, non tutae moenibus urbes,
>   invia non pelago, tristia non heremo,
> non cava, non etiam nudis[3] sub rupibus antra
>   ludere barbaricas praevaluere manus.

(2) *De Providentia Dei*, in Migne, *Patr. Gr.* lxi. c. 617 :—

> Si totus Gallos, etc.

(3) *Ad Uxorem*, in Migne, *ib.* c. 611.

> Non idem status est agris, etc.

It is possible, but I can find no direct evidence to show that the devastation had extended down the Loire. It might be considered whether the words of Orientius *invia non pelago*, which imply that the invaders attacked islands, allude to the islands of Noirmoutier, Rhé, etc.

Thus considerable regions of Gaul were a desolate wilderness, according to contemporary, rhetorical and poetical, evidence, from A.D. 408-409 to 416; and therefore, it might be argued, Gaul suits the narrative of St. Patrick in his *Confession* ($362_{22}$-$363_{34}$). He and his companions reached land three days (*post triduum*) after they left the coast of Ireland, so that our choice lies between Britain and Gaul. The data do not suit Britain. We cannot imagine what inland part of Britain they could have wished to reach, which would have necessitated a journey of twenty-eight days *per disertum*. Suppose that the crew dis-

---

[1] Edited by Brandes in the *Corp. Script. Eccl.* 1889.

[2] Compare the sketch of Professor Dill, based on these poems, in *Roman Society*, bk. iv. cap. 2 (p. 263, ed. 1).

[3] So I would amend the corrupt *metuendis*. Ellis reads *tetricis*, and suggests *mediis*. But there is greater point in *nudis*; it implies "without the crops, etc., which would naturally attract an enemy."

embarked on the south coast of Britain, and that the southern regions had been recently ravaged by the Saxons, yet a journey of a few days would have brought them to *Londinium* or any other place they could have desired to reach from a south-coast port. Moreover, if they had landed in Britain, Patrick, when he once escaped from their company, could have reached the home of his parents in a few days; whereas he did not return home for a few years (*ib.* 364). His own words exclude Britain. Having mentioned his final escape from the traders, he proceeds: *Et iterum post paucos annos in Britannis eram cum parentibus meis.* I believe that *post paucos annos* has been interpreted by some in the sense "a few years after my capture." But this is an unnatural explanation. The words naturally refer to what immediately precedes, viz. his escape. The only thing which can be alleged in favour of Britain is the intimation in the dream that he would "quickly come to his native land" (*cito iturus ad patriam tuam*). This of course represents his expectation at the time of his escape. But the very fact that he fails to say that the promise was literally fulfilled, and glides over intervening years in silence, strongly suggests that his expectation was not realised.

I observe that Mr. T. Olden, in his short history of *The Church of Ireland*, arrived at the conclusion that Patrick's *disertum* must be placed in Gaul. His subject, as a whole, lies outside my knowledge, but his chapters on Patrick would not lead one to form a favourable opinion of his work. His whole argument and narrative are vitiated by his astonishing ignorance of Imperial history. He quotes[1] a passage of Jerome to prove barbarian devastations in Gaul. He quotes it not from the original text, but at second hand from Montalembert's *Les moines d'occident*, a book which should be used with extreme caution. The passage cited by Mr. Olden has no bearing on Gaul at the time at which Mr. Olden sets St. Patrick's escape from his captivity, A.D. 395. The devastations did not begin till A.D. 407. This gross ignorance of the superficial facts of the general history of the period damages Mr. Olden's credit.

Mr. Olden, however, has made one useful contribution to the question—the only good thing in his account of St. Patrick.[2] He has brought out the significance of the dogs, which are mentioned incidentally in Patrick's narrative. He has pointed out that the dogs—which, it is implied, were numerous and valuable—must have been part of the merchandise which the traders

[1] P. 18.   [2] Pp. 16-18, and Appendix B.

shipped in Ireland. Celtic hounds were highly valued in the south,[1] and it would be probable *a priori* that they were exported from Ireland as well as from Britain. The route of this trade would have been overland through Gaul, from the north of the Loire or Garonne to a port on the coast of Provence, or to Italy.[2] Mr. Olden acutely suggests that Patrick, so long the servant of an Irish chieftain, had become skilled in the management of wolf-hounds, and that this consideration may have determined the traders to take him on board.

Thus the cargo of dogs seems to support the conclusion that it was to Gaul, not to Britain, that the traders sailed. They might have landed at either Nantes or Bordeaux. Now the only positive statement that we find anywhere as to the landing-place is in the *Life* by Probus (see above, Appendix A, ii. 9), where it is said to be Brotgalum. Bordeaux is obviously meant, and the form should probably be Bortgalum, as the Irish was Bordgal. See the instructive passage in *Vit. Trip.* p. 238, where Patrick, intending to visit Rome, is said to have waited for a ship *o Bordgail Letha* (from Bordeaux in Gaul). Probus did not invent the statement; the form of the name shows that he got it from a source of Irish origin. He adds, evidently from the same source, that the company then went to Trajectus, but we cannot identify the Gallic "Utrecht" which is intended. It is of course impossible to say whether there was any positive tradition at the back of this statement, or if it was only a deduction from the fact that Bordeaux was a regular port for travellers from Ireland to south Gaul.

Admitting, then, as a conclusion from which we can hardly escape that the landing-place was on the west coast of Gaul, it follows that if the traders marched for four weeks *per disertum*, they must have designedly avoided the beaten routes and the habitations of men. Aquitaine was at the time in an unsettled condition, on account of the barbarian invasion ; but no devastations would account for a month's wandering in a wilderness, unless such wandering was deliberate.

The corroboration of our general conclusion is supplied by Patrick himself. It was inferred above from his *Confession* that Britain was excluded; one of his Sayings, which we saw reason to believe genuine, points distinctly to Gaul (*Dicta*, i., see above, Appendix A, i. 3). It is clear that the "journey through Gaul

---

[1] Cp. Arrian's *Cynegeticus*, esp. chaps. 1, 2, 3.

[2] The nature of the cargo is another argument against the view that Britain was the destination.

and Italy" must have been one beset by particular dangers and hardships; and a little reflexion will show that we are justified in identifying it with the journey described in the *Confession*. It is a case where the argument from silence is valid. The motive of the *Confession* is to set forth the crises in his life at which the writer conceived that he was conspicuously guided by Heaven. It is clear that the "journey through Gaul and Italy," in which he used to tell his companions that he had "the fear of God as a guide," was one of those crises which had made a deep impression upon his mind, and which we should expect to find mentioned in the *Confession*. It is therefore fair to identify it with his perilous journey in the company of the traders, especially as it is not easy to imagine that at a later period, when he was at Auxerre, a journey which he might have made through Gaul would have been so memorable or exceptional. The *Dictum*, in conjunction with the other considerations which point to Gaul, justifies the conclusion that, having travelled with the traders through Gaul into Italy, he escaped from them in Italy.

The last words of the *Dictum*, "in islands in the Mediterranean," taken in conjunction with Tírechán, $302_{24}$, point to his having gone to Lérins after his escape, and a protracted stay at Lérins[1] would account for the few years which elapsed before his return to Britain.

### 7. *Palladius*

There were two readings in the MSS. of Muirchu as to the place of the death of Palladius: *in Britonum finibus* and *in Pictorum finibus*. It seems probable (see my "Tradition of Muirchu's Text," p. 205) that the author wrote *Britonum* (so *Lib. Arm.*), but that in one copy this was corrected to *Pictorum* from another source, presumably the same source which supplied W and *Vit. Trip.* with the details about Palladius. We may conclude, I think, that *Pictorum* represents the genuine tradition, and that Muirchu, taking it to refer to the Picts of north Britain—as was natural—substituted *Britonum*. But it seems most extraordinary that Palladius should have sailed off to the Picts of north Britain, seeing that he was ordained bishop for Ireland. I think we should interpret the land of the Picts or Cruithne (*V. Trip.* loc. cit., *hitirib Cruithnech*) to mean Dalaradia,

---

[1] *Annis* xxx. Tír. *loc. cit.* The numeral is less probably a mistake for iii. than the result of a mistaken attempt to account for the chronology of Patrick's life on the hypothesis that he lived to the age of 120. Other schemes assigned 30 or 40 years to the Auxerre period (Muirchu, $271_{22}$).

the land of the Picts in Ireland. As I have pointed out in cap. iv., the assumption that there were Christian communities in this part of the island makes Patrick's work there at the beginning of his bishopric more intelligible.[1]

Professor Zimmer's theory that Palladius and Patrick were one and the same person (a theory which had been already maintained by Schoell and Loofs[2]) is at variance with the distinct tradition, and does not account for the change of name.[3] It is based upon a paragraph which was added, probably by the Armagh scribe Ferdomnach, to his copy of Tírechán (Rolls ed. p. 333), where it is stated that Palladius was also called Patricius. It is also stated that Palladius suffered martyrdom among the Scots, *ut tradunt sancti antiqui*. This is at variance with W and *V. Trip.* which state that he died of disease. Muirchu says simply "died." The same notice says that Patrick was sent by Celestine. This paragraph cannot carry any weight; it is not supported by the earlier sources.

But why, we must ask, should any one have invented the assertion that Palladius was also called Patricius? The answer seems to be that the two dates for Patrick's death, the true 461 and the false 493, led, in the eighth century, to the belief in a second Patricius. This phantom is called "the other Patrick" in one of the interpolated stanzas in the hymn *Genair Patraicc*; and he came to be distinguished as *senex Patricius (Ann. Ult.* and *Chron. Scot.* 457) or *Sen Patraicc (Calendar of Oengus,* August 24).[4] One attempt to give this fictitious personage a reality may have been to identify him with Palladius.[5] Many wild and worthless speculations have been founded on this duplication of Patrick (see, for instance, Shearman's chapter on

---

[1] For the traditions and legends connecting Palladius with Scotland see Skene, *Celtic Scotland,* ii. 29 *sqq.*

[2] Schoell, *De ecclesiasticae Britonum Scotorumque historiae fontibus,* 1851, p. 77; Loofs, *De antiqua Britonum Scotorumque ecclesia,* p. 51 (1882). Compare B. Robert's criticisms on their arguments, *Étude critique,* etc., pp. 28 *sqq.*

[3] Professor Zimmer (*Early Celtic Church,* p. 38) regards Palladius as a Roman rendering of Patrick's name Sucatus (warlike), following a suggestion of Mr. O'Brien (*Irish. Eccl. Record,* 1887, pp. 723 *sqq.*). This is quite unconvincing, in the absence of any evidence that Palladius was a Briton. Why should he not have belonged to the *stirps Palladiorum* of Bourges (Apoll. Sidon. *Epp.* vii. 9, 24)? Cp. Duchesne, *Fastes épisc.* ii. p. 26, *note.*

[4] P. cxxv. ed. Stokes (1871). This calendar, Mr. Stokes has shown, cannot be earlier than the end of the tenth century.

[5] The name of Palladius does not appear in any Irish calendar of saints. It appears under July 6 in the Breviary of Aberdeen. See Todd, *St. Patrick,* p. 299.

the "History of the Three Patricks" in *Loc. Patr.* pp. 395 *sqq.*; Olden, *Church of Ireland*, Appendix A, and the article on Patrick in the *Dictionary of National Biography*, which is vitiated by the Sen Patraicc delusion). Another attempt to place the second Patrick was to connect him with Glastonbury, and thus account for the mediaeval Glastonbury tradition that the true Patrick was an abbot of that monastery (so Ussher, followed by Petrie, *Tara Hill*, p. 73).[1] But there is no evidence that the Glastonbury story has any foundation or is older than the tenth century. It is to be observed that the date August 24, given in martyrologies as the day of Old Patrick, cannot be alleged as an argument for his existence. In the *Mart. of Tallaght* (ed. Kelly), p. xxxii, we find two Patricks under this date :

> Patricii Abb. ocus Ep. Ruisdela.
> Patricii hostiarii ocus Abb. Airdmacha.

It is clear that there was an obscure but historical Patrick, abbot of Rosdela (near Durrow), whose day was August 24 ; and that his name was the motive for placing "Old Patrick" here. Compare the glosses in the *Calendar of Oengus*.[2] Armagh also wanted to appropriate "Old Patrick," and so he appears in some of the lists of its abbots.

### 8. *Patrick's Alleged Visit (or Interrupted Journey) to Rome in A.D. 432*

Muirchu's account of the events preceding Patrick's ordination as bishop has certain difficulties which involve an important question. Patrick, we are told, had left his home in Britain for the purpose of visiting Rome (*ad sedem apostolicam uisitandam*, etc.), to receive instruction there for his life-work in Ireland. But he halted on his way at Auxerre, and remained there "at the feet" of Germanus. Then when the right time came and new visions warned him : *coeptum ingreditur iter ad opus in quod ollim praeparatus fuerat utique aeuangelii* ($272_{10}$). What is the meaning of *coeptum iter*? The journey which Patrick had begun was the journey to Rome, which had been interrupted at Auxerre.

---

[1] Cp. *Chron. Scot.* pp. 24-25 ; Cormac's *Glossary* sub *Mogheime*.

[2] M. d'Arbois de Jubainville has a note on Sen Patrick in *Revue celtique*, ix. p. 111 *sqq.* He thinks a second Patricius came over to Ireland as a mere name in a copy of the Hieronymian Martyrology towards end of sixth century ; and that of him were made the two Patricks of August 24 in *Mart. of Tallaght*.

Germanus sends with him a presbyter, Segitius, as a companion and "witness." Then comes a notice of the unsuccessful mission of Palladius by Pope Celestine; but the transition to this is curious. *Certe enim erat quod Palladius*, etc., is the text of the Armagh MS., while it seems probable that other MSS. had *certi enim erant*,[1] which gives sense.

Having heard of the death of Palladius, Patrick and those who were with him *declinauerunt iter* to be ordained by "Amatorex." Assuming that they were on their way to Rome, it is clear that Muirchu did not suppose that they ever reached Rome; for, if he did, he could not have failed to say so. Accordingly, on this view, we have to suppose that the decisive news overtook Patrick somewhere between Auxerre and Rome, and that Patrick turned about and retraced his steps, making a divagation for the purpose of being ordained by "Amatorex." But if we read the whole narrative carefully up to the embarkation, we can hardly fail to see that in the writer's conception of what happened there was no reversal of direction. The only natural interpretation of Muirchu's meaning is that, met by the news about Palladius, Patrick turned from his direct route for the sake of ordination, and then resumed it. In other words, he was on his way to Ireland.

But it can be proved definitely that this was Muirchu's conception. In his table of contents to bk. i. we find a statement which throws light on *coeptum iter*. We find the items:

De inuentione sancti Germani in Galliis et *ideo non exiuit ultra* :
De *reuersione eius de Galliis* et ordinatione Palladii et mox morte eius.

Here it is (1) expressly stated that Patrick did not proceed beyond Gaul (as he had intended), and (2) implied that the journey which he undertook in the company of Segitius was a *reuersio* to Britain or Ireland.

In the light of these headings, we are compelled to interpret the words *coeptum ingreditur iter . . . aeuangelii* as meaning not the interrupted journey to Rome but the missionary journey to Ireland, which had been begun, in a sense, by the coming to Auxerre and the religious preparation there. With this interpretation, the words *certi enim erant* (which seems the probable reading : "for they knew," or "were informed") are intelligible. This explains the preceding statement that Patrick, *although setting forth for Ireland*, had not yet received episcopal ordination. They

---

[1] See Bury, "Tradition of Muirchu's Text," p. 205.

knew at Auxerre that Palladius had been ordained bishop and sent to Ireland by Celestine, and therefore Patrick was not ordained bishop. It was therefore on his way to the *mare Britannicum* that he received news of the death of Palladius. "Ebmoria," or whatever may be concealed under this form, must be sought north of Auxerre.

I have elsewhere (in the next Excursus) pointed out that Patrick was consecrated bishop by Germanus, and that Muirchu used inconsistent sources. This note aims only at showing what *Muirchu intended to convey.* [It may indeed be held that the ambiguity is due to his own misinterpretation of an older document. *Coeptum iter* may have occurred in his source, and there meant a journey to Rome; and he may have misunderstood the meaning. If it were possible to locate Ebmoria with certainty anywhere between Auxerre and Rome, this, I believe, would be the solution.]

It is, then, quite clear that, according to Muirchu's information, Patrick intended to visit Rome and study there, but that instead of doing so he was induced to study at Auxerre, and consequently did not go to Rome. It is obvious that such a statement about Patrick's purposes cannot be accepted without every reserve. Statements about a man's unfulfilled intentions, unless they can be traced clearly to himself or to an intimate friend, are in quite a different position, as historical evidence, from statements about his acts and deeds. It is equally obvious that if Muirchu had known of any evidence, oral or written, of an actual visit to Rome in A.D. 432, he would not have suppressed it. He would have had every reason to emphasise anything like a mission from the Roman see; for in the Roman controversy of his day he was on the Roman side. The stress he lays upon the unfulfilled intention only sets his silence in a stronger light.

Tírechán records a visit to Rome in later years (see below, Excursus 15), but he knows nothing of a visit in A.D. 432, and evidently did not find any notice of such a visit in the *Liber apud Ultanum*, from which he drew information about Patrick's early life. The earliest text which can be quoted for the alleged visit is the note of the ninth-century scribe of the *Liber Armachanus* ($332_{19}$), and even that note (*a Celestino—mittitur*), which, in view of the silence of the seventh-century documents, has no value, does not strictly involve the idea of a journey to Rome.

## 9. *Patrick's Consecration*

There is a difficulty as to the circumstances of Patrick's ordination as bishop which has a direct bearing on the determination of the chronology of his life. The oldest evidence—and we have no independent source to supplement it—is the account in Muirchu's *Life* (pp. 272-3). It is there stated that Patrick, learning at Ebmoria[1] of the death of Palladius, interrupted his journey (northwards) and went to a certain bishop, who conferred upon him episcopal ordination. This bishop is designated *aepiscopum Amatho rege*, and is described in terms which imply that he was eminent and well known. Now we know of no Gallic bishop called Amathorex, and we know of no Gallic bishop alive in the year 432 whose name at all resembles *Amatho regem*. But we do know of an eminent Gallic bishop named Amator, whose episcopal seat was at Auxerre, where Patrick received part at least of his ecclesiastical training. Only Amator died in 418,[2] and therefore could not have ordained Patrick bishop in 432.

Nevertheless there can hardly be a doubt that Amator is meant, for he is the only Gallic bishop, of similar name, in Patrick's time. He could be described as *mirabilis homo summus aepiscopus*; and he was bishop of Auxerre, with which, under his successor Germanus, we know that Patrick was connected. This high probability was raised into certainty when Zimmer showed that *Amatho rege* is perfectly intelligible as an Irish form.[3] The Latin colloquial casus communis *Amatore* was treated in Irish on the analogy of a name like *Ainmire*, Dat. Acc. *Ainmirig*; so that *Amatorege* represents *Amatorig*, re-Latinised (see above, Appendix A, ii. 3).

[1] The name of this place, whether in the form *Ebmoria* (*Lib. Arm.*) or in the variant form *Euboria* (for the variants see Bury, "Tradition of Muirchu's Text," p. 185) is unknown. The context shows that it lay between Auxerre and the north coast of Gaul. Ebroica = Evreux would be my guess. (It probably became the seat of a bishop before the end of the fifth century, but probably not long before. Cp. Duchesne, *Fastes ép.* ii. 226).

[2] On the evidence for this date see *note* 15 in my "Sources of Early Patrician Documents" (*E.H.R.*, July 1904), where I refer to the discussion of Dr. W. Levison in his monograph cited above, Appendix A, i. 7.

[3] *Nennius Vindicatus*, p. 123, *note*. Later compilers divided *Amatho rege*. In Irish conditions a *rex episcopus* would not sound so strange as in Gaul, though I do not know of an instance before Cormac of Cashel at the beginning of the tenth century. In *Tripartite Life* (p. 34) we get a further step in the evolution; the bishop appears as Amatho rí Románach (King of the Romans); and the final stage is reached when Patrick is ordained *coram Teodosio imperatore*.

Amator, then, is meant. The inconsistency in the chronology can be explained as due to a perfectly intelligible confusion of two different occasions. For when we come to examine closely the narrative of Muirchu we find a statement which is inconsistent with the assertion that Patrick was ordained bishop *ab Amatho rege*. We are told that when he started from Auxerre for Ireland in the company of Segitius the presbyter, he had "not yet been ordained bishop by Germanus." This clearly implies that the prelate who ordained him bishop was no other than Germanus.[1] And this is just what we should expect. If Patrick heard of the death of Palladius at some place on the road from Auxerre to the Channel, his natural course was to return to Auxerre and receive ordination from his master Germanus. How came it, then, to be stated categorically that he was ordained *ab Amatho rege*? This admits of a very simple explanation. We have only to suppose that Muirchu confounded his ordination as bishop with his ordination as deacon. This solution fits in perfectly with the interpretation of *Amatho rege* as equivalent to *Amatore*. Amator ordained Patrick deacon before (or in) A.D. 418.

A further criticism of Muirchu's text supplies a remarkable confirmation of this solution of the inconsistency of his statements. He tells us that not only was Patrick consecrated bishop, but that others, including Auxilius and Iserninus, received lesser orders *ab Amatho rege*. It is necessarily implied that Auxilius and Iserninus were of Patrick's company, and were on their way with him to Ireland. But we may ask in the first place why their ordination, whether as deacons or priests, should have been deferred till this occasion—should have depended (like Patrick's ordination as bishop) on the death of Palladius? In the second place, we have the distinct record in the Irish Annals that Auxilius and Iserninus arrived in Ireland seven years after Patrick's coming.[2] There is no reason to question that record, and the inference is that they did not accompany Patrick.

This error confirms the truth of the hypothesis that under Muirchu's account there lies a confusion between Patrick's ordination to the diaconate and his elevation to the episcopate.

[1] I pointed out this inference in "Sources of Early Patrician Documents" (*cit. sup.*).

[2] *Ann. Ult. s.a.* 439. For the separate coming of Iserninus see account in *Lib. Arm.* f. 18 r° a (342, Rolls ed.). It is there indeed supposed that they started at the same time from Gaul, but were severed by storms, and so arrived separately in Ireland. The motive for this tale is evidently the genuine record that they did not come together.

The authentic record was that Amator ordained Patrick, Auxilius, and Iserninus (Patrick as deacon, the others perhaps as deacons also). When this was taken to refer to Patrick's episcopal ordination, the association of Auxilius and Iserninus was still retained, and they were represented as accompanying Patrick.

The result of this criticism is in accordance with the general probability that Patrick had a continued connexion with one church—namely, the church of Auxerre, a connexion begun in the time of Amator and protracted in the time of Amator's successor Germanus. And it suits the chronological data derived from the *Confession* (as shown above).

### 10. *Evidence for Christianity in Ireland before St. Patrick*

The circumstances which render it antecedently probable that Christianity should have penetrated to Ireland before A.D. 430 have been set forth in the introductory chapter. The positive evidence which shows that this occurred is Prosper's notice of the mission of Palladius. It is supported by other evidence, but is in itself fully sufficient to establish the fact.

1. Prosper, *Chron. s.a.*, 431 :—

Ad Scottos in Christum credentes ordinatus a papa Caelestino Palladius primus episcopus mittitur.

It is important to observe that, if the express words *in Christum credentes* were absent, this record would establish the existence of Christian communities in Ireland. For neither Rome nor any other church would have ordained a bishop for Ireland unless there had been Christian communities there to be submitted to his authority. If all parts of Ireland had been still as entirely heathen as Scandinavia, a missionary might have been sent, but he would not have been a bishop.

Nothing can shake the inference from this record of Prosper, but some have attempted to weaken it by a statement in a later work of Prosper concerning Christianity in Ireland. In the *contra Collatorem*, written *c.* A.D. 437, Prosper, praising Celestine, says, *et ordinato Scottis episcopo dum Romanam insulam studet servare catholicam fecit etiam barbaram Christianam* (Migne, 51, 274). The expression is obviously rhetorical, and is not inconsistent with the statement in the *Chronicle*. It is quite possible that it is based on information which had reached Prosper of the progress of Christianity in the years 433-436 ; and, in a eulogy of Celestine, it was plausible to ascribe this success to his initiative in ordaining the first bishop. To infer that Prosper did not know of the death of Palladius would be unwarranted. Prosper was evidently interested in the mission of Palladius ; he probably knew him personally, as there is reason to think that he was at Rome, engaged on ecclesiastical business with the Roman see, in the year 431 ; and these considerations render it highly improbable that he would not have been aware of his death. But it was not Prosper's purpose to record the details of missionary work ; he was merely concerned to notice, and not to minimise, what Celestine had done. The passage, therefore, must not be used to support the theory that Palladius and Patricius were one and the same person (Zimmer, *Early Celtic Church*, p. 33). On the other hand, it may be added to the other evidence which shows that Patrick was not ordained by Celestine ; for in that case Prosper would not have omitted to notice that the Pope had ordained two bishops.

2. It has been generally overlooked that Patrick's expression *ad plebem* nuper *uenientem ad credulitatem* (*Conf.* 368₉) suggests, in its most natural interpretation, a spreading of Christianity before his arrival. Otherwise we should expect *primum* rather than *nuper*.

3. If Pelagius, as Zimmer holds, was born in Ireland, we might consider it probable, almost certain, that he belonged to a Christian community, and thus we should have a confirmation of the existence of such communities before the end of the fourth century. But the evidence rather points, as I have shown (see note in App. B, p. 296), to Pelagius belonging to one of the Scottic settlements in western Britain. There is, however, another piece of evidence of the same kind. An Irishman, named Fith, better known under his ecclesiastical name of Iserninus, was with Patrick at Auxerre, and was ordained by Amator (see the evidence in App. B, p. 297).

4. Certain linguistic facts are best explained, as Zimmer has ably pointed out, by the unofficial introduction of Christianity from Britain. A number of Irish ecclesiastical loan-words have forms which are "not such as we should expect if they had been borrowed straight from Latin," but can only be explained by intermediate Brythonic forms.[1] Zimmer says : "It is altogether

---

[1] There are three cases (Zimmer, *ib.* 24-26) :

1. Long ō instead of long ā : *e.g. trindōit* (=*trinitatem*) ; *altōir* (=*altāre*) ; *caindlōir* (*candelarius*) ; *notlaic* (*nātalicia*) ; *popa* (*papa*). If the Latin forms had come directly to Ireland, the ā would have been preserved ; ō for ā is characteristically British.

2. *c* for *p* : *casc* (*pascha*) ; *crubthir* (*presbyter*). Words of this kind must

incredible that the Latin loan-words in Old Irish should have been introduced by Patrick and his Romance-speaking companions from the Continent after A.D. 432. On the other hand, their linguistic form is easily explained if Christianity was gradually spread throughout Ireland in the fourth century by Irish-speaking Britons." The words, "gradually spread throughout Ireland," are far too strong, and are not required for the argument; but it is clear that the linguistic facts in question harmonise with the testimony of Prosper, and enable us to draw the further inference that the introduction of Christianity was due to intercourse with Britain. We may go further and conjecture that the transformation of the Brythonic Latin loan-words into Irish equivalents was made in the Irish settlements in western Britain, which must have been the most effective channel for the transmission of the Christian faith to Ireland.

5. The attitude of king Loigaire (see below, Appendix C, 11) to Christianity shows that it had become a force with which he had to come to terms. If it had been first brought by Patrick, he could easily have stopped its spreading in his own kingdom, and would doubtless have done so, since personally he was not well disposed to it, and the Druids were strongly against it. His policy implies that it had already taken root.

6. The circumstance that Patrick's missionary work was in the north and west of Ireland suggests that Christianity had made considerable progress in the south, and an apostle was not needed there in the same way. As Zimmer says (*ib*. 18), south-eastern Ireland in the kingdom of Laigin was "the district whence, thanks to the intercourse with the south-west of Britain, the first diffusion of Christianity in Ireland must naturally have taken place." As for the Lives of alleged pre-Patrician saints (Ailbe, Ibar, Declan, Ciaran), they are so full of contradictions and inconsistencies, as Todd demonstrated, that they are useless for historical purposes. The only hypothesis on which any significance could be ascribed to them is that there was a confusion

have been "interpreted to the Irish by British mouths," for if they had been borrowed from Latin, *p* would have been preserved. The motive for the change of *British p* to *c* in the loan-words was the observed fact that in native words Gaelic *c* corresponded to British *p* (representing the velar *q*). The treatment of Patrick's name is a significant instance. From its British form we get in Irish *Coithrige*, from its Latin form *Patraicc*. *Caille*, a veil (*caillech*, a nun), is supposed to be another case (=*pallium*). Mr. Nicholson suggests that it is Celtic, =*capillia* (*Keltic Researches*, p. 104).

3. *sr* for *fr*, *sl* for *fl*: e.g. *slechtan* (*flectionem*), *srogell* (*flagellum*). In case of a direct borrowing, *sr*, *sl* would have been kept; but coming through British they were treated on the analogy of Irish *sruth*=Br. *frut*.

between earlier and later men of the same name. This hypothesis is too uncertain to build on; but we should have to entertain it if we accepted Zimmer's remark that the contradictions in the Lives "are the natural result of attempting to varnish facts derived from *genuine local tradition* with the views universally accepted at the time when the Lives were compiled."

7. Patrick's particular interest in west Connaught is probably to be explained by his captivity there; but the appeal which this region made to him suggests that it was a specially benighted part (in a Christian's view), in contrast with other parts of the island where Christianity was known.

8. I cannot ascribe much weight to particular passages in Tírechán which Petrie (*History of Tara Hill*, p. 23) and others have cited as evidence for pre-Patrician Christianity. (1) Tír. $321_2$, *et fuit quidam spiritu sancto plenus*, etc.; (2) $329_6$, *et in quo loco quidam episcopus venit*, etc. We do not know enough of the circumstances to draw any conclusion; we do not know (assuming the records to be correct) that Patrick's acquaintance with these men began on these occasions. (3) The *altare mirabile lapideum in monte nepotum Ailello*, $313_5$; supposed to be the altar of a pre-Patrician community. To these may be added (4) the *signaculum crucis Christi*, said to have been found by Patrick in a graveyard in Roscommon ($325_8$), a story told also by Muirchu (294); and (5) the implied existence of pre-Patrician Irish Christians in the expression, *Hiberniae sanctis omnibus praeteritis praesentatis futuris*, $323_2$. There is also (6) a passage in the *Additions to Tírechán*, 337, cited by Petrie to prove pre-Patrician bishops (Colman, Bishop of Clonkeen). The story of the cross, common to Tírechán and Muirchu, and evidently a pretty early legend, has, I think, some significance, in so far as it implies that, at the time when it was invented, the existence of Christian crosses and Christian sepultures in Ireland before Patrick's preaching was taken for granted.

9. If the view put forward below in Excursus 17 as to the Paschal cycles in Ireland is correct, it is further evidence for pre-Patrician Christianity.

10. The prophecy of the Druids, which was probably not *post eventum* (see above, Chap. iv. *ad fin.*), suggests the existence of Christian worship in Ireland. If it stood alone, it would not be of much significance; but it fits in with the other evidence.

### 11. *King Loigaire and King Dathi*

The view which I have put forward of the significance of king Loigaire's reign in Irish history, and his claims to the title of statesman, is based on inferences. That his policy was pacific is an inference which may be fairly drawn from the rare mentions, in the Annals, of wars and battles during his reign of thirty-six years. The Ulster Annals record only three battles with Leinster (a victory in 453; the battle of Ath Dara, in which he was captured, in 458; and the engagement in which he met his death, *s.a.* 462). No expeditions beyond the sea are attributed to him, though the condition of Britain might have been tempting to a monarch ambitious of conquest. The great achievement of his reign was the codification of the laws of Ireland (see Excursus 12 on Senchus Mór), and the other feature for which his reign was remarkable was the spread of Christianity favoured by his attitude towards it. The record of Tírechán (308$_3$), that he did not personally adopt the new faith (*non potuit credere*), is obviously true, for it explains the coolness of ecclesiastical tradition in regard to him; and the conflicting statement of Muirchu (285$_{27}$, *credidit*, etc.), which is in a legendary context, must be rejected. It bears indeed a mark of internal inconsistency; for if the High King had been converted, it is hardly credible that Patrick would have dwelt only on his previous opposition, and prophesied that no kings of his seed would inherit the kingdom—a prophecy which was not verified. These words ascribed to Patrick in the legend (*quia resististi doctrinae meae*, etc., 285$_{29}$) seem to reflect the true tradition that Loigaire remained a pagan. If he had become a Christian, the Irish Church would have been as loud in his praises as the Roman Church in the praises of Constantine. The legend told by Muirchu represents him finally converted through fear (*melius est me credere quam mori*), as the crown and culmination of Patrick's triumphs at Slane and Tara; but at the same time it refutes itself by the cold indifference which it manifests towards the converted king.

The statesmanlike policy of Loigaire in coming to terms with Christianity is proved by the official recognition of it in the Senchus Mór (see Excursus 12), and by the toleration of it in his kingdom: see the record in Tírechán, which seems trustworthy (308$_2$), *apud illum* [Loigairium] *foedus pepigit* [Patricius] *ut non occideretur in regno illius*. (We can hardly attach much credit to the story that Patrick acted along with Loigaire in adjudicating on the inheritance of Amolngaid; Tír. 309$_{28}$. This might have been

an invention for the purpose of magnifying Patrick's importance.)
The circumstance that members of Loigaire's family were baptized
(see the conversion of Fedilmid and Fortchernn, *Add. Notices,*
334-5) was an element in the situation.

In connexion with the conclusion that Loigaire was influenced
by the prestige of the Empire, I referred to his predecessor
Dathi's expedition to Gaul. Dathi, son of Fiachra, and nephew
of king Niall, succeeded Niall as king of Ireland in 405, and was
killed by lightning near the Alps, according to the Irish Annals, in
428 (see *Ann. Ult. s.a.* 445 : through some error the entry has
been inserted under a wrong year). There is a notice of his death
in the *Lebor na hUidre,* p. 38, where he is said to have been
killed in Gaul, while besieging a town of king Fermenus (*rī Tracia*),
whose name suggests (as others have pointed out) the Faramund of
the Merovingian genealogy.[1] Zimmer (*Nennius Vindicatus,* p. 85)
dismisses the story as a reminiscence of the death of an Attacottic
chief in Roman service. But this does not account for the data,
and for the consistent tradition that Dathi met his death on the
continent ; I can see no reason to doubt the tradition, there was
no motive for its invention. Accepting it, we are obliged to infer
that Dathi went, with Irish troops, by the invitation of the Romans.
The date of the Annals for Dathi's death and Loigaire's succession,
A.D. 428, harmonises with the inference ; for just in this year the
General Aetius, on whom the defence of Gaul at this time rested,
was engaged in war with the Franks. Prosper, *s.a.* 428, *pars
Galliarum propinqua Rheno quam Franci possidendam occupaverant
Aetii armis recepta.* The name Fermenus supplies a remarkable
confirmation. As has been said, it seems to represent Faramund,
the father and predecessor of Chlojo, according to Merovingian
tradition. Chlojo, who appears a year or two later on the scene,
is the first Merovingian monarch who has a clear place in history.
Faramund has always been regarded as shadowy. The independent survival of his name in Irish tradition in connection with an
event of 428, shortly before the first appearance of his son Chlojo,
may be fairly brought forward as a piece of evidence for his
historical reality. The transference of the scene from the lower
Rhine to the regions of the Alps (due originally to vague knowledge of Gallic geography) makes the evidence more valuable, as
it shows that the name Fermenus was not introduced into the
story from Merovingian sources ; the Alps would not have
suggested to any antiquarian a connexion with a war against the
Franks in north-eastern Gaul.

---

[1] *Tracia* being an error for *Frācia.*

It is said that the corpse of Dathi was brought back by his companions to Ireland and buried in the cemetery of Rathcrochan. See the poem of Torna-Éices on the famous men and women who lay there, published by M. d'Arbois de Jubainville in *Revue Celtique*, 17, 280 *sqq.*

> Under thee is the king of the men of Fail [Ireland], Dathi son of Fiachra, the good ;
> Croghan, you have hidden him from the Galls, from the Goidels.
> Under thee is Dungalach the swift who led the king [Dathi] beyond the sea of seas.

### 12. *The Senchus Mór.*

The Irish code of law, entitled the *Senchus Mór*, preserved only in late MSS., is a work which contains a very ancient code embedded in glosses, commentaries, and accretions. Passages are quoted from it in Cormac's glossary, a work of the tenth century, and these quotations appear to be the earliest testimonia.

In the tenth century it was believed that the original code was drawn up in the reign of king Loigaire in the fifth century. Here is the note in Cormac's glossary, in Dr. W. Stokes's translation (*Trip.* p. 570).

*Nós* (customary law), the knowledge of nine [*nofis*], to wit three kings and three bishops and three sages, namely, a sage of poetry and a sage of literature and a sage of the language of the Féni. All these were composing the *Senchus Mór*. Thence it is said :—

> Loiguire, Corc, dour Daire,
> Patrick, Benén, just Cairnech,
> Ross, Dubthach, Fergus with goodness,
> Nine props, those of the *Senchus Mór*.

The same account is found in the Introduction which was prefixed in late times to the Senchus, and professes to record the circumstances of its compilation.

Was this tradition, which was current in the tenth century, genuine, or was it an invention made for the purpose of enhancing the prestige of Patrick ? In deciding this question, there are two considerations which seem to me important. (1) If the code, which evidently held such a high place in public esteem in the tenth century, had been drawn up in the seventh or eighth centuries, it is inconceivable that an event of such interest and importance as its publication should not have been recorded in the *Annals*. In my opinion this argument applies also to the sixth century. But in any case, if it be admitted that the silence of the *Annals* forbids a date later than A.D. 600 at the latest, all the probabilities are in favour of the correctness of the tradition. The entries in the *Annals* for the fifth century are extremely meagre, so that the omission of a notice of the *Senchus Mór* would not be surprising.

It may be said, however, that as a matter of fact, the *Annals* do notice the composition of the *Senchus Mór*. Under A.D. 438 we find : *Senchus mor do scribunn,* " the Senchus Mór was written." But in the first place, this entry is in Irish ; if it had been a contemporary record, it would have been preserved in Latin ; it is clearly an addition, and perhaps a comparatively late addition. In the second place, the date is suspicious. The year A.D. 438 is the very year in which the Theodosian Code was issued ; and therefore we can hardly doubt that the motive of the insertion of the Irish entry under this year was a desire to synchronise the issue of the native with that of the great Roman Code. These considerations force us to reject the entry in the *Annals* as evidence of independent value.

(2) If the story of the compilation of the Senchus in the reign of Loigaire had been a deliberate invention, say of the ninth century, it could hardly have assumed its actual shape. The persons alleged to have taken part in the compilation would naturally be those who play a prominent or well-marked part in the Patrician story. Now, leaving out Patrick and Loigaire, of the other seven only three, Daire, Benignus, and Dubthach, are conspicuous in the lives and legends of Patrick. Of the other four, Ros appears indeed, but not so conspicuously as his brother Dichu, while Corc, Cairnech, and Fergus are not mentioned at all. The case of Corc, king of Munster, is particularly to be noted, because Oengus (Corc's second successor) comes into the Patrician story, and would naturally have been selected as Patrick's colleague if the record were a pure invention.

The record, I therefore conclude, has a genuine and ancient basis. It would be rash to be confident that the number nine, and the arrangement in three classes, may not be an improvement upon the original record ; in other words, some names (*e.g.* Benignus and Daire) may conceivably be additions. The number nine was considered a number of virtue by the Gaels ; and it is conceivable that a savant of a later age might have added to the tradition in order to make up that number. But the argument is double-edged. For it is equally likely that, for just the same reason, the number of the real commission should have been fixed at nine.

The story that the occasion of the composition of the Senchus was the slaying of Odhran, Patrick's charioteer, in order to test Patrick's doctrine of forgiveness, is told in the Introduction to the *Senchus* (pp. 4 *sqq.*) and in the *Lebor na hUidre* (text and translation, in Stokes, *Tripartite*, 562 *sqq.*). A different story of the death of Odhran at the hands of Foilge is told in *Vita Quarta*, c. 77, and *Vita Tertia*, c. 59 (where the charioteer's name is not mentioned): according to this version the missile was aimed at Patrick. This version, but without reference to Foilge, is likewise noticed in the Introduction to the Senchus (p. 6).

The simplest explanation may be that a driver of Patrick was slain by an enemy, and that the incident was used by Patrick for raising the question of criminal justice; mythopoeic instinct then attributed the murder to a deliberate intention of raising the question.

The story as told in the Introduction seems to preserve a tradition that an attempt was made by Patrick to change the penalty of eric fine for murder into a penalty for death. This is the motive of the poem which is fathered upon Dubthach: "I pronounce the judgment of death, of death for his crime to every one *who kills*" (p. 13). This is to be reconciled with the Christian doctrine of perfect forgiveness by considering that the body only is killed, the soul is forgiven: the "murderer is adjudged to heaven, and it is not to death he is adjudged" (*ib.*). The commentator notices the disagreement between this principle, which in the story Patrick is assumed to have established, and the custom of eric fine which actually prevailed, and explains it on the ground that Patrick's successors had no power of bestowing heaven, hence the death penalty was discontinued, and "no one is put to death for his intentional crimes, as long as 'eric'-fine is obtained."

The historical fact underlying this story is, I submit, that the Church in Patrick's day attempted, unsuccessfully, to supersede the system of composition for manslaughter and private retaliation by making the act a public offence punishable by death.

[The questions connected with the material of the laws, and the Feine, lie quite outside my competence, and do not concern the scope of this book. I may refer to Atkinson's article "Feine," in his glossary (*Ancient Laws*, vol. vi.); Rhŷs, *Studies in Early Irish History*, pp. 52-55 (*Proc. of Brit. Acad.* vol. i.). For the legal processes and customs, the chief work is M. d'Arbois de Jubainville's *Études sur le droit celtique*, 2 vols. 1895; see also the Prefaces to the volumes of the *Ancient Laws*, and Sir H. Maine's *Early Institutions*.]

### 13. *Patrick's Visits to Connaught*

An analysis of the itinerary which Tírechán has traced for Patrick through Connaught shows that he compressed into a single journey events which must have belonged to different visits. I pointed this out in a paper on the "Itinerary of Patrick in Connaught" (*Proc. of R.I.A.* xxiv. c. 2, 1903). It was remembered that Patrick visited Connaught three times (Tír. $329_{12}$), and we may probably suppose that on the two later occasions he would have not only worked in new fields, but revisited the scenes of his earlier work. Tírechán, who used written material as well as oral information, worked all his records into the compass of a single journey. This is betrayed by a number of inconsistencies in the narrative, and it is possible to show that certain events which he ascribes to the same journey must have happened on different occasions.

1. It is clear that the expedition to Tirawley with the sons of Amolngaid was the principal motive of one visit, and that Patrick must have proceeded direct from Tara to Tirawley. Tírechán's naïve reconstruction implies that having left Tara for this purpose he engaged in a round of missionary activity, not only in Connaught, but in Meath—performing labours which would have occupied years—before he finally reached Tirawley. I have pointed out at length the absurdities involved in the story, *op. cit.* 166-7.

2. The description of the visit to Elphin implies earlier work in the same district: (*a*) perhaps the previous foundation of Senella Cella; (*b*) the presence of Assicus and Betheus, who had been settled there (*loc. cit.* 163-4).

As to Senella Cella, however, Dr. Gwynn has made a very plausible suggestion, that Tírechán confused it with Senchua = Shancough, in Sligo. The information which he gives about Senella Cella—its location in the land of the Hy Ailella, its association with Mathona, and connexion with Tawnagh—suits Senchua much better. And this comparison would account for the introduction of the statement *et exiit per montem filiorum Ailello*, etc., in $314_{18}$, as well as in $328_1$. If this view is right, it is another illustration of Tírechán's use of written sources. The difficulty is that we should expect Tírechán to have been sufficiently acquainted with the geography of Connaught as to know whether *Senella Cella* was in the land of the Hy Ailella or not. Can *Senella Cella Dumiche* be distinct from both Shankill at Elphin and Shancough?

3. An earlier visit to Tirerrill is implied by (*a*) Patrick's

knowledge of the stone altar (Tír. $313_5$); and (*b*) the fact that Tamnach had already been founded ($314_{15}$). Here indeed we can extricate a piece of Tírechán's written material, relating to Patrick's work in Tirerrill, and showing that he entered that territory from Leitrim, crossing the Bralieve hills, $314_{18}$ :—

Et exiit per montem filiorum Ailello et plantavit aeclessiam liberam hi Tamnuch,

and 328, *et exiit . . . cell Senchuae*. See Bury, *loc. cit.* 164-6.

4. In the passage in the *Liber Armachanus*, f. 9, r° (301), which Dr. Gwynn has shown (see above, p. 250) to belong to the work of Tírechán, the baptism of Hercaith and the dedication of his son Feradach = Sachellus to the church are noticed ; and it is recorded that Patrick ordained Sachellus at Rome. But immediately afterwards at Selce (319) Sachellus is already a bishop (of Baslic, *Trip.* 108). Thus two visits, separated by an interval of years, are here implied. If the statement is correct that Patrick took Sachellus with him to Rome, then our conjectural chronology for his visit to Rome (see Appendix C, 15) would give a lower limit for one of his journeys to Connaught.

5. An earlier visit to north Sligo is implied — but without inconsistency—in the account of the visit to that region (327), as well as in the presence of *bishop* Brón at Selce (and cp. $313_8$).

6. The notice of the visit to Ardd Senlis seems to imply an earlier foundation there (317).

7. Sanctus Iarnascus in Mag-n-Airniu ($320_{26}$) is introduced as if Christianity had already been planted there. It may be noticed that in this passage the words *uiris uiiii. aut xii.* show that Tírechán was using a written source ; he was doubtful about the reading.

8. Entering Tirawley, Patrick crosses the Moy. This implies that he came from the east, not from the south, as Tírechán's itinerary would imply.

If we assume as probable the correctness of the statement that Patrick's work in Connaught belongs to three different visits, we may draw tentatively the following conclusions :—

1. In the first visit, which was prior to A.D. 441, he worked (*a*) in Tirerrill, and (*b*) in north Sligo, where Bron was ordained bishop for his church (Killespugbron) under Knocknaree. Perhaps he also visited (*c*) the neighbourhood of Elphin. He visited (*d*) Mag Airthic and (*e*) the district of the Ciarrigi, and (*f*) Mag-n-Airniu. In these regions he converted the father of Sachellus.

It is possible that on this occasion he extended his journey to Mount Aigli, and fulfilled the special aim of his missionary ambition by planting a church (Ached Fobuir) near the southern limits of the forest of Fochlad.

2. On another occasion he crossed the Shannon, as described by Tírechán, at Lake Bofin; worked in Mag Glais and Mag Ái; revisited the Elphin district; founded Baslic, proceeded to Lake Tecet, revisited Mag Airthic and the Ciarrigi, etc.

3. On a third occasion, he proceeded straight (from Tara) to Tirawley in the company of Endae and the sons of Amolngaid. After his plantation of his faith in Tirawley he may have revisited other parts of Connaught. The visit falls soon after Amolngaid's death, which may have been c. 445 A.D.

It seems not at all unlikely that the second and third visits thus distinguished occurred chronologically in reverse order. It must also be borne in mind that he would have probably revisited many places in the course of the two later visits.

Conclusions very similar to mine have been reached by Dr. Gwynn, who discusses the subject in a "Supplemental Note to Chapter V." of his Introduction to the *Book of Armagh*. There are in the abbreviated memoranda (which has been described above in Appendix A, ii. 2) vestiges of the material used by Tírechán, and Dr. Gwynn points out that the first group supplies evidence of the existence of a tradition as to Patrick's work in Tirerrill, independent of the rest of the itinerary which Tírechán sketched. The first group is :—

Ailbe iSenchui. altare . . . Machet Cetchen Rodán Mathona . . .

Here, Dr. Gwynn observes, is a memorandum combining in continuous form several unconnected passages in Tírechán. "It is reasonable to infer that the tradition condensed into this memorandum was known to Tírechán; that he endeavoured to work it into his history by breaking it up into pieces and inserting them where he judged best."

### 14. *King Amolngaid : Date of his Reign*

The death of Amolngaid, king of Connaught, is not· noticed in the *Ann. Ult.*, but is recorded *s.a.* 449 in the *Annals of the Four Masters*, and must have been derived from older Annals. Probably it was given by Tigernach (this part of his work is not preserved), who generally records the changes in the succession in Connaught. We cannot indeed infer that A.D. 449 was the pre-

cise year designated in the source of the Four Masters, because
at this period their dates are not very accurate, as can be shown
by a comparison with the *Annals of Ulster*. But we can consider
it as an approximation to the date assigned by the older Annals.

The extant lists of the kings of Connaught, from Amolngaid
to Aed (son of Eochaid Tirmcharna), ob. A.D. 577, are hopelessly
confused. The material which I have examined consists of (1)
the names and dates in the Annals (*Ann. Ult.* and Tigernach);
(2) List in *Book of Leinster*, 41 a; (3) List in MS. Laud, 610, f.
116 r° b; (4) (*a*) prose list, (*b*) poetical catalogue by O'Duinn,
in *Book of Ballymote*, 57 a, 58 a. I owe the translation of
O'Duinn's poem to the kindness of Mr. E. J. Gwynn.

These sources generally agree (with the exception of 3,
which seems to be worthless) that the three kings following
Amolngaid were, in order, Ailill Molt, Duach, and Eogan Bel.
It is in regard to Duach that the chief difficulty occurs, for he
appears again in the lists as the second (or third) king after Eogan
Bel. He was son of Fergus, and is distinguished as Tenga Uma,
and is said to have fallen in the battle of Segais. The Annals
give the date of the Battle of Segais as A.D. 502 (*Ann. Ult.*,
*Ann. Inisf.*) or 500 (Tigernach); but Tigernach has a notice
of Duach Tenga Uma under 550 (p. 139, ed. Stokes), and of
his death under 556 (as well as under 500). The list of O'Duinn
distinguishes clearly two Duachs: Duach Galach, son of Brian,
who succeeded Ailill Molt, and Duach son of Fergus, seventh in
the list, who fell at the battle of Segais. (The list in the *Book
of Leinster* also distinguishes the two Duachs, designating the
first as Galach and the second as Tenga Uma).[1] This would
put the battle of Segais about 550. The earlier date of that
battle must be accepted, as Muirchertach MacErca was the victor
in it, and the notice of it in the Annals is undoubtedly independent of the lists of Connaught kings. It is also clear that
there was a fixed tradition that Duach Tenga Uma fell at
Segais, since O'Duinn, placing his reign at a later period, has to
transfer the battle of Segais along with him. We may therefore
conclude that Duach Tenga Uma preceded Eogan Bel, and fell
in the battle of Segais A.D. $\frac{500}{502}$. Now all the lists agree in
giving to the first Duach, who succeeded Ailill Molt, nineteen
or twenty years. This agrees with the circumstance that Ailill
Molt fell in the battle of Ocha A.D. 482.

---

[1] The prose list in the *Book of Ballymote* describes both Duachs as Tenga
Uma (and as slain by Muirchertach), but in the case of the first *Duach Galach*
is written above.

Eogan Bel, the sources consent, fell in the battle of Sligech. The date assigned to this battle in the Annals is A.D. 543 or 547 (both dates in *Ann. Ult.* and Tigernach). The length of his reign is given in the lists as thirty-seven (or thirty-four : the variation is obviously due to confusion of uɪɪ and ɪɪɪɪ); which is not long enough for either of the obituary dates if he followed Duach in A.D. 500-2. Tigernach, however, *s.a.* 503, gives his regnal years as forty-two; which would be consistent with A.D. 543 for the battle of Sligech.

Ailill, the Womanly, Eogan Bel's son and successor, was slain in the battle of Cuil Conaire, which is noticed in the Annals *s.a.* 550.

The remaining years up to A.D. 577, the year of Aed's death, would be just accounted for by Eochaid Tirmcharna's reign of one year and Aed's reign of twenty-five years (twenty-two years in lists 2 and 4; a confusion here too of ɪɪ and u). But at this point, after Ailill, occurs the repetition of Duach Tenga Uma : he appears in Tigernach as well as in the lists (except 4); and seven years are assigned to him. Further, the catalogue of O'Duinn inserts Eogan Srem between this second Duach and Eochaid Tirmcharna, and gives him twenty-seven years. Eogan Srem also appears in the prose list in the *Book of Ballymote*, but before Ailill.

If we take as fixed points the death of Ailill in 550 and that of Aed in 577, it is obvious that, even if Aed reigned only twenty-two years, there is no room for a second Duach and Eogan Srem in this period.

On the other hand, if we take the sum total of all the regnal years as given in O'Duinn's poem up to Aed's death, and reckon back from A.D. 577, we find that we are taken back to the neighbourhood of the death of king Dathi. It will be best to give O'Duinn's list :—

| | | | |
|---|---|---|---|
| Amolngaid . | . reigned | 20 | years |
| Ailill Molt . | . ,, | 11 | ,, |
| Duach, son of Brian | ,, | 20 | ,, |
| Eogan . . . | ,, | 37 | ,, |
| Ailill . . . | ,, | 5 | ,, |
| Eogan Srem . | . reigned | 27 | years |
| Duach, son of Fergus | ,, | 7 | ,, |
| Eochaid . . | ,, | 1 | ,, |
| Aed . . . | ., | 25 | ,, |
| Total . | | 153 | ,, |

Reckoning back 153 years from A.D. 577, we reach A.D. 424. The date of Dathi's death was A.D. 428, but if we take into account the conditions of such a calculation, where incomplete years may be set down as full years, the divergence might be consistent with the conclusion that the list was constructed on

the initial assumption that Amolngaid succeeded Dathi in 428—
which implies that Dathi was king of Connaught (but see below).

We can now see how the chronology was constructed in
O'Duinn's source. It will be simplest, for the purpose of
criticism, to tabulate the dates (approximately) implied by that
construction :—

| | | | | | | |
|---|---|---|---|---|---|---|
| Amolngaid | . | ceased to reign 444 | Eogan II. | . | ceased to reign 544 |
| Ailill I. | . | ,, 455 | Duach II. | . | ,, 551 |
| Duach I. | . | ,, 475 | Eochaid | . | ,, 552 |
| Eogan I. | . | ,, 512 | Aed | . | ,, 577 |
| Ailill II. | . | ,, 517 | | | |

These dates are entirely at variance with the chronology of
the Annals. We are entitled to criticise them on the assumption that the dates of the Annals for the battles of Segais,
Sligech, and Cuil Conaire are approximately correct. O'Duinn's
figures would place Segais *c.* 475 instead of 502 (or 500),
Sligech *c.* 512 instead of 543 (or 547), Cuil Conaire *c.* 517
instead of 550. But if we omit from his list Eogan II. and
Duach II., and then reckon back from 577, we get approximately
dates assigned in the Annals to the second and third of these
three battles, namely, 551 for Cuil Conaire, 546 for Sligech;
while the contradiction between the duration of Eogan Bel's
reign and the date of Segais is the same here as in the other
sources. If Segais was fought in 502 and Sligech in 54$^6/_7$, and
Eogan Bel reigned thirty-seven years, then seven or eight years
are left unaccounted for, and the reign of the second Duach
serves to fill this interval. But there is no room for Eogan Srem
between the battle of Segais and the death of Aed.

Again, if we take Duach I.'s death at Segais in 502 as a
fixed point, and reckon backward with O'Duinn's figures, we find
482 for the accession of Duach I., 471 for the accession of Ailill
Molt, and 451 for the accession of Amolngaid. If Amolngaid
followed Dathi in 428, this would imply an error of about twenty-
four years.

We have now the clue to the construction of O'Duinn's list.
A period of *c.* 153 years from the accession of Amolngaid to the
death of Aed had to be accounted for. The recorded regnal
years were insufficient, and the defect was supplied by an impossible interpolation in the sixth century, whereas it was in the
fifth century, in the period anterior to Duach, that the supplement was chiefly needed. Having established this point, we
need not consider further the succession of kings subsequent to
Duach Tenga Uma.

It is clear that there was a definite tradition assigning to Amolngaid twenty years, to Ailill Molt eleven years, and Duach twenty years; and that the chronologer, whom O'Duinn followed, did not venture to tamper with these numbers in order to account for the missing years. As for Ailill Molt, twenty years are assigned to him in the list in the *Book of Leinster*. But this may be at once rejected; for twenty years represent the duration of his reign as king of Ireland (462-482), and it is highly improbable that the throne of Connaught became vacant at the same moment as the throne of Ireland. Accepting then eleven years as the genuine tradition, he must have succeeded to Connaught *c.* 471, as he died in 482, and there is no reason to suppose that he resigned the kingship of Connaught before his death. The interval from 482 to 502 is exactly covered by the twenty years assigned to Duach Tenga Uma. If Amolngaid followed Dathi in 428 and reigned for twenty years, the end of his reign would fall *c.* 448, which would correspond to the record in the *Annals of the Four Masters* (449). Thus we should arrive at an interval of about twenty-four years between Amolngaid's death and Ailill Molt's succession (448-471), which is unaccounted for. [The confusion of Ailill Molt's regnal years in Connaught with his twenty regnal years in Ireland served to shorten this period by nine years; and in the list of the *Book of Leinster* the residue of the chronological error is "corrected" by adding fourteen years to the reign of Amolngaid, to whom thirty-four years are assigned.]

The question therefore is, who reigned in Connaught between Amolngaid and Ailill Molt? Now I think it can hardly be insignificant that in the Annals as well as in the lists Duach Tenga Uma is reduplicated. This must have had some motive, and the most probable explanation seems to be that two Duachs did reign in Connaught, and that O'Duinn is right in distinguishing Duach son of Brian from Duach son of Fergus, though he confuses the order and chronology. For it is clear that he had knowledge of Duach Galach son of Brian, whom he describes as falling in battle with the Cinel Eogain. His notice of this king is as follows (I use the text and translation furnished by Mr. E. J. Gwynn):—

| | |
|---|---|
| Duach mac Briain abus | Duach son of Brian next |
| XX bliadan a flaithus, | was sovereign 20 years; |
| fuair a brath, ba tennel tair, | he met his betrayal—he was a prince in the east— |
| 'sa cath re ceinel Eogain. | in battle with the cinel Eogain. |

| Ced ri cloindi Briain na mbladh | The first of the family of Brian the famed |
|---|---|
| Duach galach gargg dargiallsad, | was Duach valiant (*Galach*) fierce to whom men gave obedience ; |
| bladh don duine os gach dine | fame the man had beyond all generations |
| gurgab uile in airdrige. | so that he took the entire overkingship. |

| A secht oshein rochuala | 77 years from thence I have heard |
| secht ndeich da bliadan buadha | years of victory |
| co Seagais in Coraind cain | to Segais of fair Corand |
| co har Conaill is Eogain. | to the battle of Conall and Eogan. |

The last stanza presents a difficulty. The battle of Segais was not the "battle of Conall and Eogan," so that the preposition *co* "to" either in v. 3 or in v. 4 must be a mistake for *ó* "from." O'Curry, in his *Manuscript Material*, refers to this poem, and evidently assumes that *ó* should be read in v. 4 ; for he infers that the battle in which Duach son of Brian was killed was fought 79 [sic] years before the battle of Segais (which he dates A.D. 504 after the Four Masters), thus obtaining 425 for Duach's death, and placing his reign before Amolngaid.

Now it is to be observed that the 77 years exactly correspond to the sum total of the regnal years between the death of the first Duach and that of the second Duach, according to O'Duinn's own incorrect arrangement (37 + 5 + 27 + 7 = 76). The question therefore arises : is the statement as to the period of 77 years an inference from the arrangement, or is the arrangement determined by an independent record that 77 years elapsed between the two battles in question ? The former alternative seems less probable ; for it does not appear why this particular interval, if it were only an inference from the arrangement, should be selected for special mention. It seems much more probable that (as is suggested by the expression "I have heard") the stanza embodies a tradition independent of this particular reconstruction of the regnal list. If so, O'Curry's inference was correct, and we get (502 − 77 =) 425 as the date of the battle in which Duach MacBriain fell. There would be no difficulty in this date for Duach's death ; his father, Brian, was son of Eochaid and brother of Niall ; he was himself cousin of Loigaire and Amolngaid.[1] In this case, one of the causes of the contradictions in the Connaught succession was

[1] Dai Galach is mentioned as Brian's youngest son, and destined to reign in Connaught, in the text printed, with translation, by Dr. W. Stokes, from the *Yellow Book of Lecan* (col. 898), concerning the sons of Eochaid Muigmedoin, in *Rev. Celt.* xxiv. (1903), p. 182.

a confusion of the Duach who reigned towards the beginning of the fifth century with the Duach who reigned at the end.

If then the first Duach died *c.* 425, it seems probable that he was succeeded by Amolngaid. There seems to be no clear evidence that Dathi was king of Connaught while he was king of Ireland. It is stated in the *Genealogy of the Hy Fiachrach* (p. 90) that he ruled Connaught and Ireland. It is quite conceivable that he was king of Connaught before 405, and that in that year he secured the succession to the throne of Ireland by agreeing to transfer the kingship of Connaught to his cousin Duach. The hypothesis that Amolngaid immediately followed Duach *c.* 425 is supported by two considerations.

1. Provisionally assuming, for the purpose of the argument, that Amolngaid might have succeeded Dathi, I pointed out that the sum total of regnal years in O'Duinn's list, from Amolngaid's accession to Aed's death, would take us back to the close neighbourhood of Dathi's death in 428. But there is actually a difference of four years $(577 - 153 = 424)$. If Amolngaid succeeded Duach in 424/5, we may say that the agreement of this date with the total of years in O'Duinn's reckoning is precise.

2. On this hypothesis we are able to solve the main problem —the interval between Amolngaid and Ailill Molt.

For if Amolngaid succeeded in 424/5, and reigned 20 years, his death would fall in 444/5. There would consequently be an interval of 26 or 27 years between his death and the accession of Ailill Molt in 471. Now if Duach mac Briain had a son, we might expect to find him elected to the throne. The prose list in the Book of Ballymote designates Eogan Srem as the son of Duach Galach (that is, Duach mac Briain); and the regnal years assigned to Eogan Srem in O'Duinn's poem are precisely the number required to fill up the interval between Amolngaid and Ailill Molt. The inference therefore would be that Amolngaid was followed by Eogan, Duach's son, *c.* 444/5.

In order to show the force of the argument, I may say, at the risk of tautology, that it consists of three converging considerations. (*a*) Eogan Srem is introduced, in the lists in the Book of Ballymote, among the Kings of Connaught in the sixth century in defiance of chronology. His appearance in these lists has to be explained, and is most naturally explained by supposing that he was at one time King of Connaught, though not at the time implied in the lists. If the conclusion is right that Duach mac Briain died in 425, then his son Eogan Srem must be moved back into the fifth century. (*b*) The 27 regnal years assigned to Eogan Srem exactly occupy the vacant interval between Amolngaid and Ailill Molt. (*c*) The succession of Eogan Srem, son of Amolngaid's predecessor, is just what we might expect; it is exactly parallel to the successions in the fifth century to the throne of Ireland. Thus: Niall, Dathi, Loigaire son of Niall; Dathi, Loigaire, Ailill son of Dathi; Loigaire, Ailill, Lugaid son of Loigaire.

These considerations seem to me to outweigh the circumstance that Amolngaid's death is assigned in the Annals of the Four Masters to A.D. 449. It would be otherwise if the date were recorded in the Annals of Ulster. But a comparison of the Four Masters with the other Annals shows that the former compilation constantly deviates by several years, and, for the early period at least, a date which is found only in it, cannot be accepted as accurate with any confidence.

I have presented this investigation so as to show the steps by which I reached the conclusion, as I believe that thus it will be easier to criticise it. The reconstruction which I propose seems at least to satisfy the conditions of the problem. It may be convenient to tabulate the list of the kings, in accordance with these results, as follows:—

| | |
|---|---|
| Duach Galach, mac Briain | *d.* 424/5 |
| Amolngaid | *d.* 444/5. |
| Eogan Srem, son of Duach | *d.* 471. |
| Ailill Molt | *d.* 482. |
| Duach Tenga Uma | *d.* 502. |

### 15. *Patrick at Rome*

The evidence for a visit of Patrick to Rome A.D. 441 depends upon two records, one in the Annals, the other in Tírechán.

(1) *Ann. Ult. sub a.* 441 : Leo ordinatus est xlii<i> Romane eclesie episcopus et probatus est in fide catolica Patricius episcopus.

(2) Tírechán, (p. 301₆ : see above, p. 250) :

Et exiuit [sc. Sachellus] cum Patricio ad legendum xxx annis et ordinauit illum in urbe Roma et dedit illi nomen nouum Sachellum et scripsit illi librum psalmorum quem uidi [sc. Tírechán], et portauit [sc. Sachellus] ab illo partem de reliquis Petri et Pauli Laurentii et Stefani quae sunt in Machi.

[Cp. Tírechán, 329₂₄, where Patrick is said to have given to Olcan (ordained bishop at Dunseverick) *partem de reliquiis Petri et Pauli et aliorum et uclum quod custodiuit reliquias*].

The ordination of Leo is wrongly placed in the *Annals* in 441 ; it belongs to 440. But its close association with the notice of St. Patrick's *probatio* shows the meaning of the words *probatus est* ;[1] and in fact there is no other conceivable meaning than formal approval by the Church, and the only form which that approval was likely to take in such a case was the approval of the Church's chief representative, the Bishop of Rome. Such approval might have come in the shape of a formal epistle from the Roman bishop to the bishop in Ireland. But when we find in our seventh-century authority, Tírechán, a statement that Patrick was in Rome accompanied by Sachellus, and when we find that in his time there were relics of Peter and Paul and other martyrs at Armagh procured by St. Patrick ; and seeing that there is nothing improbable in these records, and that, on the contrary, a visit of Patrick to Rome is antecedently probable ; we may venture, I think, to combine these testimonies and conclude that Patrick did visit Rome at the beginning of Leo's pontificate. The tradition of Sachall has all the appearance of being genuine ; and Tírechán in this passage was using an older written document, as is proved by his uncertainty about a numeral (*cum uiris uiii aut uiiii*, 300₂₇ ; cp. above. App. A, ii. 1).

The notice in the Annals *probatus est in fide Catholica* is, by its brief formal character, stamped, in my judgment, as a contemporary entry, made probably in a fifth-century calendar. If it had been concocted in the sixth century, or at any later period, it could never have taken this shape ; it would have been expressed more clearly. It implies and assumes contemporary knowledge— the knowledge, as I contend, of the visit to Rome.

There is another remarkable notice in the Annals, two years later, which it seems to me may bear on the subject—*Ann. Ult. sub a.* 443 : *Patricius episcopus ardore fidei et doctrina Christi florens in nostra provincia.*[2]

*Ann. Inisf. : Patricius in Christi doctrina floruit.*

It is clear that the Ulster Annals give the entry in its original form, which is abbreviated (and translated into the past tense) by

---

[1] The notice is discussed by Todd, *St. Patrick*, pp. 469-70, but he does not attempt any explanation of *probatus est*, and by omitting the first part of the notice altogether he shows that he did not apprehend the significant association of the *probatio* with Leo.

[2] *Nostra provincia* is ecclesiastical Ireland, or north Ireland—not a particular district or kingdom.

the Annalist of Inisfallen. It has never been explained why a notice of this kind should be entered under this particular year. Such a notice, attached to a certain year, must have had a motive in some particular occurrence which happened at that date. It belongs unquestionably to that small group of contemporary entries which, preserved in calendars, found their way into the later annalistic compilations (see above, p. 282). Now Patrick's visit to Rome supplies an explanation which would fully account for it. His return from Rome, with the new prestige and authority with which the Roman bishop's approbation would have invested him, furnishes a motive which would explain a formal entry recording his activity and success at this juncture.[1]

The passage in Tírechán quoted above calls for a remark. There is obviously an error in *ad legendum* xxx *annis*. The error probably arose from some combination of the genuine tradition that Sachellus accompanied Patrick to Rome with the false idea (which had arisen before Tírechán's time through chronological confusions about Patrick's life) that Patrick studied for thirty years abroad.

### 16. *Appeal to the Roman See*

The genuineness of the canon prescribing reference to the Roman see has been sufficiently vindicated in the text (chap viii. § 4); but some observations may be added here by way of illustration. It is clear that the attitude of the Irish Church to the see of Rome in the sixth century has a very distinct value as evidence from which inferences may be made in regard to its relation to Rome in the fifth century. And for the feelings of Irish ecclesiastics towards the Roman see in the sixth century, we can have no better evidence than the letters of St. Columbanus, who was born and educated in Ireland. For on the one hand Columbanus identifies his own opinions with those of the Irish, and speaks as if he were writing in Ireland; while, on the other, he admonishes the bishops of Rome with such boldness and plainness that he cannot be accused of "Romanising" tendencies. We are therefore justified in taking the spirit which he displays towards the *Cathedra Petri* as indicative of the spirit of the Irish Church.

In the three letters which are addressed to bishops of Rome (Epp. 1, 3, 5) there is the fullest recognition of the Pope's

---

[1] The *Vit. Trip.* (Part 3, p. 238) places the visit to Rome *after* the foundation of Armagh. This order seems to be simply an inference from the fact that the relics which Patrick got at Rome were brought to Armagh.

*auctoritas* in the Western Church, and it is just this recognition which makes Columban lay such solemn weight on his own admonitions—an error (*peruersitas*, p. 175₄) committed by the Pope being one of the most serious disasters that could befall the Church. It is clear that Ireland is in no wise excluded from the general *auctoritas* of the " Apostolic Fathers " (cp. pp. 164₃₁, 165₂₃), for Pope Boniface is addressed as *omnium totius Europae Ecclesiarum capiti* (Ep. 5, p. 170₁₀). In this letter Columbanus writes : *nos enim devincti sumus cathedrae sancti Petri* (174₂₅), and *vos* (the Popes) *prope caelestes estis et Roma orbis terrarum caput est ecclesiarum, salva loci dominicae resurrectionis singulari praerogativa.* The reservation (showing that the writer is expressing his conviction and not merely using rhetorical phrases of politeness) renders this evidence all the more telling ; and the same may be said of the reservation which he makes as to the claim of the Popes as successors of the keeper of the keys of heaven (175₈₋₁₉). The attitude of Columban is briefly expressed in the wish : *Rex regum, tu Petrum, te tota sequatur ecclesia* (177₁₅).[1]

The unity of the Catholic Church is an axiom with Columbanus, and there is not the smallest reason to doubt that this idea was inculcated in Ireland. *Unius enim sumus corporis commembra, sive Galli sive Britanni sive Iberi sive quaeque gentes* (164). It is not without significance that in the story of the baptism of the daughters of King Loigaire, preserved by Tírechán, one of the five rudiments of Christianity in which the converts are required to express their belief is the *unitas aecclessiae* (316₂, Rolls ed.).

The point is that its own solidarity with the rest of Christendom, and consequent respect for the Bishop of Rome as the head of Christendom, were axioms of theory, however little they were acted on in the sixth century, in the Irish Church. And such must have been the teaching of Patrick himself. Patrick, spiritually reared in the Gallic Church, must (without direct testimony to the contrary) be presumed to have shared in the attitude of Gallic churchmen to the Roman see. It was not, indeed, the attitude of unquestioning obedience and submission of later ages. What it was has been fully explained in chap. iii. *ad fin.* and in chap. viii. § 4.

Reference must be made to another passage in Columbanus, which might be thought to prove something more (*Ep.* 5, p. 171).

Nos enim sanctorum Petri et Pauli et omnium discipulorum divinum canonem spiritu sancto scribentium discipuli sumus, toti

---

[1] The references are to Gundlach's ed., *Epp. Mer. et Kar. Aeui*, vol. i.

Iberi, ultimi habitatores mundi, nihil extra evangelicam et apostolicam doctrinam recipientes : nullus hereticus, nullus iudaeus, nullus scismaticus fuit ; sed fides catholica, *sicut a vobis primum*, sanctorum videlicet apostolorum successoribus, *tradita est*, inconcussa tenetur.

In this assertion of the orthodoxy of Ireland, the words which I have italicised might be taken to imply that Ireland received the Catholic faith directly from the Popes. This would be a misinterpretation. The words can only refer generally to the transmission and maintenance of orthodox doctrine at Rome.[1]

The text of the canon of appeal (Hibernensis, 20, 5, b) is as follows :—

Si quae difficiles[2] questiones in hac insula oriantur, ad sedem apostolicam referantur.

It is referred to in the *Liber Angueli* ($356_{11}$), where the claim of Armagh to decide a *causa ualde difficilis* is laid down ; but if Armagh does not succeed in settling the question, then *ad sedem apostolicam decreuimus esse mittendam* [sc. *causam*]. It is further stated :

hii sunt qui de hoc decreuerunt id est Auxilius Patricius Secundinus Benignus.

If these names are selected from the signatories of a synod at which the canon was passed, the presence of Secundinus, who died 447-8 (see App. B, note p. 292), shows that the synod must have been held before that year. Benignus would have been still a presbyter.[3]

## 17. *Patrick's Paschal Table*

[See Dr. B. MacCarthy's *Introduction* to the *Annals of Ulster*, vol. iv.]

The Paschal table drawn up by Dionysius (based on a cycle of 19 years like the Alexandrine) superseded the Paschal canon of Victorius of Aquitaine about 525 A.D. in the Roman Church.

---

[1] Mr. Warren rightly rejects the pregnant meaning found in this passage by Döllinger (*Liturgy and Ritual*, p. 39).

[2] *difficiles* is in three MSS., including the Coloniensis (eighth century) : it is clearly wanted, and (if there was not some stronger and fuller phrase in the original canon) it has a very pregnant meaning.

[3] I believe that the silence of Cummian in his letter to Segéne (Migne, *P.L.* 87, 970) has been urged as an objection to the authenticity of the canon. But the argument from silence in such a case as this has no cogency. It is quite possible that he was not aware of the canon.

The canon of Victorius (based on a cycle of 532 years) had been introduced in 457 A.D. and continued to be used in Gaul to the end of the eighth century. Before the reception of the Victorian system, the date of Easter was calculated in the west by a cycle of 84 years. In the time of St. Patrick, the terms between which Easter could fluctuate, according to the *supputatio Romana* based on this cycle, were the 16th and 22nd of the lunar month, the 22nd March and 21st April of the calendar. These terms were due to modifications (which had been introduced in 312 and 343 A.D.) of an older computation, in which the lunar limits were the 14th and 20th of the lunar month, the calendar limits the 25th March and 21st April.[1]

There were thus four stages, from the end of the third century, in the Paschal computation adopted at Rome :

1.  84 cycle : lunar terms, 14 × 20 : cal. terms, M. 25 × A. 21
2.  84 cycle : lunar terms, 16 × 22 : cal. terms, M. 22 × A. 21 [after 343 A.D.]
3.  532 cycle : lunar terms, 16 × 22 : cal. terms, M. 22 × A. 24 [after 457 A.D.]
4.  19 cycle : lunar terms, 15 × 21 : cal. terms, M. 22 × A. 25 [after 525 A.D.]

The Celtic Church in Britain and Ireland never adopted the Victorian cycle, and the great question of the seventh-century controversies was whether they should adopt the Dionysian computation, and abandon their old system which was based on a cycle of 84. There is no doubt that a cycle of 84 was used in Ireland in the 6th and 7th centuries, for we have the clear and express testimony of one of the great Irish churchmen of the sixth century, Columbanus of Bobbio and Luxeuil. In a letter addressed to a Gallic synod 603 or 604 A.D., he writes : *plus credo traditioni patriae meae, iuxta doctrinam et calculum octoginta quatuor annorum.*[2] The confirmation supplied by Bede, *H.E.*, 2, 2 and 5, 21, as well as by Aldhelm (ed. Dümmler, *M.G.H.*, *Epp. Mer. et Kar. Aeui*, i. 233), is superfluous.

But what surprises us is that this Paschal reckoning which prevailed in Ireland in the sixth and seventh centuries was not the *supputatio Romana* of the fourth and fifth centuries. The Paschal limits were different. The Irish celebrated Easter from the 14th to the 20th of the moon, and not before 25th March.[3] In other words, their system represented the oldest of the four stages noted above. How is the survival of this system to be explained ?

---

[1] See B. Krusch, *Der 84jährige Ostercyclus und seine Quellen*, 1880.

[2] Columbanus, *Epp.* ed. Gundlach, Ep. 4, p. 162.

[3] *Ib.* Ep. 1 (to Gregory I.), p. 157 ; *Catal. Sanct. Hib.*, *unum Pascha, quarta decima luna post aequinoctium vernale* (H. and S., *Councils*, ii. 292, 293).

If we suppose that a table of Paschal computation was brought by Patrick to Ireland in the first half of the fifth century, it is not probable that he would have introduced any other than the *supputatio Romana*. This inference does not depend on the view which we adopt as to Patrick's relations to the Church of Rome. It depends upon his connexion with the Gallic Church. There is no evidence, so far as I can discover,[1] that the Gallic Church did not agree with the Roman in the fourth and fifth centuries as to the Paschal limits. We should have to suppose that Patrick rejected both the system prevailing in western Europe, and the Alexandrine system, in favour of the older usage prevailing in his native country, Britain; and this, in view of the circumstances of his career, seems extremely unlikely.[2]

The evidence, in my opinion, suggests rather a different conclusion. It suggests that the Paschal system which prevailed in Britain in the fourth century and survived to the seventh had been introduced from Britain into Ireland, and taken root among the Christian communities there, *before the arrival of Patrick*. This is what we should expect. It is in accordance with the hypothesis of the British origin of pre-Patrician Christianity in Ireland. It is easy to comprehend that Patrick, though accustomed to the *supputatio Romana*, acquiesced in the continuance of the other system or was unable to change it. It would be not at all easy to comprehend that, if he had found Ireland a *tabula rasa* ready to receive any Paschal calculation that he might choose to inscribe, he should not have introduced the system generally received in the Western Church unless it were the system generally received in the Eastern Church. The Paschal evidence appears to be another proof of pre-Patrician Christianity in Ireland.

But if Patrick acquiesced in the continuance of the old system and did not make the fixing of the Paschal feast a crucial question in Ireland, it does not follow that he adopted it himself or may not have made some attempt to introduce another canon. There is no *a priori* objection to the possibility that, while the old method continued in the old-established communities, he

---

[1] Dr. MacCarthy's explanation (Introd. to *Annals of Ulster*, iv. p. lxxix) of an entry in the Chronicle of Marius Aventicensis (ad ann. A.D. 560), implying a survival of the old 84 cycle in Gaul, does not seem tenable (see A. Anscombe, *Z. f. Celtische Philologie*, iv. p. 333).

[2] I have omitted all reference to the abstruse technique of the computations, and the question as to the difference between the two cycles of 84 (differing in the number of the *saltus*), for which see MacCarthy, *op. cit.* pp. lxv. *sqq.* ; Krusch, *op. cit.*

may have sanctioned a different table in the new communities which he founded. This brings us to the consideration of an important piece of evidence contained in the letter of Cummian addressed to Segéne, Abbot of Hy (probably in 632 A.D.[1]), arguing for the Roman Easter. Cummian states definitely that the Pasch of Patrick differed from the Pasch of the Irish and Britons. He describes the cycle used by Patrick thus : [2]

illum [cyclum] quem sanctus Patricius, papa noster, tulit et facit (*leg.* fecit), in quo luna a xiv usque in xxi regulariter et aequinoctium a xii Kl. April obseruatur.

The Paschal lunar limits in this text are those ascribed to Theophilus and the Council of Caesarea, in the spurious *Acta* composed by an Irish computist [3] (possibly towards the beginning of the sixth century). The probability, however, seems to be that the text of Cummian has suffered corruption in the numbers, and the question is whether (1) xiv. is an error for xv.,[4] and the Alexandrine cycle is implied, or (2) xiv. and xxi. are errors for xvi. and xxii. respectively, and the *supputatio Romana* (with 84 cycle) is intended. Both these alternatives are possible, for, though we should expect Patrick to have accepted the Gallic usage, he *might* have been prepossessed in favour of the Alexandrine system at Lérins, where there was probably Eastern influence.

In any case, we can hardly feel prepared to reject the statement of Cummian [5] that Patrick "brought" and sought to introduce a different Paschal computation from that which prevailed among the Celts in Cummian's own time. We may fairly cite in confirmation the express mention of his studies of the calendar (at Auxerre) in the Hymn of Fíacc (l. 11, as interpreted by Thurneysen, *Rev. celt.* vi. 233 ; see above, p. 264).

---

[1] For dating, see MacCarthy, *op. cit.* cxl. cxli.

[2] Migne, *Patrol.* 87, 969.

[3] Krusch, 302 *sqq.* For dating, see MacCarthy, *op. cit.* cxvii., where the proof of fabrication will be found.

[4] So MacCarthy, cxxxvii., note 2.

[5] Dr. MacCarthy shows that Cummian was uncritical (cxl.), but I cannot go quite so far as he. He accepts, as genuine tradition, the statement that Patrick brought a cycle with him (rightly observing that the addition of *et fecit* cannot be pressed), but holds that it was identical with the Celtic cycle of later times. It is with much diffidence that I venture to differ from him on this point ; but I owe it to his investigations that I have been able to reach a definite conclusion.

## 18. *The Organisation of the Episcopate* [1]

Todd showed in great detail that bishops without sees were common in the Irish Church in the sixth, seventh, and eighth centuries (*St. Patrick*, pp. 1 *sqq.*). Strictly speaking, he did not prove it for the fifth century; nor did he show that there were no bishops with sees, even in the times to which his instances and illustrations apply. Loofs has maintained that both in Patrick's time and in later times there were "*episcopi paruchiales*" in Ireland. I hardly think that the positive arguments which he brings forward are very convincing; the inscription of the letter of Pope John IV. (Bede, *H.E.* 2, 19) proves nothing. But the passage which he cites from the letter of Columbanus (A.D. 603 or 604) to a synod of Gallic bishops and clergy may be quoted in this connexion. The Irish monk writes:

Inde sanctus Hieronymus haec sciens iussit episcopos imitari apostolos, monachos uero docuit sequi patres perfectos. Alia enim sunt et alia clericorum et monachorum documenta, ea et longe ab inuicem separata. [2]

Had the Abbot of Luxueil who writes with such approbation of the separate functions and ideals of sequestered monks, and active clergy (including bishops), whether regular or secular—had he been accustomed in his native country to a system in which there were no bishops who were not members of monasteries? This bears on the question whether the Irish Church in the sixth century was as exclusively monastic as it is generally represented. It is quite inconceivable that Patrick and his foreign coadjutors should have organised a purely monastic Church. Such a Church might have grown into being by degrees, but it would never have been deliberately organised in the fifth century; there was no model for it. Nor is it conceivable that Patrick would have introduced an order of bishops, none of whom were bound to any defined sphere of activity, but who might go about the island promiscuously, performing episcopal duties wherever they liked. It is incredible that he was not guided by geographical considerations in his ordination of bishops; and it is not easy to see how a geographical distribution could have been dispensed with.

[1] The learned Appendix A, pp. 123 *sqq.*, in Reeves, *Eccl. Ant.*, is valuable still.

[2] Ed. Gundlach, *M.G.H.*, *Epp. Mer. et Kar. Aeui*, i. p. 163. See Jerome, *Ep.* 58 (Migne, 22, 583).

There is indeed a total absence of evidence to suggest that there were large episcopal dioceses, and this is perfectly consistent with the tradition that Patrick ordained an immense number of bishops, variously stated, with great exaggeration, at 450 and 350.[1] Tírechán, who gives the former number, cannot mention the names of more than about forty-five. But the fact that he can record so many shows that the number of bishops under the Patrician system was not small. It does not follow that they had no dioceses ; it only follows that the dioceses were comparatively small. *A priori*, this is what we might expect. The number of small tribal territories in Ireland could not fail to affect and largely determine the ecclesiastical organisation. And when we find in the records of Tírechán, concerning the foundations of St. Patrick, that in some churches he placed presbyters, while for others he consecrated bishops, we may be sure that in this discrimination he was guided by considerations of secular geography, and that he did not wish to multiply bishops beyond necessity.

The evidence of the records and traditions preserved by Tírechán has the more weight because it is quite undesigned ; and, so far as it goes, it seems to bear out the general view of the Patrician organisation which has been indicated above. Here are the bishops who were ordained by Patrick for certain churches in Connaught :—

| | |
|---|---|
| Assicus : Elphin (313 Rolls ed.) | [Muirethachus : Killala ? (327)] [2] |
| Sachellus : Baslick (304, 320₁₄ ; cp. *Vit. Trip.* 110) | Senachus : Aghagower (322) |
| Bronus : Caisselire (327) | Cainnech : Cellola Tog (324) [3] |
| Mucneus : Donaghmore, near Fochlad (326) | Felartus : Saeoli (313) |

To these may perhaps be added the *epis prespiter bonus* (whose name is illegible in the MS. : fol. 13 r° b, l. 12) who founded a church in Imgoe Mair Cerrigi (in the barony of Costello, Mayo).

[1] 450 in Tírechán and one MS. of *Catal. Sanctorum* ; 350 in other MSS. of *Cat. Sanct.*

[2] It is not, of course, certain that Bishop Muirethachus *qui fuit super flumen Bratho*, for whom Patrick and Bronus wrote an alphabet, is identical with the *epscop Muiredaig*, "an aged man of Patrick's household," who is said in *Vit. Trip.*, p. 134, to have been left by Patrick in Cell Alaid. The foundation of Cell Alaid is not mentioned by Tírechán.

[3] The text of Tírechán leaves it doubtful whether the foundation of Cellola Tog was laid under Patrick's auspices, and whether Patrick ordained Cainnech bishop. He is not included in the author's catalogue of bishops ordained by Patrick (p. 304).

As many foundations in Connaught are recorded by Tírechán, with which no bishop is connected, it is clear that, so far as this evidence goes, Patrick proceeded on some principle in the distribution of episcopal churches. There is one passage from which it might be hastily concluded that he set two bishops in one place. He installed Assicus and his nephew Bitteus at Elphin, and both Assicus and Bitteus are described as bishops ($313$). The true interpretation obviously is that, when Assicus left Elphin (as described in $313_{29}$, *fecit profugam ad montem lapidis*), he was succeeded by Bitteus, as was natural; and that Bitteus is here ($313_{22}$) described as a bishop *proleptically*. (This accords with the part he took in the ordination of Cairell at a later time, in connexion with which Assicus is not mentioned: $314_{26}$, see below.)

There is one interesting piece of evidence for the multiplication of bishops after Patrick's death. Under his arrangement there was no bishop at Tamnach in Tirerrill; but

id cairellum

post haec autem posuerunt episcopos iuxta sanctam aeclessiam hi Tamnuch quos ordinauerunt episcopi Patricii id est Bronus et Bietheus.

The language is a little loose, but clearly means that afterwards Cairellus was ordained a bishop for Tamnach by Bronus of Caisselire and Bitteus (who had succeeded his uncle Assicus) of Elphin, and that he was succeeded by a line of bishops. Why was this innovation made? Clearly because the community of Tamnach, founded by Mathona, had grown in importance and aspired to have a bishop for itself. Here we may recognise a distinct bit of evidence for the early introduction of the system, which very soon became prevalent, of bishops without sees attached to religious houses.

There seems then to be no evidence in support of the improbable supposition that Patrick's bishops had not episcopal districts. Such districts would naturally have been determined by the tribal divisions of the country. Nor is there any difficulty in explaining the subsequent development of this episcopal church into a church which was predominantly monastic. The double position of the bishop is the clew to the development. For the bishop was not only bishop for a certain diocese, which would contain several churches and religious foundations, but he was also head of a particular community. Thus Assicus presided over a religious community at Elphin,[1] besides being episcopally

---

[1] For the *monachi* of Assicus, see $313_{33}$ and $328_{30}$.

responsible for a certain district. This system was a natural consequence of the condition of the country; there were no cities; monastic establishments were the substitute. Hence Patrick's bishops were probably in most cases monks; we have references to *monachi Patricii*,[1] from whom Patrick doubtless selected some of his bishops, just as Lérins supplied some notable bishops for the sees of Gaul. It is easy to conceive how in process of time other religious communities might aspire to be self-sufficient and have bishops of their own. If the bishop, whose jurisdiction included a number of communities, had not been himself the head of a similar community, such a tendency would not have been likely to arise. But when there were a number of monastic communities, A, B, C, etc., in one district, which was under the episcopal jurisdiction of a bishop who was the *princeps* of A, one can understand how this jurisdiction might have soon seemed to B, C, etc., an intolerable claim to superiority on the part of a neighbouring community. The bishop came to be regarded, and perhaps came to act, less as the bishop of the *paruchia* than as the *princeps* of his community. The double position of the bishop exposed him to a jealousy which would not have been aroused if he had stood outside all communities alike. The consequence was the multiplication of bishops, many communities wishing to be independent and to have bishops, each for itself. Thus the diocesan system partly broke down, and the instance of the ordination of Cairell for Tamnach seems to be an early instance.

Was there any discriminating designation to distinguish those religious settlements which were seats of bishops from those which were not? I venture on the conjecture that the name *civitas* was originally applied only to the former communities. In Gaul, in Italy, in Roman Britain, the bishop's seat was in a true *civitas*; and we can understand that in a cityless land, *civitas* might have been used in the special ecclesiastical sense of the settlement in which the bishop lived.[2]

It is worth noticing that in the Memoir of Tírechán two

---

[1] Cainnech was a *monachus Patricii*, 324₁₃. Another *mon. P.* is mentioned 329₉. The deacon Coimanus of Ardd Licce seems to have been another, 317₂₆. Gengen and Sannuch are described as *mon. P.* 305₁₇; and for the foreigners *Conleng and Ercleng*, see 313₁₂.

[2] Thus Slébte, the seat of Bishop Fíacc, would have been a *civitas*. It is called *Slebtiensis civitas* by Muirchu (271₁₉). See also *Lib. Angeli*, 355, *omnis aeclessia libera et civitas ⟨quae⟩ ab episcopali gradu uidetur esse fundata.* Cp. an Irish canon, ascribed to Patrick, in the *Hibernensis*, 29, c. 7 (p. 101 ed. Wasserschl.), *aut a sancta ecclesia aut in ciuitate intus.*

episcopal seats in Connaught seem to be distinguished as places for the ordination of *bishops* : Aghagower *in quo fiunt episcopi* ($322_7$) and perhaps Donaghmore in Fochlad.[1] Did Patrick specially mark out certain episcopal residences as places where bishops might be consecrated ?

The outcome of this discussion is that Patrick's organisation was from one point of view monastic, from another episcopal. It was monastic in so far as many of the churches in the various regions were connected with religious communities of a monastic character, and the clergy were largely monks. But this did not prevent its being episcopal, in the sense that there were episcopal districts or dioceses. There was not a body of bishops without sees, who went round visiting churches promiscuously, but each bishop had his own diocese.

There is another consideration which has not been noticed, and which seems to me of great weight. It is the position which bishops hold in the few laws in the *Senchus Mór* which touch the Church. The bishop appears in these laws as the dignitary in the Church who corresponds to the king in the State. There is no mention of presbyter abbots as sharing the privileges of the bishop, who has the same " dire " fine as a king.[2] Clearly a state of things is contemplated in which the bishops are the important administrators in the Church. Such rights could not have been established from the sixth century forward, when the bishops were of less account. This feature of the *Senchus Mór* seems to me, therefore, to have a double significance, in establishing both the antiquity of the code itself and the eminence of the episcopal office in the fifth century ; the two things hang together and mutually support each other.

A corroboration is perhaps also supplied by the *De Abusionibus Seculi*, a treatise of Irish origin, written before 700 A.D. (see App. A, i. 4), where the tenth Abuse is the *Episcopus negligens*, in which the pastoral duties of the bishop are insisted upon, and his functions as a *speculator*. It seems by no means improbable that the work is older than 600 A.D.

---

[1] $326_{21}$, *quia deus dixit illi ut legem relinquerent* [? —*et*, as Stokes suggests] *et episcopos ordinaret ibi, et prespiteros et diaconos in illa regione.* This suggests, though it does not necessitate, the inference in the text.

[2] *Senchus Mór*, i. 40. See also the following passages : i. 54 (a false-judging king and a stumbling bishop are placed on a level) ; i. 78, the king's testimony is valid against all except the man of learning, the bishop, and the pilgrim.

### 19. *The Place of Patrick's Burial*

The decisive reasons for determining the vexed question of Patrick's burial-place in favour of Saul have been given in the text; but something more may be said here in criticism of the evidence. Among the miscellaneous notices appended to Tírechán's Memoir (p. 332) by the scribe Ferdomnach, occurs a comparison of Patrick to Moses in four points, of which the fourth is: *ubi sunt ossa eius nemo nouit.* The author of this similitude has simply taken advantage, for his purpose, of the fact that there were two rival claimants, Saul and Downpatrick. It does not imply that there was no distinct and universally accepted tradition placing his burial in this district ; for if there had been any room for doubt about that, Armagh could not have failed to claim his bones.

Another notice follows, professing to tell how the place of sepulture was revealed :—

Colombcille spiritu sancto instigante ostendit sepulturam Patricii, ubi est confirmat., id est hi Sabul Patricii, id est in aeclessia iuxta mare proxima, ubi est conductio martirum id est ossuum Coluimbcillae de Britannia et conductio omnium sanctorum Hiberniae iudicii.

Whatever value we may attach to this passage as a record of an opinion of Columba, it is good evidence for the existence of a tradition that Patrick was buried at Saul. Todd (*St. Patrick*, p. 494) thinks that Downpatrick is intended, and thereby reconciles this passage (which he wrongly ascribes to Tírechán) with the statement of Muirchu that he was buried there.[1] If it were a case for reconciliation, it would be a more defensible hypothesis that Muirchu used loose language, and said that Patrick was buried at Dún, whereas he was really buried in its neighbourhood. But the two statements should have been protected against any such arbitrary attempt to reconcile them by the existence of the third statement *ubi sunt ossa eius nemo nouit*, for they afford us its explanation. Muirchu meant Dúnlethglasse, as he said ; and the writer of the notice of Columba's discovery meant Saul, as *he* said. There were two rival traditions, the Saul tradition and the Dún tradition ; and it was just the existence of these two traditions which could enable a man to say, " After all, we know not where the saint was buried ; in that too he was like Moses."

---

[1] In his treatment of the Muirchu narrative Todd does not go below the surface, but he recognises that the first part embodies a concession on the part of Armagh. The question is discussed in Reeves, *Eccl. Antiquities*, 223 *sq.*

The whole story, or collection of stories, related by Muirchu (and reproduced in the text) contain obvious marks of their growth, and internal inconsistency; though, as put together by Muirchu, they represent the account accepted at Dúnlethglasse. The first part, containing the interview with the angel, and the death and *exequiae* ($295_{18}$–$297_{25}$), does not contemplate Dúnlethglasse at all. It only contemplates Saul: *revertere ad locum unde uenis, hoc est Sabul.* It reflects, as I have said, a conciliation between the claim, or rather disappointment, of Armagh, and the actual burial at Saul; it is designed to protect, if I may say so, the countenance of Armagh, and the compromise is reflected in the two petitions representing the two interests.

After this comes the passage relating the burial at Dúnlethglasse ($298_{1-20}$). It is quite evident that it has a distinct and subsequent origin; it was manufactured in a different ecclesiastical workshop. It adds, like a sort of postscript, a new piece, a new command, to the discourse of the angel, in a new interest, namely of Downpatrick. If the whole story had been of one piece, this command would have formed part of the angel's original address; it would not be introduced as an appendix. This criticism is in itself sufficient to exhibit the falsity of Downpatrick's claim. It is to be noted that this claim had the further purpose of establishing an early date for the origin of the church of Downpatrick. It could not claim to have been founded by the saint; it alleged that it was founded in connexion with his burial.

The two stories, which Muirchu relates of the contention between the Ulidians and the men of Orior (*orientales*), supply an instructive illustration of the genesis of legends. When we have two stories of this kind, one is generally subsequent to the other, and suggested by it.[1] The common argument of both is to show how hostilities were prevented. There can be no doubt which was the genuine and primitive story. The inundation of the sea, a motive (as I pointed out in the text) characteristic of the district, furnishes a presumption in favour of the priority of the first story. The second story obviously arose out of the Dúnlethglasse legend of the oxen;[2] in fact, its point depends upon that legend. Thus was myth added to myth in the work-

---

[1] The simplest case is when an incident is reduplicated, as in the Cyclops story in the *Odyssey* (Book 9), where the second stone-casting of the Cyclops at the escaping ship is a later addition by an expander who sought to outdo the original incident but failed in his effect.

[2] I may note here that the river Cabcenne, where the Orior men discovered the deception, has not been identified, but ought naturally to be sought near their destination, Armagh. So Todd, p. 195.

shops of Irish ecclesiastics. The ecclesiastical origin is seen not only in the incident of the burning bush, but in the invention of the cart and two unyoked kine (1 Samuel vi. 7 *sqq.*).

### 20. *Legendary Date of Patrick's Death*

The true year of Patrick's death is furnished by our oldest document, Tírechán ($302_{29}$, a passione Christi . . . anni ccccxxxiii [MS. ccccxxxui]); Ann. of Ulster, *s.a.* 461 (cp. Ann. Inisf. *s.a.* 493); Nennius, *Hist. Brit.* 16 (pp. 158-9 ed. Mommsen). See the criticism of this material in Bury, *Tírechán's Memoir*, pp. 239 *sqq.*

But side by side with the true tradition, we find in the Annals another date, A.D. 493, which has been generally received and is the vulgar era of the event. It is closely connected with the legendary age of Patrick—120 years, which is as old as Muirchu's Life ($296_{19}$). The question arises, how came his age to be raised from somewhat more than 70 to 120 years, and why was A.D. 493 fixed on as the date of his death?

In the analogy which was drawn between Patrick and Moses, one of the items of resemblance is the same length of life. But the Mosaic motive cannot have been sufficient to determine originally such a marked perversion of fact. On the contrary, the age of 120 years must have been otherwise suggested and have then, in its turn, contributed to suggest the Mosaic analogy.

It is to be noted that in the *Liber Armachanus* two divergent subputations of Patrick's age are found. One of these was originally appended to the exemplar of Muirchu which was used by the Armagh scribe; the other is among the notes which are appended to his transcription of Tírechán.

In the first ($300_{21}$) it is stated that Patrick, having been captured in his 20th year, was a slave for 15 years, studied for 40, and taught for 61. Hence it is inferred that his age was 111. There must be errors in the figures.

In the second ($331_{22}$) we have the following statement:— baptized in 7th year, captured in 10th, was a slave for 7 years, studied for 30 years, and taught for 72. Hence his age at his death is inferred as 120 (10 + 7 + 30 + 72 = 119), *ut Moyses.*

It is, I venture to think, of the greatest significance that in both these cases the fictitious age is given as a total, and preceded by a statement of the items which compose it. This fact furnishes the clue. The Mosaic age, 120, was not handed down as a legend, nor was the true age of somewhat over 70 audaciously raised to the Mosaic figure for the purpose of the

Mosaic comparison. The figure 120, or something approximate, was reached by means of a computation of chronological items, and it is these chronological items that we must examine in order to discover the origin of the error.

In the two anonymous computations which I have quoted the items disagree with each other, and also disagree with the data in Patrick's *Confession*. They cannot therefore form the basis of our examination, because we may safely assume that the computation, by which 120 years (exactly or approximately) was reached and was generally accepted in Ireland, did not contravene the data of the *Confession*—data which were rightly quoted in Tírechán ($302_{17}$) from the Book of Ultan. We may safely assume that the computators, who succeeded in establishing the Mosaic age, started with the incontrovertible fact supplied by the *Confession* that Patrick was either 22 years old, or in his 22nd year, when he escaped from captivity. It is equally clear that the period which they assigned to his teaching was 60 (rather 61 years)—for that is the period from his arrival in Ireland, A.D. 433 (rather 432) to the alleged date of his death, A.D. 493. This would leave 38 (rather 37) years to be accounted for. Now Muirchu mentions two different records, 30 and 40 years, for the sojourn with Germanus (it is to be observed that, of the two computations noticed above, one reckons with 30, the other with 40 years). If either of these, 30 years must have been the period accepted in this computation for St. Patrick's studies, and an interval of 8 (or 7) years left, which agrees remarkably with the notice of Tírechán (from the *Liber apud Ultanum, ib.*): uii. *aliis annis ambulauit*, etc. The sum worked out thus—

$$22 + 7 + 30 + 61 = 120.$$

Of these items 22 had the best authority, and 30 and 7 were independent records or traditions (as we know from Muirchu and Tírechán). The problem is therefore reduced to discovering the origin of the 61 or 60 years during which the apostle is wrongly supposed to have taught. That it was due to a misinterpretation and not to a deliberate invention, there can, I think, be no question.

A list of the Armagh succession in the Book of Leinster (printed in Stokes, *Trip.* pp. 542 *sqq.*) supplies a hint which suggests an explanation of the error. The first entry is—

Patrick: 58 years *from the coming of Patrick to Ireland* till his death.

The fact that a period of 58 years is given here instead of the usual number (493–433/2) is remarkable. Now if we count back 58 years from the *true* date of Patrick's death, 461, we reach the year 403-404, which was in the close vicinity of the year in which, as we saw, he was probably taken into slavery. Hence it seems probable that in an early record it was stated correctly that 58 years elapsed between the coming of Patrick to Ireland, meaning his *first* coming as a slave, and his death, and that this notice was misinterpreted by subsequent computators who referred it to his *second* coming as a teacher. They computed: 22 + 7 (*ambulauit*) + 30 (*legit*) + 58 (*docuit*) = 117. An age so close to 120 could hardly fail to suggest Moses; the figures clamoured for a slight manipulation, and the means adopted was to increase the last period from 58 to 61. Thus the date of the death was determined: 432 + 61 = 493.

By this computation the coming to Ireland divided the whole life into two almost equal parts (59 + 61), which would naturally come to be described in round numbers as each 60 years. This probably led to the alternative date for the obit given in the *Ann. Ult.* 492 (= 432 + 60).

The computation which established 120 years for the age and A.D. 493 for the year of the death, thus involving 61 years for the Irish period, was triumphant and became authoritative. But the computations quoted above from the *Liber Armachanus* show that other theories had been propounded based on the addition of items. In the *Vita Tertia* the age is given as 132. This figure seems to have been obtained by substituting 72 instead of the (round) 60 for the last item in the sum; this is suggested by the fact that in the second computation in the *Liber Armachanus* the last item is *septuaginta duo annos docuit*, though the total 120 (119) is secured by erroneous dates for the captivity. What is the origin of this number 72? It must have come down in some form, it must have represented something, when, in order to do justice to it, one computator felt compelled to raise the Mosaic 120 to 132, and another, though holding fast to 120, modified the authentic dates of the captivity.

I suggest that this number 72 represents an old and correct record of Patrick's age at the time of his death.

### 21. *Professor Zimmer's Theory*

The general obscurity which surrounds the early history of Ireland, the difficulties which have been found in making out the period of Patrick's career from indefinite and contradictory data, the fact that while his death fell on any theory in the fifth century, no mention of him in literature is found before the seventh, these circumstances have led to a variety of theories which beset and embarrass the student who approaches Patrician literature. Patrick has been in turn eliminated and reduplicated; and, in revenge for undue magnification, his rôle has been reduced to something quite insignificant. We may say that his writings, like the poems of Homer, have been taken away from him to be ascribed to some one else of the same name. It is needless to notice here theories which are fantastic or baseless, and have never gained any general or wide acceptance, but the view which has been recently developed by the brilliant Celtic philologist, Professor Zimmer,[1] cannot be passed over without criticism.

In another note I have referred to Zimmer's identification of Patrick with Palladius. This is necessitated by, but would not necessitate, his theory. If it were demonstrated to-morrow that Patrick and Palladius were one and the same person, this would be quite as compatible with the view of Patrick adopted in the foregoing pages as with the view of Zimmer. Palladius may provisionally be left out of account for the purpose of the present criticism, though I shall have a few words to say on the subject at the end of this excursus.

Zimmer fully admits, though he had once denied, the genuineness of the *Confession* and the missive to the subjects of Coroticus; that is, he admits that they were written by Patricius, a bishop in Ireland in the fifth century. But he holds that the activity of this bishop was entirely confined to south-eastern Ireland (Laigin), that he accomplished nothing for the evangelisation or ecclesiastical organisation of the rest of Ireland, that he died (A.D. 459: Zimmer) conscious of failure, and for nearly two centuries after his death had a merely local reputation. The rejection of the traditional Patrick is, so far as I understand, based chiefly on two arguments: (1) Zimmer's interpretation of the *Confession*; and (2), if Patrick's work had at all corresponded in scope, magnitude, and import to the descriptions of it given by Irish writers of the seventh century, it would have been noticed by Bede in his *Ecclesiastical History*. As for the *Confession* I have said enough in the text, and have shown, I think, that its note is not, as Zimmer holds,

---

[1] In his article "Keltische Kirche" in the *Realencyklopädie für protestantische Theologie u. Kirche*, 1901; translated by Miss Meyer (*The Celtic Church in Britain and Ireland*), 1902.

consciousness of failure. As for the argument from the silence of Bede,[1] on which he lays much stress, I may quote what I said in reviewing his book : The value of arguments from silence "depends entirely on the cases; in some cases an argument from silence is conclusive. But can it be said to weigh much here, if we reflect that a notice of Patrick and his work in Bede's book could have been simply a defensible digression ? We can place our finger on the unproven premiss in Zimmer's argument ; he speaks of ' Bede's evidently keen interest in the early beginnings of Christianity in the British isles ' (p. 11). Substitute ' Britain ' for ' the British isles ' and the cogency of the argument disappears. Ninian and Columba are immediately relevant to his subject, Patrick is not ; and, assuming the common tradition of Patrick's work (as believed in Ireland *c.* A.D. 700) to be roughly true, it would be no more surprising to find nothing about it in Bede than it would be to find no mention of Augustine in an ecclesiastical history of Germany written on the same lines as Bede's."—*English Hist. Review*, July 1903).[2]

Zimmer's reason for restricting the sphere of work of his Patricius to Laigin, or part of Laigin, seems to be the circumstance that the author of the earliest biography, Muirchu, belonged to this part of Ireland, being connected with Slébte. [It is possible, though he does not allege it, that another reason may have been the tradition which associates Palladius (whom he equates with Patrick) with the territory corresponding to the county of Wicklow.] The suggestion is that in this neighbourhood, at Slébte, for instance, were preserved traditions and writings of the obscure Patricius, who was in the seventh century to be transformed into the great apostle of Ireland. It is obvious that the argument, even if it were based on a correct statement of facts, is quite insufficient to prove the thesis.

[1] In Bede's *Martyrology*, under March 17, we find *in Scotia S. Patricii Confessionis*. Zimmer (p. 10) accepts this, without question, as Bedan. I should like to know how far we can distinguish in this document what is Bede's from later additions.

[2] There is, however, another consideration which may be taken into account by those who wonder at the absence of any reference to Patrick in Bede's *Ecclesiastical History*. The Latin literature concerning St. Patrick only began to appear in Bede's time. Tírechán's *Memoir* cannot have been written long before his birth ; and he was nearly thirty years old when Muirchu's *Life* was composed. The older Patrician literature, as we have seen reason to believe, was in Irish, and inaccessible to Bede. The Columban church in north Britain was not concerned to propagate the fame of Patrick. There was rivalry between the Columban and Patrician communities in Ireland (cp. Tírechán, 314₈).

But the statement of facts is not correct. There is another document which, though also dating from the second half of the seventh century, may claim (see above, p. 248) to have some slight advantage in point of priority over the *Life* of Muirchu. This is the *Memoir* of Tírechán. He had nothing whatever to do with Laigin; he was connected with Connaught and Meath. His spiritual master, Ultan, was a bishop at Ardbraccan, and had in his possession a book concerning the life of Patrick. We might therefore, if we adopted Professor Zimmer's method of argument, conclude that the sphere of the true Patrick's activity was confined to a part of the kingdom of Meath. The mere existence of Tírechán's work forbids us to attach to the provenance of Muirchu's work any significance of the kind which Zimmer attributes to it.

It must also be observed in what a strange light Zimmer's theory would place the work of Muirchu. We should have to suppose that this writer, taking upon himself to be Patrick's biographer because he belonged to the province in which Patrick had worked, ignores entirely Patrick's connexion with that province (merely mentioning that he landed on the coast of Laigin), and devotes all his space to legendary adventures in other parts of Ireland.[1] As a matter of fact, a critical analysis of his work shows that a large amount of material depends on ancient local traditions of the Island-Plain in Ulidia.

This brings us face to face with the great difficulty which Zimmer has to meet. How, and why, and when was the obscure Patricius of fact transmuted into the illustrious Patricius of tradition? Zimmer's answer to the question, when? has at least the merit of precision. He finds the motive of the glorification of Patrick in the Roman controversy of the seventh century, and he dates the appearance of the legend about A.D. 625. His own words must be quoted (*Celtic Church*, p. 80):—

It would not require a long stretch of imagination if we assume that, about 625, Ireland's pious wish of having an apostle of her own was realised by reviving the memory of this Patricius, who had been forgotten everywhere except in the south-east. It was in this way, I think, that the Patrick legend sprang up with its two chief premisses: first, that Ireland was entirely pagan in 432, as the lands of the Picts and of the Saxons had been in 563 and 597 respectively; and secondly, that Patrick converted Ireland within a short time and

---

[1] As I observed above (p. 262) if Muirchu's work were anonymous and nothing were said of Aed, we should never suspect that the author belonged to the south of Ireland ; we should certainly connect him with north Ireland.

introduced a Christian Church, overcoming all obstacles and winning the favour of King Loigaire, incidents analogous to Columba's conversion of King Brude, or Augustine's of Ethelbert of Kent.

Pointing out that the first mention of Patricius is in connexion with a Paschal cycle, in Cummian's letter to Segéne, Zimmer proceeds :—

Thus the Patrick legend is characterised on its first appearance as serving the endeavours of the *Southern Irish* to enter into the *unitas Catholica* by yielding to Rome on the Easter question.

It is to be observed that Zimmer does not categorically allege that the Patrick legend was invented by the Roman party in south Ireland. He leaves this open. He says : " If this legend was not expressly invented by an Irish member of the party in favour of conformity, it was, at any rate, utilised at once by that party." Let us take in turn the two alternatives, (1) that it was invented expressly by the Roman party, (2) that it was otherwise invented, but precisely in time for them to utilise.

(1) This alternative implies that the legend was manufactured in south-eastern Ireland (the only place where, *ex hypothesi*, Patricius was remembered) for the purpose of bringing about the conformity of the northern Irish. But the legend itself, as developed in the seventh-century sources, as developed in Muirchu's work, on which Zimmer lays great stress, repudiates this origin. Southern Ireland, south-eastern Ireland, do not appear in the legend at all (except the single reference to Fiacc and the mention of the landing in Wicklow) ; and it would require the strongest direct evidence to prove that, in spite of this radical fact, the legendary story originated there. The theory implies that the south-eastern Irish, while they resuscitated Patricius, made him over entirely, and transferred all their rights in him, to the north of the island—severed him entirely from themselves. So far as the single circumstance of the conversion of Loigaire and the incidents of the first Easter is concerned, that might pass ; for in Loigaire, as High King, the south as well as the north of Ireland had part. But the point is that the whole setting connects Patrick with the north and not with the south. Zimmer's hesitation shows, I suspect, that he was to some extent conscious of this difficulty ; and so he leaves open

(2) The other possibility that the rise of the Patrick legend may have had another origin. The only motive he suggests is " Ireland's pious wish of having an apostle of her own." Now if the origin of the Patrick legend was independent of the Roman

controversy, why need it be placed in A.D. 625? How are we to determine its date? The answer, which seems to be implied by Zimmer, is that it must have been subsequent to the times of St. Columba and St. Augustine, the object being to set up a primitive apostle, to be for Ireland what Columba and Augustine were for Pictland and for England. This is, of course, the purest speculation; but setting aside the question of date, we should have to suppose—if we are not to fall into the same difficulty as in the case of the first alternative—that the idea arose in north Ireland, and that the legend was invented there. This would imply that the northern ecclesiastical mytho-poets had recourse to south-eastern Ireland to find an obscure ecclesiastic to glorify; that they detached him ruthlessly from his home and appropriated him entirely. We need not, however, consider this improbability, as Zimmer himself does not contemplate it. His view is that Patrick was resuscitated " in the district of his special activity," " with the help of his own writings and of documents about him."

It would seem far more natural that if the Irish were in search of a founder, they should seize on Palladius, whose mission was recorded by Prosper. Zimmer therefore identifies Palladius with Patricius; but the Irish had no idea of such an identity.[1] For in the oldest *Life*, Patricius and Palladius are distinguished. If, as Zimmer thinks, the creation of an apostle was due to a " specific tendency," namely, approximation to Rome, it would be strange if Palladius, for whose direct mission from Rome there existed the record of Prosper, were not chosen. The legend of the conversion, the story of the first Paschal celebration, could as easily have been spun round him as round the author of the *Confession*. Zimmer avoids the difficulty by identifying them.

For his combination of the rise of the Patrick legend with the Paschal question, Zimmer lays much stress on Muirchu. I have pointed out above (Appendix A, ii. 3) that a certain indirect con-nexion between Muirchu's work and events connected with the Roman controversy may be fairly inferred. But this inference does not furnish any support for Zimmer's daring theory. And it is important to notice in this connexion that Muirchu did not believe that Patrick went to Rome; he admits that he wished to do so,

---

[1] The particular passage on which Zimmer relies—the only *positive* evidence —is in the " Additions " to Tírechán in the *Liber Armachanus* (p. 332, Rolls ed.), where Palladius is said to have been called *Patricius alio nomine*, but is distinguished from the second Patrick. But this can be otherwise explained. The double date of Patrick's death (see Appendix C, 7) led to a duplication—a first and a second Patrick, and one attempt to fix the personality of the earlier Patrick was to identify him with Palladius.

but denies that he passed beyond Gaul. This in itself would make us hesitate to believe that the story of Patrick, as expounded by Muirchu, was a recent fabrication in the interests of the Roman cause.

But we may waive all particular criticisms of Zimmer's reconstruction, and state the general and decisive objection to his or any similar theory. It is this. The nature of the traditions which are preserved in the two seventh-century compilations written by Tírechán and Muirchu forbids the hypothesis of recent fabrication. In the first place a critical examination of the texts of these works enables us to conclude that they were largely based on older *written* material. In the second place, it is perfectly inconceivable that all the detailed traditions which Tírechán collected both from written and from oral resources concerning Patrick's work in Connaught should have been deliberately invented, between 625 and 660, in a region where Patrick's name was never known. In the third place, the really characteristic Patrician stories, the death of Miliucc, the events of the first Easter, the story of Daire, are not of the kind which are fabricated, generations after the life of the hero, for a deliberate purpose. They belong to the legends that spring up soon after the death of their hero, or even during his lifetime. I may refer to what I have said in the text (p. 111). If we had no other evidence, the tale of the first Easter at Slane and Tara would be in itself a guarantee that the "Patrick legend" could not have been deliberately invented in the seventh century.

One more observation. It would be difficult to explain how it came that, if the author of the *Confession* spent his life in Leinster, and his name was sufficiently well remembered to make his fortune in the seventh century, no particular church in that region claimed him. Zimmer may get out of the difficulty through his identification of Palladius with Patrick; he may say that Patrick's church was the Palladian Cell Fine, where memorials of Palladius were preserved. But this explanation would only serve to emphasise the improbability of the theory of identity. It is impossible to understand how Cell Fine remembered its founder as Palladius and not as Patricius, seeing that (*ex hypoth.*) the name Patricius (as used by the author of the *Confession*) had so completely superseded the name Palladius, that the bishop was not only glorified as Patricius in the seventh century, but even distinguished definitely from Palladius. Again: either it was remembered in south Ireland or it was not remembered at the beginning of that century, when the Patrician legend is alleged to have taken shape, that Palladius and Patricius were the same person. If it *was* remembered, then how came it that Palladius-Patricius was differentiated into two, when it was assuredly more in the interests of the Roman cause to glorify an apostle sent by Celestine than to discriminate a successful missionary who was not sent by a Pope, from an unsuccessful missionary who was? If it *was not* remembered, then the only passage which Zimmer can quote for the identification (*Lib. Arm.* p. 332, see above, p. 389, note) can be at once eliminated from the discussion, as resting on mere conjecture.

[The argument, which Zimmer adduces for his theory, from the statement that Patrick's burial-place was unknown, falls to the ground when the evidence in regard to his burial-place is criticised as a whole. See above, Appendix C, 19.]

# INDEX

# A CATALOG OF SELECTED
# DOVER BOOKS
## IN ALL FIELDS OF INTEREST

# A CATALOG OF SELECTED DOVER
# BOOKS IN ALL FIELDS OF INTEREST

CONCERNING THE SPIRITUAL IN ART, Wassily Kandinsky. Pioneering work by father of abstract art. Thoughts on color theory, nature of art. Analysis of earlier masters. 12 illustrations. 80pp. of text. 5⅜ x 8½.                                    23411-8 Pa. $3.95

ANIMALS: 1,419 Copyright-Free Illustrations of Mammals, Birds, Fish, Insects, etc., Jim Harter (ed.). Clear wood engravings present, in extremely lifelike poses, over 1,000 species of animals. One of the most extensive pictorial sourcebooks of its kind. Captions. Index. 284pp. 9 x 12.                                    23766-4 Pa. $12.95

CELTIC ART: The Methods of Construction, George Bain. Simple geometric techniques for making Celtic interlacements, spirals, Kells-type initials, animals, humans, etc. Over 500 illustrations. 160pp. 9 x 12. (USO)                    22923-8 Pa. $9.95

AN ATLAS OF ANATOMY FOR ARTISTS, Fritz Schider. Most thorough reference work on art anatomy in the world. Hundreds of illustrations, including selections from works by Vesalius, Leonardo, Goya, Ingres, Michelangelo, others. 593 illustrations. 192pp. 7⅛ x 10¼.                                    20241-0 Pa. $9.95

CELTIC HAND STROKE-BY-STROKE (Irish Half-Uncial from "The Book of Kells"): An Arthur Baker Calligraphy Manual, Arthur Baker. Complete guide to creating each letter of the alphabet in distinctive Celtic manner. Covers hand position, strokes, pens, inks, paper, more. Illustrated. 48pp. 8¼ x 11.        24336-2 Pa. $3.95

EASY ORIGAMI, John Montroll. Charming collection of 32 projects (hat, cup, pelican, piano, swan, many more) specially designed for the novice origami hobbyist. Clearly illustrated easy-to-follow instructions insure that even beginning papercrafters will achieve successful results. 48pp. 8¼ x 11.        27298-2 Pa. $3.50

THE COMPLETE BOOK OF BIRDHOUSE CONSTRUCTION FOR WOODWORKERS, Scott D. Campbell. Detailed instructions, illustrations, tables. Also data on bird habitat and instinct patterns. Bibliography. 3 tables. 63 illustrations in 15 figures. 48pp. 5¼ x 8½.                                    24407-5 Pa. $2.50

BLOOMINGDALE'S ILLUSTRATED 1886 CATALOG: Fashions, Dry Goods and Housewares, Bloomingdale Brothers. Famed merchants' extremely rare catalog depicting about 1,700 products: clothing, housewares, firearms, dry goods, jewelry, more. Invaluable for dating, identifying vintage items. Also, copyright-free graphics for artists, designers. Co-published with Henry Ford Museum & Greenfield Village. 160pp. 8¼ x 11.                                    25780-0 Pa. $10.95

HISTORIC COSTUME IN PICTURES, Braun & Schneider. Over 1,450 costumed figures in clearly detailed engravings—from dawn of civilization to end of 19th century. Captions. Many folk costumes. 256pp. 8⅜ x 11¾.        23150-X Pa. $12.95

STICKLEY CRAFTSMAN FURNITURE CATALOGS, Gustav Stickley and L. & J. G. Stickley. Beautiful, functional furniture in two authentic catalogs from 1910. 594 illustrations, including 277 photos, show settles, rockers, armchairs, reclining chairs, bookcases, desks, tables. 183pp. 6½ x 9¼.                                23838-5 Pa. $9.95

AMERICAN LOCOMOTIVES IN HISTORIC PHOTOGRAPHS: 1858 to 1949, Ron Ziel (ed.). A rare collection of 126 meticulously detailed official photographs, called "builder portraits," of American locomotives that majestically chronicle the rise of steam locomotive power in America. Introduction. Detailed captions. xi + 129pp. 9 x 12.                                27393-8 Pa. $12.95

AMERICA'S LIGHTHOUSES: An Illustrated History, Francis Ross Holland, Jr. Delightfully written, profusely illustrated fact-filled survey of over 200 American lighthouses since 1716. History, anecdotes, technological advances, more. 240pp. 8 x 10¾.
25576-X Pa. $12.95

TOWARDS A NEW ARCHITECTURE, Le Corbusier. Pioneering manifesto by founder of "International School." Technical and aesthetic theories, views of industry, economics, relation of form to function, "mass-production split" and much more. Profusely illustrated. 320pp. 6⅛ x 9¼. (USO)                                25023-7 Pa. $9.95

HOW THE OTHER HALF LIVES, Jacob Riis. Famous journalistic record, exposing poverty and degradation of New York slums around 1900, by major social reformer. 100 striking and influential photographs. 233pp. 10 x 7⅞.
22012-5 Pa. $10.95

FRUIT KEY AND TWIG KEY TO TREES AND SHRUBS, William M. Harlow. One of the handiest and most widely used identification aids. Fruit key covers 120 deciduous and evergreen species; twig key 160 deciduous species. Easily used. Over 300 photographs. 126pp. 5⅜ x 8½.                                20511-8 Pa. $3.95

COMMON BIRD SONGS, Dr. Donald J. Borror. Songs of 60 most common U.S. birds: robins, sparrows, cardinals, bluejays, finches, more–arranged in order of increasing complexity. Up to 9 variations of songs of each species.
Cassette and manual 99911-4 $8.95

ORCHIDS AS HOUSE PLANTS, Rebecca Tyson Northen. Grow cattleyas and many other kinds of orchids–in a window, in a case, or under artificial light. 63 illustrations. 148pp. 5⅜ x 8½.                                23261-1 Pa. $4.95

MONSTER MAZES, Dave Phillips. Masterful mazes at four levels of difficulty. Avoid deadly perils and evil creatures to find magical treasures. Solutions for all 32 exciting illustrated puzzles. 48pp. 8¼ x 11.                                26005-4 Pa. $2.95

MOZART'S DON GIOVANNI (DOVER OPERA LIBRETTO SERIES), Wolfgang Amadeus Mozart. Introduced and translated by Ellen H. Bleiler. Standard Italian libretto, with complete English translation. Convenient and thoroughly portable–an ideal companion for reading along with a recording or the performance itself. Introduction. List of characters. Plot summary. 121pp. 5¼ x 8½.
24944-1 Pa. $2.95

TECHNICAL MANUAL AND DICTIONARY OF CLASSICAL BALLET, Gail Grant. Defines, explains, comments on steps, movements, poses and concepts. 15-page pictorial section. Basic book for student, viewer. 127pp. 5⅜ x 8½.
21843-0 Pa. $4.95

BRASS INSTRUMENTS: Their History and Development, Anthony Baines. Authoritative, updated survey of the evolution of trumpets, trombones, bugles, cornets, French horns, tubas and other brass wind instruments. Over 140 illustrations and 48 music examples. Corrected and updated by author. New preface. Bibliography. 320pp. 5⅜ x 8½. 27574-4 Pa. $9.95

HOLLYWOOD GLAMOR PORTRAITS, John Kobal (ed.). 145 photos from 1926-49. Harlow, Gable, Bogart, Bacall; 94 stars in all. Full background on photographers, technical aspects. 160pp. 8⅜ x 11¼. 23352-9 Pa. $12.95

MAX AND MORITZ, Wilhelm Busch. Great humor classic in both German and English. Also 10 other works: "Cat and Mouse," "Plisch and Plumm," etc. 216pp. 5⅜ x 8½. 20181-3 Pa. $6.95

THE RAVEN AND OTHER FAVORITE POEMS, Edgar Allan Poe. Over 40 of the author's most memorable poems: "The Bells," "Ulalume," "Israfel," "To Helen," "The Conqueror Worm," "Eldorado," "Annabel Lee," many more. Alphabetic lists of titles and first lines. 64pp. 5³⁄₁₆ x 8¼. 26685-0 Pa. $1.00

PERSONAL MEMOIRS OF U. S. GRANT, Ulysses Simpson Grant. Intelligent, deeply moving firsthand account of Civil War campaigns, considered by many the finest military memoirs ever written. Includes letters, historic photographs, maps and more. 528pp. 6⅛ x 9¼. 28587-1 Pa. $11.95

AMULETS AND SUPERSTITIONS, E. A. Wallis Budge. Comprehensive discourse on origin, powers of amulets in many ancient cultures: Arab, Persian Babylonian, Assyrian, Egyptian, Gnostic, Hebrew, Phoenician, Syriac, etc. Covers cross, swastika, crucifix, seals, rings, stones, etc. 584pp. 5⅜ x 8½. 23573-4 Pa. $12.95

RUSSIAN STORIES/PYCCKNE PACCKA3bI: A Dual-Language Book, edited by Gleb Struve. Twelve tales by such masters as Chekhov, Tolstoy, Dostoevsky, Pushkin, others. Excellent word-for-word English translations on facing pages, plus teaching and study aids, Russian/English vocabulary, biographical/critical introductions, more. 416pp. 5⅜ x 8½. 26244-8 Pa. $8.95

PHILADELPHIA THEN AND NOW: 60 Sites Photographed in the Past and Present, Kenneth Finkel and Susan Oyama. Rare photographs of City Hall, Logan Square, Independence Hall, Betsy Ross House, other landmarks juxtaposed with contemporary views. Captures changing face of historic city. Introduction. Captions. 128pp. 8¼ x 11. 25790-8 Pa. $9.95

AIA ARCHITECTURAL GUIDE TO NASSAU AND SUFFOLK COUNTIES, LONG ISLAND, The American Institute of Architects, Long Island Chapter, and the Society for the Preservation of Long Island Antiquities. Comprehensive, well-researched and generously illustrated volume brings to life over three centuries of Long Island's great architectural heritage. More than 240 photographs with authoritative, extensively detailed captions. 176pp. 8¼ x 11. 26946-9 Pa. $14.95

NORTH AMERICAN INDIAN LIFE: Customs and Traditions of 23 Tribes, Elsie Clews Parsons (ed.). 27 fictionalized essays by noted anthropologists examine religion, customs, government, additional facets of life among the Winnebago, Crow, Zuni, Eskimo, other tribes. 480pp. 6⅛ x 9¼. 27377-6 Pa. $10.95

FRANK LLOYD WRIGHT'S HOLLYHOCK HOUSE, Donald Hoffmann. Lavishly illustrated, carefully documented study of one of Wright's most controversial residential designs. Over 120 photographs, floor plans, elevations, etc. Detailed perceptive text by noted Wright scholar. Index. 128pp. 9¼ x 10¾. 27133-1 Pa. $11.95

THE MALE AND FEMALE FIGURE IN MOTION: 60 Classic Photographic Sequences, Eadweard Muybridge. 60 true-action photographs of men and women walking, running, climbing, bending, turning, etc., reproduced from rare 19th-century masterpiece. vi + 121pp. 9 x 12. 24745-7 Pa. $10.95

1001 QUESTIONS ANSWERED ABOUT THE SEASHORE, N. J. Berrill and Jacquelyn Berrill. Queries answered about dolphins, sea snails, sponges, starfish, fishes, shore birds, many others. Covers appearance, breeding, growth, feeding, much more. 305pp. 5¼ x 8¼. 23366-9 Pa. $8.95

GUIDE TO OWL WATCHING IN NORTH AMERICA, Donald S. Heintzelman. Superb guide offers complete data and descriptions of 19 species: barn owl, screech owl, snowy owl, many more. Expert coverage of owl-watching equipment, conservation, migrations and invasions, etc. Guide to observing sites. 84 illustrations. xiii + 193pp. 5⅜ x 8½. 27344-X Pa. $8.95

MEDICINAL AND OTHER USES OF NORTH AMERICAN PLANTS: A Historical Survey with Special Reference to the Eastern Indian Tribes, Charlotte Erichsen-Brown. Chronological historical citations document 500 years of usage of plants, trees, shrubs native to eastern Canada, northeastern U.S. Also complete identifying information. 343 illustrations. 544pp. 6½ x 9¼. 25951-X Pa. $12.95

STORYBOOK MAZES, Dave Phillips. 23 stories and mazes on two-page spreads: Wizard of Oz, Treasure Island, Robin Hood, etc. Solutions. 64pp. 8¼ x 11. 23628-5 Pa. $2.95

NEGRO FOLK MUSIC, U.S.A., Harold Courlander. Noted folklorist's scholarly yet readable analysis of rich and varied musical tradition. Includes authentic versions of over 40 folk songs. Valuable bibliography and discography. xi + 324pp. 5⅜ x 8½. 27350-4 Pa. $9.95

MOVIE-STAR PORTRAITS OF THE FORTIES, John Kobal (ed.). 163 glamor, studio photos of 106 stars of the 1940s: Rita Hayworth, Ava Gardner, Marlon Brando, Clark Gable, many more. 176pp. 8⅜ x 11¼. 23546-7 Pa. $12.95

BENCHLEY LOST AND FOUND, Robert Benchley. Finest humor from early 30s, about pet peeves, child psychologists, post office and others. Mostly unavailable elsewhere. 73 illustrations by Peter Arno and others. 183pp. 5⅜ x 8½. 22410-4 Pa. $6.95

YEKL and THE IMPORTED BRIDEGROOM AND OTHER STORIES OF YIDDISH NEW YORK, Abraham Cahan. Film Hester Street based on Yekl (1896). Novel, other stories among first about Jewish immigrants on N.Y.'s East Side. 240pp. 5⅜ x 8½. 22427-9 Pa. $6.95

SELECTED POEMS, Walt Whitman. Generous sampling from *Leaves of Grass.* Twenty-four poems include "I Hear America Singing," "Song of the Open Road," "I Sing the Body Electric," "When Lilacs Last in the Dooryard Bloom'd," "O Captain! My Captain!"–all reprinted from an authoritative edition. Lists of titles and first lines. 128pp. 5³⁄₁₆ x 8¼. 26878-0 Pa. $1.00

THE BEST TALES OF HOFFMANN, E. T. A. Hoffmann. 10 of Hoffmann's most important stories: "Nutcracker and the King of Mice," "The Golden Flowerpot," etc. 458pp. 5⅜ x 8½.                                                                                21793-0 Pa. $9.95

FROM FETISH TO GOD IN ANCIENT EGYPT, E. A. Wallis Budge. Rich detailed survey of Egyptian conception of "God" and gods, magic, cult of animals, Osiris, more. Also, superb English translations of hymns and legends. 240 illustrations. 545pp. 5⅜ x 8½.                                                            25803-3 Pa. $13.95

FRENCH STORIES/CONTES FRANÇAIS: A Dual-Language Book, Wallace Fowlie. Ten stories by French masters, Voltaire to Camus: "Micromegas" by Voltaire; "The Atheist's Mass" by Balzac; "Minuet" by de Maupassant; "The Guest" by Camus, six more. Excellent English translations on facing pages. Also French-English vocabulary list, exercises, more. 352pp. 5⅜ x 8½.                       26443-2 Pa. $8.95

CHICAGO AT THE TURN OF THE CENTURY IN PHOTOGRAPHS: 122 Historic Views from the Collections of the Chicago Historical Society, Larry A. Viskochil. Rare large-format prints offer detailed views of City Hall, State Street, the Loop, Hull House, Union Station, many other landmarks, circa 1904-1913. Introduction. Captions. Maps. 144pp. 9⅜ x 12¼.                                 24656-6 Pa. $12.95

OLD BROOKLYN IN EARLY PHOTOGRAPHS, 1865-1929, William Lee Younger. Luna Park, Gravesend race track, construction of Grand Army Plaza, moving of Hotel Brighton, etc. 157 previously unpublished photographs. 165pp. 8⅞ x 11¾.
23587-4 Pa. $13.95

THE MYTHS OF THE NORTH AMERICAN INDIANS, Lewis Spence. Rich anthology of the myths and legends of the Algonquins, Iroquois, Pawnees and Sioux, prefaced by an extensive historical and ethnological commentary. 36 illustrations. 480pp. 5⅜ x 8½.                                                                        25967-6 Pa. $8.95

AN ENCYCLOPEDIA OF BATTLES: Accounts of Over 1,560 Battles from 1479 B.C. to the Present, David Eggenberger. Essential details of every major battle in recorded history from the first battle of Megiddo in 1479 B.C. to Grenada in 1984. List of Battle Maps. New Appendix covering the years 1967-1984. Index. 99 illustrations. 544pp. 6½ x 9¼.                                                                   24913-1 Pa. $14.95

SAILING ALONE AROUND THE WORLD, Captain Joshua Slocum. First man to sail around the world, alone, in small boat. One of great feats of seamanship told in delightful manner. 67 illustrations. 294pp. 5⅜ x 8½.                          20326-3 Pa. $5.95

ANARCHISM AND OTHER ESSAYS, Emma Goldman. Powerful, penetrating, prophetic essays on direct action, role of minorities, prison reform, puritan hypocrisy, violence, etc. 271pp. 5⅜ x 8½.                                                      22484-8 Pa. $6.95

MYTHS OF THE HINDUS AND BUDDHISTS, Ananda K. Coomaraswamy and Sister Nivedita. Great stories of the epics; deeds of Krishna, Shiva, taken from puranas, Vedas, folk tales; etc. 32 illustrations. 400pp. 5⅜ x 8½.     21759-0 Pa. $10.95

BEYOND PSYCHOLOGY, Otto Rank. Fear of death, desire of immortality, nature of sexuality, social organization, creativity, according to Rankian system. 291pp. 5⅜ x 8½.
20485-5 Pa. $8.95

A THEOLOGICO-POLITICAL TREATISE, Benedict Spinoza. Also contains unfinished Political Treatise. Great classic on religious liberty, theory of government on common consent. R. Elwes translation. Total of 421pp. 5⅜ x 8½. 20249-6 Pa. $9.95

MY BONDAGE AND MY FREEDOM, Frederick Douglass. Born a slave, Douglass became outspoken force in antislavery movement. The best of Douglass' autobiographies. Graphic description of slave life. 464pp. 5⅜ x 8½. 22457-0 Pa. $8.95

FOLLOWING THE EQUATOR: A Journey Around the World, Mark Twain. Fascinating humorous account of 1897 voyage to Hawaii, Australia, India, New Zealand, etc. Ironic, bemused reports on peoples, customs, climate, flora and fauna, politics, much more. 197 illustrations. 720pp. 5⅜ x 8½.    26113-1 Pa. $15.95

THE PEOPLE CALLED SHAKERS, Edward D. Andrews. Definitive study of Shakers: origins, beliefs, practices, dances, social organization, furniture and crafts, etc. 33 illustrations. 351pp. 5⅜ x 8½.    21081-2 Pa. $8.95

THE MYTHS OF GREECE AND ROME, H. A. Guerber. A classic of mythology, generously illustrated, long prized for its simple, graphic, accurate retelling of the principal myths of Greece and Rome, and for its commentary on their origins and significance. With 64 illustrations by Michelangelo, Raphael, Titian, Rubens, Canova, Bernini and others. 480pp. 5⅜ x 8½.    27584-1 Pa. $9.95

PSYCHOLOGY OF MUSIC, Carl E. Seashore. Classic work discusses music as a medium from psychological viewpoint. Clear treatment of physical acoustics, auditory apparatus, sound perception, development of musical skills, nature of musical feeling, host of other topics. 88 figures. 408pp. 5⅜ x 8½.    21851-1 Pa. $10.95

THE PHILOSOPHY OF HISTORY, Georg W. Hegel. Great classic of Western thought develops concept that history is not chance but rational process, the evolution of freedom. 457pp. 5⅜ x 8½.    20112-0 Pa. $9.95

THE BOOK OF TEA, Kakuzo Okakura. Minor classic of the Orient: entertaining, charming explanation, interpretation of traditional Japanese culture in terms of tea ceremony. 94pp. 5⅜ x 8½.    20070-1 Pa. $3.95

LIFE IN ANCIENT EGYPT, Adolf Erman. Fullest, most thorough, detailed older account with much not in more recent books, domestic life, religion, magic, medicine, commerce, much more. Many illustrations reproduce tomb paintings, carvings, hieroglyphs, etc. 597pp. 5⅜ x 8½.    22632-8 Pa. $11.95

SUNDIALS, Their Theory and Construction, Albert Waugh. Far and away the best, most thorough coverage of ideas, mathematics concerned, types, construction, adjusting anywhere. Simple, nontechnical treatment allows even children to build several of these dials. Over 100 illustrations. 230pp. 5⅜ x 8½.    22947-5 Pa. $7.95

DYNAMICS OF FLUIDS IN POROUS MEDIA, Jacob Bear. For advanced students of ground water hydrology, soil mechanics and physics, drainage and irrigation engineering, and more. 335 illustrations. Exercises, with answers. 784pp. 6⅛ x 9¼.    65675-6 Pa. $19.95

SONGS OF EXPERIENCE: Facsimile Reproduction with 26 Plates in Full Color, William Blake. 26 full-color plates from a rare 1826 edition. Includes "The Tyger," "London," "Holy Thursday," and other poems. Printed text of poems. 48pp. 5¼ x 7.    24636-1 Pa. $4.95

OLD-TIME VIGNETTES IN FULL COLOR, Carol Belanger Grafton (ed.). Over 390 charming, often sentimental illustrations, selected from archives of Victorian graphics—pretty women posing, children playing, food, flowers, kittens and puppies, smiling cherubs, birds and butterflies, much more. All copyright-free. 48pp. 9¼ x 12¼.    27269-9 Pa. $7.95

PERSPECTIVE FOR ARTISTS, Rex Vicat Cole. Depth, perspective of sky and sea, shadows, much more, not usually covered. 391 diagrams, 81 reproductions of drawings and paintings. 279pp. $5\frac{3}{8}$ x $8\frac{1}{2}$. 22487-2 Pa. $7.95

DRAWING THE LIVING FIGURE, Joseph Sheppard. Innovative approach to artistic anatomy focuses on specifics of surface anatomy, rather than muscles and bones. Over 170 drawings of live models in front, back and side views, and in widely varying poses. Accompanying diagrams. 177 illustrations. Introduction. Index. 144pp. $8\frac{3}{8}$ x$11\frac{1}{4}$. 26723-7 Pa. $8.95

GOTHIC AND OLD ENGLISH ALPHABETS: 100 Complete Fonts, Dan X. Solo. Add power, elegance to posters, signs, other graphics with 100 stunning copyright-free alphabets: Blackstone, Dolbey, Germania, 97 more–including many lower-case, numerals, punctuation marks. 104pp. $8\frac{1}{8}$ x 11. 24695-7 Pa. $8.95

HOW TO DO BEADWORK, Mary White. Fundamental book on craft from simple projects to five-bead chains and woven works. 106 illustrations. 142pp. $5\frac{3}{8}$ x 8. 20697-1 Pa. $4.95

THE BOOK OF WOOD CARVING, Charles Marshall Sayers. Finest book for beginners discusses fundamentals and offers 34 designs. "Absolutely first rate . . . well thought out and well executed."–E. J. Tangerman. 118pp. $7\frac{3}{4}$ x $10\frac{5}{8}$. 23654-4 Pa. $6.95

ILLUSTRATED CATALOG OF CIVIL WAR MILITARY GOODS: Union Army Weapons, Insignia, Uniform Accessories, and Other Equipment, Schuyler, Hartley, and Graham. Rare, profusely illustrated 1846 catalog includes Union Army uniform and dress regulations, arms and ammunition, coats, insignia, flags, swords, rifles, etc. 226 illustrations. 160pp. 9 x 12. 24939-5 Pa. $10.95

WOMEN'S FASHIONS OF THE EARLY 1900s: An Unabridged Republication of "New York Fashions, 1909," National Cloak & Suit Co. Rare catalog of mail-order fashions documents women's and children's clothing styles shortly after the turn of the century. Captions offer full descriptions, prices. Invaluable resource for fashion, costume historians. Approximately 725 illustrations. 128pp. $8\frac{3}{8}$ x $11\frac{1}{4}$. 27276-1 Pa. $11.95

THE 1912 AND 1915 GUSTAV STICKLEY FURNITURE CATALOGS, Gustav Stickley. With over 200 detailed illustrations and descriptions, these two catalogs are essential reading and reference materials and identification guides for Stickley furniture. Captions cite materials, dimensions and prices. 112pp. $6\frac{1}{2}$ x $9\frac{1}{4}$. 26676-1 Pa. $9.95

EARLY AMERICAN LOCOMOTIVES, John H. White, Jr. Finest locomotive engravings from early 19th century: historical (1804–74), main-line (after 1870), special, foreign, etc. 147 plates. 142pp. $11\frac{3}{8}$ x $8\frac{1}{4}$. 22772-3 Pa. $10.95

THE TALL SHIPS OF TODAY IN PHOTOGRAPHS, Frank O. Braynard. Lavishly illustrated tribute to nearly 100 majestic contemporary sailing vessels: Amerigo Vespucci, Clearwater, Constitution, Eagle, Mayflower, Sea Cloud, Victory, many more. Authoritative captions provide statistics, background on each ship. 190 black-and-white photographs and illustrations. Introduction. 128pp. $8\frac{7}{8}$ x $11\frac{3}{4}$. 27163-3 Pa. $13.95

EARLY NINETEENTH-CENTURY CRAFTS AND TRADES, Peter Stockham (ed.). Extremely rare 1807 volume describes to youngsters the crafts and trades of the day: brickmaker, weaver, dressmaker, bookbinder, ropemaker, saddler, many more. Quaint prose, charming illustrations for each craft. 20 black-and-white line illustrations. 192pp. 4⅝ x 6. 27293-1 Pa. $4.95

VICTORIAN FASHIONS AND COSTUMES FROM HARPER'S BAZAR, 1867–1898, Stella Blum (ed.). Day costumes, evening wear, sports clothes, shoes, hats, other accessories in over 1,000 detailed engravings. 320pp. 9⅜ x 12¼.
22990-4 Pa. $14.95

GUSTAV STICKLEY, THE CRAFTSMAN, Mary Ann Smith. Superb study surveys broad scope of Stickley's achievement, especially in architecture. Design philosophy, rise and fall of the Craftsman empire, descriptions and floor plans for many Craftsman houses, more. 86 black-and-white halftones. 31 line illustrations. Introduction 208pp. 6½ x 9¼. 27210-9 Pa. $9.95

THE LONG ISLAND RAIL ROAD IN EARLY PHOTOGRAPHS, Ron Ziel. Over 220 rare photos, informative text document origin ( 1844) and development of rail service on Long Island. Vintage views of early trains, locomotives, stations, passengers, crews, much more. Captions. 8⅞ x 11¾. 26301-0 Pa. $13.95

THE BOOK OF OLD SHIPS: From Egyptian Galleys to Clipper Ships, Henry B. Culver. Superb, authoritative history of sailing vessels, with 80 magnificent line illustrations. Galley, bark, caravel, longship, whaler, many more. Detailed, informative text on each vessel by noted naval historian. Introduction. 256pp. 5⅜ x 8½.
27332-6 Pa. $7.95

TEN BOOKS ON ARCHITECTURE, Vitruvius. The most important book ever written on architecture. Early Roman aesthetics, technology, classical orders, site selection, all other aspects. Morgan translation. 331pp. 5⅜ x 8½. 20645-9 Pa. $8.95

THE HUMAN FIGURE IN MOTION, Eadweard Muybridge. More than 4,500 stopped-action photos, in action series, showing undraped men, women, children jumping, lying down, throwing, sitting, wrestling, carrying, etc. 390pp. 7⅞ x 10⅝.
20204-6 Clothbd. $25.95

TREES OF THE EASTERN AND CENTRAL UNITED STATES AND CANADA, William M. Harlow. Best one-volume guide to 140 trees. Full descriptions, woodlore, range, etc. Over 600 illustrations. Handy size. 288pp. 4½ x 6⅜.
20395-6 Pa. $6.95

SONGS OF WESTERN BIRDS, Dr. Donald J. Borror. Complete song and call repertoire of 60 western species, including flycatchers, juncoes, cactus wrens, many more–includes fully illustrated booklet. Cassette and manual 99913-0 $8.95

GROWING AND USING HERBS AND SPICES, Milo Miloradovich. Versatile handbook provides all the information needed for cultivation and use of all the herbs and spices available in North America. 4 illustrations. Index. Glossary. 236pp. 5⅜ x 8½.
25058-X Pa. $6.95

BIG BOOK OF MAZES AND LABYRINTHS, Walter Shepherd. 50 mazes and labyrinths in all–classical, solid, ripple, and more–in one great volume. Perfect inexpensive puzzler for clever youngsters. Full solutions. 112pp. 8⅛ x 11.
22951-3 Pa. $4.95

PIANO TUNING, J. Cree Fischer. Clearest, best book for beginner, amateur. Simple repairs, raising dropped notes, tuning by easy method of flattened fifths. No previous skills needed. 4 illustrations. 201pp. 5⅜ x 8½. 23267-0 Pa. $6.95

A SOURCE BOOK IN THEATRICAL HISTORY, A. M. Nagler. Contemporary observers on acting, directing, make-up, costuming, stage props, machinery, scene design, from Ancient Greece to Chekhov. 611pp. 5⅜ x 8½. 20515-0 Pa. $12.95

THE COMPLETE NONSENSE OF EDWARD LEAR, Edward Lear. All nonsense limericks, zany alphabets, Owl and Pussycat, songs, nonsense botany, etc., illustrated by Lear. Total of 320pp. 5⅜ x 8½. (USO) 20167-8 Pa. $6.95

VICTORIAN PARLOUR POETRY: An Annotated Anthology, Michael R. Turner. 117 gems by Longfellow, Tennyson, Browning, many lesser-known poets. "The Village Blacksmith," "Curfew Must Not Ring Tonight," "Only a Baby Small," dozens more, often difficult to find elsewhere. Index of poets, titles, first lines. xxiii + 325pp. 5⅝ x 8¼. 27044-0 Pa. $8.95

DUBLINERS, James Joyce. Fifteen stories offer vivid, tightly focused observations of the lives of Dublin's poorer classes. At least one, "The Dead," is considered a masterpiece. Reprinted complete and unabridged from standard edition. 160pp. $5\frac{3}{16}$ x 8¼. 26870-5 Pa. $1.00

THE HAUNTED MONASTERY and THE CHINESE MAZE MURDERS, Robert van Gulik. Two full novels by van Gulik, set in 7th-century China, continue adventures of Judge Dee and his companions. An evil Taoist monastery, seemingly supernatural events; overgrown topiary maze hides strange crimes. 27 illustrations. 328pp. 5⅜ x 8½. 23502-5 Pa. $8.95

THE BOOK OF THE SACRED MAGIC OF ABRAMELIN THE MAGE, translated by S. MacGregor Mathers. Medieval manuscript of ceremonial magic. Basic document in Aleister Crowley, Golden Dawn groups. 268pp. 5⅜ x 8½. 23211-5 Pa. $8.95

NEW RUSSIAN-ENGLISH AND ENGLISH-RUSSIAN DICTIONARY, M. A. O'Brien. This is a remarkably handy Russian dictionary, containing a surprising amount of information, including over 70,000 entries. 366pp. 4½ x 6⅛. 20208-9 Pa. $9.95

HISTORIC HOMES OF THE AMERICAN PRESIDENTS, Second, Revised Edition, Irvin Haas. A traveler's guide to American Presidential homes, most open to the public, depicting and describing homes occupied by every American President from George Washington to George Bush. With visiting hours, admission charges, travel routes. 175 photographs. Index. 160pp. 8¼ x 11. 26751-2 Pa. $11.95

NEW YORK IN THE FORTIES, Andreas Feininger. 162 brilliant photographs by the well-known photographer, formerly with *Life* magazine. Commuters, shoppers, Times Square at night, much else from city at its peak. Captions by John von Hartz. 181pp. 9¼ x 10¾. 23585-8 Pa. $12.95

INDIAN SIGN LANGUAGE, William Tomkins. Over 525 signs developed by Sioux and other tribes. Written instructions and diagrams. Also 290 pictographs. 111pp. 6⅛ x 9¼. 22029-X Pa. $3.95

ANATOMY: A Complete Guide for Artists, Joseph Sheppard. A master of figure drawing shows artists how to render human anatomy convincingly. Over 460 illustrations. 224pp. 8⅜ x 11¼. 27279-6 Pa. $10.95

MEDIEVAL CALLIGRAPHY: Its History and Technique, Marc Drogin. Spirited history, comprehensive instruction manual covers 13 styles (ca. 4th century thru 15th). Excellent photographs; directions for duplicating medieval techniques with modern tools. 224pp. 8⅜ x 11¼. 26142-5 Pa. $12.95

DRIED FLOWERS: How to Prepare Them, Sarah Whitlock and Martha Rankin. Complete instructions on how to use silica gel, meal and borax, perlite aggregate, sand and borax, glycerine and water to create attractive permanent flower arrangements. 12 illustrations. 32pp. 5⅜ x 8½. 21802-3 Pa. $1.00

EASY-TO-MAKE BIRD FEEDERS FOR WOODWORKERS, Scott D. Campbell. Detailed, simple-to-use guide for designing, constructing, caring for and using feeders. Text, illustrations for 12 classic and contemporary designs. 96pp. 5⅜ x 8½.
25847-5 Pa. $2.95

SCOTTISH WONDER TALES FROM MYTH AND LEGEND, Donald A. Mackenzie. 16 lively tales tell of giants rumbling down mountainsides, of a magic wand that turns stone pillars into warriors, of gods and goddesses, evil hags, powerful forces and more. 240pp. 5⅜ x 8½. 29677-6 Pa. $6.95

THE HISTORY OF UNDERCLOTHES, C. Willett Cunnington and Phyllis Cunnington. Fascinating, well-documented survey covering six centuries of English undergarments, enhanced with over 100 illustrations: 12th-century laced-up bodice, footed long drawers (1795), 19th-century bustles, l9th-century corsets for men, Victorian "bust improvers," much more. 272pp. 5⅜ x 8¼. 27124-2 Pa. $9.95

ARTS AND CRAFTS FURNITURE: The Complete Brooks Catalog of 1912, Brooks Manufacturing Co. Photos and detailed descriptions of more than 150 now very collectible furniture designs from the Arts and Crafts movement depict davenports, settees, buffets, desks, tables, chairs, bedsteads, dressers and more, all built of solid, quarter-sawed oak. Invaluable for students and enthusiasts of antiques, Americana and the decorative arts. 80pp. 6½ x 9¼. 27471-3 Pa. $8.95

HOW WE INVENTED THE AIRPLANE: An Illustrated History, Orville Wright. Fascinating firsthand account covers early experiments, construction of planes and motors, first flights, much more. Introduction and commentary by Fred C. Kelly. 76 photographs. 96pp. 8¼ x 11. 25662-6 Pa. $8.95

THE ARTS OF THE SAILOR: Knotting, Splicing and Ropework, Hervey Garrett Smith. Indispensable shipboard reference covers tools, basic knots and useful hitches; handsewing and canvas work, more. Over 100 illustrations. Delightful reading for sea lovers. 256pp. 5⅜ x 8½. 26440-8 Pa. $7.95

FRANK LLOYD WRIGHT'S FALLINGWATER: The House and Its History, Second, Revised Edition, Donald Hoffmann. A total revision—both in text and illustrations—of the standard document on Fallingwater, the boldest, most personal architectural statement of Wright's mature years, updated with valuable new material from the recently opened Frank Lloyd Wright Archives. "Fascinating"—*The New York Times*. 116 illustrations. 128pp. 9¼ x 10¾. 27430-6 Pa. $11.95

PHOTOGRAPHIC SKETCHBOOK OF THE CIVIL WAR, Alexander Gardner. 100 photos taken on field during the Civil War. Famous shots of Manassas Harper's Ferry, Lincoln, Richmond, slave pens, etc. 244pp. 10⅝ x 8¼.          22731-6 Pa. $9.95

FIVE ACRES AND INDEPENDENCE, Maurice G. Kains. Great back-to-the-land classic explains basics of self-sufficient farming. The one book to get. 95 illustrations. 397pp. 5⅜ x 8½.          20974-1 Pa. $7.95

SONGS OF EASTERN BIRDS, Dr. Donald J. Borror. Songs and calls of 60 species most common to eastern U.S.: warblers, woodpeckers, flycatchers, thrushes, larks, many more in high-quality recording.          Cassette and manual 99912-2 $9.95

A MODERN HERBAL, Margaret Grieve. Much the fullest, most exact, most useful compilation of herbal material. Gigantic alphabetical encyclopedia, from aconite to zedoary, gives botanical information, medical properties, folklore, economic uses, much else. Indispensable to serious reader. 161 illustrations. 888pp. 6½ x 9¼. 2-vol. set. (USO)          Vol. I: 22798-7 Pa. $9.95
          Vol. II: 22799-5 Pa. $9.95

HIDDEN TREASURE MAZE BOOK, Dave Phillips. Solve 34 challenging mazes accompanied by heroic tales of adventure. Evil dragons, people-eating plants, blood-thirsty giants, many more dangerous adversaries lurk at every twist and turn. 34 mazes, stories, solutions. 48pp. 8¼ x 11.          24566-7 Pa. $2.95

LETTERS OF W. A. MOZART, Wolfgang A. Mozart. Remarkable letters show bawdy wit, humor, imagination, musical insights, contemporary musical world; includes some letters from Leopold Mozart. 276pp. 5⅜ x 8½.          22859-2 Pa. $7.95

BASIC PRINCIPLES OF CLASSICAL BALLET, Agrippina Vaganova. Great Russian theoretician, teacher explains methods for teaching classical ballet. 118 illustrations. 175pp. 5⅜ x 8½.          22036-2 Pa. $5.95

THE JUMPING FROG, Mark Twain. Revenge edition. The original story of The Celebrated Jumping Frog of Calaveras County, a hapless French translation, and Twain's hilarious "retranslation" from the French. 12 illustrations. 66pp. 5⅜ x 8½.
          22686-7 Pa. $3.95

BEST REMEMBERED POEMS, Martin Gardner (ed.). The 126 poems in this superb collection of 19th- and 20th-century British and American verse range from Shelley's "To a Skylark" to the impassioned "Renascence" of Edna St. Vincent Millay and to Edward Lear's whimsical "The Owl and the Pussycat." 224pp. 5⅜ x 8½.
          27165-X Pa. $4.95

COMPLETE SONNETS, William Shakespeare. Over 150 exquisite poems deal with love, friendship, the tyranny of time, beauty's evanescence, death and other themes in language of remarkable power, precision and beauty. Glossary of archaic terms. 80pp. 5³⁄₁₆ x 8¼.          26686-9 Pa. $1.00

BODIES IN A BOOKSHOP, R. T. Campbell. Challenging mystery of blackmail and murder with ingenious plot and superbly drawn characters. In the best tradition of British suspense fiction. 192pp. 5⅜ x 8½.          24720-1 Pa. $6.95

THE WIT AND HUMOR OF OSCAR WILDE, Alvin Redman (ed.). More than 1,000 ripostes, paradoxes, wisecracks: Work is the curse of the drinking classes; I can resist everything except temptation; etc. 258pp. 5⅜ x 8½. 20602-5 Pa. $5.95

SHAKESPEARE LEXICON AND QUOTATION DICTIONARY, Alexander Schmidt. Full definitions, locations, shades of meaning in every word in plays and poems. More than 50,000 exact quotations. 1,485pp. 6½ x 9¼. 2-vol. set.
Vol. 1: 22726-X Pa. $16.95
Vol. 2: 22727-8 Pa. $16.95

SELECTED POEMS, Emily Dickinson. Over 100 best-known, best-loved poems by one of America's foremost poets, reprinted from authoritative early editions. No comparable edition at this price. Index of first lines. 64pp. 5 3/16 x 8¼.
26466-1 Pa. $1.00

CELEBRATED CASES OF JUDGE DEE (DEE GOONG AN), translated by Robert van Gulik. Authentic 18th-century Chinese detective novel; Dee and associates solve three interlocked cases. Led to van Gulik's own stories with same characters. Extensive introduction. 9 illustrations. 237pp. 5⅜ x 8½. 23337-5 Pa. $6.95

THE MALLEUS MALEFICARUM OF KRAMER AND SPRENGER, translated by Montague Summers. Full text of most important witchhunter's "bible," used by both Catholics and Protestants. 278pp. 6⅝ x 10. 22802-9 Pa. $12.95

SPANISH STORIES/CUENTOS ESPAÑOLES: A Dual-Language Book, Angel Flores (ed.). Unique format offers 13 great stories in Spanish by Cervantes, Borges, others. Faithful English translations on facing pages. 352pp. 5⅜ x 8½.
25399-6 Pa. $8.95

THE CHICAGO WORLD'S FAIR OF 1893: A Photographic Record, Stanley Appelbaum (ed.). 128 rare photos show 200 buildings, Beaux-Arts architecture, Midway, original Ferris Wheel, Edison's kinetoscope, more. Architectural emphasis; full text. 116pp. 8¼ x 11. 23990-X Pa. $9.95

OLD QUEENS, N.Y., IN EARLY PHOTOGRAPHS, Vincent F. Seyfried and William Asadorian. Over 160 rare photographs of Maspeth, Jamaica, Jackson Heights, and other areas. Vintage views of DeWitt Clinton mansion, 1939 World's Fair and more. Captions. 192pp. 8⅞ x 11. 26358-4 Pa. $12.95

CAPTURED BY THE INDIANS: 15 Firsthand Accounts, 1750-1870, Frederick Drimmer. Astounding true historical accounts of grisly torture, bloody conflicts, relentless pursuits, miraculous escapes and more, by people who lived to tell the tale. 384pp. 5⅜ x 8½. 24901-8 Pa. $8.95

THE WORLD'S GREAT SPEECHES, Lewis Copeland and Lawrence W. Lamm (eds.). Vast collection of 278 speeches of Greeks to 1970. Powerful and effective models; unique look at history. 842pp. 5⅜ x 8½. 20468-5 Pa. $14.95

THE BOOK OF THE SWORD, Sir Richard F. Burton. Great Victorian scholar/adventurer's eloquent, erudite history of the "queen of weapons"–from prehistory to early Roman Empire. Evolution and development of early swords, variations (sabre, broadsword, cutlass, scimitar, etc.), much more. 336pp. 6⅛ x 9¼.
25434-8 Pa. $9.95

AUTOBIOGRAPHY: The Story of My Experiments with Truth, Mohandas K. Gandhi. Boyhood, legal studies, purification, the growth of the Satyagraha (nonviolent protest) movement. Critical, inspiring work of the man responsible for the freedom of India. 480pp. 5⅜ x 8½. (USO) 24593-4 Pa. $8.95

CELTIC MYTHS AND LEGENDS, T. W. Rolleston. Masterful retelling of Irish and Welsh stories and tales. Cuchulain, King Arthur, Deirdre, the Grail, many more. First paperback edition. 58 full-page illustrations. 512pp. 5⅜ x 8½. 26507-2 Pa. $9.95

THE PRINCIPLES OF PSYCHOLOGY, William James. Famous long course complete, unabridged. Stream of thought, time perception, memory, experimental methods; great work decades ahead of its time. 94 figures. 1,391pp. 5⅜ x 8½. 2-vol. set.
Vol. I: 20381-6 Pa. $12.95
Vol. II: 20382-4 Pa. $12.95

THE WORLD AS WILL AND REPRESENTATION, Arthur Schopenhauer. Definitive English translation of Schopenhauer's life work, correcting more than 1,000 errors, omissions in earlier translations. Translated by E. F. J. Payne. Total of 1,269pp. 5⅜ x 8½. 2-vol. set. Vol. 1: 21761-2 Pa. $11.95
Vol. 2: 21762-0 Pa. $12.95

MAGIC AND MYSTERY IN TIBET, Madame Alexandra David-Neel. Experiences among lamas, magicians, sages, sorcerers, Bonpa wizards. A true psychic discovery. 32 illustrations. 321pp. 5⅜ x 8½. (USO) 22682-4 Pa. $8.95

THE EGYPTIAN BOOK OF THE DEAD, E. A. Wallis Budge. Complete reproduction of Ani's papyrus, finest ever found. Full hieroglyphic text, interlinear transliteration, word-for-word translation, smooth translation. 533pp. 6½ x 9¼.
21866-X Pa. $10.95

MATHEMATICS FOR THE NONMATHEMATICIAN, Morris Kline. Detailed, college-level treatment of mathematics in cultural and historical context, with numerous exercises. Recommended Reading Lists. Tables. Numerous figures. 641pp. 5⅜ x 8½.
24823-2 Pa. $11.95

THEORY OF WING SECTIONS: Including a Summary of Airfoil Data, Ira H. Abbott and A. E. von Doenhoff. Concise compilation of subsonic aerodynamic characteristics of NACA wing sections, plus description of theory. 350pp. of tables. 693pp. 5⅜ x 8½. 60586-8 Pa. $14.95

THE RIME OF THE ANCIENT MARINER, Gustave Doré, S. T. Coleridge. Doré's finest work; 34 plates capture moods, subtleties of poem. Flawless full-size reproductions printed on facing pages with authoritative text of poem. "Beautiful. Simply beautiful."–*Publisher's Weekly.* 77pp. 9¼ x 12. 22305-1 Pa. $6.95

NORTH AMERICAN INDIAN DESIGNS FOR ARTISTS AND CRAFTSPEOPLE, Eva Wilson. Over 360 authentic copyright-free designs adapted from Navajo blankets, Hopi pottery, Sioux buffalo hides, more. Geometrics, symbolic figures, plant and animal motifs, etc. 128pp. 8⅜ x 11. (EUK) 25341-4 Pa. $8.95

SCULPTURE: Principles and Practice, Louis Slobodkin. Step-by-step approach to clay, plaster, metals, stone; classical and modern. 253 drawings, photos. 255pp. 8⅛ x 11.
22960-2 Pa. $11.95

THE INFLUENCE OF SEA POWER UPON HISTORY, 1660–1783, A. T. Mahan. Influential classic of naval history and tactics still used as text in war colleges. First paperback edition. 4 maps. 24 battle plans. 640pp. 5⅜ x 8½. 25509-3 Pa. $12.95

THE STORY OF THE TITANIC AS TOLD BY ITS SURVIVORS, Jack Winocour (ed.). What it was really like. Panic, despair, shocking inefficiency, and a little heroism. More thrilling than any fictional account. 26 illustrations. 320pp. 5⅜ x 8½. 20610-6 Pa. $8.95

FAIRY AND FOLK TALES OF THE IRISH PEASANTRY, William Butler Yeats (ed.). Treasury of 64 tales from the twilight world of Celtic myth and legend: "The Soul Cages," "The Kildare Pooka," "King O'Toole and his Goose," many more. Introduction and Notes by W. B. Yeats. 352pp. 5⅜ x 8½. 26941-8 Pa. $8.95

BUDDHIST MAHAYANA TEXTS, E. B. Cowell and Others (eds.). Superb, accurate translations of basic documents in Mahayana Buddhism, highly important in history of religions. The Buddha-karita of Asvaghosha, Larger Sukhavativyuha, more. 448pp. 5⅜ x 8½. 25552-2 Pa. $12.95

ONE TWO THREE . . . INFINITY: Facts and Speculations of Science, George Gamow. Great physicist's fascinating, readable overview of contemporary science: number theory, relativity, fourth dimension, entropy, genes, atomic structure, much more. 128 illustrations. Index. 352pp. 5⅜ x 8½. 25664-2 Pa. $8.95

ENGINEERING IN HISTORY, Richard Shelton Kirby, et al. Broad, nontechnical survey of history's major technological advances: birth of Greek science, industrial revolution, electricity and applied science, 20th-century automation, much more. 181 illustrations. ". . . excellent . . ."–*Isis.* Bibliography. vii + 530pp. 5⅜ x 8¼. 26412-2 Pa. $14.95

DALÍ ON MODERN ART: The Cuckolds of Antiquated Modern Art, Salvador Dalí. Influential painter skewers modern art and its practitioners. Outrageous evaluations of Picasso, Cézanne, Turner, more. 15 renderings of paintings discussed. 44 calligraphic decorations by Dalí. 96pp. 5⅜ x 8½. (USO) 29220-7 Pa. $4.95

ANTIQUE PLAYING CARDS: A Pictorial History, Henry René D'Allemagne. Over 900 elaborate, decorative images from rare playing cards (14th–20th centuries): Bacchus, death, dancing dogs, hunting scenes, royal coats of arms, players cheating, much more. 96pp. 9¼ x 12¼. 29265-7 Pa. $11.95

MAKING FURNITURE MASTERPIECES: 30 Projects with Measured Drawings, Franklin H. Gottshall. Step-by-step instructions, illustrations for constructing handsome, useful pieces, among them a Sheraton desk, Chippendale chair, Spanish desk, Queen Anne table and a William and Mary dressing mirror. 224pp. 8⅛ x 11¼. 29338-6 Pa. $13.95

THE FOSSIL BOOK: A Record of Prehistoric Life, Patricia V. Rich et al. Profusely illustrated definitive guide covers everything from single-celled organisms and dinosaurs to birds and mammals and the interplay between climate and man. Over 1,500 illustrations. 760pp. 7½ x 10⅛. 29371-8 Pa. $29.95

*Prices subject to change without notice.*

Available at your book dealer or write for free catalog to Dept. GI, Dover Publications, Inc., 31 East 2nd St., Mineola, N.Y. 11501. Dover publishes more than 500 books each year on science, elementary and advanced mathematics, biology, music, art, literary history, social sciences and other areas.

Issues:

1. Synthesis of power/planning.

2. Crucial but limited place of Rome in the west.  p183/216/222

3. Hard-core 'facts' on Patrick

4. Critical place of social/political factors in evangelism
   a. Internal to Ireland
   b. Favor of Rome.

5. Place of ritual/rite in evangelism  193

6. What does the hagiography/legendary material show?  p102/8  205

7. Place of creed  139

8. Relics  151

9. Pelagius - Irish  350